THIRD EDITION

Designing Professional Development for Teachers of Science and Mathematics

We dedicate this edition to our friend and coauthor Susan Loucks-Horsley (1947–2000) whose seminal ideas and leadership continue to significantly impact our work and our lives.

THIRD EDITION

Designing Professional Development for Teachers of Science and Mathematics

Susan Loucks-Horsley
Katherine E. Stiles
Susan Mundry
Nancy Love
Peter W. Hewson

CORWIN
A SAGE Company

For information:

Corwin
A SAGE Company
2455 Teller Road
Thousand Oaks, California 91320
(800) 233-9936
Fax: (800) 417-2466
www.corwinpress.com

SAGE Pvt. Ltd.
B 1/I 1 Mohan Cooperative
    Industrial Area
Mathura Road, New Delhi 110 044
India

SAGE Ltd.
1 Oliver's Yard
55 City Road
London EC1Y 1SP
United Kingdom

SAGE Asia-Pacific Pte. Ltd.
33 Pekin Street #02-01
Far East Square
Singapore 048763

Printed in the United States of America

Library of Congress Cataloging-in-Publication Data

Designing professional development for teachers of science and mathematics / Susan Loucks-Horsley . . . [et al.]. — 3rd ed.
    p. cm.
Includes bibliographical references and index.
ISBN 978-1-4129-6360-2 (cloth)
ISBN 978-1-4129-7414-1 (pbk.)
    1. Science teachers—In-service training—United States. 2. Mathematics teachers—In-service training—United States. I. Loucks-Horsley, Susan. II. Title.

Q183.3.A1D47 2010
507.1′073—dc22   2009029612

This book is printed on acid-free paper.

            12   13   10   9   8   7   6   5   4   3   2

Acquisitions Editor:	Dan Alpert
Associate Editor:	Megan Bedell
Production Editor:	Veronica Stapleton
Copy Editor:	Cynthia Long
Typesetter:	C&M Digitals (P) Ltd.
Proofreader:	Dennis W. Webb
Indexer:	Molly Hall
Cover Designer:	Michael Dubowe

Contents

Foreword

Educators who are committed to high levels of learning for all students and who understand the link between student learning and educator learning will find guidance and inspiration in this third edition of *Designing Professional Development for Teachers of Science and Mathematics* by Susan Loucks-Horsley, Katherine E. Stiles, Susan Mundry, Nancy Love, and Peter W. Hewson. Like its predecessors, this edition places the design of professional development firmly within the context of standards-based reform and a performance-based culture that seeks to continuously improve professional practice and student achievement.

The third edition continues in the tradition of its predecessors by linking professional learning and student achievement, with a particular focus on closing the achievement gaps that exist between rich and poor students, and students of color and White and Asian students. As *Designing Professional Development for Teachers of Science and Mathematics* points out, the planning and implementation of effective professional development efforts always occur within a particular setting that presents unique goals, strengths, resources, and barriers. Because there are no formulas, successful planning and implementation require—as the authors make clear—the blending of research, "practitioner wisdom," and "a repertoire of strategies from which to choose," with the emphasis always on "a process of thoughtful, conscious decision making."

This edition extends the groundbreaking work presented in the first two editions by expanding its discussion regarding the intended outcomes of professional development strategies, including developing leadership, and ways to combine approaches to serve various purposes; extending its discussion on the role of evaluation in promoting continuous reflection and improvement; updating its discussion of knowledge, beliefs, and recent research; and elaborating on the contextual factors that influence professional development, with a new emphasis on practical approaches for assessing context in relationship to each factor. Of particular interest to readers of the third edition will be the authors' discussion of professional learning communities, an approach that has taken hold in many K–12 schools in the past few years.

Although Susan Loucks-Horsley passed away in 2000, she remains the first author of this book, an ongoing testament to the power of her ideas and colleagueship. The high regard in which she was held by her coauthors and the effects she had on their professional lives and that of countless others (including myself) clearly demonstrate the influence Susan continues to have on the field of professional development a decade after her untimely death.

Dennis Sparks
Emeritus Executive Director
National Staff Development Council
Ann Arbor, Michigan

Acknowledgments

From its conception, this book has been a complex undertaking. The first edition originally represented a year of collaboration among people from vastly different "communities": practitioners and researchers; scientists, mathematicians, and educators; people working in elementary, middle, and high schools and higher education settings; and those with school, district, state, and national perspectives. Our challenge was to avoid simply gathering and describing efforts to support professional learning but rather to examine and understand those efforts, search for common themes and struggles, and write a book that represented the collective wisdom of the field. The success of the first and second editions of this book rests in large part on the contributions of hundreds of voices.

Hearing these voices was originally made possible by a five-year grant from the National Science Foundation (NSF) for the creation and funding of the National Institute for Science Education (NISE). The NISE was a partnership between the Wisconsin Center for Education Research at the University of Wisconsin–Madison and the National Center for Improving Science Education, now at WestEd. It was headquartered in Madison, Wisconsin, from 1996 to 2001. The work of the NISE was carried out by several different teams, one of which was the Professional Development Team, whose members authored the first edition of this book.

First and foremost, we are grateful to our original collaborators: Hubert Dyasi, who, along with Rebecca Dyasi, contributed the case on the Workshop Center at City College, New York; Susan Friel, who contributed the case on Teach-Stat; Judy Mumme, who contributed the case on the Mathematics Renaissance; Cary Sneider, who contributed the Global Systems Science case; and Karen Worth along with Melanie Barron, who contributed the case on the Cambridge public schools. These exceptional professional developers shared their learning, their struggles, and their enthusiasm for their work. Their stories, updated for this edition, illustrate the main ideas we formulated together.

We thank our colleagues for their careful reviews and substantive contributions to the first edition (Joan Ferrini-Mundy, Iris Weiss, Deborah Schifter, Josefina Arce, Ed Silver, Ned Levine, Mark St. John, and Vernon Sells) and to the second edition (Harold Pratt, Page Keeley, Susan Koba, Gay Gordon, and Kathy DiRanna). In support of the first and second editions, we are grateful for the vision and guidance of the leadership of the NISE—Andy Porter, Terry Millar, and Denice Denton—and the National Center for Improving Science Education—Senta Raizen and Ted Britton. We appreciate the original support from the National Science Foundation, especially that of Susan Snyder, Margaret Cozzins, Larry Suter, and Daryl Chubin.

In the years following the publication of the first and second editions, many projects and individuals were instrumental in extending the work of *Designing Professional Development for Teachers of Science and Mathematics*. The relatively lengthy list of those we want to thank reflects the sustained impact of the book on our and our colleagues' work in professional development.

- The NISE Cases Group—Ned Levine, Ed Silver, Margaret Smith, and Mary Kay Stein—worked with the NISE Professional Development Team to develop four cases of professional development practice that elucidated the ways in which the design framework is implemented in different contexts.
- Through their participation in the NISE Strategies Working Group, Carne Barnett-Clarke, Virginia Bastable, Mark Driscoll, David Hartney, Barbara Miller, Judy Mumme, Lynn Rankin, Ann Rosebery, Susan Jo Russell, Mary Kay Stein, and Jo Topps enriched our understanding of three professional development strategies—curriculum implementation, immersion in inquiry and problem solving, and case discussions.
- The NISE professional development cadre disseminated the first book to thousands of educators, and we thank them for their commitment to getting the ideas in the book into the hands of so many practitioners.
- We are grateful to the many professional developers who opened their doors to video cameras so that WestEd and WGBH's Teachers as

Learners project could capture images of effective professional development in action and teach us all more about teachers as learners.

- Our colleagues in WestEd's National Academy for Science and Mathematics Education Leadership have greatly enhanced our understanding of what it takes to translate the ideas in this book into action in districts and schools across the country, and we thank this community of learners for contributing to our own learning over the last 11 years.

- The National Science Foundation continues to support our work through a current grant to develop a professional development simulation and accompanying learning modules designed to bring the research and foundational ideas in this book to life through active engagement and learning. We especially thank Robert Gibbs at NSF for his guidance and support, as well as the members of our simulation development team, Carol Bershad, Eliza Spang, and Nancy Hurley; and the design team, Anita Bernhardt, Brenda CampbellJones, Stephen Getty, Margaret Holzer, Mike Klentschy, Susan Koba, Carolyn Landel, Ramon Lopez, and Jim Short. We also thank the numerous professional developers who have field-tested the simulation and contributed to our reflections on the content in this third edition.

We want to thank our colleague Eliza Spang for her contributions to several chapters in this book. She updated literature reviews and helped us revise the professional development design framework. Jennifer Novakoski diligently stuck with us through each iteration of the development of the graphics in the third edition and constantly challenged us with thoughtful questions. Deanna Maier once again worked her magic and formatted the manuscript with meticulous attention to detail. For his enduring patience and encouragement as our editor, we heartily thank Dan Alpert at Corwin Press.

Finally, for their patience and support through the lengthy period of writing yet another book, we thank our families. Without your constant encouragement none of this would be possible.

The contributions of the following reviewers of the third edition are gratefully acknowledged:

Nan Dempsey, Regional Coordinator
Upstate Mathematics and Science Regional Center
Duncan, SC

Mark Kaufman, Director
Regional Alliance for Mathematics and Science Education TERC
Cambridge, MA

Susan Koba, Science Education Consultant
Omaha, NE

Douglas Llewellyn, Professor
St. Johns Fisher College
Rochester, NY

About the Authors

 **Susan Loucks-Horsley** was the lead author of the first edition of *Designing Professional Development for Teachers of Science and Mathematics,* and she directed the professional development research group for the National Institute for Science Education on which the book is based. At the time of her death in 2000, Susan was associate executive director of Biological Sciences and Curriculum Study (BSCS) and senior research associate for Science and Mathematics at WestEd. She had previously served as director of Professional Development and Outreach at the National Research Council's Center for Science, Mathematics, and Engineering Education, where she promoted and monitored standards-based education, especially the *National Science Education Standards.* Susan was a leading researcher, writer, and professional developer who enjoyed collaborating with others to address education's toughest problems. She was the senior author of several books, including *Continuing to Learn: A Guidebook for Teacher Development* (1987), *An Action Guide for School Improvement* (1985), and *Elementary School Science for the 90s* (1990). In addition, she wrote numerous reports on teacher development for the National Center for Improving Science Education, as well as chapters and articles on related topics. While at the University of Texas/Austin Research and Development Center for Teacher Education, she worked on the development team of the Concerns-Based Adoption Model (CBAM), a classic framework for understanding and leading change efforts. Susan remains the first author on this third edition of the book in recognition of her seminal ideas that are still the foundation for the book.

Katherine E. Stiles is currently a senior program associate at WestEd in the Mathematics, Science, and Technology Program, where she leads projects focused on enhancing leadership and professional development in science and mathematics education and conducts evaluation of state and district education initiatives. She is codirector of WestEd's National Academy for Science and Mathematics Education Leadership and several other projects designed to enhance the knowledge and skills of leaders. She is coauthor of books and articles focused on professional development and leadership, including *Designing Professional Development for Teachers of Science and Mathematics* (Corwin, 2003) and *Leading Every Day: 124 Actions for Effective Leadership* (Corwin, 2002, 2006), which received the National Staff Development Council's 2003 Outstanding Book of the Year Award, and is lead author of the *Facilitator's Guide to Leading Every Day* (Corwin, 2006). Katherine is project director for an NSF-funded project to develop a simulation game and learning modules based on the research that is the foundation for the Professional Development Design Framework and the content of the third edition of this book.

As a senior staff member on the Using Data Project, a collaboration between TERC and WestEd, she codeveloped the professional development program to support teachers and leaders as they engaged in collaborative inquiry into data and is coauthor of the book that resulted from the project's work, *The Data Coach's Guide to Improving Learning for All Students: Unleashing the Power of Collaborative Inquiry* (Corwin, 2008). Katherine has over 10 years of experience evaluating science and mathematics education and professional development programs, including NSF-funded statewide projects and state-funded Mathematics and Science Partnerships. In 2002, Katherine was awarded the Paul D. Hood Award for Distinguished Contribution to the Field from WestEd. Prior to joining WestEd in 1995, Katherine worked at the National Science Resources Center in Washington, D.C., as a science curriculum developer and authored four curriculum units for the Science and Technology for Children program. With degrees in psychology, special education, and education, and teaching experience in elementary programs, she brings 20 years of experience to her current work in science and mathematics education and professional development.

Susan Mundry is currently deputy director of Learning Innovations at WestEd and associate director of WestEd's Mathematics, Science, and Technology Program. She directs several national and regional projects focused on improving educational practice and oversees the research and evaluation projects of Learning Innovations. She was codirector of a research study examining the distribution of highly qualified teachers in New York and Maine for the Northeast and Islands Regional Education Laboratory and project director for the evaluation of the Intel Mathematics Initiative, a professional development program for elementary and middle grade teachers aimed at increasing student outcomes in mathematics. She is also a principal investigator for two National Science Foundation projects that are developing products to promote the use of research-based practice in science and mathematics. Since 2000, Susan has codirected the National Academy for Science and Mathematics Education Leadership, which provides educational leaders with training and technical assistance on professional development design, leading educational change, group facilitation, data analysis and use, and general educational leadership, as well as access to research-based information to improve teaching and learning. Building on this work, she provides technical assistance to several large urban school districts engaged in enhancing leadership and improving math and science programs.

As a senior research associate for the National Institute for Science Education (1997–2000), Mundry conducted research on attributes of effective professional development. She served on the national evaluation team for the study of the Eisenhower Professional Development program led by the American Institutes for Research where she worked on the development of national survey instruments and the protocols for case studies. From 1982 to 1997, Mundry served in many roles from staff developer to associate director at The NETWORK Inc, a research and development organization focused on organizational change and dissemination of promising education practice. There, she managed the work of the National Center for Improving Science Education and the Center for Effective Communication, provided technical assistance to schools on issues of equity and desegregation, oversaw national dissemination programs, and codeveloped the "Change Game" (Making Change for School Improvement), a simulation game that enhances leaders' ability to lead change efforts in schools and districts.

Susan has written several books, chapters, and articles based on her work. She is coauthor of *A Leader's Guide to Science Curriculum Topic Study* (Corwin, 2009), *Designing Effective Professional Development for Teachers of Science and Mathematics* (second edition) (Corwin, 2003), *Leading Every Day: 124 Actions for Effective Leadership* (Corwin, 2002, 2006), which was named a National Staff Development Council Book of the Year in 2003, and *The Data Coach's Guide to Improving Learning for All Students* (Corwin, 2008).

Nancy Love is director of Program Development at Research for Better Teaching in Acton, Massachusetts, where she leads this education-consulting group's research and development. She is the former director of the Using Data Project, a collaboration between TERC and WestEd, where she led the development of a comprehensive professional development program to improve teaching and learning through effective and collaborative use of school data. This program has produced significant gains in student achievement as well as increased collaboration and data use in schools across the country. Love has authored several books and articles on data use, including *The Data Coach's Guide to Improving Learning for All Students: Unleashing the Power of Collaborative Inquiry* (Corwin, 2008) and *Using Data to Improve the Learning for All: A Collaborative Inquiry Approach* (Corwin, 2009). She is also well-known for her work in professional development both as a presenter and author of articles. In 2006, she was awarded the Susan Loucks-Horsley Award from the National Staff Development Council in recognition of her significant national contribution to the field of staff development and to the efficacy of others.

 **Peter W. Hewson** is professor of Science Education at the University of Wisconsin–Madison. He teaches in the undergraduate science teacher education and graduate science education programs and coordinates a professional development school in Madison. He has been deeply involved in the development of a conceptual change framework that informs the teaching and learning of science; the framework also has major implications for teacher education and professional development. He has published extensively on these and related topics. He played a major role in opening a dialogue between researchers in South Africa and the United States; this led to the establishment of an annual Research School in South Africa with particular emphasis on the professional development of new researchers in science and mathematics education. In 2009, he received the Distinguished Contributions to Science Education Through Research Award from the National Association for Research in Science Teaching. He received his DPhil in theoretical nuclear physics from Oxford University and taught physics and science education in South Africa before moving to the United States.

Introduction

Writing the third edition of *Designing Professional Development for Teachers of Science and Mathematics* has given us a chance to reflect on our learning from colleagues, new research and literature, and our work with dedicated and thoughtful professional developers in the field who have been using the ideas in this book since the first edition.

The intention of this introduction is to make visible for you, the reader, our process of reflecting and revising. If you are familiar with the first and second editions, you can take this retrospective look with us. If you are new to the book, you will understand its evolution into this revised edition. In either case, you will know why we took on the work of revising *Designing Professional Development for Teachers of Science and Mathematics* and how it has changed.

WHAT HAS HAPPENED SINCE
THE FIRST AND SECOND EDITIONS

Since 1998, we have been watching with a sense of wonder and delight how *Designing Professional Development for Teachers of Science and Mathematics* has taken on a life of its own. We are professional developers. As such, we knew that writing the book was only the beginning, the easy part, as Susan Loucks-Horsley would say. The hard part, the "real work," was getting it used well. For the past 11 years, we have been on the ground actively disseminating and engaging others with the ideas in *Designing*

Professional Development for Teachers of Science and Mathematics along with many colleagues and collaborators.

Even so, when we first put fingers to keyboards 11 years ago, we could never have anticipated how well the book would be used. We have seen dog-eared, sticky note–marked copies in the hands of professional developers all over the country, some of whom fondly refer to it as the "yellow book" or the "clouds book" because of the first edition's cover design. With equal gratification, we have worked elbow-to-elbow with professional developers who have made the principles and processes come to life in the purposeful and imaginative professional development designs they have created—designs that are paying off in powerful learning for teachers and their students.

A long list of products and research that built on and extended the original work resulted from the first edition. For example, *Teachers as Learners: A Multimedia Kit for Professional Development in Science and Mathematics* (Corwin, 2003) is a set of videos and learning activities that provide visual examples of powerful professional learning strategies based on those identified in the 1998 edition of this book. The WestEd authors are currently developing a science professional development simulation and accompanying learning modules, with support from the National Science Foundation, to bring the professional development design framework and conceptual ideas in the book to life in the form of an engaging set of materials.

One of our reasons for updating the earlier editions of the book was to collect and bring together in one place all that we have learned through many people's efforts to translate the principles, framework, and strategies of the first and second editions into practice and to deepen our understanding of professional development design through further research and new resources. The original editions evolved by synthesizing and codifying what outstanding and effective professional developers do when they design programs. This edition has the design work of more professional developers from which to draw. It is truly from the field, to the field.

In addition to what we have learned through work that grew directly out of the earlier editions, the field as a whole is advancing. With a wide-angle lens, we have observed some encouraging changes that have influenced our thinking and informed our revisions.

The knowledge bases about learning, teaching, the nature of science and mathematics, professional development, and educational change are growing. A veritable explosion of cognitive research has occurred since the first edition of this book, increasing our understanding about how children and adults construct knowledge in mathematics and science. More also is known about what constitutes and supports transformative learning for teachers and how to combine professional learning strategies to address a multiplicity of teachers' learning needs. We now better understand when and how professional development improves practice and student learning. Reports and studies emerge almost daily (e.g., Blank, de las Alas, & Smith, 2008; Carnegie Corporation of New York, 2009; Wei, Darling-Hammond, Andree, Richardson, & Orphanos, 2009) that outline the current status of science and mathematics education and professional development and provide recommendations for continuous improvement. We are learning more and more about how professional learning communities support continuous improvement and their role in sustaining teachers' professional learning. Research is emerging on the impact of coaches and mentors on teachers' practice and the benefits generated through teacher induction programs. The knowledge base on evaluation of professional development programs, paired with ongoing monitoring, has influenced our thinking about the design framework and how designers collect data to improve programs. These developments and learnings are reflected throughout the chapters in the book, as well as in the professional development design framework itself.

National, state, and local standards are more widely known and consulted as school districts shape their vision of teaching and learning. Since we first convened as a team of authors and collaborators in 1996, the National Council of Teachers of Mathematics (NCTM) standards were only three years old, and the National Research Council's (NRC) National Science Education Standards had just been published. "The 1990s," we wrote, "are certain to be known as the decade in which standards became commonplace among educators and policymakers in the United States" (Loucks-Horsley, Hewson, Love, & Stiles, 1998, p. 215). We were right; standards are now commonplace. Most states and many school districts have adopted standards, some more closely aligned with national standards than others. In fact, as we write this introduction, the Common Core State Standards Initiative, led by the National Governors Association and the Council of Chief State School Officers (CCSSO), has the commitment of 49 states and territories to develop common academic standards in mathematics and English language arts (CCSSO, 2009).

For the most part, today the debate has shifted from whether or not standards should guide mathematics and science education to how to implement them and how to ensure that they are met. There are many recent resources to help guide the efforts to implement the standards, including NCTM's *A Research Companion to Principles and Standards for School Mathematics* (2003a) and *Curriculum Focal Points for Prekindergarten Through Grade 8 Mathematics: A Quest for Coherence* (2006), new tools from the American Association for the Advancement of Science (AAAS) such as the two volumes of the *Atlas of Science Literacy* (2001, 2007), the work under development at the National Science Teachers Association (NSTA) on the Science Anchors project, as well as other publications supporting standards and research-based mathematics and science education. The consensus that has been reached around standards sets the context for the other advances in the field we discuss below.

Professional development has become more purposeful and is being designed more often with the clear intention of improving student learning. While "hodgepodge" and "hit-and-run style" professional development are far from a thing of the past, we find more examples than we did 11 years ago of professional development that is being designed and implemented for the purpose of helping students to achieve standards. In these programs, goals for student learning are determined by studying standards and analyzing student learning data; student goals influence the purpose and content of professional development, which is tied to improving practice. Teachers have access to meaningful data and are better prepared to engage in data-driven dialogue processes to design instructional interventions to address their students' learning needs. Designers have become more intentional in their efforts to create teacher learning opportunities that align with their contexts and cultures. It has been especially gratifying for us to witness the design framework described in this book being widely used to stimulate dialogue about important inputs into the design process and to produce more thoughtful and powerful professional development programs. We have seen the design framework used to guide the development of programs of many grain sizes, from single institutes to complex multiyear programs.

Science and mathematics content and pedagogical content knowledge are playing a greater role in professional development programs. Another positive development has been a shift from providing teachers with opportunities to learn generic instructional strategies, such as cooperative learning, to designing professional development around the essential knowledge teachers need to teach the mathematics and science embodied in the standards. The national mandate to ensure a highly qualified teacher in every classroom has contributed to the progress made in helping teachers develop the in-depth science and mathematics content knowledge they need to improve student learning. We see more examples of professional development that engages teachers in understanding the content they teach, deepening their knowledge about how to teach this content in particular, and learning about ways that students think about and learn this content. For example, *Science Curriculum Topic Study* (Keeley, 2005) and *Mathematics Curriculum Topic Study* (Keeley & Rose, 2006) along with *A Leader's Guide to Science Curriculum Topic Study: Designs, Tools and Resources for Professional Learning* (Mundry, Keeley, & Landel, 2010) provide structured opportunities for teachers to "bridge the gap between standards and practice" by creating awareness of the mathematics and science content needed for basic adult literacy. These resources also provide opportunities to set goals for deepening content knowledge in areas that are weak, for understanding what research suggests about teaching different science and mathematics topics, for becoming facile at identifying the recommended grade spans for teaching certain mathematics and science content, for becoming aware of common misconceptions students' hold and gain insight into how to spot them, and to better understand how science and mathematics ideas develop across grades K–12.

Research indicates that leadership for teaching and learning has a direct impact on student learning. Leadership is widely recognized as one of the most important factors in teacher and student learning. Schools and districts that are going somewhere—toward improved student learning—have effective leaders who behave in specific ways that impact success. Leithwood and his colleagues found that only classroom instruction has a greater impact on student learning than school leadership (Leithwood, Louis, Anderson, & Wahlstrom, 2004). In their meta-analysis of school leadership, Marzano, Waters, and McNulty (2005) reaffirm the link between leadership and student learning: "Our basic claim is that research over the 35 years provides strong guidance on specific leadership behaviors for school administrators and that those behaviors have well-documented effects on student achievement" (p. 7). Summing up decades of research in two words, Dennis Sparks (2005) says, "Leaders matter" (p. vii). We have seen many national, state, and local initiatives started in the last several years to develop the knowledge and abilities of leaders in district and school contexts, most relying on recent research to guide the content for the leaders' learning.

THE ENDURING CHALLENGES OF PROFESSIONAL DEVELOPMENT

As noted earlier in this introduction and explored in-depth in Chapter 2, there is widespread consensus regarding what constitutes effective professional learning: It is directly aligned with student learning needs; is intensive, ongoing, and connected to practice; focuses on the teaching and learning of specific academic content; is connected to other school initiatives; provides time and opportunities for teachers to collaborate and build strong working relationships; and is continuously monitored and evaluated. Despite the improvements made in teachers' professional learning that reflect what is known about effective professional development, the challenges are greater than ever.

Of paramount importance is raising the performance of all students in mathematics and science and closing achievement gaps that exist between rich and poor, and students of color and White and Asian students. Given that future innovation, global finance, and our very standard of living depend on mathematics and science knowledge, our students' unacceptable performance in these subjects constitutes nothing short of a national crisis. The report from the National Commission on Mathematics and Science Teaching for the 21st Century (2000; also known as the Glenn Commission), aptly named *Before It's Too Late,* states:

> Our children are not just losing the ability to respond to the challenges already presented by the 21st century but to its potential as well. We are failing to capture the interest of our youth for scientific and mathematical ideas. We are not instructing them to the level of competence they will need to live their lives and work at their jobs productively. Perhaps worst of all, we are not challenging their imaginations deeply enough. (pp. 4–5)

Most alarming are gaps in performance that exist between rich and poor students, and students of color and White and Asian students, which, after a decade of investment in systemic reform, are maddeningly persistent. The challenge we face is to make breakthroughs in educating an increasingly diverse student population with different histories and cultural perspectives, experiences and expectations, and styles and approaches to learning and organizing information—"before it's too late."

Enhanced Goals for Student Learning

According to the Glenn Commission, "Students' grasp of science as a process of discovery, of mathematics as the language of scientific reasoning is often formulaic, fragile, or absent altogether" (National Commission on Mathematics and Science Teaching for the 21st Century, 2000, p. 10). Moving students beyond superficial understanding requires a fundamental shift in the goals that school communities embrace for their diverse students: goals proposed in national standards that focus on deep understanding, inquiry, and problem solving rather than on acquisition of facts; application of knowledge across subject areas; collaboration among learners; and alternatives to traditional assessment that measure progress of individuals in relation to new learning goals while providing accountability for the effectiveness of teaching and schools.

Ongoing, Sustained, Collaborative Learning Beyond Workshops and Institutes

Although many schools throughout the country have implemented structures and processes that focus on teachers' collaborative learning, 90% of U.S. teachers have participated in professional learning consisting primarily of short-term conferences or workshops (Wei et al., 2009). Too often, teachers are not provided with time or opportunities to observe in each other's classrooms, engage in sustained learning with mentors and coaches, or convene in small groups to reflect on practice. Many schools have embraced the tenets of professional learning communities (PLCs) and embedded the processes of continuous improvement within their cultures. However, many other schools have latched onto such an approach with minimal attention to changing mind-sets or cultures, reflected in such statements as "we are doing PLCs." In addition, we know from research that a substantial amount of time (typically, 50 or more hours) of professional development is needed before teachers make substantial changes in their practices, but most professional development opportunities are of much shorter duration (Wei et al., 2009). This suggests that districts and schools continue to view teachers' professional learning as independent, disconnected workshops, rather than interconnected, sequential learning experiences.

Professional Development That Is Directly Connected to Teaching Practices

Although there have been changes in the extent to which professional development is driven by students' learning needs, there has not been concurrent improvement in focusing those learning experiences on what teachers do in their classrooms. We have seen teachers engaged in meaningful exploration of their teaching practices, but too often, this is not prevalent in schools. For example, teachers report that much of the professional development available to them is not useful (Wei et al., 2009, p. 92), implying that their learning is disconnected from their practice. This aspect of teachers' learning frequently appears on federal, state, and organizational reports as a recommendation for improvement, as is the case with the 2009 Carnegie Corporation of New York's report:

> Cease support for professional development in science and math that is disconnected from teaching practices in schools; replace with investment in strategic and coherent collaborative offerings that link coherent, sustained professional learning, rich in relevant science and math content, to direct changes in instruction in schools. (p. 9)

Professional Learning That Is Facilitated by High-Quality Professional Developers and Teacher Leaders

In an economic environment where districts and schools are eliminating structured, off-site "professional development days," it is increasingly critical to develop school-based capacity for facilitation of teacher learning within the school day and culture. However, developing facilitators of teacher learning is often left by the wayside, with facilitators who either receive little or no professional learning of their own, or are "pressed into service before they are fully prepared for their roles" (Banilower, Boyd, Pasley, & Weiss, 2006, p. 86). With coaching and mentoring gaining popularity in many districts, it is equally important to develop the knowledge, skills, and abilities of these facilitators of adult learning and to provide them with ongoing, sustained opportunities to reflect on and make improvements in their practice. Research is beginning to demonstrate the impact of teacher-to-teacher learning approaches, and it is imperative to ensure that these leaders are afforded the same quality professional development that they offer to other teachers.

These are not easy problems to solve; they are systemic and reflect the wide gap between what we know about effective professional development and what actually happens in practice. It was our sense of urgency about closing that gap that led us to write the first edition of this book. The fact that many of the same challenges persist indicates that our original purpose for the book has yet to be fulfilled and is more urgent than ever. Our hope is that providing designers with updated guidance on what we know to be effective in professional development will continue to move the field closer to narrowing the gap between what we know and what we do in schools to support the teaching and learning of science and mathematics.

CARRYING ON SUSAN LOUCKS-HORSLEY'S WORK

Our commitment to contributing to improvements in the field of professional development relates to another of our reasons for undertaking the third edition revisions: to carry forward the work of our close friend, mentor, and coauthor, Susan Loucks-Horsley, who died in a tragic accident in 2000. *Designing Professional Development for Teachers of Science and Mathematics* was Susan's vision. In her usual generous way, she brought collaborators into the process so that we could learn with her. Learning was Susan's passion—students' learning, teachers' learning, her colleagues' learning, and her own continuous growth. The project grew out of her commitment to create "thick and rich descriptions of robust professional development" that could transform old notions of what she called cafeteria-style or hit-and-run professional development. She led the project with extraordinary clarity of thinking and purpose, yet surprised us with her eagerness to listen and learn from us. Susan did more than write about collegial learning; she created it wherever she went. When anyone would call *Designing Professional Development* Susan Loucks-Horsley's book, she was quick to correct them, saying, "It is *our* book." Benjamin Disraeli said that the mark of a truly great person was not just someone who gave her gifts, but someone who brought out the gifts in others. Because Susan brought out our gifts, we produced this new edition—"*our* book"—as our gift to her.

In describing the central idea for *Designing Professional Development for Teachers of Science and Mathematics,* Susan Loucks-Horsley used the simile of a bridge. She wrote, "A bridge, like professional development, is a critical link between where one is and where one wants to be" (1999, p. 2). We find her simile apt in several ways. Susan was herself a bridge builder—building bridges between the research and practitioners, between the professional development and the science and mathematics education communities, and between educators and scientists and mathematics. She intended for *Designing Professional Development for Teachers of Science and Mathematics* to build strong bridges as well.

The book's organizing principle is that professional development is a complex design undertaking. Susan wrote: "Each bridge requires careful design that considers its purpose, who will use it, the conditions that exist at its anchor points (beginning, midway, and end), and the resources required to construct it" (1999, p. 2). In part, *Designing Professional Development* is a practical manual for bridge building. While there is consensus about the characteristics of effective professional development, there is still a prevalent gap between knowledge and practice. The book, like Susan's life, bridges research and practice by providing rich descriptions of effective programs constructed in various contexts addressing common challenges in unique ways. By carrying on her work, we as Susan's coauthors and friends serve as a bridge, connecting our readers to her prodigious legacy and profound vision.

PURPOSE OF THE BOOK

The book is intended to help professional developers construct strong bridges—between theory and practice, professional development and mathematics and science education, and the current and desired state of teaching and learning these subjects. It brings together in one place a rich discussion of the practices and issues of professional development for mathematics and science education. It is at once a "primer" on principles of effective professional development and a conversation among experienced professional developers about ways they address the many barriers to creating programs that emulate those principles. The book gets inside the thinking of designers, illuminating their purposes, strategies, triumphs, and failures.

The idea behind this book—and the professional development project at the National Institute for Science Education that produced it—evolved as experienced professional developers examined their practice. The purpose of the book as originally conceived was to offer a few distinct and robust models of professional development, ones that provided alternatives to traditional formats such as inservice workshops. As we examined the "models" in use by each of the project's collaborators, we realized that, rather than offering distinctly different approaches, each program or initiative was a unique combination of professional development strategies whose choice was influenced by the professional learning goals and the particular context—and those strategies changed over time as learning occurred, goals and context changed, and various issues developed. We determined that professional development, like teaching, is about decision making—designing optimal learning opportunities tailored to the unique situation. Rather than offering a few models for professional developers to adopt or adapt, we could instead provide guidance about professional development design. Drawing on research, the literature, and the wisdom of experienced professional developers, we could offer multiple "best practices" to assist professional developers in designing and strengthening their programs. More specifically, this book is designed to

- offer a framework to assist professional developers in considering key inputs and combining strategies uniquely tailored for their contexts and their particular goals in improving science and mathematics teaching and learning;
- summarize key knowledge, such as the characteristics of effective professional development for teachers of science and mathematics, that informs professional development design;
- provide guidance on how to assess one's context to prepare to design professional development;
- discuss critical issues that cut across professional development programs and initiatives and ways these issues can be addressed;
- describe different strategies for professional learning that go beyond the most common workshops and institutes;
- provide examples of how elements of the design framework were used to create real-life professional development initiatives for teachers of mathematics and science; and
- offer references and resources for further exploration and inquiry.

CHANGES IN THE THIRD EDITION

This third edition of the book *Designing Professional Development for Teachers of Science and Mathematics* reflects new ideas and updates and expands the core concepts presented in the first and second editions. The discussion of the professional development design framework in Chapter 1 reflects the authors' deeper understanding of the relationship and interaction among the implementation processes and the inputs into designing professional development. We also expanded the discussion of the role of evaluation on impact and the continuous cycle of reflection and revision. We have updated the design framework graphic to emphasize where the different professional development inputs are most influential as well as to emphasize that reflection and revision are ongoing and that evaluation focuses on understanding the results that are achieved.

A core idea we continue to build on in this edition is the idea that professional developers should have a basic understanding of research findings that influence their work. In Chapter 2, we update the discussion of knowledge and beliefs, including recent research, and how they influence the professional development program, and the actions of professional development designers. In Chapter 5, we added a new professional development strategy, curriculum topic study, that is focused on helping teachers learn and apply knowledge from research and standards.

Over the past several years, we have learned even more about the importance of understanding the context for the professional development, and Chapter 3 discusses the context factors that influence professional development, with a new emphasis on practical approaches for assessing your own context in relationship to each factor.

A major message in the other editions of the book was the need to shift professional development from one-time workshops and institutes to more ongoing and job-embedded professional learning. In the past decade, many educators have made this shift and are working in continuously improving learning organizations in which teachers expand their expertise and work with colleagues to share best practice in an ongoing way. In this edition of the book, we expand on this message and include more on the role of professional development in building professional cultures that support and sustain ongoing improvement and the use of best practice. For example, Chapter 4 includes a discussion of the critical issues that influence professional development, with an emphasis on building leadership and cultures that sustain learning. Chapter 5 provides more guidance about professional development strategies with an emphasis on their purposes, intended outcomes, and ways in which to combine strategies to address diverse contextual needs and provide an array of different experiences tied to teachers' and students' learning needs. Chapter 6 is updated to reflect our original collaborators' cases and includes discussions of how their thinking and programs have evolved over time.

THE AUDIENCE FOR THIS BOOK

The primary audience for this book is professional developers: those who design, conduct, and support professional development for practicing teachers of mathematics and science and those learning to do so through coursework, mentoring, and collegial support groups. Our focus is at the *inservice* level, although many of the ideas presented in the book can be used to redesign preservice teacher education programs. These professional developers are found in schools (as teacher leaders, advisers, mentors, coaches, administrators, members of leadership teams); school district offices (as curriculum supervisors, coordinators, staff developers); intermediate and state agencies; colleges and universities in faculties of education, science, and mathematics; professional associations, such as the National Science Teachers Association (NSTA) and the National Council of Teachers of Mathematics (NCTM), and their affiliated leadership organizations; state and federally funded projects and initiatives, such as those focused on teacher enhancement, systemic reform, and materials development, funded by the National Science Foundation, the U.S. Department of Education, and individual states; independent training and development firms; museums and other informal education organizations; and research labs and other organizations. There are several secondary audiences for the book: funders, sponsors, evaluators, policymakers, and mathematics and science teachers in their roles as consumers of professional development. All should find this book useful as it depicts best practices and how critical issues can be dealt with within different contexts.

ORGANIZATION OF THE BOOK

Chapter 1, A Framework for Designing Professional Development, introduces the design orientation of this book. This chapter discusses why, with the wide variety of professional development goals and contexts in which they are pursued, it is most fruitful to think of professional development as a dynamic decision-making process rather than as a static set of models. The design framework, which can be used to design new programs or analyze and improve existing programs, is described. Driving the process is a commitment to a vision for students and their learning and analysis of student learning and other data to set specific goals for professional development. These goals serve as the basis for implementing and evaluating the program and continuously reflecting on changes and refining the professional development. Inputs of knowledge and beliefs, context factors, and critical issues influence the professional development design process and inform the design of the overall program. Each subsequent chapter delves more deeply into each of the inputs.

Chapter 2, Knowledge and Beliefs Supporting Effective Professional Development, describes what is currently known about learning, teaching, the nature of science and mathematics, adult learning and professional development, and the change process—knowledge that forms the foundation for a professional development initiative.

Chapter 3, Context Factors Influencing Professional Development, discusses several factors within local contexts that influence the design and nature of professional development, including the nature of the students and teachers (their needs, backgrounds, abilities, motivations, etc.); current curriculum, instruction, and assessment practices including the learning environment; the nature of the organizational culture and importance of developing professional culture; the critical role of leadership for professional development; national, state, and local policies that constrain or support professional learning; resources that are available to support professional development; and the role of families and communities in supporting, as well as contributing to, science and mathematics education and professional development. How differences in these dimensions influence design and implementation of professional development is illustrated by a variety of examples from different contexts.

Chapter 4, Critical Issues to Consider in Designing Professional Development, discusses seven issues that need to be addressed in professional development initiatives if they are to be effective and successful over time. These issues include building capacity for sustainability, making time for professional development, developing leadership, ensuring equity, building a professional learning culture, garnering public support, and scaling up. Each of the issues is defined and illustrated (what it is and why it is an issue), the existing literature is cited, and questions and actions are suggested for professional developers to consider as they grapple with these issues.

Chapter 5, Strategies for Professional Learning, describes 16 strategies that are widely used for professional development of mathematics and science educators. They are grouped into four clusters based on their primary purposes and focus: immersion in content, standards, and research; examining teaching and learning; aligning and implementing curriculum; and professional development structures. Each strategy is described according to its key elements and intended outcomes, and we explore how the strategy can be combined with other strategies to create a coherent program, as well as how the strategy lends itself to developing leadership and some of the issues to consider when selecting the strategy. Examples of each strategy in action are provided via a vignette, with resources suggested to guide designers to learn more.

Chapter 6, The Design Framework in Action, illustrates how the different parts of the design framework influenced the decisions and professional development designs in five settings. The five settings are summarized as cases of professional development, written by the book's original collaborators: Hubert Dyasi and Rebecca Dyasi of City College of New York; Susan Friel of the University of North Carolina at Chapel Hill; Judy Mumme of the Mathematics Renaissance at WestEd; Cary Sneider of the Museum of Science, Boston; and Karen Worth of the Educational Development Center (EDC) and Melanie Barron of the Cambridge (Massachusetts) public schools. These cases are referred to throughout the book.

HOW TO USE THIS BOOK

There are a variety of ways this book can be used. The design framework itself, introduced in Chapter 1 and discussed with illustrations in Chapter 6, can be used by professional developers to design new programs or improve current programs. Beginning with these chapters will immerse the reader immediately into the dynamic world of decision making about professional development. An alternative is reading the chapters sequentially, in which case different inputs into professional development programs are introduced one by one—the knowledge base, context, critical issues, and strategies—combining increasingly more considerations about professional development design by the time the actual planning and implementation process is illustrated in Chapter 6. Another alternative, one that may be more immediately helpful to professional development planners, is to review the section in Chapter 2 on the knowledge base in professional development and then to turn to Chapter 5, which describes each of the 16 strategies and suggests under what circumstances they might be best used. Because professional development is a complex and dynamic process, we believe that each chapter has something new to offer the reader, but the order in which chapters are read is not critical.

VALUES SHARED BY THE AUTHORS

Early in framing the first edition of this book, we realized that what we were creating was based very much on our shared beliefs and that a book by another set of authors might read quite differently. Therefore, we decided it was important to be explicit about our beliefs, as a form of "truth in packaging." Readers who share these beliefs should find the contents quite compatible; we hope that those who do not will be challenged to consider an alternative perspective and direction and its value in their work. The values that underlie this book include the following:

1. *Professional development experiences need to have students and their learning at their core.* And by that we mean every student. Science and mathematics education reforms and the national standards on which they are based share a common commitment to learning for all, not the privileged or talented few. This not only implies a whole new perspective on the content that students should learn but also the teaching and learning strategies that need to be employed by their teachers (especially ways of knowing what students know). We believe that, given the scarcity of resources, including time, for teacher learning, all those resources must be focused on learning and developing the best means for reaching every student.

2. *Excellent science and mathematics teachers have a very special and unique kind of knowledge that needs to be developed through their professional learning experiences.* Pedagogical content knowledge, that is, knowing how to teach specific scientific and mathematical concepts and principles to children at different developmental levels, is the unique province of teachers and must be the focus of professional development. Knowledge of content, although critical, is not enough, nor is knowledge of general pedagogy. There is something more to professional development for science and mathematics teachers than generic professional development opportunities are able to offer.

3. *Principles that guide the reform of student learning should also guide professional learning for educators.* Professional development opportunities need to "walk their talk." People teach as they are taught, so engaging in active learning, focusing on fewer ideas more deeply, and learning collaboratively—all of these principles—must characterize learning opportunities for adults.

4. *Teachers as leaders exert a powerful force for school improvement.* In roles such as coaches, mentors, professional development facilitators, instructional specialists, and content or grade-level team leaders, teacher leaders benefit schools by increasing expertise in teaching and learning, strengthening collaborative cultures and internal accountability, and building capacity. Through the development of their own expertise in leading adult learning, teacher leaders also increase their own sense of professionalism and empowerment.

5. *Professional development must both align with and support system-based changes that promote student learning.* Professional development has long suffered from separation from other critical components of education, with the common result that new strategies and ideas are not implemented. While professional development cannot be expected to cure all the ills of the system, it can support changes in such areas as standards, assessment, and curriculum, creating a culture and capacity for continuous improvement so critical to facing current and future challenges.

With these values explicit, the reader is now invited to explore a new direction for professional development for mathematics and science. We hope that you will, as we have in revising this edition, see with fresh eyes the possibilities for powerful professional learning.

1

A Framework for Designing Professional Development

This book introduces the big idea that effective professional development is carefully designed and implemented based on a number of important factors or inputs. It offers a conceptual framework for thinking about, planning, and implementing professional development called the *professional development design framework.* This chapter introduces the framework and its components. The subsequent chapters in this book discuss, in detail, each of the components and how to apply them in your work.

The framework emerged originally from collaborative reflection with outstanding professional developers about their programs for mathematics and science teachers. These professional developers felt very strongly that what they had to offer were not "models" that others could admire and adopt. Their programs were more complex than that, combining elements of different models, evolving and changing over time. They emerged out of and were uniquely suited to their own particular goals and context.

Equally complex was the process they used to develop their programs. As professional development "designers," they consciously drew on research and "practitioner wisdom" and were guided by their own passionate beliefs about the nature of mathematics and science and student and adult learning. They had a repertoire of strategies from which to choose. They grappled with challenging, critical issues related to the "big picture" of mathematics and science education reform. When confronted with critical issues that threatened to block their progress, they worked with other educators to problem solve and generate creative new solutions. They analyzed student learning data and student work and studied their own unique contexts to deliberately set goals to improve student and teacher learning and classroom practice. They thought carefully about what approach would be best in a particular time and place to advance their goals. Drawing on all of these elements, they carefully crafted their goals and plans. Once implemented, their designs never stopped evolving. They evaluated their programs not only in terms of teacher satisfaction but also on the basis of whether teacher and student learning goals were met. They reflected on results and made revisions based on what they learned. For these designers, professional development was not about importing models or following formulas. They engaged in a process of thoughtful, conscious choices and decision making.

It is this process of careful consideration and decision making by professional developers that we have attempted to capture, albeit greatly simplified, in Figure 1.1. At the center of the framework, illustrated in the boxes connected with horizontal arrows, is the professional development design and implementation process, incorporating the following actions: commit to a vision and standards, analyze student learning and other data, set goals,

Figure 1.1   Professional Development Design Framework

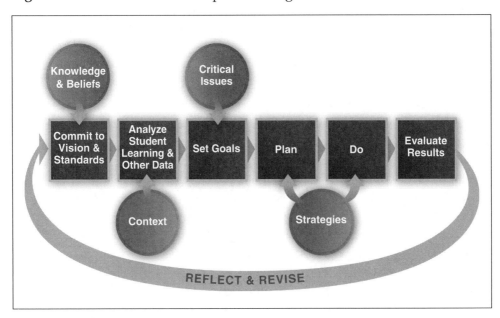

plan, do, and evaluate results. Each action in the design and implementation process is influenced by several inputs.

INPUTS INTO THE DESIGN PROCESS

The circles above and below the design and implementation process represent four important inputs into the design process that help professional developers make informed decisions. They cue designers to consider the following:

1. *Knowledge and beliefs.* "Stand on the shoulders of giants" by consulting the extensive knowledge bases that can inform the professional development work, and consider how the beliefs operating in your context align with the research.

2. *Context.* Understand the unique features of the local context and use that information to inform the design.

3. *Critical issues.* Pay attention to issues that may influence the success and impact of any professional development, and plan ahead to address them.

4. *Strategies.* Consider a wide range of professional development strategies; choose ones most aligned with your goals, match the needs of the audience, and support teachers to learn and grow over time.

Another way of thinking about these four inputs is that the first, *knowledge and beliefs,* helps answer the question, "What knowledge should inform us, based on the research?" The second, *context,* signals the designer to ask, "What is needed most in our local site, and what resources and conditions may support or threaten us?" The next, *critical issues,* leads us to consider "how certain conditions should be addressed to better ensure our success." The fourth, *strategies,* provides an opportunity to explore the question, "Which strategies, and in what combination, will contribute to enhanced teacher learning and practice?"

The arrows from the input circles into the design and implementation process boxes indicate when in the process these four inputs are most important to start to consider. For example, note that strategies are most important to consider after goals are clearly established. Otherwise, there is the danger of selecting trendy strategies that may not align with your goals, meet your student learning needs, or fit your context. Once an input is considered, it is assumed that it will continue to inform all subsequent stages in the process. For example, the input of knowledge and beliefs informs *commit to vision and standards* and every subsequent step, including how the plan is designed, implemented, and evaluated. The input context determines the data you consider in the *analyze student learning and other data* step and helps identify the student, teacher, and organizational needs the professional development should address. Plans are made and implemented based on a solid understanding of contextual factors such as available time, resources, leadership, and school culture and are evaluated, in part, by the extent to which these and other context factors are positively impacted. Planners next consider critical issues like equity, scaling up, and building capacity to inform the *set goals* and *plan* steps, and they continue to attend to these critical issues as they are implementing and evaluating the program.

The input strategies has two arrows connecting it to both the *plan* and *do* steps in the design framework. At the plan step, one considers which strategies would best address the identified goals and outcomes, based on all prior inputs and implementation processes, and selects a combination of strategies. In the do step, those strategies are implemented based on the plan. However, this is also the point at which the final design and implementation process, *evaluate results,* plays a critical role. During the plan and do steps, designers develop plans for how they will evaluate the effectiveness and impact of the professional development plan and anticipate the data that will be gathered. Throughout the do step, designers monitor implementation based on data and refine the implementation of the selected strategies. For example, ongoing monitoring may reveal that teachers have achieved an intended outcome, and then additional strategies may be implemented to address new and emerging needs. Monitoring might also alert designers to the emergence of additional critical issues that need to be addressed in the plan.

Designers also engage in summative evaluation, again using data, to determine the extent to which the entire professional development plan has impacted changes in the context, facilitated achievement of the goals, addressed the critical issues, and contributed to closing the gap from the current status to the achievement of the vision. This formal step of evaluating results leads the designer into the *reflect and revise* process, indicated by the arrow that connects the final process box back into the commit to vision and standards process box. The reflection on results guides revision and refinement of the overall plan as designers continue to implement professional development. The reflect and revise arrow illustrates the cyclical and continuous process of designing, implementing, evaluating, and refining professional learning programs.

The process mapped out in the design framework can be used to design both small- and large-scale professional learning programs, ranging from those in an individual school to those for a statewide or national initiative. It can guide designs that involve a single strategy, such as a workshop or study group, or a complex program, combining several strategies either simultaneously or over time. Whatever the grain size, the design framework provides a map for crafting professional development to achieve the desired goals for students and teachers.

The framework describes professional development design at its best—an ideal to strive toward, rather than an accurate depiction of how it always happens or a lockstep prescription for how it should happen. Given limited resources, especially time, professional developers may not always have the luxury of giving their full attention to every one of the four inputs and the six design and implementation process steps in the model. The professional developers who helped to create the framework extracted its components from what they actually did and what they wished they had done better. With the benefit of hindsight, they helped to construct the framework that alerts planners to important bases to cover and pitfalls to avoid. For programs just being designed, planners can take advantage of the knowledge and experience of others who have preceded them down the path.

If professional development programs are already underway, the framework can stimulate reflection and refinement. Wherever planners are in their process, they can hone in on the parts of the framework that best serve their purposes, knowing that no planning process is perfect and that even the "best-laid plans" are always subject to change. For example, if you are in the midst of setting goals, you might scan the research to see how your goals align. Is there evidence in the research that supports your goal? Also consider whether the contextual data support the goals. Are you inviting the right teachers, and have you targeted the areas of highest student learning need? If you are already providing the professional development, turn to the discussion of strategies to learn how different strategies might support your existing program. Reflect on your results, and then consider the inputs that are of most interest to you. Perhaps it would be a good time to think through critical issues that you have not yet addressed. The design framework supports such reflection and refinement wherever a program is in the process.

These next sections of this chapter briefly describe each element of the design framework. Chapters 2, 3, 4, and 5 provide more detail on each of the four major inputs into the design process. While the design framework looks rational and analytical, professional development design is more art than science. It is fueled by vision and passion; requires great skill, knowledge, and creativity; and continues to evolve as all of us who work in professional development strive for better results for students, teachers, and schools.

Knowledge and Beliefs

Figure 1.2   Professional Development Design Framework: Knowledge and Beliefs

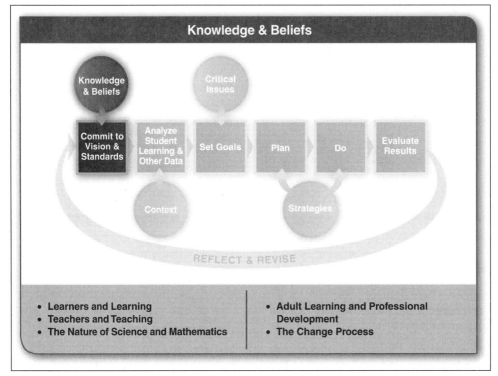

We have a lifetime of knowledge to draw upon when planning professional development, and that is why the first input designers consider is the existing knowledge and beliefs about improving science and mathematics education. In the design framework, knowledge and beliefs are delineated as an important input into every phase of design, from the initial vision to the evaluation.

Much is known about effective professional development for mathematics and science education, and more is being learned every day. For those of us who design and provide learning programs for teachers, the knowledge and beliefs we have constitute our specialized expertise. They help shape our professional judgment about what to do and not do and inform every decision we make as we design and conduct professional development. By *knowledge* we mean those things that are supported by solid facts and research; *beliefs* refer to those things we are coming to know or believe based on personal experiences, observations, and convictions. We must consider both knowledge and beliefs and how they influence the design and implementation of professional development. Taking advantage of this knowledge can help planners jump-start their efforts, put them on solid footing, and avoid unnecessary and costly mistakes. The professional development design framework suggests that designers start by consulting knowledge and beliefs reflected in five distinct, but related *domains* (see Figure 1.2).

The first domain is *learners and learning.* An explosion of cognitive research in the past few decades has resulted in a rich body of knowledge about how people learn in general and in mathematics and science in particular (Anderson, 1995; Bransford, Brown, & Cocking, 1999; Cobb, 1994; Donovan & Bransford, 2005; Driver, Asoko, Leach, Mortimer, & Scott, 1994; Duschl, Schweingruber, & Schouse, 2007; Mezirow, 1997). Professional developers use this knowledge to guide decisions about the content and the activities for professional learning.

A second domain is what is known about *teachers and teaching.* This includes how teachers develop their specialized knowledge and skills and learn to use effective instructional practices (Shulman, 1986). This domain further informs the decisions a designer makes about the content for the professional development (e.g., what should teachers know about the topics they teach, and what kinds of instructional strategies should teachers be learning?).

The third domain is *the nature of science and mathematics* (American Association for the Advancement of Science, 1989; Hazen & Trefil, 1991; National Council of Teachers of Mathematics, 2000; Paulos, 1992). Knowing that science and technology often entail investigation, design, and discovery and that mathematics involves problem solving and communication and both reflect unique dispositions, such as being analytical, skeptical, and inquiring, raises the question of how the professional development can model these actions and habits of mind so that teachers experience the true nature of the disciplines and consider how to provide similar experiences for their students.

The fourth domain is what is known about effective *adult learning and professional development* (Blank, de las Alas, & Smith, 2008; Darling-Hammond, 2000; Garet, Porter, Desimone, Birman, & Yoon, 2001; National Staff Development Council, 2001b; Wei et al., 2009). It guides designers to use research-based principles on effective teacher learning, such as making sure professional learning is linked to classroom practice; provides ample support for teachers to try out new learning in the classroom; and ensures programs are of an adequate duration and engage teachers as adult learners.

The last important domain is the knowledge base on *the change process* (Fullan, 1993, 2002; Hall & Hord, 2006; Wagner et al., 2006). Understanding this domain helps designers think about professional development as a process of individual and organizational change through which teachers transform their knowledge and apply new ideas to changes in practice. An understanding of the change process enables designers to anticipate and plan for how teachers will be supported to move from awareness to implementation to sustainability of new practices. When change involves deeply held beliefs, special actions are needed to open up new ways of thinking and support teachers to integrate new knowledge and abandon or reframe ideas that no longer work.

Having an understanding of these domains helps professional developers clarify what they know and believe about learners and learning, teachers and teaching, the nature of the discipline, effective professional development, and the educational change process. They may identify areas where their own experiences and beliefs or those of their colleagues are not aligned with the research. This is a good opportunity to talk about and clarify what knowledge and beliefs will be reflected in a professional development program. As designers clarify and articulate their beliefs, these beliefs become the "conscience" of the program. They shape goals, drive decisions, create discomfort when violated, and stimulate ongoing critique.

In Chapter 2, we discuss in detail the growing consensus about what is known in each of these domains and summarize key points that professional development designers need to keep in mind.

Context

Figure 1.3   Professional Development Design Framework: Context

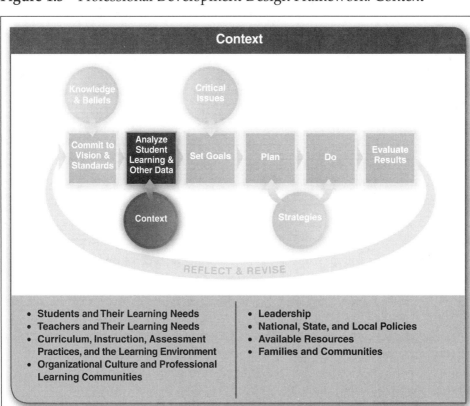

There is no prescription for which designs are right for which situations—no "paint by numbers kit" for professional development. Skilled professional developers have one foot planted firmly in theory (knowledge and beliefs and vision) and the other in action (the local context, data about students, issues faced, and planning and doing professional development). As professional developers design their programs, they are influenced by their vision of what science and mathematics teaching, learning, and professional development should look like. They are equally concerned with providing teacher learning programs that are relevant, so they must carefully analyze and study their own context. There are *eight* important aspects of the local context that designers need to consider (see Figure 1.3).

Designers must know who the students are, what learning results have been attained, and what learning problems exist. For example, designers should ask an array of questions, such as "Are students underperforming in certain subjects or specific topics?" "Are there achievement gaps between rich and poor, different student populations, males and females, and what practices are contributing to these gaps?" Designers also need to know about the teachers they will work with. They consider questions like "What knowledge do our teachers have, and what new knowledge do they need?" "What are their beliefs about teaching and learning, and how do they teach?" "Do they collaborate with other teachers?"

Designers also rely on information about current curriculum, instruction, and assessment practices and the kinds of learning environments created for students. It is also important to understand the culture and the extent to which there is a professional learning community among teachers. This information serves as the basis for professional development goals for students, teachers, instruction, and the organization and helps to ensure that professional development is linked with learning results. Other features of the context that are important to consider are the leadership; national, state, and local policies that must be observed; available resources such as time, money, and expertise; and families and communities. Considering these factors helps designers make better decisions as they plan, implement, and evaluate programs.

In Chapter 3, we provide more in-depth discussion of each of the eight contextual factors and help designers think about the unique ways in which their local contexts inform the professional development program.

Critical Issues

Figure 1.4   Professional Development Design Framework: Critical Issues

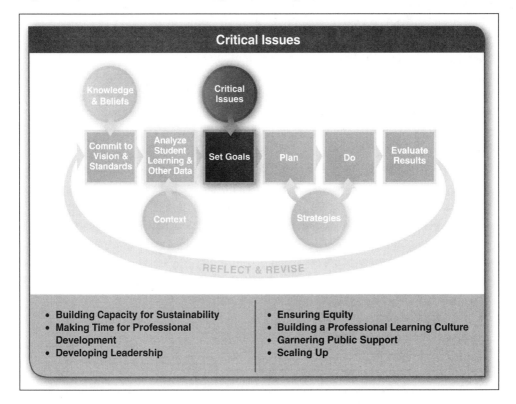

As we looked at professional development programs throughout the country, we discovered some common issues that designers were facing. These issues were critical to the success of programs everywhere, regardless of the context (although context will heavily influence how they take shape). We called these *critical issues* because it is essential for professional developers to consider how to address them as part of their planning, or they are likely to create problems for them later on.

There are seven critical issues: (1) building capacity for sustainability, (2) making time for professional development, (3) developing leadership, (4) ensuring equity, (5) building a professional learning culture, (6) garnering public support, and (7) scaling up (see Figure 1.4). Proactive planners anticipate these issues and begin grappling with them in the initial design phase. As the program is implemented, they keep these issues in the forefront, confronting obstacles and creating opportunities to better respond to these challenges. The critical issues defy easy solutions. They are the "tough nuts" that professional developers work to crack as they design and provide learning experiences for teachers.

Chapter 4 examines these issues in all of their complexity, summarizing research, offering examples of best practice, and posing enduring, unresolved questions.

Strategies for Professional Learning

Figure 1.5 Professional Development Design Framework: Strategies

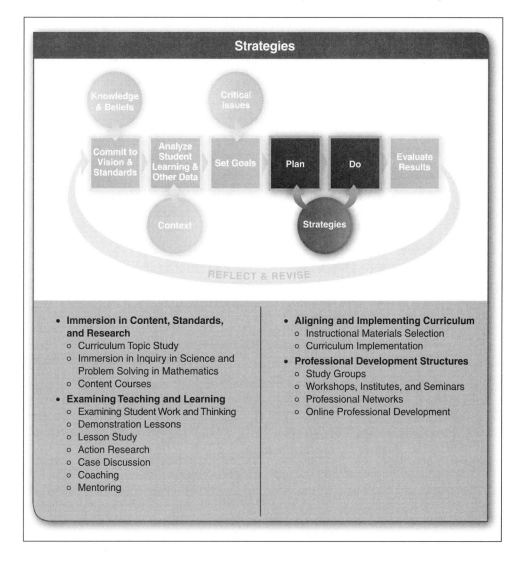

After setting program goals, professional developers plan how they will implement the program. At this point, they consider another important input—the strategies they can use for professional learning (see Figure 1.5). Like classroom teachers, effective professional developers have a variety of

strategies to draw on and skillfully select and combine to achieve their goals and to support change over time. With a repertoire of strategies, professional developers can design programs that address different goals and embed professional learning into the daily lives of teachers. For example, if the goals are to build content knowledge and increase teachers' understanding of student thinking and learning progressions, the professional developer might choose two different strategies—a content course combined with sessions for groups of teachers to examine and reflect on student work and thinking.

In this book, we identify 16 professional development strategies that can be used in a variety of contexts for different purposes. The 16 strategies are organized into four clusters that define the set of strategies in that cluster (see Figure 1.5). The clusters are (1) immersion in content, standards, and research; (2) examining teaching and learning; (3) aligning and implementing curriculum; and (4) professional development structures. The fourth cluster includes strategies that are generic structures for providing professional development (e.g., study groups, workshops, institutes, seminars, professional networks, and online professional development). When planning, one considers which of the strategies will be used to provide professional development, and more important, what content and learning activities will be provided within the strategies to support the learning goals of the professional development.

A professional development program can be made up of multiple strategies offered simultaneously to groups of teachers to meet their different needs or accommodate varied learning styles. For example, novice teachers might benefit from a multiday immersion in science inquiry followed by mentoring by an experienced teacher to learn to teach through inquiry. More expert teachers might follow up on the immersion experience with an action research project to study what students learn through inquiry. Different strategies can also be phased in over time, such as working with external experts initially and then moving to more teacher-directed strategies such as study groups, demonstration lessons, and action research as teachers' confidence and skill increase. Rather than models, these 16 strategies are the palette from which professional developers can select and blend individual colors to give life and form to their professional development programs.

Each of the clusters and strategies is further described in Chapter 5. For each cluster, we provide a discussion of the underlying assumptions that are foundational to the strategies within the grouping and the implementation requirements for the cluster of strategies. Each strategy is then illustrated through a vignette, followed by discussion of the key elements, the way in which the strategy addresses specific intended outcomes, suggestions for combining with other strategies, reflections on the issues to consider, and a list of resources to gain more in-depth information about the strategy and how to implement it within a program. The information about the clusters and strategies contained in Chapter 5 is intended to assist planners in selecting and combining strategies to align with their specific goals and contexts.

THE DESIGN AND IMPLEMENTATION PROCESS

Figure 1.6 Professional Development Design Framework: The Design and Implementation Process

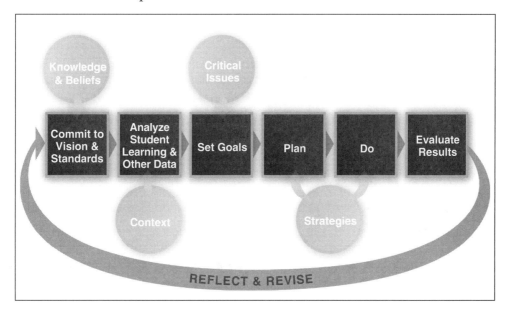

The important inputs in the framework described above—knowledge and beliefs, context, critical issues, and strategies—influence the professional development design process. While it is essential to take each of these into account, the design process has a life of its own. It sometimes follows a logical sequence from committing to a vision, to analyzing student learning data, to setting goals, planning, doing, and evaluating as the framework suggests. Yet most professional developers are already in the midst of implementing their programs. They can enter the step or stage of the framework wherever they find themselves and loop back to prior steps to consider how they may influence future decisions.

A brief look at each of the phases of the design and implementation process (commit to vision and standards → analyze student learning and other data → set goals → plan → do → evaluate results → reflect and revise) follows (see Figure 1.6).

Commit to Vision and Standards

Figure 1.7   Professional Development Design Framework: The Design and Implementation Process: Commit to Vision and Standards

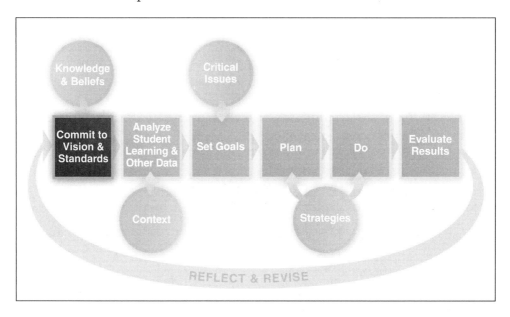

The reform of mathematics and science education rests firmly on a commitment to enhance teaching and learning to reach much higher levels of learning as reflected in national and international standards for all students. The vision of mathematics and science teaching and learning, based on the standards developed by the National Council of Teachers of Mathematics (NCTM, 1989, 1991, 1995, 2000), the National Academy of Science's National Research Council (National Research Council [NRC], 1996), and the American Association for the Advancement of Science (AAAS, 1993), is one in which all students engage in inquiry into significant questions in science and investigate complex problems in mathematics in supportive, collegial communities. Students come to deeply understand important science and mathematics ideas and master complex skills and reasoning processes that are essential to scientific and mathematical literacy. To achieve this vision, teachers need strong content knowledge and the skills, behaviors, and dispositions of the science and mathematical disciplines. Teachers need to have ownership in the vision of high standards and quality education for all and feel competent to create appropriate learning environments for their students. This includes feeling secure in the knowledge of the content they will help their students learn and possessing a wide array of instructional strategies known to support successful learning.

For this to happen, teachers need opportunities for ongoing professional growth—ones in which they learn what they need to know to achieve the vision, in ways that model how they can work with their students. Schools need to break down the barriers to teacher collaboration and promote the sharing of effective practice. Schools themselves must become learning communities. The National Staff Development Council's (2001b) professional development standards and the teaching standards and professional development standards in the NCTM and NRC documents clearly articulate a vision for science and mathematics teaching and professional development. Because it is difficult, if not impossible, to teach in ways that one has not learned, teachers also need opportunities to inquire into significant questions in science and to learn challenging mathematics and reflect on their own learning and teaching in supportive, collegial communities. That is why effective professional development programs start with committing to a vision of quality teaching and learning and begin the design process by asking: "What do classrooms in which the vision of science and mathematics teaching and learning, based on local, state, and national standards, is playing out look like?" And following from that question, "What do professional development opportunities in which teachers learn in that way and learn to teach in that way look like?"

Supporting standards is more than an issue to be considered; standards set the course for professional development (see Figure 1.7). Providing teachers with the knowledge and skills they need to help every student achieve high standards is the central purpose of professional development. Standards guide the selection of content for professional development, which helps teachers explore the "big ideas" of the disciplines and deepen their content knowledge. Standards themselves are often the subject of professional development, as teachers immerse themselves in studying what the standards mean and what their implications are for learning and teaching and professional development. And standards serve as the foundation of the vision that inspires the professional development design process from beginning to end.

Dennis Sparks (1997) wrote, "It's been said that someone who has a 'why' can endure any 'how'; few things are more important to motivation than purpose that is regarded as profoundly and morally compelling" (pp. 24–25). The vision of learning, teaching, and professional development based on standards is the "why" of professional development design. It is the desire to reach the vision that motivates professional developers to create powerful learning opportunities for teachers. It is the tension between the vision and the current reality that fuels goal setting and planning, drives the desire to change, and gives meaning to the daily tasks of implementing professional development programs. And as professional developers reflect on and evaluate their programs, they gauge how well the school community is moving closer to its vision and recommit to the future they want for students, teachers, and schools.

What actually happens in the phase "commit to vision and standards" of the design process? How does a school community solidify its commitment to a vision and a set of standards for science and mathematics reform? Many educators have experienced the process of developing a vision as a meaningless exercise of putting words on paper that are either promptly ignored, written and embraced by only a few, or so general as to inspire no one. Because the vision for science and mathematics reform is rooted in deeply held beliefs and assumptions, developing a truly shared and compelling vision is a complex and long-term process. Notice in the design framework that an important input into the vision is knowledge and beliefs—the knowledge bases about learning, teaching, the nature of science and mathematics, professional development, and the change process. It is important that the vision statements are based on shared knowledge, not shared ignorance, and that school staff take the time to study relevant research and national standards and supporting documents. Without exception, the professional developers who worked on this book reported drawing on these knowledge bases to formulate the purpose, guiding principles, and core outcomes for their work. Schools can do the same by asking a few key questions (see Table 1.1).

Table 1.1   Committing to a Vision and Standards: Questions to Consider

Questions to Consider
1. What is our vision for science and mathematics teaching and learning?
2. What do students need to know and be able to do in mathematics and science?
3. How will we know if they have gained this knowledge?
4. What will we do if they do not gain this knowledge?
5. What do classrooms in which this new vision is playing out look like?
6. What do teachers need to know and be able to do if students are to achieve these standards?
7. What is our vision for teachers' learning?
8. What does professional development in which this new vision is playing out look like?
9. To support this vision of science and mathematics teaching, learning, and professional development, what kind of an organization do we need to be?

Creating opportunities for constructive dialogue around the questions in Table 1.1 can contribute to developing a shared vision for education in schools, but it is important to keep in mind that this is not just a one-time, linear process. Designers may not get everyone on the same page before they need to move ahead. It is important to start the process and then move ahead, revisiting these questions at different points. Very often, the shared vision and commitment to creating an educational environment that is based on research and the standards is generated over time as teachers engage in professional development experiences. It is important not to wait to provide professional development until the entire school community is united around a common vision. Michael Fullan (1993) reminds us that "vision emerges from, more than it precedes, action" (p. 28) and that "ready, fire, aim" may be a more productive sequence (p. 31). *Ready* implies that professional development design starts with some notion of purpose, especially for those designing the effort, but does not bog down in perfecting the shared vision. *Fire* is implementing the professional development program. It is through doing, learning, reflecting, evaluating, and applying new knowledge and skills that the vision is clarified. *Aim,* according to Fullan, is crystallizing new beliefs and clarifying and strengthening the sense of shared purpose. While commitment to vision and high standards for all students comes first in the sequence of the design framework, this phase is in fact iterative and interactive with all other phases of the process.

Analyze Student Learning and Other Data

Figure 1.8   Professional Development Design Framework: The Design and Implementation Process: Analyze Student Learning and Other Data

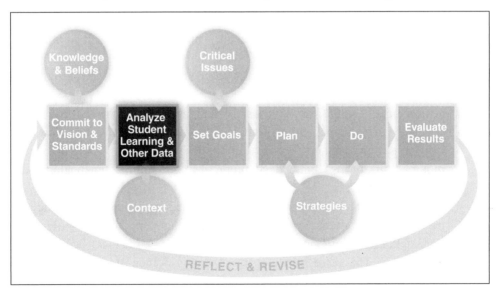

Relevant Student Learning and Other Data

- Demographic data about students and teachers
- Multiple measures of students' achievement of standards
- Student learning data disaggregated by race and ethnicity, economic status, English language learners, students with special needs, and gender
- Data about classroom practice and students' opportunity to learn
- Data about professional development, the school culture, and leadership

In this phase of the professional development design and implementation process, professional developers take stock of their reality as they explore the gap between the current and the desired state—based on the vision and standards—and set targets for improvement (see Figure 1.8). When a school community has a shared commitment to high standards for all students, it is better prepared to take an honest look at student learning data and is more likely to experience dissatisfaction with results that fall short of its commitments, rather than complacency, resignation, or defensiveness (Love, Stiles, Mundry, & DiRanna, 2008). The purpose of analyzing student learning and other data is to identify specific targets for improving student learning that will determine the goals for teacher learning and form the basis for a professional development program clearly focused on results for students. When designing professional development for a local school or district, it is crucial that the professional development plan is linked with school or district goals for improving mathematics or science learning.

Student Learning Data

Most important in this phase, professional developers examine multiple sources of student learning data to determine what essential knowledge and skills students are and are not learning and what performance gaps exist between rich and poor, males and females, and different student populations. Data analysis can begin with readily available data such as state and district assessments, including both standards-based and norm-referenced test results.

These assessments, however, do not provide adequate evidence of achievement of all the knowledge, skills, and dispositions that local communities may value and that national standards and many state and local standards call for, such as mathematical reasoning, problem solving, communication, inquiry skills, or in-depth understanding of important mathematical and scientific concepts.

An important part of enacting a vision based on standards is putting into place a comprehensive local assessment system that complements high-stakes tests with more formative assessments tied to local standards and curriculum. This assessment system would include performance tasks, portfolios, and scoring and examination of student work as well as short-answer and multiple-choice tests. In addition to classroom and school or district local assessments, common assessments administered periodically by teachers who teach the same grade level or course can provide teachers with timely and relevant feedback on the extent to which students are mastering agreed-on standards (Love et al., 2008). Figure 1.9 illustrates the different types of data and the frequency of analysis that schools and districts will want to use during this step in the design process.

By using multiple measures, professional developers verify their perceptions of student learning needs with more than one data source. Goals for professional development are not arbitrary or based on the latest fad but instead are grounded in the needs that are showing up consistently in the

Figure 1.9   The Data Pyramid

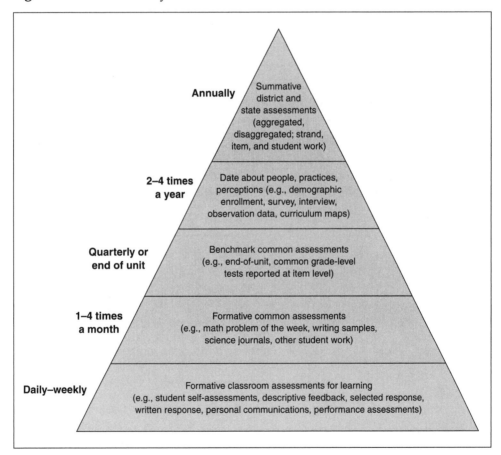

Source: Love, N., Stiles, K. E., Mundry, S., and DiRanna, K. (2008). *The Data Coach's Guide to Improving Learning for All Students: Unleashing the Power of Collaborative Inquiry* (p. 129). Thousand Oaks, CA: Corwin. Used with permission.

data. Another advantage of using both classroom and common grade-level assessments along with state and district assessments to target needs is that teachers become actively involved in analyzing results and reflecting on how they can be enhanced. When teachers embrace the problems and identify potential solutions, they are more willing participants in the professional development programs designed to solve them. They also become active agents in testing out new instructional strategies and monitoring progress toward improvement (DiRanna et al., 2008; Love et al., 2008).

It is important not only to use multiple sources of assessments of student learning but also to go beyond superficial analyses of summary or aggregate reports to derive the maximum value for goal setting. Figure 1.10 illustrates a process for digging deeply into state- and local-assessment results to get a better idea of the learning goals and, therefore, what areas professional development needs to address. The process begins with examining aggregate or summary reports. These reports provide the headlines such as, overall, what percentage of students met standards in mathematics or science. Aggregated data, examined over time, also provide information that reveals trends, such as progress in increasing the percentage of students who meet standards.

To explore performance gaps, professional developers need to go beyond the aggregate or summary reports to examine disaggregated results, results separated out by different populations of students, such as students receiving lunch assistance and those not, racial and ethnic groups, language groups, and males and females.

Figure 1.10   Drill Down Into Student Learning

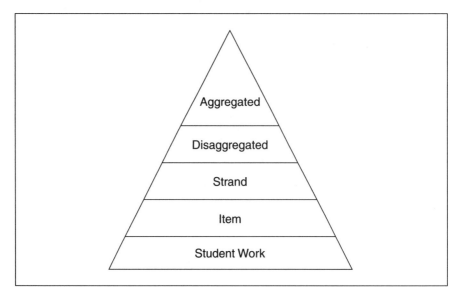

Source: Love, N., Stiles, K. E., Mundry, S., and DiRanna, K. (2008). *The Data Coach's Guide to Improving Learning for All Students: Unleashing the Power of Collaborative Inquiry* (p. 132). Thousand Oaks, CA: Corwin. Used with permission.

Digging deeper into the data in this way enables professional developers to uncover achievement and performance gaps so that equity issues take center stage in the professional development plan. Often, schools do not even recognize that they have racial, economic, or cultural performance gaps until they examine disaggregated data. By uncovering these gaps, professional developers can direct attention to improving the achievement of specific groups of students who are not learning well. Their designs may include opportunities for teachers to diversify their instructional strategies, to better understand the racial and cultural backgrounds of their students, and to surface educators' beliefs, practices, and policies that may act as obstacles to some students' achievement of standards.

The next two levels of analysis are examining strand and item data. These levels of analysis require looking at how students performed on strands, such as geometry or physical science, and on particular test items within the strands. Getting inside the assessment and analyzing the actual items enables designers to identify the knowledge and skills the assessment items are actually measuring and to look for patterns in correct and incorrect answers. This level of analysis helps planners gain a much better sense of what knowledge and skills students are struggling with (e.g., not just mathematics problem solving in general but specific aspects of problem solving that are most challenging for students) and to pinpoint needs more precisely. Finally, examining student work often proves to be the most fruitful data source, providing rich insights into students' thinking. Examining student work is both a way to set goals for professional development and a way to engage teachers in professional development. Having them examine student work often creates many insights into what students are learning and what areas need improvement.

Opportunities-to-Learn Data

Performance gaps are often the result of inadequate opportunities for particular student populations to learn a rigorous mathematics and science curriculum. A study by Weiss, Banilower, McMahon, and Smith (2001) found that ability grouping was still widely practiced in mathematics and science and that classes labeled low ability are more likely to contain a high proportion of students of color. Another study by Weiss, Matti, and Smith (as cited in Weiss, 1997) found that students in low-ability classes had fewer opportunities to engage in inquiry-based science or write about reasoning when solving mathematical problems. Professional development programs should be geared not just to closing achievement gaps, but also to closing opportunities-to-learn gaps. In this phase of the design process, professional developers can also use data about course enrollment, special program placement, teachers' qualifications, and curriculum, instruction, and assessment practices to uncover what practices may be preventing some students from achieving standards (Love, 2002).

Data About Practice

Complementing data about student achievement and opportunities to learn are data about teachers' needs. What knowledge and skills do teachers need if students are going to reach specific standards? Identifying teachers' specific learning needs as they directly relate to student learning needs forms the basis for setting the goals and outcomes for the professional development program. In addition, data about the school, district, or organization can help designers assess the quality of leadership, the strength of the professional learning community, and the capacity of the organization to implement and sustain mathematics and science reform. Equally important is obtaining data related to prior professional development efforts. These data enable planners to consider what has been successful in the past to address teachers' and students' learning needs. These data can also help planners steer clear of efforts that did not result in changes in teachers' knowledge or practices.

As a result of engaging in the "analyze student learning and other data" step in the design process, professional developers have delved into data about student learning, opportunities to learn, and classroom practice to ensure that their goals focus on critical areas of need for student and teacher learning.

Set Goals

Figure 1.11   Professional Development Design Framework: The Design and Implementation Process: Set Goals

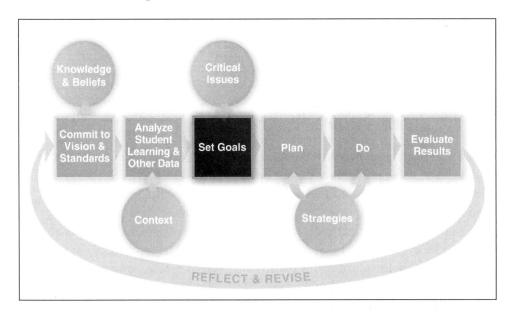

Rigorous analysis of student learning and other data sets the stage for setting goals for the professional development program (see Figure 1.11). If the vision describes the desired future and the data analysis describes the current reality, goals are the benchmarks or milestones to assess progress toward the vision. "Vision may inspire, but goals foster immediate accountability," says Richard DuFour and Robert Eaker (1998), who liken goals to the "ports of call on the journey toward improvement" (p. 203). A few clear, concrete, and attainable goals motivate, energize, and focus professional development and school improvement. On the other hand, according to Michael Schmoker (1999), the absence of explicit learning goals is "the most striking, self-defeating, contradictory characteristic of schools and our efforts to improve them" (p. 23). Since professional development is to be linked to student achievement, four kinds of goals are relevant: goals for student learning, goals for teacher learning, goals for teaching practice, and goals for the organization, such as developing leadership and building a professional community focused on student learning results.

> **Four Goals for Professional Development**
>
> - Goals for student learning
> - Goals for teacher learning
> - Goals for teaching practice
> - Goals for the organization

1. *Goals for student learning.* The driving force behind a professional development program is a small number of specific, attainable, and measurable student learning goals. Learning goals, according to Schmoker (2002), should target the lowest-scoring subjects or courses and target specific standards where achievement is low. Improvement efforts can bog down with long laundry lists of goals or vague or overly ambitious goals. As designers set goals for student learning, they tap into knowledge about teaching and learning and the nature of mathematics and science treated explicitly in the national and some state standards. In addition, setting goals for students involves analyzing students' needs and confronting disparities in achievement between different populations of students. It is essential that goals for student learning specifically address closing achievement gaps where applicable and expanding learning opportunities to all students.

2. *Goals for teacher learning.* Goals for teachers flow directly out of goals for students. If students are going to develop a set of understandings, skills, and predispositions, then what do teachers need to know to

realize those outcomes for students? Learning goals for teachers are also informed by referring to the standards, as well as data about teacher performance, knowledge and skills, needs, and supports available. These goals should attend equally to teachers' need to enhance their content knowledge of the discipline they teach and their pedagogical content knowledge (their understanding of how to make content accessible to their students).

3. *Goals for teaching practice.* Professional development that is linked to improving student learning should also set goals for teacher practice. How will teachers translate the new knowledge they are gaining into classroom practice? For example, many professional development programs focus on increasing teachers' content knowledge, and this is important. However, they often lack a clear emphasis on how teachers should translate their new knowledge into the classroom. For programs that aim to increase science or mathematics content knowledge, designers need to clarify what practices they would expect to see in the classroom and communicate these expectations to the teachers.

4. *Goals for the organization.* Professional development goals can also encompass goals for the organization, such as the development of leadership or the strengthening of the professional learning community. Often these goals are set to support the central goal of improving teaching and learning. For example, the professional development program may set goals to establish a core of teacher leaders who will support other teachers' growth through coaching and other collaborative work to improve practice. The inputs of knowledge and beliefs and critical issues also suggest that having explicit goals for leadership development and for building a professional learning community are essential for sustaining any changes in practice that the professional development program is designed to bring about.

Clarifying clear and worthwhile outcomes for student learning, teacher learning, teaching, and the organization not only brings focus and coherence to the professional development program but also lays the groundwork for future program evaluation. An important part of the goal-setting process, according to Guskey (2000), is to consider how goals will be assessed and what evidence will be used to determine whether goals are met.

Plan

Figure 1.12 Professional Development Design Framework: The Design and Implementation Process: Plan

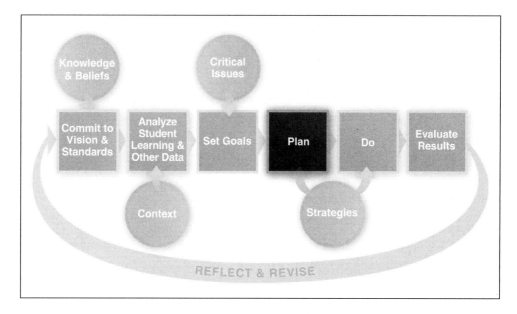

Once goals are set, planners begin to sketch out their design and think about how they will measure results. They ask themselves, "Given our goals, what is the best combination of strategies we should implement?" "If our goals are focused on increased content knowledge, what strategies should we use?" "What strategies will help teachers translate their new knowledge into improved classroom practice?" "Do we have the leadership we need to make it all happen, and if not, what strategies do we need to develop leaders?" Planners revisit what they know about the context, unearthing important factors to consider as they tailor their program to their own circumstances and review the student learning and other data they have collected to connect plans to goals.

This is when they may decide they need more information about learning, teaching, mathematics or science, professional development, or the change process. Having a research-based vision of what effective programs can look like can generate some ideas for their plans. Learning about similar districts' plans and consulting the education literature can also be helpful. Planning is the time to revisit and clarify the beliefs that underlie the program. Critical issues enter in as planners consider how to confront challenges such as "How will we scale up the program to reach large numbers of teachers or build leadership to sustain changes in teacher practice?" This is also the process step where the program would develop its plan and timeline for how to gather evaluation data and what data to gather.

The design framework has been used to plan small- and large-scale programs. Planners for small-scale efforts pick and choose among the contextual factors, critical issues, and knowledge and beliefs that are most relevant for their initiative and use the design and implementation steps in the framework to be more thoughtful and deliberate about their planning. For a small-scale effort such as one institute, professional developers do not consider every context factor but think carefully about the most relevant ones, especially about the participants' backgrounds and their learning needs. For example, when they are working with teams of teachers who have little planning time back in their districts, they are sure to provide productive planning time within the institute. Whether large- or small-scale, short- or long-term, professional developers draw on the most relevant inputs into the design process to develop their plans for the professional development program.

Do

Figure 1.13   Professional Development Design Framework: The Design and Implementation Process: Do

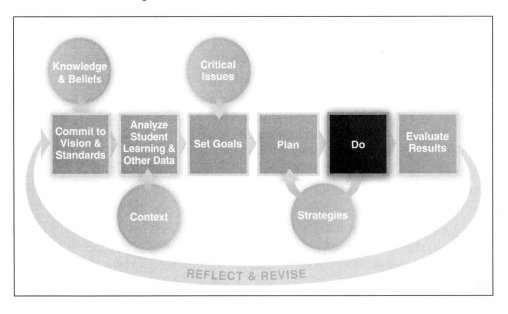

Having made the best decisions they can, designers move from "sketching" to "painting"—the actual implementation of their plan (see Figure 1.13). In this phase, they draw on their skills as content experts and facilitators and their knowledge about implementation and the change process (e.g., Fullan, 1991, 2001; Hall & Hord, 2006; Kegan & Lahey, 2009). For fundamental change to happen, teachers need to experience learning the way they will implement it in the classroom and experiment with new behavior and gain new understandings, and that takes time. They will move through predictable developmental stages in how they feel and how they are using new approaches (Hall & Hord). Frequently, things get worse before they get better, as teachers experience what Fullan calls the "implementation dip." Teachers try new instructional strategies, and they struggle to get it right. Without help and the opportunity to talk with others experiencing the same struggle, they may just go back to doing things the old way. This is when it is critical to provide follow-up help, classroom visits, and other support structures to help teachers make corrections and commit to changing their practice.

What is most important for professional developers in the do stage is to pay close attention and monitor how the professional development is working: "How are the teachers reacting to and engaging with the content?" "What adjustments do we need to make?" "What are they learning?" "What are they having difficulty with?" "How will we reteach content they are having difficulty learning?" "How can we support them to set realistic goals for taking their learning back to the classroom?" "What new teacher learning needs are emerging, and how will we address them?"

Despite the best-laid plans, it is impossible to predict how the initial design will work. As the action unfolds, designers discover what works and what doesn't. Like artists stepping back from the canvas and examining their work from different perspectives, professional developers continuously monitor their plan using a variety of data sources. They ask questions such as "Is this working?" "Are we moving toward our goals of improved student learning in mathematics and science?" "Are we meeting participants' needs?" "Is our program, in fact, a good match with our context?" "What conditions, if any, have changed, and how should we respond?" "What critical issues do we need to address now?" Sometimes their reflection is enhanced by interested visitors (sometimes called "critical friends") who sensitize professional developers to important aspects of their programs seen from different perspectives.

Based on this feedback, planners often go back to the drawing board. It is rare that an entire program is carried out exactly as planned. As the examples in this book will illustrate, the most successful programs do not start out with flawless designs. They begin with a sound idea that then goes through many revisions and continues to evolve. Programs change over time both because planners figure out a better way and because conditions change, sometimes as a direct result of the professional development program. There is a live interplay between context and implementation. Far from linear or lockstep, implementing professional development is recursive and usually messy, demanding flexibility and continuous learning throughout the process.

Evaluate Results

Figure 1.14   Professional Development Design Framework: The Design and Implementation Process: Evaluate Results

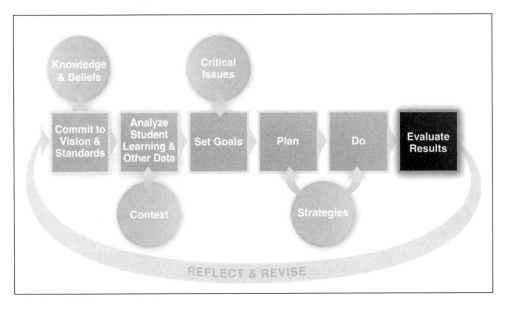

An essential but often overlooked or underused part of the professional development design process is evaluation of results (see Figure 1.14). Professional development opportunities are designed for a wide variety of purposes and to achieve specific goals. It is the role of evaluation to determine whether and in what ways they are successful in meeting the goals.

Fulfilling that role, however, is rarely easy for several reasons. First, regardless of the purpose of a given program, people typically jump to measure what is easiest: satisfaction of participants. Because of this norm, it is difficult to get people to think more broadly about outcomes and measures. Second, there is increasing demand to assess the value of professional development based on the achievement of the students of those teachers who participate. This demand is well-founded, given the large investment of resources that has been made in professional development and the critical need to improve student learning and close achievement gaps. The challenge here is not to expect student learning outcomes prematurely, before the professional development program has been fully implemented and teacher learning and change in practice have been well supported and documented over time. Nonetheless, it is important that professional developers broaden the valued outcomes for in-depth, long-term professional development to include changes in classroom practice and in student learning results. Finally, evaluation needs attention because it is underused as a valuable learning experience for professional developers, participants, and others. Reflection on evaluation results, as they are being gathered as well as when synthesized, is an important contributor to continuous improvement. There are several questions that professional developers can ask themselves that may help them address the challenges of evaluation of their programs and initiatives:

- What are the goals or desired outcomes of the program or initiative?
- What evidence would demonstrate accomplishment of the program's outcomes?
- How do you gather data on program outcomes and evaluate changes in practice over time?
- How do you take advantage of evaluation as a learning experience?

What are the goals or desired outcomes of the program or initiative?

Professional developers typically have a wide range of goals, but they are often not skilled at articulating them as outcomes. "What would you see if you were successful?" "What would have changed and for whom?" It is easier to think of activities than accomplishments; for example, conducting a summer institute and a series of follow-up problem-solving sessions is often cited as a goal, rather than teachers using inquiry-based strategies in their classrooms as a result of the summer institute and follow-up programs. The range of possible outcomes is quite large: development of new abilities (knowledge, skills, strategies, dispositions) by a variety of people (teachers, students, administrators) and organizations (departments, teams, schools, districts) in a variety of areas (teaching, leadership, change management). Being clear about desired outcomes and articulating what they would look like if they were present not only lays important groundwork for evaluation but also results in a more focused and purposeful program.

What evidence would demonstrate accomplishment of the program's outcomes?

Evaluation helps collect evidence of the extent to which a program's aims have been met. A wide range of instruments and sources of information are often used to amass evidence that teachers learn or gain something from professional development, that they later apply the learning to their practice, and that ultimately there is some change in the classroom. Content assessments, interviews, observations, document analysis (e.g., lesson plans), performance tasks, focus groups—all can contribute evidence. Teachers, students, colleagues, administrators, scientists, and mathematicians—all can be sources of information about the outcomes of a professional learning experience. Obviously there are trade-offs for every instrument and source of information, for example, in cost, time, degree of self-report, or amount of inference required (Guskey, 2000). These are all considered in designing an evaluation keyed to a particular purpose, audience, and budget.

The framework for data collection includes the quality of the professional development activities; extent of teacher involvement in the activities; changes in teacher attitudes and beliefs; changes in science and mathematics curriculum, instruction, and assessment; nature of the culture or context for teaching; and the sustainability of the professional development system (Horizon Research Inc., 2001). There are several tested evaluation instruments in the public domain that can be used to gather information. Horizon Research, Inc.'s Web site (www.horizon-research.com/instruments) provides a set of evaluation instruments they developed for National Science Foundation projects. There are also a number of content and pedagogical content knowledge assessments in science and mathematics that can be used. Some examples are the *Learning Mathematics for Teaching Assessment* from the University of Michigan and the *Diagnostic Science Assessment* and the *Diagnostic Mathematics Assessment for Middle School Teachers* from the University of Louisville. These can be used as a pretest prior to starting the professional development and as a posttest after the program is complete to assess teacher gains. Teachers can be actively involved in looking at the results in their own classrooms by using formative assessments that provide evidence of what students know prior to and after instruction (e.g., Keeley, Eberle, & Farrin, 2005; Keeley, Eberle, & Tugel, 2007).

How do you gather data on program outcomes and evaluate changes in practice over time?

The impact of professional learning activities looks different at different times. This is why it is foolhardy to either expect or focus on measuring student learning when teachers have just begun to learn and experiment with new ideas and strategies. Well-designed evaluations unfold with expectations for change. For example, one might focus on measuring participants' satisfaction and whether they are developing basic understanding early in a program; change in classroom behavior and in the professional culture midway; and then on various kinds of student change, beginning with attitudes and evolving to demonstrating new, deeper understandings of concepts.

To address this issue, evaluators have used concepts and tools of the Concerns-Based Adoption Model (Hall & Hord, 2006) to answer questions about the implementation of changes in mathematics and science education (Loucks-Horsley et al., 1990; Pratt & Loucks-Horsley, 1993). Three kinds of questions can be asked: "How do teachers' concerns about the new program or teaching strategy change over time?" "How does their use of the new program or teaching strategy change over time?" "To what extent do teachers implement the critical components of the new program or teaching strategy over time?" Two developmental scales—Stages of Concern (assessed using paper-and-pencil instruments) and Levels of Use (assessed through a focused interview procedure)—provide criteria for assessing progress along the change continuum. Components of the program or strategy can also be defined and assessed using a combination of interview and observation; the different configurations that the program components take on in different classrooms can then be represented and monitored over time.

After sufficient time has elapsed for teacher change to result in improvement in student learning, students are an appropriate focus for professional development evaluation. A unique evaluation scheme was used by the Mathematics Renaissance (see Chapter 6) in its final and fifth year to evaluate the impact on students of the professional development it provided to middle school teachers throughout the state of California. As part of the Third International Mathematics and Science Study (TIMSS), hundreds of hours of classroom instruction have been videotaped in mathematics classrooms throughout the United States (U.S. Department of Education, 1996), which have been compared to those of classrooms in Japan and Germany using a very sophisticated coding and analysis procedure. Videotapes of classrooms of teachers participating in Mathematics Renaissance professional development were made, and similarly coded and analyzed. They were compared with a sample of the TIMSS tapes of U.S. classrooms to address the question, "Do students of Mathematics Renaissance teachers have a greater opportunity to develop the kinds of mathematical understandings, skills, and attitudes called for in the NCTM Standards and the California Mathematics Framework than do students of teachers not involved in Mathematics Renaissance?"

A valuable resource for guiding the evaluation of professional development is the book *Evaluating Professional Development* (Guskey, 2000), which identifies five critical levels of professional development evaluation ranging from simple to more complex. Each level builds on the one before it:

- Level 1: Participants' reaction
- Level 2: Participants' learning
- Level 3: Organizational support and change
- Level 4: Participants' use of new knowledge and skills
- Level 5: Student learning outcomes (p. 82)

For each level, Guskey lays out what questions are addressed, what information will be gathered through which evaluation methods, what is measured or assessed, and how the information will be used.

How do you take advantage of evaluation as a learning experience?

Increasingly, evaluators are becoming partners with professional developers in a commitment to continuous improvement of programs and their results. Involvement is the key word here, through such activities as

- engaging program staff, as well as participants, in specifying and discussing desired outcomes and identifying and prioritizing evaluation questions;
- involving staff and participants in the design or review of instruments or procedures for assessing outcomes;
- sharing responsibility with staff and participants for collecting data;
- engaging staff in analyzing and interpreting data; and
- sharing responsibility for reporting learning from the evaluation with a variety of audiences using a variety of formats.

Each of these activities can contribute to staff and participant understanding of their own learning and that of others, of a variety of methods to assess important learning outcomes as well as interpret information gathered, of ways to specify and then to investigate the answers to important questions, and of how to communicate to a variety of audiences and develop arguments for new ways of acting.

Reflect and Revise

Figure 1.15   Professional Development Design Framework: The Design and Implementation Process: Reflect and Revise

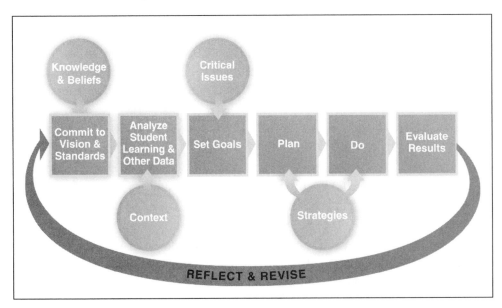

Although the professional development design framework illustrates this step in the process as emerging out of the "evaluate results" step (see Figure 1.15), reflecting and revising is a step that is continuous, ongoing, and embedded throughout all other process steps. For example, none of the inputs remain static over time. The knowledge base about learning, teaching, the nature of mathematics and science, professional development, and the change process is constantly growing. Designers, therefore, need to continuously reflect on emerging research and ask, "How does this new information influence our professional development?" Beliefs change, too. Seeing the impact of their work, professional developers begin to think differently about students, teachers, their disciplines, professional development, and change. These changes can influence the ways in which the plan is implemented. Critical issues are just as dynamic. Experience may lead designers to consider new issues or gain deeper understandings of the ones they have grappled with.

Continuous monitoring for evidence of impact and effectiveness of the overall program often leads planners back into prior steps in the process. Often programs may have an outside evaluator or internal "critical friend" who can support this ongoing reflection by providing timely feedback about how the program is meeting teacher needs, what is being learned, and what is needed next. For example, data gathered from pre- and postassessments of teachers' content knowledge may indicate achievement of a specific goal. Feedback forms and "exit cards" that teachers complete after each learning experience provide critical input into whether the design is on track or if it has missed the mark for some teachers.

Designers use this formative feedback to ask, "How is the program working?" "Is it aligned with our goals and research, and what additional learning needs are emerging for teachers?" "Do they need more in-depth content learning of a specific concept or immersion into a different concept?" "What additional strategies for professional learning should we consider?" "Do some teachers need direct assistance in the classroom to apply learning, and if so, how will this be provided?" When data indicate goals are being met, designers may reflect on how to document what is being accomplished to share their successful results with others and to scale up the program to reach new teachers.

The reflection and revision process keeps designers out of a simplistic mind-set that can lead people to implement plans that are not working. Too often, professional development plans are so set in stone they prevent the kind of reflexive action needed to be effective. This process step reminds us all that even the best-laid plans must often be revised and sometimes even scrapped when the goals of professional learning are not being met. Reflecting and revising throughout the process can help to avoid costly mistakes and a waste of limited resources and demonstrate to teachers that you are willing to adjust your plans in the service of their learning.

The design framework presented here in Chapter 1 is not perfect. It creates artificial distinctions among components like critical issues and context, which are far more interconnected than separate circles depict. It simplifies an enormously complex process. And it may miss important feedback loops and connections. With that disclaimer, allow us to advocate strongly for the use of a design framework such as this to guide professional development. Since the publication of the first edition of this book in 1998, we have seen the design framework lead to more purposeful and reflective professional development designs. It has been used to look back on a program and ask, "How did our program reflect each of the inputs and approach each of the steps in the process?" "What would we do differently next time?" Its use helps professional developers make conscious choices and resist the quick-fix approach. We are more convinced than ever that only through thoughtful and careful design, based on sound principles and strategies, can professional development be elevated from its current state, treat all teachers as the professionals they are, and make the vision of schools as places of professional learning and quality science and mathematics education a reality in the United States.

2

*Knowledge and Beliefs
Supporting Effective
Professional Development*

Figure 2.1   Knowledge and Beliefs Supporting Effective Professional
Development

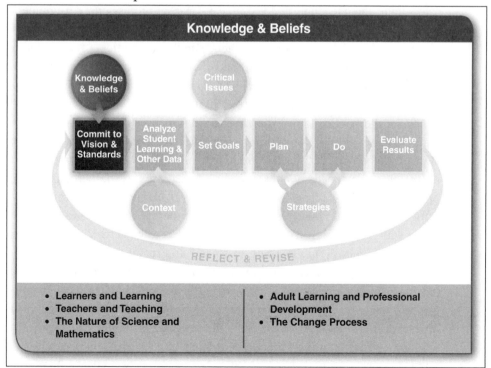

Chapter 1 introduces and describes the components of a comprehensive framework for designing and implementing professional development. One of the first and very important inputs into the design process is the knowledge base on key topics related to professional development for science and mathematics teachers. The *knowledge base* refers to two different kinds of information—*knowledge* and *beliefs.* Knowledge refers to information that is sure, solid, dependable, and supported by research. It is distinct from opinions or points of view that may not be supported by evidence. Beliefs reflect what we think we know (Ball, 1996) or may be coming to know based on new information. They are supported by experience, and people are strongly committed to them. What people know and believe influences their sense making and informs the choices they make in their everyday lives. Beliefs also inform how teachers engage in and learn from professional development. In a perfect world, research knowledge and people's beliefs would be in alignment, but this is rarely the case. It takes time for new knowledge to be translated into beliefs and changes in practice. The professional developer's job is to know and apply the research base to all work with teachers and to create opportunities for teachers to examine and reflect on the alignment between their beliefs about teaching and learning of science and mathematics and the education knowledge base.

In recent years, new knowledge and changing beliefs based on research discoveries and reflection on practice have begun to transform the way educators think about teaching and learning and teacher professional development. Significant findings in the five areas of (1) learners and learning, (2) teachers and teaching, (3) the nature of science and mathematics, (4) adult learning and professional development, and (5) how educational change occurs provide valuable insights for shaping decisions about the design and provision of professional development (see Figure 2.1).

Since the publication of the first edition of this book, we have worked with educators across the nation to promote the idea that effective professional development designs are grounded solidly in research knowledge and on the particular needs, contexts, and circumstances of the participants. As part of this work, we have asked scores of people what makes learning powerful in mathematics and science. Time after time their responses are right on target with the research. They say: "Learning has to be active," or "You need to connect what you are learning to what you already think and know, and challenge what you already believe to make room for new ideas," or "Learners have to want to learn—it has to be meaningful and relevant to them." Then we ask how many of them consistently have professional development opportunities with these same features. The usual response is "none" or "a few."

The fact remains that the field of education is living in a paradox of knowing one thing and doing another. For example, we say we know that learning experiences should be active, coherent, and relevant, yet too much of student learning and teacher professional development is still not interactive or reflective and remains disconnected from practice. Research finds that schools that promote teacher collegiality and collaboration around learning have higher achievement rates than teachers who work in more isolated settings, yet there are still many schools that have not adopted these practices (Lee, Smith, & Croninger, 1995; Marks, Louis, & Printy, 2000; McLaughlin & Talbert, 2001; Newmann & Wehlage, 1995). We need to make common knowledge common practice, starting with providing professional development that better reflects the knowledge base. At every juncture, professional development designers and providers should ask themselves, "What does the research say?" "How well does our design reflect the knowledge from research?" "What are the implications for the classroom?" and "What are the implications for the professional development design?"

In the rest of this chapter, we discuss the essential knowledge and beliefs that are important for professional developers to consider as they begin to move through the professional development design and implementation process shown in Figure 2.1. Regarding the common knowledge identified in this chapter, it is essential that professional developers take into account two perspectives—a professional developer perspective and a teacher participant perspective—when designing and implementing programs. The professional developer perspective recognizes that teachers engaged in professional development are learners who bring their own knowledge and beliefs about teaching and learning to their professional development experiences. The teacher participant perspective acknowledges that teachers engaging in professional development often think about what they are learning in terms of their students and how to support them as learners of mathematics and science. Using these two perspectives, professional developers will better understand how the interactions between the five knowledge bases discussed in this chapter influence their professional development programs.

LEARNERS AND LEARNING

All professional development programs need to consider the knowledge base on learners and learning as a major input to their designs. This consideration is critical on at least two levels. First, when teachers experience and reflect on how students learn, they are better able to understand why certain instructional strategies are more effective than others, thus enabling them to provide powerful learning experiences for their students. Second, we need professional development designs that reflect how people learn so that the teachers themselves are supported to learn in a sustained and in-depth way. Too often the cognitive research on learning is forgotten when it comes to designing teachers' learning.

Major findings from cognitive research are summarized in several widely used research syntheses, including *How People Learn* (Bransford, Brown, & Cocking, 1999), *Knowing What Students Know: The Science and Design of Educational Assessment* (Pellegrino, Chudowsky, & Glaser, 2001), *How Students Learn History, Mathematics, and Science in the Classroom* (Donovan & Bransford, 2005), and *Taking Science to School* (Duschl, Schweingruber, & Schouse, 2007). The Institute for Education Science summarized a subset of the research as principles for organizing instruction (Pashler et al., 2007). Extensive research on student ideas in science and mathematics can be found in *Making Sense of Secondary Science: Research into Children's Ideas* (Driver, Squires, Rushworth, & Wood-Robinson, 1994), *Benchmarks for Science Literacy* (American Association for the Advancement of Science, 1993), and *A Research Companion to Principles and Standards for School Mathematics* (National Council of Teachers of Mathematics, 2003a). These are documents that all professional developers should have on their shelves to help design professional development that reflects the research on learning.

With the caveat that we are learning more all the time, currently five general concepts summarize the knowledge base on how people learn:

Learners and Learning

- New knowledge is built on the learner's prior knowledge.
- Learning is an active process.
- Knowledge is constructed through a process of change.
- New knowledge comes from experiences and interaction with ideas and phenomena.
- Learning needs to be situated in meaningful and relevant contexts.
- Learning is supported through interaction among students about the ideas of science and mathematics.

SOURCE: Bransford, Brown, and Cocking (1999).

---

1. What learners already know influences their learning.

The myth that students are empty vessels waiting to be filled with new ideas has been dispelled by research. We now know that what students already know and believe influences what and how they learn (Bransford, et al., 1999; Chi, 2005; Vosniadou & Brewer, 1992). The research suggests that what learners know is an important foundation for their future learning. When consistent with conceptions that are currently accepted by mathematics and science communities, this prior or informal knowledge is a strong base on which to build new understandings. Sometimes, however, learners' conceptions are inconsistent with accepted knowledge and are called naïve conceptions or alternative conceptions.

Alternative conceptions are tenacious and resistant to change using conventional teaching strategies. The existing ideas interact with and even filter new knowledge, resulting in a variety of learning outcomes—some desired by the teacher and others unintended. What learners already know or think they know plays a much more important role in teaching and learning than previously recognized. We know that learning involves building on or modifying existing ideas, rather than just adding new disconnected information (Bransford et al., 1999; Wandersee, Mintzes, & Novak, 1994). This understanding of how prior knowledge influences how learners interpret and interact with new ideas and information has had a profound influence on the design of learning experiences. Students' prior knowledge and naïve conceptions must be taken into account to support them to develop deeper understanding. To do so, teachers need skills for assessing and challenging students' ideas and connecting new knowledge to what students already know and believe (Pashler et al., 2007).

Learning is also influenced by the learners' expectations, attitudes, and beliefs about themselves and about learning, schooling, and the community in which they live (Fredericks, Blumenfeld, & Paris, 2004). When individuals are learning effectively, they are engaged in what they are doing and expect that it will make sense to them. They do not expect learning to be easy and instantaneous, but have confidence that understanding will come from persistence, interaction with ideas and natural phenomena, dialogue with peers and teachers, attention to other possible ideas, and a willingness to change their view on the basis of compelling new evidence.

Since learning is influenced by what learners already know and think they know, and by their view of themselves as learners, it is essential that learning experiences be designed to elicit and connect with or challenge prior knowledge and provide opportunity for interaction with people and ideas. The use of carefully developed formative assessments that probe student thinking about science and mathematical ideas is highly effective in informing teaching and learning and supporting teachers to link new knowledge with students' prior conceptions (Keeley, Eberle, & Farrin, 2005; Keeley, Eberle, & Tugel, 2007; Rose, Minton, & Arline, 2007; Wiliam, 2007).

2. Learners construct new knowledge.

Learning is a process through which learners construct their knowledge by modifying or revising existing ideas (Bransford et al., 1999; Cobb, 1994; Driver, Asoko, Leach, Mortimer, & Scott, 1994). This idea is based on the view of learning as a personal and active process through which the learner interacts with information and experiences and filters them through what they already know (Bruner, 1966). Learning comes from thinking through and often struggling with problems and situations to arrive at new understandings, which are built on learners' current ideas. The learner interacts in a very active sense with ideas and experiences, rather than just passively taking in facts or memorizing data (Bransford et al., 1999).

The research on learning suggests that learners need to develop conceptual understanding as well as procedural information and learn to apply and transfer knowledge of the content flexibly (Bransford et al., 1999). When people only learn the procedures or the "what" and "how" and not the "why," they may lack the understanding needed to generalize their knowledge to novel situations. The "why" involves understanding the explanatory principles of a discipline, the big ideas that relate concepts to one another and lead to explanations of disciplinary phenomena. The AAAS *Atlas of Science Literacy* (2001; 2007) includes concept maps that show how science and some mathematics concepts develop across grades K–12 and indicates connections among different ideas. These tools focus teachers on the big ideas in science and mathematics that are important for students to understand and point out the connections that should be made across the concepts. Understanding concepts deeply helps learners better integrate their knowledge and know when ideas can by applied in different contexts (Goldstone & Son, 2005; Kaminski, Sloutsky, & Heckler, 2006). For example, if learners understand that air moves from regions of higher pressure to lower pressure, they can group several phenomena together (deflating tires or balloons, certain weather patterns, understanding how lungs inflate and deflate), understand them as examples of the same underlying principle, and use that principle when faced with new situations involving airflow. This type of principled understanding makes knowledge usable and permits flexible application to new situations. The likelihood of achieving deep understanding is increased when learners go beyond mere rote memorization and actively process information to understand connections and underlying explanatory principles (Chi, Bassok, Lewis, Reimann, & Glaser, 1989; Chi, DeLeeuw, Chiu, & LaVancher, 1994; Chi, Feltovich, & Glaser, 1981; Hmelo-Silver, Marathe, & Liu, 2007).

Developing conceptual understanding is more complex than memorizing a procedure and involves experience (e.g., engaging in many science investigations or solving many mathematics problems), metacognition, and developing and revising ideas over time. Students who understand the discipline have a command of the knowledge base: the known facts, concepts, procedures, and principles of that discipline. They are able to use the knowledge to address new questions and to refine, extend, and justify explanations. They can choose and apply appropriate knowledge and tools to their questions and generate and explain findings. They understand the "language" of the discipline, including the agreed-on norms of using evidence to propose hypotheses and to make arguments in the discipline (Duschl & Osborne, 2002; Gee, 1990; Lemke, 1990). With respect to learners in science, the publication *Taking Science to School* (Duschl et al., 2007) defined four key, intertwined competencies students should develop:

- Know, use, and interpret scientific explanations of the natural world.
- Be able to construct and evaluate scientific evidence and explanations.
- Understand the nature of scientific knowledge and how such knowledge advances.
- Be able to productively engage in scientific practices and discourse as part of understanding science as a way of knowing that involves observation, measurement, pattern identification, models, and explanations.

To achieve these outcomes, teaching involves drawing out the ideas learners hold and making useful connections between scientifically and mathematically correct ideas and existing ones.

Another important aspect of learning is the process of personal reflection. Effective learners are able to monitor their own ideas and thought processes, compare and contrast them with those of others, and provide reasons why they accept one point of view over another. The research literature also supports the idea that learning is mediated by the culture and the social environments in which learners interact with their peers, teachers, families, and others. It is from this interaction that learners acquire (very often implicitly) the norms, expectations, and values that influence whether, how, and what they learn (Silver, Kilpatrick, & Schlesinger, 1990).

Learning in this way is both individualistic and dependent on interactions with other learners. These two concepts have greatly challenged the perspective that people acquire concepts by receiving and memorizing information from other people who know more than they do, that students will learn what their teachers know by listening to what they say, and that the presence of other students is incidental to learning (Schifter, 1996a).

Research on Cognition Reveals Useful Guidelines for Professional Development

- Make useful connections between teachers' existing ideas and new ones.
- Provide opportunity for active engagement, discussion, and reflection to challenge existing ideas and construct new ones.
- Situate the learning in contexts teachers find familiar.
- Challenge current thinking by producing and helping to resolve dissonance between new ideas and existing ones.
- Support teachers to develop strategies for eliciting prior knowledge and use formative assessment information to guide instruction.
- Use formative assessments to elicit teachers' prior knowledge, and build from there.
- Develop teachers' understanding of research on learning, so they become intentional in their selection of effective instructional strategies.
- Use a learning cycle such as the 5Es—engage, explore, explain, elaborate, evaluate to support learning (Bybee, 1997).

3. Knowledge is constructed through a process of change.

Learners evolve from their current state of knowledge in four different ways: (1) when new ideas fit naturally with existing ideas and are added to them; (2) when learners create a new idea out of existing knowledge; (3) when new ideas extend and challenge existing knowledge, leading to its minor modification or wholesale restructuring; and (4) when learners see that new ideas are powerful but irreconcilable with existing knowledge, leading to the rejection of their existing knowledge.

As learners confront new information, their initial questions relate to defining it. They ask: "What is it?" "Do I know what it means?" "Can I represent it?" Once a new perspective becomes clear to learners, they can consider whether it is plausible and useful. They ask: "Do I believe it?" "Does it fit with other things I believe to be true?" "Does it achieve anything for me?" "Does it solve problems I have been grappling with?" "Does it suggest approaches I hadn't thought of?" (Posner, Strike, Hewson, & Gertzog, 1982). If all these conditions are met, the new idea will gain higher status for the learner. This entire process happens as learners assess, adopt, or reject new ideas, often unconsciously.

Even if learners find that a proposed change has a high status for them, they may still not consider it worth the trouble and effort to adopt it. Individuals are more likely to change, reject their existing ideas and adopt new ones—that is, transform their thinking—when the new idea has high status *and* they have reason to be dissatisfied with their existing ideas (Hewson & Thorley, 1989). Learners may become dissatisfied with their current knowledge when they confront new ideas that do not support their current thinking, also referred to as experiencing *cognitive dissonance*. For example, a teacher may examine student work and see that the students did not learn the concepts the teacher thought she taught. The teacher may ask herself whether the methods she is using can really be effective when so many students failed to learn. She may then begin to question her practice or become dissatisfied with her current ideas about how to teach.

When such dissatisfaction emerges, the learner works hard to resolve it by either rejecting the new information (this

---

Learning Is a Process of Change

When learners engage with new information and ideas they may

- add new knowledge that fits easily with their existing ideas,
- create new ideas out of their existing knowledge,
- modify existing ideas based on new information,
- reject existing knowledge in the face of powerful new ideas, and
- build on prior knowledge to understand more and more complex knowledge.

is often the case) or by beginning a process of reorganizing prior knowledge (Bransford et al., 1999; Thompson & Zeuli, 1999). Transformational learning occurs when learners reject deeply held ideas, reorganize what they know, and restructure and question their basic assumptions and frameworks for learning (Mezirow, 1991, 1997).

Furthermore, as students transform their thinking, they build on prior knowledge. This process of building on prior knowledge to understand more complex knowledge and develop more sophisticated ways of thinking is called a *learning progression* (Duschl et al., 2007). The time frame for a learning progression is multiple years (6–8 years), not one school year. Researchers in this area of learning emphasize the need to change standards to accommodate learning progressions and change teachers' work to be collaborative both within grade level and across grade levels. Engaging teachers in thinking about learning progressions provides them with another view of teaching one student as a long-term endeavor involving many teachers, rather than a one-year experience involving one teacher. Learning is, therefore, both a short-term and long-term change process.

4. New knowledge comes from experiences.

Learning arises in different ways as learners inquire into natural phenomena, grapple with challenging problems, raise and address questions, interact with people and resources (e.g., books or video), and reflect on their thoughts and ideas. In support of using a diverse array of instructional activities, research shows that hands-on activities, analyses of preexisting data, and direct instruction support student learning of science (Klahr & Nigam, 2004; Magnusson & Palincsar, 2005; Wenglinsky, 2000). By including direct observation of and experience with phenomena, ideas and instructional materials, and input from teachers and experts in the field, such as mathematicians and scientists, teachers provide numerous experiential pathways toward learning for their students.

5. Everyone is able to understand and do science and mathematics.

National standards for mathematics and science education reflect a vision in which all students are provided with opportunities and support to develop mathematics and science literacy and the essential skills needed for productive life in the twenty-first century. The rich knowledge base on learners and learning shows that all learners from very young ages come to school with conceptions about the world, are curious about phenomena, and can inquire into them and make meaning of them. When all children have access to quality teaching and high expectations, they are able to meet standards for content learning, and young children are capable of learning much more than educators usually expect (Campbell, 1995; Duschl et al., 2007; NCTM, 2000; National Research Council, 1996). Schools keep the flame of learning alive by challenging all students to learn these subjects that are most critical for the future.

Educational equity and opportunity for learning are enhanced when teachers, students, and families hold high expectations for student learning. High expectations, however, are not enough (NCTM, 2000). To support all learners means creating access to courses and effective teaching and support structures for English learners and students with disabilities (Carr et al., 2009; Carr, Sexton, & Laganof, 2007; Lee & Fradd, 1998; Rosebery, 2008; Warren, Ballenger, Ogonowski, Rosebery, & Hudicourt-Barnes, 2001). It means having diversity among faculty and adults to act as role models, and it means ensuring that children in high-poverty districts have access to the curriculum and instructional and laboratory materials needed for them to succeed in science and mathematics (Bransford, Darling-Hammond, & LePage, 2005; Britton, Raizen, Kaser, & Porter, 2000).

TEACHERS AND TEACHING

What is the vision of teaching and of the role of teachers that your professional development program will embody? Drawing on research and standards documents, this section outlines the knowledge teachers need, the role they ideally play in promoting learning, and considerations for their own professional learning.

Teaching is the act of organizing and shaping learning experiences for students. In recent years, higher standards for student learning have caused educators to reexamine the teaching routines common in our schools. Many do not support students to reach high standards. For example, from an in-depth look at the teaching of mathematics in eighth-grade classrooms in the United States, Japan, and Germany, researchers found American mathematics teaching to be focused narrowly on having students develop isolated skills through repeated practice (Stigler & Hiebert, 1999). Educators have worked to reform mathematics teaching by encouraging students to use multiple solution strategies and by increasing emphasis on conceptual understanding and mathematical discourse in the classroom. Similarly in science, reforms have focused on increasing students' opportunity to engage in scientific investigations, to think and communicate scientifically, and to use technological tools. These changes have ramped up demands on teachers to become more proficient in their content areas, understand how students learn, and have a wider range of instructional strategies to facilitate learning for all students (Duschl et al., 2007; NCTM, 2000; NRC, 2001). Furthermore, teachers must be skilled at assessing student learning and using assessment information to make hundreds of instructional decisions every day. Quality professional development focuses on supporting the improvement of teaching by enhancing knowledge and skills in these critical areas.

Three general concepts frame what we currently know about teachers and teaching: (1) The purpose of teaching is to facilitate learning; (2) teaching is a profession requiring specialized knowledge; and (3) the practice of teaching is complex. Together, these concepts support a view of teaching that is reflected in national standards and that many schools are working hard to bring about. It is a view of teaching that coherently builds on the concepts of learners and learning previously described. In particular, this view contrasts sharply with teaching approaches used in the past in which teachers outlined procedures they expected students to follow, provided authoritative explanations they expected students to memorize, and evaluated students' work only to see whether information had been reproduced correctly (Schifter, 1996a). It also underscores the requirement that teachers be highly skilled and knowledgeable in their subject matter so they can create coherence and connections across the content, know the next best questions to ask, and facilitate learning with understanding (Schifter, 1999).

1. The purpose of teaching is to facilitate learning.

This may seem so obvious that there is no need to state it. Yet there are still many examples of teacher learning that focus on preparing teachers to "deliver" content without attention to whether their students have learned this content (Sparks, 2002). Increasingly, educators are interested in linking teaching to learning and using ongoing assessment to adjust and enhance teaching and to increase student learning.

Learning lies at the heart of any conception of teaching. Teachers need to match learners and what they know with the intended curriculum in ways that make learning achievable. A teacher cannot assume it is solely the learners' responsibility to make the necessary connections between where they are and where the teacher intends them to go. Rather, effective teaching involves continually assessing where the learners are, choosing appropriate learning activities based on the assessment, offering scaffolding to support learning, and assessing again to inform the next instructional decisions (Black, Harrison, Lee, Marshall, & Wiliam, 2003). This includes engaging the students in self-assessment and monitoring of their own learning and using informal assessment to drive instruction (Carlson, Humphrey, & Reinhardt, 2003; DiRanna et al., 2008).

This view of teaching has obvious implications for professional development. Teachers need opportunities to develop advanced knowledge in their content, an understanding of what they can learn by examining student work and thinking, a diverse array of assessment strategies, and a range of instructional strategies. All of these are key focus areas for effective professional development.

2. Teaching is a profession requiring specialized knowledge.

Practice of any profession is complex and uncertain and draws upon expert knowledge bases particular to the profession (Schön, 1983, 1988). The complexity and uncertainty stem from the fact that professionals are constantly being called on to make decisions in unique circumstances without "absolute" knowledge. Past experience and expert knowledge do not provide a set of fixed rules to follow but only heuristics that can guide professional judgment and decision making. To make decisions that are informed rather than reactive, reflection on past and current actions (a key characteristic of professional practice) is employed to inform future decisions.

The current view of teaching as a profession requiring specialized knowledge is in sharp contrast with the outmoded perspective of teachers as skilled technicians who, rather than have their own body of knowledge, simply apply bodies of disciplinary knowledge produced by others. It is now recognized that the teaching profession constitutes its own large body of knowledge. This includes knowledge of the content of the disciplines (including national and state content standards), of students, and of a variety of instruction and assessment strategies (Coble & Koballa, 1996; National Commission on Mathematics and Science Teaching for the 21st Century, 2000; National Commission on Teaching and America's Future [NCTAF], 1996, 2003; NCTM, 2000; NRC, 1996).

The Math and Science Partnership Knowledge Management and Dissemination (KMD) project (2007) discussed the relationship between teachers' mathematics and science content knowledge and their instructional practice and students' achievement, citing evidence that teacher content knowledge is related to student learning. Summarizing a number of research studies, they point out that a teacher's content knowledge influences how teachers engage their students in the subject matter and how they evaluate, choose, and use instructional materials. There are many dimensions for content knowledge needed for teaching. For example, the KMD project identifies several domains for teachers' content knowledge, including disciplinary content; knowledge that there are alternative frameworks for thinking about the content; knowledge of the relationship between big ideas and supporting ideas; understanding of how students think about the content; knowledge of activities or tools that can be used to diagnose student thinking; knowledge of how to sequence ideas; and content-specific strategies such as activities, representations, analogies, and questions.

In addition to having a deep understanding of the dimensions of content knowledge, teachers also have specialized pedagogical knowledge. Shulman's (1986) and others' research on teacher knowledge (Cochran, DeRuiter, & King, 1993; Fernández-Balboa & Stiehl, 1995; Grossman, 1990; Loughran, Mulhall, & Berry, 2004; Magnusson, Krajcik, & Borko, 1999; van Driel, Verloop, & de Vos, 1998) refer to teachers' specialized knowledge as *pedagogical content knowledge*. It is an understanding of what makes the learning of specific concepts easy or difficult for learners, an awareness of what concepts are more fundamental than others, and knowledge of ways of representing and formulating subject matter to make it accessible to learners. Developing pedagogical content knowledge requires subject matter knowledge (Clermont, Krajcik, & Borko, 1993; Smith & Neale, 1989). In order for teachers to demonstrate high levels of pedagogical content knowledge, they must have sufficient subject matter knowledge. With limited content knowledge, teachers' pedagogical content knowledge is restricted.

> **Expert Teachers**
>
> - Know the structure of the knowledge in their disciplines
> - Know the conceptual barriers that are likely to hinder learning
> - Have a well-organized knowledge of concepts (content knowledge) and inquiry procedures and problem solving strategies (based on pedagogical content knowledge)
> - Continuously assess their own learning, knowledge, and practices
>
> SOURCE: Bransford, Brown, and Cocking (1999, p. 230).

Like other professionals, teachers expect to continue learning throughout their careers to deepen their expertise and enhance their practice. They recognize that they practice in uncertain circumstances; that much of their knowledge is embedded in their practice rather than in codified bodies of knowledge; and that their extensive, complex knowledge, particularly with respect to their understanding of how learners learn, profoundly influences how they teach (Loughran et al., 2004). Based on this, teachers need learning opportunities that focus on their practice. They need to engage with other teachers in conversations to learn what works under what circumstances, examine examples of practice, and reflect on their own practice and their students' learning to become "connoisseurs" of effective practice. As Ball and Cohen (1999) write,

> The opportunity to engage in such conversation can provide a means for teachers to represent and clarify their understandings, using their

own and others' experiences to develop ideas, learn about practices, and gain a more solid sense of themselves as contributing members of a profession, as participants in the improvement of teaching and learning and their profession, and as intellectuals. (p. 17)

3. The practice of teaching is complex.

Teaching involves a complex cycle of planning, acting, observing, and reflecting. It occurs in a highly dynamic atmosphere characterized by interactions that change from one second to the next. It requires teachers to process information on multiple levels simultaneously and make decisions constantly. To do so, they must draw on their ability to apply knowledge about students, content, the curriculum, instruction, assessment, and their schools and communities (Bransford et al., 2005). Researchers (Bransford et al., 1999) have identified four learning environments that teachers need to create in their classrooms:

- *Learner-centered environments* that focus on the knowledge and experiences learners bring to the situation
- *Knowledge-centered environments* that emphasize teaching new content and concepts in ways that align with how people learn the discipline
- *Assessment-centered environments* that provide learners with ongoing feedback on their learning and promote self-reflection on learning
- *Community-centered environments* that nurture learning communities characterized by collaboration, collegial interaction, and reflection

Schools that develop these environments provide a learning-enriched experience for all. To succeed in creating such environments, teachers need opportunities to develop their pedagogical content knowledge, engage in critical reflection on their own and others' classroom practice, and develop rich repertoires of practice that support them through the complexity of teaching and learning. Currently, there is a growing emphasis on professional development that engages teachers in building a professional learning culture and examining practice with experts and colleagues to develop the specialized knowledge of the profession (Loughran et al., 2004; Shulman & Shulman, 2004; Smith, 2001; Stigler & Hiebert, 1999; Weiss & Pasley, 2009). Specifically, professional development strategies such as lesson study, case discussion, and examination of student work (see Chapter 5) are contributing to the development of a rich appreciation for the complexity of teaching and have been shown to develop teachers' content knowledge and sophisticated pedagogical reasoning skills and to increase student achievement (Barnett & Tyson, 1993; Heller, Kaskowitz, Daehler, & Shinohara, 2001).

Teaching is complex because learning is complex. Developing rote and factual knowledge is simpler than developing in-depth understanding of science and mathematics concepts. The latter requires teaching characterized by posing challenging tasks more often than providing succinct explanations. Teachers encourage their students to articulate their ideas and to question each other about their reasons for holding them, rather than only correct their mistakes. Teachers and students set goals for instruction and create appropriate contexts for classroom activities. Students engage in meaningful projects, problems, and inquiries.

Teachers who embrace the complexity of teaching organize activities in which students do much of the talking and doing, often in small groups without the teacher. They watch students' actions and listen carefully to students' arguments and explanations in order to understand what sense the students are making. They monitor classroom activities and decide if, when, and how to intervene. When they intervene, they frequently do so by opening the topic up in ways that elicit more questions rather than prompting premature closure. Their knowledge of the subject matter and the students' developmental level helps them ask the next best question. They facilitate different levels of discourse needed in the classroom, being concerned not only with what students say about the topic but also why they say it. They establish and maintain a classroom environment that provides opportunities for students to explore their own and others' ideas individually and collectively without fear of ridicule or sanction. Teachers build on and guide students to new understanding by challenging their thinking and recognizing and addressing their confusion (NCTM, 2000; NRC, 1996).

These teachers create opportunities for all students to learn. They know learning is not simple and that students all learn differently. They establish the learning environment as a place where students are respected and engaged, where students' questions and ideas are valued and respectfully challenged, and where students have the time, resources, and space necessary to explore and learn. They know that if students are not thinking they are not learning, so they construct experiences in which the students are doing the work and the thinking and actively sharing their thoughts with their peers. They have a repertoire of strategies for responding appropriately to the variety of knowledge and experience brought by their students, and they work to ensure equal access to equitable teaching for all students by using proven strategies.

THE NATURE OF SCIENCE AND MATHEMATICS

As professional developers plan activities to increase teachers' abilities to teach science and mathematics in ways consistent with national standards and state frameworks, it is important for them to keep the nature of the disciplines in mind. Just as professional development programs should reflect what is known about learning and teaching, so too should they reflect the nature of the disciplines. For example, national standards documents call for these subjects to be experienced and learned in ways that reflect how they are practiced in the real world (NCTM, 2000; NRC, 1996).

> ### The Nature of Science and Mathematics
>
> - Mathematics and science are dynamic disciplines that continue to produce new knowledge.
> - Science is practiced through active engagement and inquiry into phenomena in the world.
> - Mathematics involves complex reasoning, problem solving, and communication.

Mathematics and science were long viewed as bodies of established knowledge, comprising true facts known for a long time. Science of this kind has been called a rhetoric of conclusions and final-form science (Duschl, 1990). It represented a static conception of the discipline. People expressed similar conceptions of mathematics.

In the past few decades, there has been explosive development in technology leading to new understanding and applications of science and mathematics that have challenged and changed the view of these disciplines as static bodies of knowledge. They have come to be seen as dynamic disciplines that are a necessity for all to learn (AAAS, 1989).

With regard to mathematics, the need to be able to think and reason mathematically has become essential for everyday life (NCTM, 2000). Mathematics develops the ability to reason, to solve complex problems—often from different perspectives—and to analyze and communicate about patterns and relationships. It is used to answer fundamental questions and find solutions to practical problems (AAAS, 1993). The ability to understand and manipulate quantitative information is a basic skill for all.

Due to the impact of complex advances in science on everyday life, the ability to understand new scientific knowledge and make judgments of whether it is valid knowledge is essential for everyone (AAAS, 1989). Beyond the personal level, the dependence of the U.S. economy on scientific and technological advances places an additional demand on science educators to help develop the future innovators of this country (NRC, 2006). Careers in science and technology require knowledge of mathematics, science, and engineering as well as skills in observing, describing, conjecturing, testing, designing, and explaining. Furthermore, more and more jobs of the twenty-first century are requiring additional skills, such as "thinking critically and making judgments, solving complex, multidisciplinary, open-ended problems, and communicating and collaborating" (Partnership for 21st Century Skills, 2008, p. 10).

The characteristics of the work of scientists and mathematicians are finding their way into classrooms in which students solve challenging mathematical problems, engage in scientific inquiry, and tackle challenging design tasks to solve real-world problems (NCTM, 2000; NRC, 1996). Educators have come to appreciate that the learning of mathematics and science should reflect what it means to apply mathematics and science and an understanding of where knowledge comes from. This is a dynamic conception of these disciplines, recognizing science and mathematics as human pursuits—as much invention as discovery—with a long history in which schools of thought compete, fashions change, and some questions may never be settled (Duschl, 1990). Beliefs about science and mathematics and their processes shape people's approaches to the disciplines (Brickhouse, 1990; Lemberger, Hewson, & Park, 1999). In one study of teachers with specific views about the nature of science and how students learn science, evidence emerged linking these views to teaching practices observed in classrooms (Lemberger et al.). Teachers who saw science as composed of facts frequently used lecturing, memorization, and surface-level questioning in the classroom. Other teachers who thought students constructed their own understandings used more discovery-oriented practices. These differing views about the nature of science and how students learn influenced teaching practices and the opportunities made available to students to construct understandings of science.

Therefore, it is essential that effective professional development in science and mathematics reflect the nature of the disciplines. For example, teachers engage in solving challenging science and mathematics problems. They dialogue with each other and with their facilitators about what they are observing and learning. They speak, listen, and respond as they construct new meanings and formulate arguments. They explain their solutions and conclusions and ground their explanations in correct mathematics or science concepts and ideas. Through this process, they grapple with fundamental concepts in the discipline, not only learning what they are but also why they take the form that they do. In the process of developing these higher-order ideas and capabilities, teachers are also learning important information such as facts and formulas and doing exercises and procedures. These facts and procedures are not, however, ends in themselves but serve as integral parts of a broader context that gives these pieces of information their meaning. Teachers, in turn, can create experiences with their students in the classroom that reflect the nature of doing and learning science and mathematics.

ADULT LEARNING AND PROFESSIONAL DEVELOPMENT

The knowledge base on professional development has grown considerably since the first edition of this book. We now have more evidence linking quality professional development and teacher expertise with students' opportunity to learn challenging mathematics and science (Blank, de las Alas, & Smith, 2008; Cohen & Hill, 1998; Darling-Hammond, 1997; Garet et al., 1999; Weiss, Banilower, McMahon, & Smith, 2001). Furthermore, more research is now focusing on the relationship between quality professional development, such as specific induction programs, and teacher retention (Ingersoll & Kralik, 2004; Johnson & The Project on the Next Generation of Teachers, 2007). Contextual factors, such as professional culture, leadership, systemic support, and time for teacher learning, influence the type and quality of professional development (Darling-Hammond, 1997; Sparks, 2001; Wei, Darling-Hammond, Andree, Richardson, & Orphanos, 2009).

Effective Professional Development

- Is designed to address student learning goals and needs
- Is driven by a well-defined image of effective classroom learning and teaching
- Provides opportunities for teachers to build their content and pedagogical content knowledge and reflect on practice
- Is research based and engages teachers as adult learners in the learning approaches they will use with their students
- Provides opportunities for teachers to collaborate with colleagues and other experts to improve their practice
- Supports teachers to develop their professional expertise and to serve in leadership roles
- Links with other parts of the education system
- Is continuously evaluated and improved

Professional development has remained a key strategy in the educational reform movement, yet its focus and means of delivery have shifted and continue to shift in some fundamental ways. For example, science and mathematics reform initiatives have been challenged to increase the content and pedagogical content understanding of teachers. They have reached out to highly competent mathematics and science specialists to build this understanding, often immersing teachers in mathematical problem solving and scientific inquiry and sustained programs that increase teachers' understanding of their curriculum. They are realizing that simply providing different and more collegial forms of professional development is not the answer. Rather, the professional development must address substantive content and pedagogy within the teacher learning program (Ball, 1996; Garet et al., 1999; Weiss & Pasley, 2009). In one case, when teachers participated in professional development programs emphasizing science and mathematics content, more teachers seemed to understand these content areas to be dynamic bodies of knowledge and felt more prepared to teach the content (Banilower, Boyd, Pasley, & Weiss, 2006).

Educators now see the value of placing learning and student thinking at the center of professional development and, as a result, have adopted many practice-based strategies such as examining student work and using cases of student learning to deepen understanding of content and how children learn it (Ball & Cohen, 1999; Smith, 2001). These practices flow from a new appreciation of what it takes to develop what was described previously as teachers' specialized pedagogical content knowledge.

Professional development programs, such as the curriculum-support initiatives at organizations like the Education Development Center, TERC, and Biological Sciences and Curriculum Study (BSCS), use knowledge from how people learn not only to help teachers add new skills but also to transform their thinking and deeply held beliefs about teaching and learning. From the hallmark study of mathematics reform in California, educators learned that reform focused only on adding new materials and changing some practice resulted in a patchwork quilt of reform where some reform practices—often the ones that fit with a teacher's prior ideas—were adopted and others ignored (Cohen & Hill, 1998). What is needed is for teacher learning programs to engage teachers in strategies that produce "transformative" learning, that is, "changes in deeply held beliefs, knowledge, and habits of practice" (Thompson & Zeuli, 1999, p. 342). According to Thompson and Zeuli, transformative learning experiences for teachers have five requirements.

Requirement 1: Create a high level of cognitive dissonance to upset the balance between teachers' beliefs and practices and new information or experiences about students, the content, or learning. Teachers need to engage in learning more about subject matter, instructional strategies, or how students learn in ways that cause them to start thinking that there are better ways to teach, thereby creating cognitive dissonance.

Requirement 2: Provide sufficient time, structure, and support for teachers to think through the dissonance they experience. They need opportunities to discuss, challenge, read about, and make sense of what they experienced.

Requirement 3: Embed the dissonance-creating and dissonance-resolving activities in teachers' own situations and the practices of teaching and learning by using student work, videotaping, or engaging in student investigations as a learner.

Requirement 4: Enable teachers to develop a new repertoire of practice that fits with their new understanding. This moves teachers from new understanding to change in practice. Teachers need to answer the questions: "Now that you have new understanding, what will you do differently in the classroom?" and "What could you do to help students come to new understanding?"

Requirement 5: Engage teachers in a continuous process of improvement, including (a) identifying new issues and problems with teaching and learning, (b) engaging with these to come to new understanding, (c) making changes in their practice, and (d) recycling through this process. (Thompson & Zeuli, 1999, pp. 355–357, citing Huberman, 1995)

Requirements for Transformative Learning Experiences

- Create a high level of cognitive dissonance.
- Provide sufficient time, structure, and support for teachers to think through the dissonance experienced.
- Embed the dissonance-creating and -resolving activities in teachers' situations and practices.
- Enable teachers to develop a new repertoire of practice that fits with their new understanding.
- Engage teachers in a continuous process of improvement.

SOURCE: Thompson and Zeuli (1999, pp. 355–357).

Transformative learning is different from "additive" learning through which teachers develop new skills or learn new things to integrate with what they currently know (Thompson & Zeuli, 1999). Historically, professional development has focused on only adding new skills and knowledge without helping teachers to rethink and discard or transform thinking and beliefs. Many teachers have reported that this practice leaves them overwhelmed with an increasingly overflowing plate of new things to know and do. There is a place for both additive and transformative learning in teacher professional development, but there needs to be conscious choices of what is being added and what is being discarded or transformed, and why. Unless teachers have learning opportunities that help them see the basic intentions of reform and of their curriculum and how both fit with knowledge of how people learn, they run a high risk of inadvertently making choices that detract from student learning. For example, teachers may use "activities that work" from a kit-based science program without using these activities to build students' conceptual understandings of overarching themes within science (AAAS, 2001; Appleton, 2003).

These new developments in the knowledge base on effective professional development are quite significant. They enrich the basic principles of effective professional development that are reflected in earlier works (Loucks-Horsley, Love, Stiles, Mundry, & Hewson, 2003) and support the common vision of effective science and mathematics education (NCTM, 1989, 2000, 2006; NRC, 1996) and standards for teacher professional development (National Staff Development Council, 2001b). The common vision is of several principles that are present in quality professional development experiences:

- *Effective professional development is designed to address student learning goals and needs.* Based on data that provide evidence of areas for students' growth, professional learning strategies are combined and sequenced in ways to help teachers develop the knowledge and skills to focus on enduring and important content and to improve students' learning.

- *Effective professional development experiences are driven by a well-defined image of effective classroom learning and teaching.* This image includes, for example, a commitment to all children learning mathematics and science, an emphasis on inquiry-based learning, investigations, problem solving, and applications of knowledge, an approach that emphasizes in-depth understanding of core concepts and challenges students to construct new understandings and clear means to measure meaningful achievement.

- *Effective professional development experiences provide opportunities for teachers to build their content and pedagogical content knowledge and skills and examine and reflect on practice critically.* They help teachers develop in-depth knowledge of their science or mathematics, as well as pedagogical content knowledge (understanding how children learn the content, listening to students' ideas, posing questions, recognizing misconceptions), and help in choosing and integrating curriculum and learning experiences.

- *Effective professional development experiences are research based and engage teachers as adult learners in the learning approaches they will use with their students.* For example, start where teachers are and build from there; provide ample time for in-depth investigations, collaborative work, and reflection; and connect explicitly with teachers' other professional development experiences and activities.

- *Effective professional development provides opportunities for teachers to work with colleagues and other experts in learning communities to continually enhance their practice.* Continuous learning is a part of the school norms and culture, teachers are rewarded and encouraged to take risks and learn, and teachers learn together and share best practices.

- *Effective professional development experiences support teachers to deepen their professional expertise throughout their career and serve in leadership roles.* For example, teachers serve as supporters of other teachers, as agents of change, and as promoters of reform.

- *Effective professional development experiences provide links to other parts of the education system.* For example, professional development is integrated with other district or school initiatives, district or state curriculum frameworks, and assessments and has active supports within the community.

- *Effective professional development experiences are continuously evaluated to ensure a positive impact on teacher effectiveness, student learning, leadership, and the school community.*

These principles demonstrate how beliefs about professional development have changed over the last four decades. In the early 1970s, professional development was called inservice training; its goal was to bring outside expertise to teachers to increase their knowledge, often about a discrete new program or approach. Programs often used what were called "teacher proof" materials that provided the simplistic "recipes" for learning. This was strictly additive learning with little attention to engaging teachers in thinking or changing underlying assumptions or building professional culture. Professional developers were often called "trainers" and primarily used lecture and sometimes demonstration of procedures as their learning tools. Much of this has changed today, but there are still vestiges of the old paradigm that prevail. More work is needed to shift away from such narrowly focused professional development.

For example, more and more attention is being paid to providing professional development that is embedded into the regular structure of schools through arrangements such as study groups, professional learning communities, and grade-level teams. There are many good reasons for schools to organize as ongoing learning communities. Research suggests such arrangements can increase coherence, reduce isolation, develop teacher knowledge, and establish systems that allow early intervention for students (Mundry & Stiles, 2009). Hord and Sommers (2008, p. 9) examined extensive literature on learning communities and identified five overall attributes:

1. *Shared Beliefs, Values, and Vision.* The staff share an "unrelenting attention to student learning success" (Hord & Sommers, 2008, p. 10). They focus on learning—student learning as well as adult learning.

2. *Shared and Supportive Leadership.* The staff share in the decision making and authority for taking action. Schools are clear about their processes for decision making.

3. *Collective Learning and Its Application.* Staff are organized to learn together and apply what they learn to their work with students.

4. *Supportive Conditions.* Schools make sure teachers have the structure, including time, location, resources, leadership, and support, to form a learning community and the interpersonal skills needed to be open, honest, and caring contributors.

5. *Shared Personal Practice.* A hallmark of schools organized as learning communities is that they bring educational practice out into the public. Teachers observe and provide feedback to one another and have a shared understanding of their approaches to education. They continually make enhancements in practice.

The important role of facilitators in contextualizing professional development programs to optimize teacher learning is also gaining recognition in the research literature (Remillard & Geist, 2002). A recent report suggests that the knowledge, skills, and preparation of facilitators may influence the quality of a professional development program more than the roles of facilitators—that is, scientists, professors, or teacher leaders (Banilower et al., 2006). There is also a growing recognition that the ways in which teachers learn the content and curriculum that they will use in the classroom need to differ from how they will teach it to students. This requires going beyond simply doing the same lesson one would do with students with the teachers. It requires adapting the material to meet conditions of adult learning. Adult learners need to see the relevancy of something before they learn it; they learn most effectively when new knowledge is presented in the real contexts, and they need time to connect new ideas and skills to their already diverse background (Knowles, Holton, & Swanson, 2000). Facilitators of professional learning experiences for teachers must have highly developed facilitation skills, knowledge of the content and how teachers think about the content, and effective strategies for engaging teachers with the content (Carroll & Mumme, 2007). They need to be able to engage adult learners in activating their prior knowledge and setting goals for their own learning and provide experiences that allow teachers to interact with new information, resources, ideas, and phenomena. Similar to the need for a learning cycle in the classroom, adult learning benefits from a purposeful design with distinct stages of learning from invitation to learn (or engagement) to experience to reflection and evaluation. Effective facilitators also pay attention to creating the learning environment needed for teachers by establishing group norms or ground rules that respect teachers as adults and professionals, providing ample time for adult interaction and processing of information in many different ways, drawing on multiple learning styles, and providing time to both think and talk (Garmston & Wellman, 2009).

Many schools now see that ongoing teacher learning must become a permanent part of a school's systems and structures to support continuous learning and professional growth (Sparks, 2002; Supovitz & Christman, 2003). To sustain professional growth in a school, professional developers and school leaders often integrate teacher career paths into their design of professional development programs. More specifically, different professional development strategies and goals may be needed depending on whether a teacher is a novice teacher, an experienced teacher, or a master teacher. New, or novice, teachers are often supported in their first three years' of teaching through induction or mentoring programs. Second-stage teachers, those in their fourth through tenth years who are more experienced, are often engaged in sustaining their learning through development as teacher leaders, mentors, or coaches. Recognizing the strengths, in addition to the needs, of teachers based on their experience can influence the specific strategies that teachers either participate in or are invited to facilitate and lead (Johnson & The Project on the Next Generation of Teachers, 2007).

In addition, it is helpful for professional development designers to consider how novice and expert teachers learn. For example, we know from research that experts "notice features and meaningful patterns of information; have a great deal of content knowledge that is organized, and their organization of information reflects a deep understanding of the subject matter; and are able to retrieve important aspects of their knowledge with little additional effort" (Bransford et al., 1999, p. xiii). When selecting and combining strategies to develop teacher expertise, it is helpful to consider a range of opportunities that have certain features, including

- activities explicitly designed to develop science and mathematics content knowledge with a deep understanding of the underlying concepts and principles,
- opportunities to help teachers understand how students think about and learn science and mathematics,
- new learning that is based on prior knowledge and learning,
- time and structures for collaboration and interactions with colleagues,
- reflection and analysis of learning, and
- ample opportunities for translating new learning into teaching strategies (Stiles & Mundry, 2002, p. 150).

Understanding the research on how experts learn can also help designers recognize that "even when experts and novices are in the same professional development situation, their learning is different because of how they process the experience" (Stiles & Mundry, 2002, p. 140). For example, when viewing a video of classroom teaching, the novice might focus more on the way in which the classroom is organized and the specific moves the teacher makes. The expert, on the other hand, might focus more on what the students are doing and saying and how the teacher responds to individual students' understanding of the content. For the professional development designer, knowing that novices and experts will experience learning in different ways can influence the design and how facilitators decide to group teachers for learning.

Designing professional development so that it promotes continuous teacher and organizational learning requires ensuring that it fits with a school's vision and goals, that it is equitable for teachers and students, that it builds the leadership and infrastructure needed, that it fits with the school context, and that it gives teachers the range of experiences they need to learn. The design framework presented in this book is aimed at guiding schools to create such effective systems and structures for professional development.

THE CHANGE PROCESS

Professional developers can be guided by the research and practice knowledge about how effective change happens in education settings (Evans, 1996; Fullan, 1991, 1993, 2001, 2007; Hall & Hord, 2006; Reeves, 2009). Change is both an individual and an organizational phenomenon, affecting each and every educator, as well as the schools, districts, universities, and other organizations to which they belong. Principles that derive from the knowledge base on change include those shown in the box titled "The Change Process."

All educational changes of value require individuals to act in new ways (demonstrated by new skills, behaviors, or activities) and to think in new ways

> **The Change Process**
>
> - Change is a process that takes time and persistence.
> - At different stages in the change process, individuals need different kinds of support and assistance.
> - Change efforts are effective when the change is clearly defined and communicated, support and assistance are available, and leaders and policies support the change.
> - Most systems resist change.
> - Organizations engage in continuous cycles of improvement when they analyze data, set goals, take action, assess their results, and make adjustments.

(demonstrated by new beliefs, understandings, or ideas). The question of the relationships between thoughts and actions is therefore important for professional development. The conventional wisdom has been that changing teacher beliefs should be the primary work of professional development, for when one believes differently, new behaviors will follow. Research on teacher change, however, indicates that changes in beliefs often come later when teachers use a new practice and see the benefits to their students (Ball & Cohen, 1999). Instead of being linear, changes in ideas and attitudes, and actions and behaviors, occur in a mutually interactive process. On the one hand, people's current thoughts influence what choices they make and what they attend to as they plan and carry out educational activities. On the other hand, people's reflections on these activities and their outcomes influence their thoughts about educational matters. Change in attitudes and behaviors is iterative; well-conceived professional learning experiences address both, knowing that change in one brings about and then reinforces change in the other.

A study of sites engaged in mathematics or science reform found that when the intervention was focused primarily on changing teachers' philosophy and beliefs, changes in actual practice and use of new curriculum were disappointing. Likewise, in sites where the intervention focused only on how to use new curriculum to the exclusion of developing new philosophy and beliefs needed to embrace new curriculum, the desired changes were not achieved. Only in sites where the professional development provided a balance between pragmatic application and development of new philosophy did the use of new curriculum take root (Mundry & Loucks-Horsley, 1999).

Fundamental beliefs are formed over time through active engagement with ideas, understandings, and real-life experiences. This explains why many teachers find it difficult to change how they teach. For example, many teachers learned mathematics or science in ways that are very different from those reflected in the national science and mathematics standards, and they learned by memorizing information and others' explanations through a transmission model. These experiences served as powerful models for their own teaching and created a script that they followed in their own teaching (Stigler & Hiebert, 1999). Deep change occurs only when beliefs are restructured through new understandings and experimentation with new behaviors.

Effective professional development experiences are designed to help teachers build new understandings of teaching and learning and try the teaching strategies that help students learn in new ways. They guide teachers to construct knowledge in the same ways as do effective learning experiences for students. Yet it is surprising to note how often the principle of constructivism is conveyed to teachers in the context of how they should help their students learn, without its being the basis for how they learn themselves (e.g., there are still too many lectures on, as opposed to experience in, constructivism in professional development programs). Experiencing learning in ways that hold to constructivist principles is the only way for teachers to understand deeply why it is important for their students to learn in this way and for them to break their old models of teaching (Little, 1993; Loucks-Horsley et al., 1990).

It should come as no surprise, then, that when change occurs, it does not happen in one step, but is progressive. Studies of individuals who change their practice over time report that individuals go through stages in how they feel about the change and how knowledgeable and sophisticated they are in using it. The questions that people ask evolve from early questions that are more self-oriented (What is it? How will it affect me?) to questions that are more task-oriented (How do I do it? How can I use these materials effectively? How can I organize myself? Why is it taking so much time?) to questions focused on impact (Is this change working for my students? Is there something that will work even better?) (Hall & Hord, 2006).

Professional development initiatives that are designed with the change process in mind have distinct characteristics (Fullan, 1991, 2007; Hall & Hord, 2006; Loucks-Horsley & Stiegelbauer, 1991; Sparks, 2002). First, they are informed by the ongoing monitoring of the concerns, questions, teaching contexts, and needs of teachers and focus interventions and support on what is learned. Second, they pay attention to implementation for several years in order for teachers to progress from an early focus on management to a later focus on measuring student learning. Tied to this is the way they create real-istic expectations in the system. It can take three to five years for teachers to fully implement a new practice or program, and therefore, expecting student achievement to change in a short period of time is unrealistic. Yet clear expectations for student learning should be established from the beginning and data collected to assess student growth over this time. Third, once changes in teachers' practice become routine, other demands on their time may distract them from focusing on student learning. Effective professional development designs anticipate this and build in opportunities for organiza-tional priority setting and ongoing monitoring of student learning (Loucks-Horsley, 1995; Sparks, 2002).

Although a major focus of change initiatives is on the individuals chang-ing, professional development can succeed only with simultaneous attention to changing the system within which teachers and other educators work. In the earlier wave of mathematics and science reform, impact studies reported the disturbing finding that many teachers who had experienced exemplary profes-sional development returned to their schools to find no support for the kinds of changes they wanted to make and, therefore, no change ultimately occurred. Education and businesses alike have learned a great deal from similar experi-ences over the past two decades, and what has emerged is new attention to the structures in the system that support or block innovation and change. In orga-nizations, five factors contribute to successful change efforts: leadership, effective communication, a tight alignment of people and organizational goals, adequate training and funding, and a clear definition of the compelling reasons for change (Kotter, 1996). As discussed in Chapter 3, the school leaders must be involved in the design of professional development so that there is coher-ence among the many different initiatives and priorities in a school. Ideally, leaders will work with the professional developers and the teachers to clearly define what will change and what will stay the same. Rather than layer new practices on top of old, leaders thoughtfully consider what practices teachers should abandon to make way for new approaches (Reeves, 2009). They will document both what practices are expected in the classroom and what support and development teachers will have to make the necessary changes.

Change cannot happen in isolation—it must be a coherent part of the strategic direction of the school or district (Sparks, 2002). With organiza-tional change, the unit of change is the system and not the individual. A major premise of systems thinking is that the behavior of individuals in sys-tems is dictated by underlying structures in organizations such as incentive systems, culture, and rules. Individuals are not to blame for breakdowns in the system caused by the system itself (Patterson, 1993; Senge, 1990). Effective change thus requires the organization to strive for continuous learning and to adopt new approaches and strategies quickly in response to new needs in the system. Educators at all levels are seeing the need to pay attention to "systemic change" by aligning components of the system, strengthening the relationship of the components to one another, and focusing their efforts on high standards for student learning. Professional development is viewed as a critical component of reform, one that must be linked to those same clear goals for students, as well as assessment, preservice teacher education, school leadership, and resources and staffing (NCTAF, 1996).

The knowledge base discussed in this chapter provides important guidance for the design of effective professional development experiences. It encourages professional developers to know the knowledge base on the relevant areas affecting professional development and to embed this knowledge into the visions and designs for teacher learning in science and mathematics.

3

Context Factors Influencing Professional Development

Figure 3.1   Context Factors Influencing Professional Development

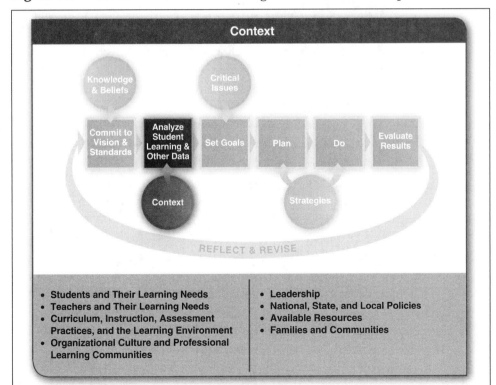

A group of teachers from a large urban center's archdiocese schools attended a two-day professional development session on peer coaching. They were excited about the peer-coaching session, but when it came time to attend a follow-up meeting, most admitted they had not tried peer coaching at all. In talking with the teachers, the staff development coordinator discovered that several barriers were at play. School schedules made it extremely difficult for teachers to be released from their classrooms for observations and pre- and post-conferences. Teachers had high anxiety about being observed by other teachers. School leaders were not clear about the purposes or benefits of peer coaching or their role in supporting it. An organizational culture, with strong norms of risk taking and collegiality, had not been established. Even though the program itself was a fine one, the context provided insurmountable obstacles to its implementation. Peer coaching was dead in the water.

This example highlights the systemic nature of professional development. It is important to keep in mind that professional learning occurs within people who have extensive experience and who live and work in unique contexts that can either thwart or support professional development (Blank, de las Alas, & Smith, 2008; Guskey, 2000; Sparks, 1996). In the example above, the strategy, peer coaching, and the larger organizational context were mismatched, and the program never got off the ground. Context is one reason why a program that is a great success in one place may fail in another. Richard DuFour (2001) writes, "In the right school context, even flawed professional development activities (such as the much maligned single-session workshop) can serve as a catalyst for professional growth. Conversely, in the wrong school context, even programs with solid content and training strategies are unlikely to be effective" (p. 14). Effective professional development is tailored to fit into the unique, local context in which teachers teach and students learn. Often the context itself must be adapted for the professional development to be implemented successfully.

Professional developers collect information and get to know the contexts of the schools and districts where they work to guide them in designing professional development that is appropriate and realistic and can thrive in and strengthen the systems in which they work. They do what business leader Max DePree (1989) calls the "first responsibility of leaders"—to define and assess their current reality (p. 11). In their synthesis of research on school leadership, Marzano, Waters, and McNulty (2005) identified "situational awareness" as the responsibility of principals most highly correlated with student achievement (p. 20). Effective school leaders use their keen awareness of the details and undercurrents in the school to address current and potential problems. In the same way, professional developers use situational awareness to scan their environment, developing awareness of current practice and culture, anticipating problems, accurately predicting what will support or undermine their efforts, and designing professional development that will work in the context.

This chapter introduces eight context factors that need careful consideration as one designs professional development. They are (1) students and their learning needs; (2) teachers and their learning needs; (3) curriculum, instruction, assessment practices, and the learning environment; (4) organizational culture and professional learning communities; (5) leadership; (6) national, state, and local policies; (7) available resources; and (8) families and the community (see Figure 3.1).

For each of these factors, we discuss

- its importance in shaping professional development,
- examples of how to tailor professional development to address that context factor,
- tips for considering each factor as you plan, and
- questions to help you investigate the factor in your own context.

Resources, including data-analysis tools and processes, survey instruments, rubrics, and observation protocols, are provided at the end of this chapter for investigating these factors in your own schools and districts.

Professional developers use information about their context throughout the design process. In the planning stage, they use data about student and teacher learning as the basis for setting program goals. They also look broadly at their school or district as a system to consider what factors might support or constrain their efforts, such as the organizational culture, leadership, or local, state, and national policies. From their analysis of the context, professional development designers may set goals for the organization, as well as for professional learning, such as strengthening leadership, enhancing opportunities for collegial work, or creating learning communities. In some cases, a particular constraint in the context will need to be addressed before implementing the professional development program to increase the likelihood of achieving the desired impact. For example, if there is not adequate time for professional development, that roadblock will need to be addressed before launching the program so that resources are not squandered. During implementation, it is important to continue to scan the context, noticing and responding to changes and attending to new conditions or constraints that may arise. For example, you may be alerted to the need to increase family and community engagement when you learn that there are misconceptions in the community about why teachers are participating in professional development, or you may find a greater need to focus on building teachers' leadership skills as the program is implemented, so the teachers can play a larger role in the next phase of the program. As professional development progresses, the designers pay attention to the evaluation data showing what impact the program is having on the context, especially on teacher and student learning, organizational culture, and leadership. Through reflection and revision these data inform the next round of planning and goal setting.

It is difficult to draw sharp lines between context factors and the other inputs into designing professional development. For example, the discussion of the input knowledge and beliefs reinforces how important contextual factors such as professional culture, leadership, systemic support, and time are to providing powerful teacher learning. Contextual factors of time, professional culture, and public support are also reflected in the section on critical issues, which regardless of the particularities of local context will need to be addressed successfully. The reader will find that these important inputs are revisited many times in this book just as good designers reassess them often in their work. The intent of considering contextual factors is to consciously guide professional developers to choose teacher learning approaches that are well matched to the context (i.e., approaches that both address the needs of the context and fit into or help change the culture as needed) and to use context data to fine-tune their designs to the needs and realities of their schools. Below we discuss each of the context factors, starting with one that is at the very core of all professional development planning.

STUDENTS AND THEIR LEARNING NEEDS

Effective professional development is designed to help teachers meet the specific needs of real students in real classrooms.

—Thomas B. Corcoran, 2007, p. 5

The eighth-grade team analyzed their assessments results in mathematics, indicator by indicator. The data were clear: Many students were struggling with three areas in the state standards: (1) applying algebra to measure angles formed by or contained in parallel lines cut by a transversal and by intersecting lines; (2) adding and subtracting polynomials (integer coefficients); and (3) multiplying a binomial by a monomial or a binomial (integer coefficients). They also were dismayed to see that large numbers of their English language learners were underperforming in these and other math standard areas. Using this context data about students and their learning needs, the mathematics coaches and teachers identified areas where they thought they needed to improve teaching of lessons. In response, the mathematics coaches worked with the eighth-grade teachers using lesson study to develop a series of lessons targeted to the areas of low performance. The teachers examined research on teaching the math concepts and on scaffolding learning for English language learners. They worked together to revise their lessons to better reflect the research. The group observed a few teachers teaching the revised lessons. They then debriefed and refined the lessons again. Next, all teachers taught the lessons to their own students. They gathered formative assessment data as they were teaching. They examined student work gathered from teaching the revised lessons, evaluated the effectiveness of the lessons in enhancing students' learning, and identified aspects of the lesson in need of further refinement. They came together again to reflect on the changes they had made to instruction and why they needed those changes and to plan how to use what they learned to continue to improve learning in mathematics.

One of the most important context factors to consider when designing professional development is student learning. Designers need to engage teachers in considering the questions, "Who are our students?" "How well are we serving them?" "What are the implications for teacher learning?" The vignette above illustrates the alignment between student learning results and professional development planning. In the example, the mathematics coaches started by engaging the eighth-grade teachers in analyzing student learning data to identify areas where instruction might need to be enhanced. The data provided a clear focus for the professional development—improving students' mastery of the indicators on which they performed poorly. The professional development strategy chosen, lesson study, was targeted to improve the teaching of mathematics lessons in the areas where student knowledge was weakest and to address needs of a special student population. Goals for the teachers' learning connected directly with the student learning goals: teachers were learning how to design research-based lessons, trying out and reflecting on new instructional approaches, and using formative assessment to address the student learning goal. Student learning data were used before, during, and after the professional development, and teachers were actively engaged in that analysis.

Understanding students and their learning needs is at the heart of professional development design. It is the key to establishing and sustaining a clear focus on student learning goals. According to Tom Guskey (2000), "Of all the variables related to effective professional development, goal clarity is perhaps the most important. It is essential that we be explicit about the goals of professional development, especially in terms of the classroom or school practices that we hope to see implemented and the results that we would like to attain in terms of students" (p. 17).

The professional development design process begins with a commitment to a vision for students and a set of desired outcomes or standards. The next step is to analyze student learning results to uncover gaps between the desired learning results and the current reality. The gaps uncovered in this analysis inform the specific student learning goals for the professional development program. For example, the goal may be focused on improving student learning in physical science, K–12, or in algebraic thinking in the upper elementary and middle schools. Or it may be more narrowly focused on improving understanding of a particular topic or standard within a grade or a school. Goals based on analysis of student learning needs not only give coherence and focus to the plan, but they set the stage for ongoing monitoring and evaluation, which rely on clear targets. Highlighting the link between initial assessment of student learning and professional development design, Fishman and his colleagues researched a professional development model focused on wide-scale science curriculum implementation in a large urban district (Fishman, Marx, Best, & Tal, 2003). The process began with analysis of standards documents and evidence of current status of student performance based on artifacts, classroom behaviors, and pre- and posttests. Professional development was then designed to help teachers acquire the knowledge they needed to enact the curriculum units, particularly in those areas where student performance was weak. Researchers then evaluated the professional development based on teacher reflection, classroom observation, and student performance. When student learning results indicated that students were having difficulty with a particular part of the curriculum, such as map-reading skills, professional development was redesigned to help teachers focus on areas of student difficulty. Fishman and his colleagues documented teachers using new strategies learned in the redesigned professional development and the results they had on student learning.

In addition to targeting a specific content area or set of standards upon which to focus improvement, analysis of student learning data serves other purposes. When analyzed by demographic factors—by race or ethnicity, economic, language, special education status, gender, and mobility—the data bring to light inequities in how student groups are being served. Underlying achievement gaps are disparities in educational opportunities, resource allocation, and discipline based on race and economic status (Betts, Rueben, & Danenberg, 2000; Darling-Hammond, 2004; National Center for Education Statistics, 2001; Oakes, 1990, 2005; Oakes & Saunders, 2002). A primary purpose of professional development is to bring about the organizational and individual changes that will result in more

Tips for Aligning Professional Development With Students and Their Learning Needs

- Coordinate your professional development with school-improvement planning.
- Establish clear goals for professional development based on priorities for student learning.

culturally proficient practices in schools and classrooms. These practices include a broad set of teaching strategies for working with diverse student groups as well as ongoing examination of deeply held cultural assumptions that shape practice (Banks et al., 2005; Nuri Robins, Lindsey, Lindsey, & Terrell, 2006). Student learning data—disaggregated by relevant demographic groups—provide a window into how inequities manifest in your own context and a rallying cry for professional development aimed at eradicating them.

In additional to achievement data—formative, summative, and disaggregated by student-demographic groups—other data about students' learning needs, including surveys about their perceptions, interviews, examination of student work, and course-taking patterns provide a fuller picture of students and how well they are being served. Such data inform professional development plans. For example, the J. Eric Johnson Community School near Dallas, Texas, collected data about student engagement, which were shared widely with teachers. Their reflection stimulated teachers to make changes in practice to improve student engagement in the classroom (Minnett, Murphy, Nobles, & Taylor, 2008).

Frequent and in-depth data analysis is not just a professional development planning tool. It is professional development in itself—giving teachers insights into standards, content, and students' thinking; fueling continuous improvement in instruction; and keeping professional learning communities riveted on results. Table 3.1 suggests questions to consider about students and their learning needs as you design professional development.

- Do not choose a program or strategy unless you are clear how it addresses your schools' student learning needs.
- Do the "nest test," making sure that professional and organizational development goals are connected directly with student learning goals.
- Keep student learning data or goals for improving learning prominently displayed when you meet for professional learning activities and in other locations, such as the faculty room, as a constant reminder of the student learning goals you are pursuing.
- If your school lacks capacity in analyzing student learning results, set a professional development goal to increase teachers' capacity to analyze and use data to improve their teaching.
- Make sure your data are disaggregated so that you can identify unique needs and patterns across all student populations. Disaggregate student-achievement data, course-taking patterns, resource allocations, special program assignments, and other factors by race, cultural background, gender, poverty, and disability to bring equity issues to the forefront.
- Document which students are being taught by uncredentialed teachers or teachers teaching out of their subject area. Prioritize these teachers to participate in professional development and course work.
- Frequently monitor student learning through benchmark assessments aligned with curriculum and standards, and use results to consider what new professional learning may be needed.
- Support teachers' use of ongoing formative assessments and establish mechanisms for teachers to work together to examine student work and thinking.

Table 3.1   Students and Their Learning Needs: Questions to Consider

---

Questions to Consider

1. Who are our students? What are their cultural backgrounds? Learning styles?

2. What standards are in place for student learning?

3. How are students performing in relation to standards? What particular concepts, skills, and dispositions are students learning well or not learning well?

4. What gaps in achievement—by race, socioeconomic status, language status, educational status, and gender—exist among students?

5. What are the top priority goals for improving student learning and closing achievement gaps?

6. How is student learning monitored on a regular basis? To what extent are formative assessments guiding teachers to improve instruction and students to improve their learning?

TEACHERS AND THEIR LEARNING NEEDS

Of all the things that are important to having good schools, nothing is as important as the teacher and what that person knows, believes, and can do. . . . Teacher effects dwarf all others on student learning.

—Jon Saphier (Saphier, Haley-Speca, & Gower, 2008, p. v)

Once student learning goals are clearly established based on analysis of student learning and other data, the next context factor to explore is teachers and their learning needs. The driving question designers ask now is "If students are going to meet the learning goals we have established, what new knowledge, practices and beliefs do teachers need, and how will they acquire them?"

Decades of research leave little doubt that what teachers know and do exerts the biggest influence on what students learn. "The most direct route to improving mathematics and science achievement for all students is better mathematics and science teaching," concluded The National Commission on Mathematics and Science Teaching for the 21st Century (2000, p. 7). Researchers have linked teacher content knowledge in mathematics and science with higher student performance in these disciplines (Darling-Hammond, 2000;

Goldhaber & Brewer, 2000). There is also strong evidence that teacher knowledge of pedagogical content and generic pedagogy as well as their beliefs and dispositions about teaching, learning, and students have an effect on student learning (Blank et al., 2008; Mendro & Bembry, 2000; Muijs & Reynolds, 2001; Sanders & Rivers, 1996).

Cohen, Raudenbush, and Ball (2003) describe three relationships as the focal point for professional learning that supports students' learning: (1) teacher understanding of the subject domains, (2) teachers' grasp of student thinking, and (3) teachers' understanding of and responsiveness to the students they teach. Bransford, Darling-Hammond, and LePage (2005) frame the domains of teacher learning as (1) knowledge of learners and their development, (2) knowledge of subject matter and curriculum goals, and (3) knowledge of teaching. Professional developers look for the levers for improving student learning within these domains of teacher knowledge.

Taking stock of who the teachers in your setting are and what they need to learn is as important to professional development design as knowledge of students and their learning needs in the classroom. It lays the groundwork for setting realistic and meaningful goals tied to student learning goals that are grounded in what teachers actually need to know to improve their teaching. It allows for designs to be differentiated to meet the needs of a diversity of teachers—from the most experienced to the most novice—who need different learning at different times delivered in different ways. Knowing what teachers know and what they want to learn also enables professional developers to build on teachers' prior knowledge respectfully, uncover common naïve ideas, and adjust the program as specific concerns arise. As in the classroom, assessment of teachers and their needs shapes initial goals and strategies as well as ongoing adjustments in professional development.

Increasingly, professional development programs are collecting information on what content and pedagogical content knowledge teachers have and how they are changing their practices over time to inform professional development planning. Several teacher surveys, such as the *Learning Mathematics for Teaching, Assessing Teacher Learning About Science Teaching, Diagnostic Teacher Assessments in Mathematics and Science*, and *Misconception-Oriented Standards-Based Assessment Resource for Teachers,* are being used to provide teachers with feedback on the knowledge needed for teaching. (For more information on these surveys, see "Resources for Investigating Context" at the end of this chapter.) Other tools focus on helping to guide the change process and see how well teachers are implementing changes. For example, in Madison, Wisconsin, district leaders used the *Stages of Concern (SoC) Questionnaire* from the Concerns-Based

Adoption Model (Hall & Hord, 2006) to guide the design of districtwide professional development in support of standards-based instruction. The questionnaire revealed that many teachers had a superficial awareness of standards-based instruction or even disagreed with it. "We fundamentally changed the way we went about allocating resources," reported Lisa Wachtel, executive director of Teaching and Learning in the Madison Metropolitan School District (personal communication, September 2008).

The district developed a differentiated professional development program to respond to teachers' range of concerns. They prepared DVD- and Web-based professional development materials, guiding questions, and facilitator guides aligned with the specific concerns that surfaced in the questionnaire. At the same time, they developed a cadre of teacher leaders in each of the content areas who could facilitate study groups with teachers, targeting their specific concerns. For some teachers, what were needed were sessions focused on "unpacking" and getting a deeper understanding of standards. For others, who did not agree with the stance of standards-based instruction, reflective dialogue about beliefs about students and their ability to achieve standards was provided. By making use of a continuous flow of information about teachers and the concerns among teachers, teacher leaders, and district leaders, the district has been able to deepen the implementation of standards-based instruction and report cards. "Standards-based education is shifting away from downtown initiatives; it is becoming more of a building-based initiative carried out through teacher leaders, and becoming increasingly evident in the classroom," Wachtel (personal communication, September 2008) reported.

Sometimes taking into consideration teacher learning needs happens "in the moment." Remillard and Geist (2002) describe how mathematics professional developers supported teacher learning through "openings in the curriculum" (p. 7). The curriculum in their research was Developing Mathematical Ideas, a program for elementary teachers to examine key ideas in mathematics and student thinking through

> **Tips for Considering Teachers and Their Learning Needs in Professional Development Design**
>
> - Set explicit teacher learning goals tied to student learning goals.
> - Assess teacher learning before and during professional development.
> - Use tools such as validated knowledge surveys and questionnaires such as from the Concerns-Based Adoption Model to gain insight into what teachers know and think.
> - Look for evidence that teachers are applying their learning in the classroom.
> - Provide opportunities for teachers to talk with one another about their goals for students and their beliefs about learning.

teacher-developed cases of students' mathematical thinking, group discussions, and immersion in mathematics. "Openings in the curriculum" refer to "unanticipated and at times awkward points in the conversation through which facilitators had to navigate" (p. 13) in response to pedagogical or mathematical issues that arose during the sessions. While challenging for the facilitator, these openings provided rich opportunities to foster learning based on the actual questions, challenges, observations, or actions of participating teachers.

As designers consider the contextual issue of teachers and their learning needs, it is helpful to explore the questions listed in Table 3.2.

Table 3.2   Teachers and Their Learning Needs: Questions to Consider

---

Questions to Consider

1. Who are the teachers (demographics, years of experience, cultural background)?

2. How well prepared are teachers to teach challenging science and mathematics content (course work, credentials, professional development experiences, perceptions)? What percentage are teaching subjects for which they are not certified?

3. How are new teachers inducted and supported?

4. What goals do teachers have for their learning?

5. What are teachers' beliefs, perceptions, and concerns related to the professional development? To mathematics and science improvement based on research and standards?

6. What are teachers' strengths in mathematics and science content and pedagogy? What specific content knowledge and pedagogical skills do teachers need if students are to achieve the desired learning goals?

7. What specific goals is the professional development program targeting for teachers? What will they learn, and how will they apply their learning in the classroom?

8. What is the current capacity of teachers and administrators to use student learning and other data effectively?

9. What has been teachers' experiences implementing new practices in the classroom and with past professional development? What are their expectations for professional learning?

CURRICULUM, INSTRUCTION, ASSESSMENT PRACTICES, AND THE LEARNING ENVIRONMENT

The educational core—curriculum,
instruction, assessment and professional
development—is where our time, money,
and effort should be focused.

—*Rodger W. Bybee, 2006, p. 159*

If professional development is going to improve mathematics and science learning, then it must address the "educational core" and improve classroom practice. However, helping teachers make the leap from learning something new to implementing it in the classroom is one of the biggest challenges professional developers face. As Tom Guskey (2000) puts it, "If there is one thing on which both behaviorists and cognitivists agree, it is that no one expects new learning to transfer immediately into more effective practice" (p. 180). Designing quality professional development involves paying thoughtful attention to teachers' concerns, providing coaching in the classroom and requisite instructional materials and sufficient time for job-embedded learning, and engaging in ongoing problem solving and support so that transfer can take place (Hall & Hord, 2001; Joyce & Showers, 1988; Loucks-Horsley & Stiegelbauer, 1991; Wei et al., 2009; Weiss & Pasley, 2009).

To meet this challenge, professional developers assess the current state of mathematics and science classroom practice—the curriculum, instruction, and assessment practices and learning environments. Knowledge of current classroom practices guides them in setting appropriate and realistic goals for professional development and later in monitoring and evaluating its impact. It helps them identify and plan to address the obstacles teachers will face. It gives them data to differentiate professional development goals and approaches based on what different teachers need. For example, if beginning teachers are preoccupied with classroom management, they will need additional support in how to manage student groups and materials in an inquiry-based science program before they can successfully engage students in investigations. Teachers with more experience implementing inquiry-based approaches may need professional development that is focused on helping them to examine student work to hone their instruction and assess how well the curriculum is working. When professional developers keep their fingers on the pulse of practice, they can match content and delivery to the next challenge teachers face.

As discussed in Chapter 2, the compendium *How Students Learn: History, Mathematics, and Science in the Classroom* describes four key elements of effective classroom environments, which draw on principles of learning and serve as lenses through which professional developers can examine teaching practice (Donovan & Bransford, 2005). The first, the *learner-centered environment,* encourages attention to students' ideas, knowledge, skills, and attitudes as the foundation upon which new knowledge builds. Second is the *knowledge-centered environment,* which focuses on what is to be taught (curriculum), why it is taught (understanding), and what mastery looks like. Related to the first two is the third, the *assessment-centered environment,* in which ongoing formative assessments, designed to make student thinking visible, guide students and teachers in their learning. The fourth is a *community-centered environment* in which norms of risk taking, questioning, and respect shape the culture of the classroom. In assessing the current context, professional developers seek to determine the extent to which these four essential environments exist in the schools' classrooms, and if they are not present, set goals to put them in place. As they do so, it is important to ask whether each and every student, regardless of racial, economic, or educational status, has access to the best possible learning environments.

How do professional developers gather information about these dimensions of classroom practice and assess teachers' use of new knowledge and skills? Thomas Guskey (2000), in his book *Evaluating Professional Development,* suggests the following methods:

- Direct observation
- Teacher interviews or conferencing
- Supervisor interviews or conferencing
- Student interviews or conferencing
- Questionnaires
- Focus groups
- Implementation logs and reflective journals
- Participant portfolios (p. 202)

Over the past several years, a variety of tools have been developed to assess classroom practice, monitor changes, and evaluate the impact of reform on curriculum, instruction, and assessment practices and learning environments, including surveys and observation protocols. (See "Resources for Investigating Context" at the end of this chapter.) When observing classrooms, it is important that those observing have trained "eyes" so that they know what to look for and how to accurately interpret what they are seeing. For example, the Lenses on Learning program provides an in-depth, video-based

Tips for Considering Curriculum, Instruction, Assessment Practices, and Learning Environments in Professional Development Design

- Build classroom coaching and observation into the professional development program so you are gathering data about practice at the same time you are supporting teachers.
- Provide professional development for principals so they are prepared to observe for the classroom practices the professional development intends teachers to implement. Help principals develop mechanisms to offer growth-oriented feedback rather than debilitating criticism.
- Be aware of the limitations of quick walkthroughs and checklist observations, which can create incomplete impressions about classroom practices. All walkthroughs should be guided by clearly defined protocols that have growth-oriented debriefings to help teachers strengthen their teaching.
- Communicate with principals, coaches, and other instructional leaders about what they are seeing in their classroom observations.
- Develop and discuss clear goals for improving practice with teachers, and share clear examples of how the new practices should be implemented in the classroom.
- Do not underestimate what it takes to change classroom practice. Build ongoing support for teachers and monitoring of how they are doing.
- Develop a description or profile of what effective classroom practice looks like. See, for example, Innovation Configurations (Hall & Hord, 2006) that can be used to clearly articulate what classroom practices are intended.

professional development program for educational leaders on how to observe standards-based elementary mathematics classrooms (Grant et al., 2002). Many school districts are also using their own protocols for classroom observation to identify how well teachers implement desired instructional practices. Mathematics and science coaches often observe and provide help and feedback for teachers. Assessing the curriculum, instruction, and assessment practices requires that professional developers get into classrooms to gather direct evidence of teacher practice and use the information to inform plans for teacher learning.

Monitoring classroom practice is especially important as programs are underway to uncover whether change in practice is occurring, what variations in the intended practice are being implementing, and what is needed next. For example, the Katz Elementary School in Las Vegas, Nevada, adopted a National Science Foundation funded mathematics curriculum that emphasized nonroutine problem solving. A few years later, teachers on the school data team were surprised to uncover in their data analysis that many students were struggling with problem solving. This led the team to collaborate with the principal in surveying teachers and observing classrooms to assess the implementation of the curriculum. When they discovered that the curriculum was not being implemented consistently, they designed professional development strategies to help teachers, including vertical teaming, workshops targeted to curriculum units, and development of common rubrics and weekly assessments for mathematics problem solving (Love et al., 2008).

As the above example illustrates, ongoing monitoring of curriculum, instruction, assessment, and the learning environment is key to bridging the gap between professional development and the classroom practice. Table 3.3 lists questions to guide investigation of curriculum, instruction, and assessment practices and learning environments as you design professional development.

- Initiate the professional development program by collecting baseline data using the same tools you will use to evaluate the impact of professional development in classroom practice.
- Take advantage of quick hallway chats, team and faculty meetings, and meetings with teacher leaders and building-based coaches to learn what is happening in classrooms.

Table 3.3   Curriculum, Instruction, Assessment Practices, and the Learning Environment: Questions to Consider

Questions to Consider

1. To what extent is the curriculum clearly defined and aligned with standards? Is the written curriculum implemented as intended? How are the specific content areas you hope to improve addressed in the written and taught curriculum? To what extent is the curriculum focused, rigorous, and coherent?

2. To what extent do some students (e.g., those living in poverty, students of color, second language learners, special needs students, and girls) have less opportunity to learn a rigorous curriculum than others? Is tracking practiced? Who is taking advanced placement (AP) courses?

3. To what extent are students in science classes involved in active, hands-on learning approaches? Are some groups of students receiving more of this type of instruction than others?

4. To what extent are students in mathematics classes engaged in problem solving and reasoning skills and learning how to apply knowledge to novel problems? Are some groups of students receiving more of this kind of instruction than others?

5. What methods of student assessment are used in class, and are the strategies consistent with goals of learning in content standards? Are varied assessment strategies being used more with some student groups than others?

6. Is the learning environment respectful of students and their diversity and conducive to all students' active participation and collaboration?

ORGANIZATIONAL CULTURE AND PROFESSIONAL LEARNING COMMUNITIES

Today the most promising context for continuous professional learning is the professional learning community.

—*Shirley Hord, 2008, p. 10*

The concept of schools organized as professional learning communities has caught fire in the last decade, and for good reason (Mundry & Stiles, 2009). A growing body of research has found that when schools function as professional learning communities, establish clear goals, measure student learning regularly, work collaboratively to support learning, and intervene when students fail to learn, students learn (Berry, Johnson, & Montgomery, 2005; Bolam, McMahon, Stoll, Thomas, & Wallace, 2005; Louis & Marks, 1998; Phillips, 2003; Strahan, 2003; Supovitz, 2002; Supovitz & Christman, 2003). This research underscores why it is important to consider organizational culture as an important factor as you plan professional development. Professional learning communities (PLCs) by their definition are focused on learning whatever is needed to enhance practice and student learning. PLCs thrive in a collaborative culture, which provides a nurturing environment for professional learning (Eaker & Keating, 2008; Hord & Sommers, 2008). At the same time, professional development that is collaborative, focused on student learning, and closely linked to classroom practice, strengthens the collaborative culture. Because school culture and professional development enjoy a symbiotic relationship, professional developers focus on both. As Hord and Boyd (1995) explain, "Attending to this aspect of context (culture), assessing its strengths and weaknesses and planning accordingly, can yield a rich harvest for both professional and organizational development" (p. 10).

In order for professional learning communities to take hold, profound changes in school culture must occur. Eaker and Keating (2008) define culture as the "assumptions, beliefs, expectations, and habits that constitute the norm for those working in it" (p. 15). They argue that professional learning communities rest on at least three major cultural shifts. The first is a shift in purpose from a focus on teaching to a focus on learning, a "seismic" change, in their words, that has ripple effects throughout a school (p. 15). The second is a shift in the work of teachers from isolation to collaboration. The third is a shift in focus from inputs to outcomes, where evidence of student learning drives improvements in professional practice. A central goal of professional development is to help bring about these shifts.

Anchored in these cultural shifts, robust professional learning communities share a set of defining characteristics. Hord and Sommers (2008) identify the following features:

- Shared values and vision
- Shared and supportive leadership: administrators and faculty hold shared power and authority for making decisions
- Collective learning and its applications
- Supportive conditions for the maintenance of the community, such as time and a place to meet, resources and policies that support collaboration, and relational factors such as openness and truth telling
- Shared personal practice (p. 9)

Kruse and Louis (2009) identify four similar principles of professional learning communities: "(1) Focusing on values and norms that you hold in common: What is important to us? (2) Reflective discussion: How can we embody what we value in our work? (3) Shared practice: What is hard for us to do? Can we help each other? (4) Collective responsibility: We all own the effectiveness of this school" (p. 64). Other characteristics cited in the research literature are mutual trust, inclusive schoolwide membership, and networks and partnerships external to the school (Stoll, Bolam, McMahon, Wallace, & Thomas, 2006).

Professional developers apply their understanding of the underlying cultural shifts and the characteristics of professional community described above to design programs that are attuned to and help to strengthen organizational culture. For example, many of the professional development strategies described in Chapter 5, such as case discussions and lesson study, depend on the presence of the supportive conditions described by Hord and Boyd (1995), such as a time and place for teachers to meet regularly. Before embarking on such strategies, it is important to establish the climate and structures that will help to ensure their success. However, structural changes such as new schedules or team time do not in themselves result in professional learning communities. As Phil Schlechty (1997) concludes, "Structural change that is not supported by cultural change will eventually be overwhelmed by the culture" (p. 136). Richard DuFour (1999) adds, "Schools make a major mistake when they settle for creating team structures. The real challenge is developing teams with a high 'group IQ,' teams that are effective in working together to solve problems and to renew their school" (p. 62).

In addition to examining the culture for its capacity to be a collaborative learning community, professional developers examine the extent to which the school culture is committed to achieving educational equity.

When designing professional development for data coaches to lead school-based data teams, Love, Stiles, Mundry, and DiRanna (2008) found that building shared commitments and a common language around equity was foundational to the work of data teams and learning communities. Especially when examining disaggregated data by race and socioeconomic, educational, or language status, they observed that some data-team members fell into "culturally destructive " behaviors—blaming their students and their backgrounds—or "culturally blind" practices, denying that differences in performance among demographic groups were important to address (Lindsey, Roberts, & CampbellJones, 2005, p. 85). The developers realized that professional development is often needed to increase cultural proficiency—the ability to interact knowledgably and respectfully among diverse cultural groups. It is difficult to implement changes in the classroom focused on learning for all students until faculty can learn to talk about their cultural assumptions and challenge the thinking that has led to wide achievement gaps among student populations. Cultural proficiency is at least as or even more important to develop as a core competency for leaders of professional learning communities as data literacy, collaborative inquiry skills, and content and pedagogical content knowledge (CampbellJones, CampbellJones, & Love, 2009). School staff who have not worked to develop this competency may need to start here with their professional development planning.

These examples point to the many challenges of creating effective school cultures and putting professional learning communities into practice. As with other educational innovations, wildly popular does not translate into widely implemented—although in the case of professional learning communities, success stories are growing (Vescio, Ross, & Adams, 2008.). However, DuFour

---

Tips for Considering Organizational Culture and Professional Learning Communities in Professional Development Design

- Establish clear goals for both professional development and school culture.
- Identify school structures that may deter teachers from meaningful collaboration (e.g., schedule, competitive or fearful culture, rewards).
- Monitor changes in school culture as well as changes in teacher and student learning.
- Develop the capacity for staff to communicate effectively by establishing strong norms of collaboration (Garmston & Wellman, 2009) and effective teamwork skills.
- Develop leaders' capacity to lead collaborative professional communities.
- Attend to cultural proficiency as an important dimension of high-performing school culture.

Table 3.4   Organizational Culture and Professional Learning
Communities: Questions to Consider

Questions to Consider

1. To what extent are shared values and vision evident in the school culture?

2. Are school structures in place that support collaborative practice, for example, time for teachers who teach the same content and/or grade levels to meet during the school day, ready access to relevant student learning data, opportunities for professional learning tied to classroom practice?

3. How are school and district leaders supporting schools to work as professional learning communities? How could their support be strengthened?

4. How much conversation in teacher teams is focused on mathematics and science teaching and learning? Do teachers share a vision and common language about teaching and learning goals?

5. What norms exist for making instruction research- and standards-based? Do teachers use evidence from student learning data or research when they discuss practice?

6. How safe is it for teachers to share their own practice with one another? Is reflective dialogue a norm? Have teachers been supported or criticized when they share ideas with colleagues?

7. Is there ongoing inquiry into beliefs about students and their capacities? Are assumptions about race, class, educational, and linguistic differences among students talked about openly and critically examined?

8. Is there attention to developing teachers' collaborative and problem-solving skills?

9. Are there clear answers to the questions: (a) What do we want students to learn? (b) How will we know? (c) What will we do if they don't learn? Are a set of interventions for students in place to both prevent and remediate failure? (DuFour, R., DuFour, R., Eaker, R., & Karhanek, G., 2004)

10. What professional development efforts are currently under way? How are multiple efforts coordinated? How are teachers and others being helped to address multiple and conflicting priorities?

(2004) cautions, "The term has been used so ubiquitously that it is in danger of losing all meaning" (p. 6). Declaring a school a professional learning community does not make it so, nor does establishing the structures such as team time without attending to the much more difficult changes in the underlying assumptions and norms of the culture. Hord and Sommers (2008) detail the many "rocks in the road" those leading professional communities navigate, including bringing together individuals who have worked in isolation into a community, staying focused on what is important in the daily operations of a school, finding time, being overloaded with initiatives, monitoring implementation, and protecting team time from intrusions.

Table 3.4 (see page 97) suggests questions to ask as you investigate what changes may be needed in the organizational culture to support learning for all.

LEADERSHIP

Leaders are responsible for building the capacity in individuals, teams, and organizations to be leaders and learners.

—*Stephanie Hirsh and Joellen Killion, 2007, p. 25*

In our professional development sessions with leaders, the authors often ask participants to make connections between school improvement and an image depicting an open-bed truck overloaded with bundles. On closer examination, participants notice that the truck has no driver. They quickly see the analogies: Our school can be loaded with good intentions, professional development initiatives, and a wide variety of school data, but if there is no driver, the school is going nowhere.

Leadership is widely recognized as one of the most important factors in teacher and student learning. Schools and districts that are going somewhere—toward improved student learning—have effective leaders who behave in specific ways that impact success. Leithwood, Louis, Anderson, and Wahlstrom (2004) found that only classroom instruction has a greater impact on student learning than school leadership. In their meta-analysis of school leadership, Marzano, Waters, and McNulty (2005) reaffirm the link between leadership and student learning: "Our basic claim is that research over the 35 years provides strong guidance on specific leadership behaviors for school administrators and that those behaviors have well-documented effects on student achievement" (p. 7). Summing up decades of research in two words, Dennis Sparks (2005) says, "Leaders matter" (p. ii). They matter for students' learning, for teachers' learning, and for our schools and districts as learning organizations.

Fullan (2005) calls for a critical mass of leaders at all levels of the system who are skilled in putting systemic change into action. Kaser, Mundry, Stiles, and Loucks-Horsley (2006) identified four key areas for leaders: They must possess research-based leadership skills, understand how to lead and manage change, be leaders of learning, and be effective facilitators of groups and teamwork. Hirsh and Killion (2007) add that it is the role of leaders to develop others' leadership. They describe a cascade of leadership knowledge, skills, and dispositions—from teachers developing students' leadership, to coaches developing teacher leadership, to principals distributing responsibilities throughout the staff, to central offices creating learning communities for aspiring leadership. Their conclusion: "Sustaining change means sustaining leadership and spreading it widely throughout the system" (p.40).

At the district level, Waters and Marzano (2006) found that the following actions of superintendents and other district personnel, including curriculum leaders and school boards, correlated with improved student learning:

- Collaborative goal-setting processes, involving key stakeholders
- Clear and nonnegotiable goals
- Board alignment with and support of district goals
- Monitoring the goals for achievement and instruction
- Use of resources to support goals for achievement and instruction (p. 11)

District leaders also play an important role in developing principals. Saphier (2008) describes the role of those supervising principals, such as zone or regional superintendents in large districts. He recommends that these district leaders convene principals in learning communities to study and problem solve on instructional leadership issues in schools; observe and provide feedback about the principals' classroom observation and conferring skills; observe and provide principals with feedback on their leadership actions; and conduct regular school visits and walkthroughs.

Principals play a highly influential role in supporting effective teaching and learning in schools. From their review of research studies that link leadership and student learning, Marzano and others (2005) found 21 school leadership behaviors associated with student learning, the top five follow:

1. Use situational awareness of what is happening in the school for problem solving.

2. Exhibit flexibility in adapting to needs.

3. Discipline in a manner that protects teachers from distractions.

4. Monitor and evaluate school practices and their impacts on student learning.

5. Reach out to the community.

Principals also have a crucial role to play in supporting professional development, developing teacher leadership, and nurturing learning communities. Evaluators of the NSF Local Systemic Change projects cited principal support as the most important factor in teacher participation and supportive contexts for reform. Some of the concrete ways in which principals supported reform were to actively participate in professional development themselves, support teacher leaders, budget new resources, create schedules and structures for teacher collaboration, and educate parents about new mathematics and science programs (Banilower et al., 2006). Research on professional learning communities further illuminates the multiple roles that principals play in creating the cultural conditions that allow teaching and learning to thrive: integrating fragmented subcultures, attacking incoherence, establishing trust, keeping the focus on improving teaching and learning, distributing leadership, creating networks of support for their own learning, modeling and promoting cultural proficiency, and engaging families and communities (Fullan, 2002; Hord & Sommers, 2008; Kruse & Louis, 2009; Lindsey, Robins, & Terrell, 2003).

In the realm of school leadership, teacher leaders exert a powerful force for school improvement. They do so as classroom teachers and in leadership roles outside the classroom as coaches, mentors, professional development facilitators, instructional specialists, team leaders, or department chairs (Silva, Gimbert, & Nolan, 2000). Whether formally or informally, teacher leaders benefit schools by increasing expertise in teaching and learning, strengthening collaborative cultures and internal accountability, building capacity, and increasing teachers' sense of professionalism and empowerment. They also impact student learning by implementing new practices in their own classrooms (Hirsh & Killion, 2007; Killion & Harrison, 2006; Murphy, 2005; York-Barr & Duke, 2004). Killion and Harrison (2006) define 10 roles for teacher leaders, including resource provider, data coach, curriculum specialist, instructional specialist, mentor, and catalyst for change.

Because of the crucial role that leadership plays in promoting student and teacher learning, professional developers carefully study their own context and consider leadership in several ways as they design programs. Drawing on the research described above, they analyze the strengths and weaknesses of leadership throughout the system. They look for ways to capitalize on quality leadership where it exists. For example, schools with effective principals might be asked first to pilot new programs so they can be tried out under more favorable conditions. Professional developers also look for ways in which teachers are providing leadership, such as those described above, and design programs that will capitalize on teacher leadership in schools. For job-embedded professional development strategies such as examining student thinking, curriculum topic study, or lesson study, having local teacher leadership is essential.

Professional developers work to mobilize leadership at all levels in support of mathematics and science education improvement. At the district level, they look to district leaders to articulate

Tips for Considering Leadership in Professional Development Design

- Set leadership-development goals for all levels—among district personnel, principals, and teachers.
- Identify legitimate teacher leader roles to support the goals of the professional development program.
- Determine what knowledge, skills, and support leaders need, and plan professional development to meet those needs.
- Engage principals and district leaders in supporting teachers' professional development.
- Help principals develop the "eyes" to recognize good mathematics and science teaching.

Table 3.5   Leadership: Questions to Consider

Questions to Consider
1. How is teacher leadership being developed and supported? Principal leadership? District leadership?
2. To what extent are district leaders providing direction and support for mathematics and science education reform? Engaging in research-based practices found to improve student learning? Developing principals to be instructional leaders?
3. To what extent are principals using research-based leadership practices found to improve student learning? Providing direction and support for mathematics and science reform? Building learning communities? Supporting teacher leadership? Effectively observing and coaching teachers in the classroom?
4. What leadership roles are teachers playing—formally and informally (e.g., mentors, instructional coaches, study group facilitators, team leaders, or other such roles)?
5. What knowledge, skills, and support are most needed by leaders to strengthen their role in supporting effective mathematics and science learning?
6. How will the professional development program capitalize on strengths of leadership while strengthening leadership at all levels?

clear goals for mathematics and science education and follow through with the resources to implement. At the school level, they mobilize principals to strengthen learning communities and support teachers in implementing new ways of teaching mathematics and science in the classroom and build essential teacher leadership to support other teachers to implement new practices successfully. Table 3.5 (see page 101) provides questions to examine leadership in your own context.

NATIONAL, STATE, AND LOCAL POLICIES

Good policy promotes good practice.

—*National Staff Development Council*
2008, para. 6

Professional development programs swim in a stream of state and national policies as well as local mandates and regulations. Standards and accountability systems, testing, certification requirements and procedures, incentive systems, union contracts, school schedules and calendars, teacher education and induction, teacher quality mandates, professional development and recertification procedures, time for teacher learning—these and other policies at all levels exert a strong influence on professional development.

Recognizing the strong link between good policy and good practice, the National Staff Development Council (2008) has recently set the goal of advancing effective policies at the national, state, and local level as one of the top priorities of its strategic plan. Policies that support professional development are grounded in the knowledge and beliefs outlined in Chapter 2, including (1) one of the most significant influences on student achievement is teacher quality; (2) professional development improves student achievement and teacher quality; and (3) high-quality professional development is sustained over time, collaborative, linked to student learning goals, tied to daily practice of teachers, and focused on developing teachers' content and pedagogical content knowledge. Examples of policies include (1) induction systems for beginning teachers, (2) funding and time for professional development, (3) a definition of professional development that recognizes and values job-embedded and collaborative learning for teachers, (4) evaluation systems that promote professional learning and align with teaching and learning standards, and (5) professional development linked to school-improvement goals (Sparks & Hirsch, 2000).

Research on educational policy provides us with additional insights into how policies impact teaching and learning. For example, in their study of 10 years of mathematics reform in California, researchers David Cohen and Heather Hill (2001) found that the state standards and accountability system positively impacted student learning when teachers had new curriculum, new assessments, and good professional development in how to use them. Linda Darling-Hammond (2000) in her research found that states experiencing progress in increasing student learning took two clear policy steps: (1) They identified teaching standards for what teachers should know and be able to do at different points in their career, and (2) they used these standards to develop more thoughtful certification and licensing systems, more productive teacher education and induction programs, and more effective professional development.

Despite these encouraging examples from research and practice, mathematics and science educators often face an unfriendly policy environment in which professional development is undervalued, underfunded, or narrowly defined as workshops or courses. State and local policies related to school schedules and use of teacher time pose barriers to the development of professional learning communities. Federal mandates and accountability requirements have had a mixed impact on teaching and learning, according to a study of the No Child Left Behind (NCLB) Act of 2001, which found a narrower emphasis on tested content and skills, less time for some subjects, diminished creativity in the classroom, and increased stress among teachers, among other impacts (Rentner et al., 2006). While good policies promote good practice, others pose challenges to professional learning.

To meet these challenges, professional developers first seek to understand the policy environment in which they work. Shirley Hord and William Sommers suggest that studying relevant policies can become a valuable professional development activity in itself (2008). Once they are grounded in an understanding of relevant policies, educators get creative about leveraging policies to their advantage when possible. For example, many districts have effectively used the federal education laws as the impetus to improve the quality of professional development and student learning. Rentner et al. (2006) also found that NCLB has led some schools to offer more professional development, revise school calendars to expand time for professional development, focus professional development on academics and leadership development, and move toward school-site rather than districtwide professional development. Weiss and Pasley (2009) suggest that "rather than ignoring district policy that may not reflect the vision, a more prudent approach would be to view current policies as not necessarily the 'final word.' Program leaders should constantly be on the lookout for opportunities to modify key district policies in favor of greater alignment with the program vision: working on standards documents, selection criteria for instructional materials, assessments, teacher recruitment, professional development requirements, and teacher evaluation practices" (p. 86).

The Denver Public Schools provide a good example of a district that is leveraging policy to promote and deepen implementation of inquiry-based science programs districtwide. The district has actively involved teachers in piloting and selecting curriculum. Staff offer summer institutes and ongoing support for teachers in how to implement the units in the curriculum. District policy now requires high school students to have three years of science, and a new science resource center provides kit refurbishment. The district has developed a series of "best practices" documents that describe in detail what the program should look like when implemented well and is monitoring both implementation and results. Instead of shying away from inquiry-based instruction in an accountability environment, Denver has embraced it, with promising results, including growth on state assessments that exceeded that of the state (P. Kinkaid, personal communication, September 2008).

District policies, regulations, and union contracts are also part of the context of professional development to be considered. Even when local regulations or union contracts appear to be obstacles, solutions can be found. Richard DuFour and his colleagues (2004) describe how the teachers' contract at Adlai Stevenson High School in suburban Chicago might have prevented them from putting a teacher advisory program into place, where freshmen would meet with their faculty adviser four days each week for 25 minutes. This program was part of a comprehensive system of interventions to prevent student failure, but the additional assignment for teachers was in violation of the contract. Rather than give up, supporters of the program figured out how to cut the number of teachers assigned to study halls so that teachers could function as advisers without taking on an extra assignment.

In addition to studying and working within current policies, it is also important that educators become active advocates for policy changes at the local, state, and national levels. The National Staff Development Council offers an

> **Tips for Considering National, State, and Local Policies in Professional Development Design**
>
> - Study union contracts and involve union representatives in professional development planning.
> - Find creative ways to work around policies that constrain professional development.
> - Use policies such as federal accountability mandates to your advantage whenever possible.
> - Involve teachers and administrators in learning about and influencing policy as part of their professional learning.
> - Request that all-school or all-district staff development days be redirected to professional development focused on specific curricular or content areas that are most in need of improvement.

advocacy toolkit for staff developers on their Web site with tips on how to advocate for effective professional development at the state and national level. In Washington state, the Center for Strengthening the Teaching Profession combines professional development for teacher leaders with advocacy for state policies that support teacher quality. Through the center's programs, teacher leaders statewide learn advocacy skills such as how to write and speak to policymakers and then put those skills to work in their district or at the statehouse.

However, influencing policy does not just happen at the statehouse or in Washington, D.C. As Dennis Sparks (2003) writes, "The influence of policy decisions about professional development made in Washington or state capitols cannot be negated. But many of the most critical decisions that affect the quality of professional learning are made when teachers and principals gather around meeting room tables to determine student achievement targets, staff learning goals, professional development

Table 3.6   National, State, and Local Policies: Questions to Consider

Questions to Consider

1. What policies impact professional development at the local, state, and national levels? What accountability systems are in place?

2. What local district policies, contracts, incentive systems, calendars, and schedules impact professional development? What accountability systems are in place at the state and national levels? How do they support or impede teacher learning?

3. What are state and local policies for recertification? For support of beginning teachers? For attracting and retaining qualified mathematics and science teachers?

4. How do policies impede or support collegial learning? A focus on core problems of teaching and learning? Equity? Teacher leadership?

5. How is professional development defined by local, state, and national policies? Does the definition focus on workshop hours? Designate who will "deliver" professional development? Allocate or restrict time for professional development?

6. What incentives are provided for professional development, both extrinsic and intrinsic?

processes, and assessment methods to determine if they are making progress toward meeting those goals. Educators make hundreds of thousands of such decisions each year in more than 100,000 schools and district offices that cumulatively determine the quality of professional learning in schools" (p. 2). When mathematics and science leaders take these kinds of actions in their schools and districts, they keep a close read on the policies impacting their program while helping to shape a supportive context for reform.

In sum, professional developers pay attention to and use current policies to their advantage while advocating for new policies that promote high-quality professional development. Table 3.6 (see page 105) offers questions to guide exploration of national, state, and local policies.

AVAILABLE RESOURCES

> *Today, more than ever before, science holds the key to our survival as a planet and our security and prosperity as a nation. It's time we once again put science at the top of our agenda and work to restore America's place as the world leader in science and technology.*
>
> —*President Barack Obama, 2008, para. 2*

No one who plans professional development needs to be reminded about the urgency to ensure a quality science and mathematics education for all students in the current times and the need for adequate resources, especially time, money, materials, and expertise to do so. As demands for school accountability increase, so too must the resources allocated to professional development to ensure that all student have this opportunity. The National Staff Development Council (NSDC) recommends that at least 10% of a school district's budget be devoted to professional development and that 25% of an educator's workday be used for staff development (NSDC, 2001b). If professional learning is to become embedded in the fabric of the school day, teachers need pupil-free time to engage in learning and collegial interaction. An important insight from the recent study *Professional Learning in the Learning Profession: A Status Report on Teacher Development in the U.S. and Abroad* (Wei et al., 2009) supports the findings from the Third International Mathematics and Science Study (U.S. Department of Education, 1996) that in most European and Asian countries direct student contact takes up less than half of teachers' working time. The other half of their time is spent on teaching-related tasks, such as collaboration with other teachers, lesson design, and improving instructional practices. In contrast, "U.S. teachers spend about 80 percent of their total working time engaged in classroom instruction" (Wei et al., p. 20). The study also found that many countries, including Singapore, Sweden, and the Netherlands, require 100 or more hours of professional development beyond time spent in collaborative learning with other teachers during the school day.

Professional developers themselves need time to design professional development in the thoughtful way this book advocates. They cannot be burdened with so many responsibilities that they are unable to give professional development the attention it requires. They need time and other resources to plan, implement, monitor, and evaluate professional development as well as time for their own professional growth in order for U.S. schools to produce the scientifically and mathematically literate citizens needed for this century.

Time is not the only resource that is necessary for professional development. Teachers need professional materials, teaching materials, computers and advanced technology for themselves and their students, and laboratory facilities. Hands-on science kits need to be refurbished and restocked in a timely fashion. Expertise is another valuable resource that can be found in many places. University and community college faculty, scientists and mathematicians from industry, government agencies (e.g., geological surveys and agricultural extension offices), and museums and environmental organizations can provide valuable content expertise. The Web now puts rich mathematics and science content expertise as well as professional development content at educators' fingertips. And, of course, there is always the need for dollars to purchase materials, refurbish kits, fund substitutes, and buy expertise. Taking stock of what time, materials, and expertise is available helps professional developers take advantage of what they have and plan for what they need.

> ## Tips for Considering Available Resources in Professional Development Design
>
> - Anticipate resources that will be needed to not only initiate but also follow through and sustain professional development programs.
> - Plan for how to build local capacity, such as teacher leaders or coaches.
> - Take advantage of Internet resources when they are good matches for your context.
> - Explore partnerships with education and community agencies and groups and collaboration with other school districts to identify science and math resource people or to share costs for professional development.
> - Make sure time is provided for teachers to work together.
> - Document and report on results of professional development to advocate for needed resources.
> - Look for creative ways to reallocate resources for professional development such as using all-staff meeting days for school-based professional learning.

One of the most valuable resources schools have is their own teachers, coaches, and leaders. As they plan professional development, they take into consideration who within their school or district has skills and knowledge that can be mobilized for the effort. Are there instructional coaches? Data coaches? Mentors? Are there teachers who have expertise in particular areas of mathematics or science content or pedagogy that can be used? Who has had experience with professional development strategies such as lesson study or case discussions? Internal capacity is one of the first places professional developers look to draw upon the expertise and leadership needed for their programs.

Mathematics and science educators become masterful at meeting the challenge of scarce resources. One strategy is to collaborate with other school districts to share expenses for professional development programs. Increasingly, the Internet is providing quick and easy access to professional development programs, Webinars, online courses, and other resources—allowing

Table 3.7   Available Resources: Questions to Consider

Questions to Consider
1. How much time do teachers have available for professional development and collegial work?
2. Does professional development happen mostly during the school day? What percentage of the school day is devoted to professional development?
3. What resources are allocated in the budget for professional development? What additional resources, including those currently designated for courses, credit reimbursements, or teacher evaluation, could be rechanneled for professional development?
4. What grant funds are available?
5. What community support, partnerships (such as universities or businesses), collaboratives, and other sources of external expertise are available?
6. What local expertise, including teacher leadership, can be tapped?
7. What instructional and professional development materials, equipment, supplies, and technology do teachers have? What do they need?
8. What internet-based resources and delivery mechanisms can you use to meet your goals?
9. What classroom materials, for example, software, science kits, mathematics manipulatives, and texts, are needed? How will consumable materials be refurbished? How will teachers receive materials in a timely fashion and over time?

for more flexible scheduling and cost savings. While requiring an initial investment, developing teacher leaders, coaches, and mentors ultimately is another cost-effective way to sustain mathematics and science education reform by building internal capacity to provide professional development for teachers. Partnerships with universities, education agencies, families, and community groups can also help provide needed resources.

Professional developers are, simultaneously, visionaries and realists. They work toward a vision of professional development that is adequately supported. In the short run, they scan their environment for available resources, make efficient use of what they have, reallocate resources to where the payoff for teaching and learning are greater, and aggressively seek out more. They consider what resources they need and what resources they have available as input into the design of their program. Table 3.7 (opposite page) offers questions to assess available resources.

FAMILIES AND COMMUNITIES

The more families participate in schooling . . . the better for student achievement.

—Michigan Department of Education, 2001, p. 1

The final contextual factor to be considered when planning professional development is families and communities. Researchers have found a compelling relationship between involvement of families of all economic, racial, ethnic, and educational backgrounds and improved academic achievement for all ages of students (Henderson & Mapp, 2002). Specific benefits follow:

- Higher grade point average
- Enrollment in more challenging programs
- More classes passed and credits earned
- Better attendance
- Improved behavior at home and at school
- Better social skills and adaptation to school (p. 24)

The kind of family involvement that is associated with student-achievement gains is a "far cry from room mothers and cupcakes," as Pat Roy writes in an article on the topic (Roy, 2006, p. 3). Joyce Epstein and her colleagues (2009) at the Center on School, Family, and Community Partnerships at

Johns Hopkins University define family, community, and school collaboration broadly to include six dimensions organized in the following framework:

Type 1: Parenting—helping families establish supportive home environments for children

Type 2: Communicating—establishing a two-way exchange about school programs and children's progress

Type 3: Volunteering—recruiting and organizing parent help at school, home, or other locations

Type 4: Learning at home—providing information and ideas to families about how to help students with homework and other curriculum-related materials

Type 5: Decision making—Having parents from all backgrounds serve as representatives and leaders in school communities

Type 6: Collaborating with the community—identifying and integrating resources and services from the community to strengthen school programs (p. 16)

To put the research findings and this expanding notion of family and community involvement into practice, a report from the Southwest Educational Development Laboratory (Henderson & Mapp, 2002) makes the following recommendations for administrators, teachers, and other school staff:

- Recognize that all families, regardless of income, education level, or cultural background, are involved in their children's learning and want their children to do well in school.
- Create programs that will support families to guide their children's learning, from preschool to high school.
- Work with families to build their social and policy connections, including connecting families with each other and with community groups and helping them to develop their political knowledge and skills to strengthen their voice in decision making.
- Develop the capacity of school staff to work with families and community members, e.g., professional development that helps staff develop trusting and respectful relationships with diverse families.
- Link family and community engagement efforts to student learning through programs such as afterschool programs and mathematics and science family nights.
- Focus efforts to engage families and community members in developing trusting and respectful relationships by respecting cultural and class differences, allocating resources to this effort, and taking simple steps such as face-to-face meetings.

- Embrace a philosophy of partnership and be willing to share power with families. Make sure that families, school staff, and community members understand that the responsibility for children's educational development is a collaborative enterprise.
- Build strong connections between schools and community organizations (pp. 61–69).

The research and recommendations summarized here can help professional developers to assess the strength of family and community participation in their own context and to explicitly plan for how to strengthen it. This work takes on particular significance in mathematics and science education reform, which has a unique set of challenges. Because mathematics and science reform calls for major shifts in how and what students learn, it is important that leaders carefully consider the views of families and community members, involve them in the ways recommended, and garner their participation and support for reform. A study of families' perceptions about mathematics and science education reform conducted in Kansas and Missouri (Kadlek, Friedman, & Ott, 2007) found that parents surveyed were typically complacent about mathematics and science education improvement, primarily because they assumed schools were doing a good enough job now. Citing an "urgency gap" between reform leaders and families, the report urges leaders to make a stronger case for why high levels of mathematics and science learning are essential for all, not just a few students (p. 7). If families are not aware of the need for all students to have a quality mathematics and science education and the role ongoing teacher learning plays in providing up-to-date and research-based instruction, they may not understand why schools need to support professional development in these subject areas.

In other contexts, families and community members actively challenge changes in the ways teachers teach mathematics and science because they are concerned that their children will not develop necessary basic skills to get into college or perform well on high-stake assessments. When leading the Workshop Center at City College of New York, an inquiry-based science professional development program for teachers in Harlem, Hubert Dyasi (see Chapter 6, "Professional Development Case A") reported that parents were concerned that "experimenting" on their children with inquiry-based science was discriminatory. Dyasi's experience underscores the critical need for professional developers to communicate with and involve families in understanding current research on learning, as well as the goals for professional development, and how teacher learning ultimately benefits children's learning.

When professional developers pay attention to this context factor, they examine current practices regarding communication and engagement with families and people in the community and seek to strengthen them. They solicit families' and community members' views about mathematics and

> **Tips for Considering Families and Communities in Professional Development Design**
>
> - Make families and communities a priority in your plan. Be proactive.
> - Strive for two-way communication—listening and talking.
> - Examine cultural biases that might stand as barriers to building trusting relationships.
> - Provide professional development for educators in family and community engagement.
> - Monitor progress and communicate results to families and community members.

science education through surveys, open forums, and other means. Striving for two-way communication—listening and talking—they bring families and community members into the dialogue as they plan. If families or community members have resisted a mathematics or science initiative before, they seek to understand the different points of view and offer evidence and engage in discussion to avoid the same reaction again. Throughout implementation, professional developers monitor public perceptions informally and formally through surveys, interviews, or focus groups. They include in their designs strategies for proactively engaging the public rather than just responding to criticism and attacks. For example, many school districts involved in districtwide reform of their mathematics and science programs incorporated parent outreach efforts such as "awareness workshops,

Table 3.8   Families and Community: Questions to Consider

Questions to Consider
1. What are parents' and the community's interests and concerns about science and mathematics education?
2. To what extent do families, school board, and community members understand and support the vision of science and mathematics teaching, learning, and professional development found in research and in national, state, and local standards?
3. To what extent have the broad definition of family and community involvement and the recommendations described in this chapter been put into practice? What is a next step in your own context? How can professional development help?
4. How well prepared are teachers and administrators to communicate and work effectively with families and community members and build trusting relationships by respecting cultural and class differences?
5. What efforts have been made to involve families and communities in mathematics and science education in the past? What has been successful? Unsuccessful? Why? What changes are needed?

leadership development seminars for parents, and Family Math and Science Nights" (Banilower et al., 2006, p. 22). One project included community members in reviewing instructional materials. Another used an outside consultant to organize small groups of parents, offered child care, and involved business volunteers (Banilower et al., 2006). A final crucial role for professional developers is to design learning experiences that build administrators' and teachers' capacity to build trusting and productive relations with families and the community and engage them as partners in students' learning of mathematics and science.

Table 3.8 (opposite page) offers questions to consider regarding family and community engagement.

Having scanned these eight contextual factors, designers now have a better sense of what they need to consider in their own settings as they plan for professional development. In answering the questions posed for each factor, they learn about the constraints and the supports operating within their systems. They know which aspects of their context are givens—the mountains that cannot be moved (at least for now)—and what "landscaping" needs to happen as they develop their professional development programs. They are ready to design professional development that fits their context.

RESOURCES FOR INVESTIGATING CONTEXT

AllThingsPLC Web Site: www.allthingsplc.org (AllThingsPLC provides access to research, tools, and a blog for building professional learning communities.)

Commissioner's Parent Advisory Council. (2007). *The missing piece of the proficiency puzzle: Recommendations for involving families and community in improving student achievement* (Final Report to the Kentucky Department of Education). Frankfort: Kentucky Department of Education. (This report contains a comprehensive rubric entitled "Kentucky Family and Community Involvement Guide to Student Achievement," pp. 18–23.)

Council of Chief State School Officers & the Wisconsin Center for Education Research. (2003). *Surveys of enacted curriculum.* Available from www.ccsso.org/ (The authors provide surveys for all grade levels in both mathematics and science that examine instructional activities, assessments, instructional influences, preparation, and expectations for students.)

DuFour, R., DuFour, R., Eaker, R., & Karhanek, G. (2004). *Whatever it takes: How professional learning communities respond when kids don't learn.* Bloomington, IN: National Educational Services. (The appendix includes a professional learning continuum that can be used to assess progress toward sustaining learning communities.)

Hall, G., & Hord, S. (2001). *Implementing change: Patterns, principles, and potholes.* Boston: Allyn & Bacon. (Hall and Hord describe the three Concerns-Based

Adoption Model [CBAM] Tools: Stages of Concern, Levels of Use, and Innovation Configurations.)

Hord, S., Hirsh, S., & Roy, P. (2005). *Moving NSDC's staff development standards into practice: Innovation configurations* (Vol. 2). Oxford, OH: National Staff Development Council & Southwest Educational Development Laboratory. (See Roy & Hord, 2003.)

Hord, S. M., Meehan, M. L., Orletsky, S., & Sattes, B. (1999). Assessing a school staff as a community of professional learners. *Issues About Change, 7*(1). Retrieved from www.sedl.org/change/issues/issues71/ (This article includes a validated 17-item instrument for assessing five research-based attributes of professional learning communities.)

Horizon Research, Inc. (2006). *2005–06 Data collection manual.* Retrieved from www.horizon-research.com/LSC/manual (This manual includes a guide to Horizon Research, Inc.'s surveys of classroom practice and observation protocols.)

Horizon Research, Inc. & American Association for the Advancement of Science Project 2061. (2009). *Assessing Teacher Learning About Science Teaching (ATLAST).* Available from horizon-research.com/atlast (ATLAST is a project in development by Horizon Research, Inc. in collaboration with American Association for the Advancement of Science Project 2061, with funding from the National Science Foundation. ATLAST provides assessments to measure teachers' content knowledge in three areas: force and motion, plate tectonics, and flow of matter and energy in living systems.)

Johnson, R. (2002). *Using data to close achievement gaps: How to measure equity in our schools.* Thousand Oaks, CA: Corwin. (Tools for analyzing student learning and other data to uncover and address inequities in opportunities to learn are included.)

Kansas Teaching, Learning & Leadership Survey (Kan-TeLL) Web site: www.kan-tell.org (This site provides access to surveys that collect data from teachers and principals to help districts and schools assess and improve teaching and learning conditions.)

Keeley, P. (2005). *Science curriculum topic study: Bridging the gap between standards and practice.* Thousand Oaks, CA: Corwin. (This resource, and the Keeley & Rose, 2006, resource, provide guidelines for using the national standards and several adult trade books to help designers examine their contextual factor of the curriculum, instruction, and assessment practices.)

Keeley, P., & Rose, C. M. (2006). *Mathematics curriculum topic study: Bridging the gap between standards and practice.* Thousand Oaks, CA: Corwin. (See Keeley, 2005.)

Kruse, S. D., & Louis, S. K. (2009). *Building strong school cultures: A guide to leading change.* Thousand Oaks: CA: Corwin. (This guide contains a chapter on diagnosing professional culture and additional self-assessment instruments throughout the book on leadership and families and communities.)

Learning Mathematics for Teaching. (2009). *Learning Mathematics for Teaching (LMT) Project.* Available at http://sitemaker.umich.edu/lmt/faq_teachers (The Learning Mathematics for Teaching assessment instruments include problems based on authentic mathematics tasks teachers may encounter in the classroom, such as "assessing a student's mathematical work, representing numbers and operations in the context of instruction, or explaining common mathematical rules" [LMT, 2009, para.1]. The instruments have been used to measure the effectiveness of professional development focused on enhancing mathematics knowledge.)

Lindsey, R., Graham, S., Westphal, R. C., & Jew, C. L. (2008). *Culturally proficient inquiry: A lens for identifying and examining educational gaps.* Thousand Oaks, CA: Corwin. (This includes information on using the cultural proficiency continuum for self-assessment of responses to diversity in curriculum and instruction, assessment, parents and community, and professional development.)

Love, N. (2002). *Using data/getting results: A practical guide for school improvement in mathematics and science.* Norwood, MA: Christopher-Gordon. (This guide contains tools for collecting and analyzing data about student learning, curriculum instruction, and assessment practices and equity.)

Love, N., Stiles, K. E., Mundry, S., & DiRanna, K. (2008). *A data coach's guide to improving learning for all students: Unleashing the power of collaborative inquiry.* Thousand Oaks, CA: Corwin. (This comprehensive guide includes data tools and collaborative processes for analyzing student learning and other data to guide school improvement.)

Mid-continent Research for Education and Learning. (2005). *Balanced Leadership Profile.* Available from www.mcrel.org (McREL offers the *Balanced Leadership Profile,* a subscription-based online survey and professional development tool based on 21 principal-leadership responsibilities.)

Mundry, S., & Stiles, K. E. (2009). *Professional learning communities for science teaching: Lessons from research and practice.* Arlington, VA: National Science Teachers Association. (An overview of the research on professional learning communities and seven chapters written by leaders of PLCs in various contexts, from an urban high school to district, regional, and state initiatives are included.)

National Network of Partnership Schools at Johns Hopkins University Web site: www.csos.jhu.edu/P2000/index.htm (This site offers a variety of resources and publications for engaging parents and communities, including specific resources for mathematics and science educators.)

National Staff Development Council. (2006, September). Parent involvement checklist. *The Learning Principal, 2*(1), 4–5. (This issue features a parent involvement checklist that can be used to guide improvements.)

President and Fellows of Harvard College. (2006). *Misconceptions-Oriented Standards-Based Assessment Resources for Teachers (MOSART).* Available from www.cfa.harvard.edu/smgphp/mosart/about_mosart.html (The project has developed several sets of student assessments, linked to the K–12 physical and earth science national standards, to measure changes in students' conceptual understanding of science concepts.)

Roy, P., & Hord, S. (2003). *Moving NSDC's staff development standards into practice: Innovation configurations* (Vol. 1). Oxford, OH: National Staff

Development Council & Southwest Educational Development Laboratory. (This resource, and the Hord, Hirsh, & Roy, 2005, resource [Volume 2] describe in detail what best professional development practice looks like, organized by professional roles.)

The Tripod Project Web site: www.tripodproject.org (This project provides surveys of students' perceptions of engagement and classroom learning conditions.)

University of Louisville Center for Research in Mathematics and Science Teacher Development. (n.d.). *The projects: Mathematics assessments for middle school teachers, mathematics assessments for elementary teachers, and science assessments for middle school teachers.* Available from http://louisville.edu/education/research/centers/crmstd (The center's Web site includes pre- and post-assessments of middle school science teachers' content knowledge in physical, earth/space science, and life science, as well as assessments of elementary and middle school mathematics teachers' content knowledge.)

WestEd. (2002). *Healthy Kids Surveys.* Available from www.wested.org/cs/chks/print/docs/chks_home.html (WestEd provides access to several surveys for students regarding their learning environment.)

4

Critical Issues to Consider in Designing Professional Development

Figure 4.1 Critical Issues Influencing Professional Development

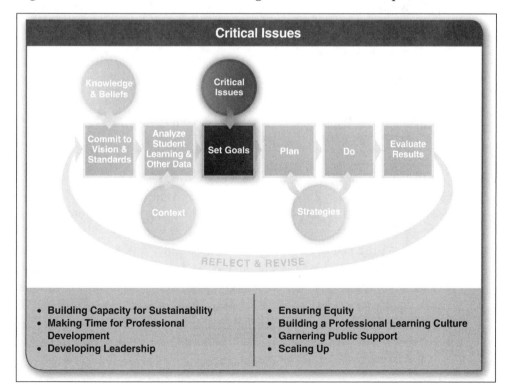

even critical issues need to be considered as one designs and provides professional development for teachers. These issues are (1) building capacity for sustainability, (2) making time for professional development, (3) developing leadership, (4) ensuring equity, (5) building a professional learning culture, (6) garnering public support, and (7) scaling up (see Figure 4.1).

All seven issues discussed in this chapter are important, and lack of attention to any one of them can ultimately doom a professional development initiative. As Susan Loucks-Horsley repeatedly warned when sharing the design framework with professional developers, "Ignore these at your own peril." The seven critical issues play an important role at different stages in the life of a professional development program or initiative, but designers can be assured that each will influence the effectiveness of the program at some point. For this reason, it is important to consider how each one of these issues may influence your choices during the "set goals" stage in the design process, as well as throughout the rest of the planning and implementation of the program. For example, when setting goals and identifying specific learning outcomes, it is imperative to consider the issue of making time for professional learning. If designers intend to conduct collaborative study groups with grade-alike teachers during the school day, such a strategy will fail if policies and schedules are not adjusted beforehand to provide the necessary time. As another example, it will be important to work on developing a professional learning culture if the design calls for teachers to examine student work and thinking or engage in collaborative lesson study in a school in which isolation is the prevalent norm.

As we discuss each critical issue, we recognize that entire books have been written on each one. The intent of this chapter is to raise the awareness level of professional development designers to ensure that the issues are not ignored and to suggest questions for professional developers to ask themselves as they design or reflect on their programs.

BUILDING CAPACITY FOR SUSTAINABILITY

Research suggests that professional development programs are more likely to reach goals and impact student learning schoolwide when they address multiple dimensions of school capacity, rather than focus only on developing individual teacher learning (Newmann, King, & Youngs, 2000). While building teacher knowledge is seen as essential, this research suggests that attention must also be paid to building collective knowledge across a school that supports learning for all. Components of school capacity that need attention include teachers' knowledge, skills and dispositions, professional community, program coherence, technical resources, and principal leadership—and all are essential.

Focusing only on building teachers' knowledge, skills, and dispositions without attending to the other capacity areas (building professional community, ensuring coherence and buffering teachers from competing demands, providing research-based programs and resources, and developing principal leadership) may result in incomplete implementation, confusion about priorities, or abandonment of the use of new programs or practices. The findings suggest that professional development plans should address all of the components of school capacity based on what is needed in a particular context. For example, one school may need a focus on building expertise of individual teachers, while another might need to focus on program coherence and reducing fragmentation in professional development.

Schools with high capacity are in a better position to support the comprehensive use of professional development over time. Lower capacity schools face more difficulty in implementing comprehensive professional development (Newmann et al., 2000). These findings underscore the importance of carefully assessing capacity prior to initiating professional development and of using the occasion of program planning to set goals to strengthen not only teacher knowledge but also other aspects of school capacity that are weak.

In the next section are questions that professional developers can use to consider what goals they may need to set to build or enhance the capacity of their systems to sustain professional development in science and mathematics education.

> **Building Capacity for Sustainability: Critical Reflection Questions**
>
> - Would you know capacity if you saw it?
> - Do you have leaders who can work with teachers to support their learning and teaching?
> - Do you have support systems for professional development providers?
> - Do you recognize, study, and apply the knowledge base of professional development theory and practice and help others do so?
> - Do you work to create and influence policies, resources, and structures that make professional development a central rather than a marginal activity?

Would you know capacity if you saw it?

A conference of mathematics and science educators reflecting on this question concluded that components of capacity, which can be present at any system level from local to national, are the following:

- People who can work with teachers in supporting their learning and teaching
- Support systems for professional development providers

- A knowledge base of professional development theory and practice
- Supported cultures in which professional development flourishes
- Policies, resources, and structures that make professional development a central rather than a marginal activity (Friel & Bright, 1997, p. 41–46)

These elements constitute an "infrastructure" for professional development. Without a strong infrastructure, professional development can be of uneven quality and insufficient quantity, is not cost-effective, and comes in the form of projects that are not sustainable, accessible, or inclusive. As noted in the introduction to this critical issue, research suggests that lack of capacity can negatively impact the success of the professional development.

The Consortium for Policy Research in Education (CPRE) conducted a study of 22 school districts to examine the ways in which the districts effectively supported sustained capacity for student and teacher learning. This report (Massell, 2000) notes four strategies that were common to all of the districts: (1) interpreting and using data to drive decisions about teaching and learning, (2) building teacher knowledge and skills through professional development, (3) aligning curriculum and instruction with both state policies and other education efforts and initiatives in the schools and districts, and (4) targeting additional interventions on low-performing students or schools.

Do you have leaders who can work with teachers to support their learning and teaching?

In this chapter, leadership is discussed as another critical issue for professional development. With respect to building capacity, the importance of leadership cannot be underestimated. First, principals play a key role in their schools' capacity by ensuring coherence, establishing clear goals, and creating organizational arrangements for teacher collaboration. Too many professional development programs fail to enlist principals in carrying out these key functions. Capacity also involves having other school leaders. The current view of professional development calls for building a much broader range of leadership capacity within schools to lead professional development experiences. These include teachers who are in leadership positions, science and mathematics resource teachers, and staff developers within school systems. (See the section on "Developing Leadership" in this chapter for ideas for building leadership capacity.)

Do you have support systems for professional development providers?

Staff or outside consultants and resource people who are providing professional development also need support and opportunities for ongoing learning and development. The development of a larger and more cohesive cadre of professional development providers is of critical importance to sustaining effective professional development. They need opportunities to learn, to network with others in similar roles, and confront challenges and solve problems together. Building capacity and sustainability for mathematics and science education thus means developing and maintaining a diverse array of structures to provide this ongoing support. For example, instructional coaches meet together regularly to review and discuss student work to support their work with teachers. They might review and critique lessons to deepen their own understanding of what to look for in classrooms and how to help the teachers they are coaching. Leaders also participate in national and regional events sponsored by the major professional organizations for their own continued development (e.g., National Science Teachers Association, National Science Education Leadership Association, National Council of Teachers of Mathematics, National Council of Supervisors of Mathematics, and National Staff Development Council).

Do you recognize, study, and apply the knowledge base of professional development theory and practice and help others do so?

As described in Chapter 2, there is a substantial knowledge base for professional development theory and practice that covers a wide range of both the contexts for professional development and the kinds of professional development experiences that can occur. This knowledge base includes studies of teachers in the process of changing their beliefs, mathematics and scientific knowledge, and classroom practice; research on the process of professional development itself; studies of teachers in subject matter collaboratives and networks; studies of a variety of strategies for professional development; and teachers' own writing about their practice and about changed classrooms.

In addition, the national standards documents are a comprehensive collection of the knowledge base in mathematics and science. They offer a vision of the content and processes for teaching these subjects and considerations from research on the development of teachers, and the school or system supports necessary for effective learning. Professions are defined, in part, by shared knowledge, both practical and theoretical, that becomes a common language with which to communicate and improve. In fact, creating and sharing knowledge is one of the key roles of leaders (Fullan, 2000). Building capacity in the system to initiate and sustain ongoing learning requires that the knowledge base be known and used. Through leadership development programs, study groups for leaders and curriculum topic study, a professional development strategy discussed in Chapter 5, teachers and leaders are learning and applying the knowledge base to their work.

Do you work to create and influence policies, resources, and structures that make professional development a central rather than a marginal activity?

In addition to adding a variety of structures and activities to what is currently available for teachers' learning, it is clear that certain state and local policies and financial arrangements constrain the degree to which teachers can participate thoughtfully in the professional development opportunities available. This means that to increase what is available to teachers, it is necessary to identify and institute policies that increase the capacity of teachers and schools to take advantage of what is available. As long as structures and financial policies marginalize professional development, whatever capacity can be built will be underused.

For example, education systems are plagued by schedules that impede professional development during the school day, a major obstacle to promoting job-embedded and practice-based learning. Schedules also challenge teachers' ability to work in teams. Schools and districts often lack a commitment to long-term and consistent priorities for teacher learning that would support teachers to develop in any one content area over time. Instead, multiple programs are offered which can distract teachers and reduce program coherence.

Professional developers must work with policymakers at all levels to develop and institute policies that recognize that professional development for all education personnel is an essential component of an effective school system, rather than an add-on activity that can be eliminated in difficult times. Strategies for developing supportive policies are also addressed in Chapter 3 and in this chapter in the sections "Making Time for Professional Development" and "Garnering Public Support."

MAKING TIME FOR PROFESSIONAL DEVELOPMENT

For science and mathematics professional development to be effective, teachers need ample time for in-depth investigation, reflection, and continuous learning. Making adequate quality time available to effectively carry out professional development programs is a challenge faced by every professional developer. In fact, time has emerged as one of the key issues in virtually every analysis of school change (Fullan & Miles, 1992; Garet et al., 1999; Little, 1993; Loucks-Horsley et al., 1987; Loucks-Horsley, Stiles, & Hewson, 1996; National Council of Teachers of Mathematics, 2000; National Research Council, 1996; Sparks, 1994; Yoon, Duncan, Lee, Scarloss, & Shapley, 2007).

The issue, however, is not just *making* time for professional development but assessing how time is used, allocated, and distributed throughout the school day and throughout the academic year. Simply making more time does not ensure more effective professional development opportunities for teachers. It is also essential to use time in creative and unique ways to provide diverse and productive learning opportunities for teachers. As the National Partnership for Excellence and Accountability in Teaching (2000) notes, "The one major reason for failure of schoolwide change models is the lack of teacher time focused on the right things. Districts actually may be providing sufficient support and time for professional development, but the results are less than desired because the time is not used well" (p. 11).

One challenge educators face is overcoming the traditional ways in which teachers, administrators, and the public view how time is spent in schools. Most schools are organized around the value—whether explicitly or implicitly acknowledged—that the most worthwhile use of time in schools is spent in direct contact with students.

As we know, student learning *is* the most valuable outcome of schools, but teachers' learning is a major contributor to student learning that is not yet fully acknowledged as a valuable goal of schools. Until the view of learning for all—including teachers and students—changes, educators will continue to bemoan the fact that "there isn't enough time!" As Tom Guskey (1999) notes, "If the additional time for professional development is to yield truly meaningful improvements, we must ensure that time is used wisely, efficiently, and effectively. This will require deep and profound changes in the organizational culture of most schools and in the perspectives of educators who work within them" (p. 11).

Advocating for quality time for teacher learning in schools is the responsibility of all educators. Fortunately, mounting evidence and research exist that support educators in their efforts to find time for teacher learning. Research documents a positive relationship between time for teachers to engage in professional learning and quality instruction and student learning (e.g., Council of Chief State School Officers, 2008). Another recent review of professional development studies by Yoon and colleagues (2007) found a positive relationship between sustained professional development programs and student achievement. The sustained professional development programs included 30 to 100 contact hours over a time period ranging from 6 to 12 months. These findings substantiate the importance of making time for sustained professional development opportunities.

Although changes have been made in numerous schools and districts throughout the country, professional developers still face challenges in reallocating time for professional development. One barrier is the current structure of schools. Teachers typically have only their lunch or planning periods designated as time away from their students. Rarely are teachers able to use this time to collaborate or consult with their peers, reflect on either their teaching or their students' learning, or connect with others outside of the school environment. Implied in this statement is that teachers' own time is

Making Time for Professional Development: Critical Reflection Questions

- How do you find ways to make more effective use of time currently available within the school calendar?
- How can you work toward influencing state policies and public perceptions that support professional development?

"designated" for them; rarely, however, are teachers empowered, or trusted, to decide how to use the designated time on their own.

Given the organizational structure of schools and the perception of how teachers should spend their working hours, what can professional developers do? How do professional developers design programs and initiatives that overcome the obstacles and allocate the necessary time needed to create continuous learning opportunities for teachers of science and mathematics? The following section suggests questions for professional developers to ask themselves as they tackle the issues surrounding time for professional development.

How do you find ways to make more effective use of time currently available within the school calendar?

Even with the current structure and organization of schools, professional developers have been able to find ways to "creatively restructure" the time that is already available to teachers within the school day and the calendar year. A review of the literature finds that the solutions being implemented fall into several categories: released time, restructured or rescheduled time, common time, better-used time, and purchased time (Darling-Hammond, 2000; Guskey, 1999; Murphy & Lick, 2001; Wei et al., 2009; WestEd, 2000; Yoon et al., 2007).

Released Time

This strategy entails freeing teachers from their regular instructional time with students. The most obvious approach is to provide substitute teachers so that teachers can participate in professional development, although there are some downsides to frequent use of substitutes unless they are qualified to teach rather than just supervise students. Some schools have regular substitute teachers who know the learning routines and can step into the teacher's role. Other schools draw upon principals and other administrators, family members, and volunteers to serve as substitute teachers; other schools use specialist teachers, such as art or music, or part-time teachers. Other options include team teaching and instituting community-based learning experiences or library research for students, or partnerships with community organizations, informal learning settings (such as museums), and libraries to provide project-based learning opportunities for students that free individual teachers from instructional time.

Restructured or Rescheduled Time

This solution requires formally altering overall instructional time—the school day, the school calendar year, or teachers' schedules. For example, some schools are implementing schedules in which students attend school one hour longer on four days and are released early on the fifth day or in which students arrive one hour later in the morning one day each week, providing time in the morning for teachers to meet with one another. Some schools combine this approach with teachers arriving 30 minutes early, creating additional nonteaching time. Others have combined and reallocated the small amount of time that teachers are required by contract to stay after school each day to "buy" one or two 45-minute periods for collegial work before school starts each week. Others group students and teachers, using a team teaching approach, so that groups of teachers have scheduled time outside of the classroom. The school schedule can also be used to restructure time. Block scheduling, with periods that often extend from 90 to 120 minutes, creates a longer planning period for teachers where they can have time for their own work and collaboration with other teachers. Several districts find that by adding just five minutes a day to the school schedule they can gain four to five early release days for teacher learning. Year-round scheduling is increasingly being used by many districts, which can create large blocks of time during semester breaks (e.g., three or four weeks) for professional development.

Common Time

To move teachers out of individual preparation time, schools are reorganizing time so that teachers have "common" free time. Such scheduled collaborative time enables teachers to meet by grade level, by discipline, by subject area, or as interdisciplinary teams. This time is also being used by learning communities to inquire into their students' results and teaching and to create a regular time for mentor and mentee teachers to conference. Many schools are organizing collaborative time to follow or precede lunchtime, giving teachers as much as 90 minutes of nonteaching time when they can interact with colleagues informally or in learning activities such as study groups, case discussions, and examining student work.

Better-Used Time

Often, teachers' time outside of the classroom during the school day is consumed by faculty meetings and administrative tasks that limit their opportunities for collaborating with peers. Schools are finding ways to reduce the administrative nature of this time by using e-mail for routine communication between teachers and administrators and even for communicating with students and families. Some schools designate that one staff meeting each month be used for professional development. A unique solution has been to move "nonessential" student-oriented activities, such as assemblies and club meetings, to afterschool time or to recruit staff other than teachers to participate in these activities, thus providing more time for teachers to meet. Some schools are using testing proctors to supervise students while they take state assessments, providing teachers with additional blocks of time each year for collaboration.

Working with local educators, professional developers can help to find time by examining the days that are formally scheduled for professional development and reassessing whether they are being used optimally. Schools and districts that investigate their current professional development practices (inservice days, Saturday workshops, and afterschool presentations) often find that they do not meet the teachers' needs. By reallocating this time to job-embedded experiences, such as demonstration lessons, case discussions, or action research conducted in the classroom or even summer months spent in a research project or course, schools can find the time for in-depth and relevant professional development.

In addition to examining existing professional learning time, professional developers are finding more ways to better use time by turning to technology for teachers' professional development. This avenue for learning allows teachers to engage in reflective, in-depth, and collegial learning via online courses, online study groups, or online book study, often at any time of the day, which is appealing for teachers who are fitting their learning in late at night or in the early morning hours as they juggle work and family responsibilities.

Purchased Time

Many schools and districts have taken advantage of the funding opportunities for professional development by obtaining grants from state and federal agencies, such as the Math and Science Partnership (MSP) programs supported by the U.S. Department of Education and the National Science Foundation or private foundations. In these cases, teachers are given stipends for working beyond their regular hours, often on weekends and during the summer. This is an ideal way to make time, as it does not take away from student time and values the teachers by paying them for the additional time spent outside of school hours. Some schools and districts have used grants to establish a "pool" to pay permanent substitutes or provided these stipends for teachers to attend professional development activities outside of the school day, on weekends, and in the summer.

How can you work toward influencing state policies and public perceptions that support professional development?

The suggestions described above primarily focus on implementing solutions at the school or district level. Inherent in those solutions is the assumption that schools and districts have control over their own programs, have some existing time and funding for professional development, and can institute the kinds of restructuring discussed, that is, reorganizing school days and calendar years. Many professional developers, however, are faced with policies and perceptions that further impede their efforts to create meaningful learning opportunities for teachers, such as limited numbers of days allocated by state boards of education for professional development or public concern about teachers' time out of classrooms. In these cases, more outreach is needed. One step is presenting the research evidence to key stakeholders and policymakers that in-depth professional development is essential to support improved student learning and that providing time for professional development is critical. To accomplish this, professional developers must identify and define what is considered professional development at their local sites. Increasing public awareness of and support for teachers' professional development includes conveying the importance of teachers' ongoing learning outside of the classroom and emphasizing how this enhances student learning. Changing perceptions about what professional development "looks like" and how it benefits student learning can increase understanding of its importance among families and community members.

For time for professional development to be valued, all involved— including teachers, administrators, policymakers, and the public—must begin to reconceptualize how to use school time. As Margaret Wheatley (2002) states, "Schools that are truly learning communities for students and teachers alike require time for teachers to study and collaborate during the school day. If we want our world to be different, our first act needs to be reclaiming time to think" (p. 99).

DEVELOPING LEADERSHIP

Leadership is a critical issue in professional development for two reasons. First, leadership development is often an explicit goal of a large majority of professional development initiatives in science and mathematics. Numerous science and mathematics projects provide professional development experiences focused on enhancing leadership skills for principals and administrators, teacher leaders, and other educators involved in the improvement of science and mathematics education. Second, from research on professional development and change in schools it is clear that leadership and support are required for professional development experiences to result in changes in teaching and learning practice (Bybee, 1993; Fullan, 1991; Houston, Blankstein, & Cole, 2007; Lieberman & Miller, 2004; St. John & Pratt, 1997; Weiss & Pasley, 2009).

Teacher leadership has also been shown to be associated with increased teacher learning and with creating more collaborative professional cultures (Talbert & McLaughlin, 1994; York-Barr & Duke, 2004). Given the critical need in mathematics and science to retain new teachers and support more experienced teachers (National Commission on Mathematics and Science Teaching for the 21st Century, 2000), developing teacher leaders and professional developers can renew and challenge teachers and contribute to the cultural shift in schools toward learning communities. As Katzenmeyer and Moller (1996) note, "Restructuring the school as a workplace for teacher leaders to have collegial interactions is one initiative that can encourage talented teachers to remain in the profession. Teacher leadership opportunities can promote teaching as a more desirable career and help to retain outstanding teachers who can assist in the complex tasks of school change" (p. 93).

Furthermore, effective school leadership is positively related to increased student achievement (Waters, Marzano, & McNulty, 2003). Leadership plays a significant role in cultivating a culture of teacher and student learning and ensuring that teachers have the support they need to make needed changes in practice. Thus, the development, support, and advocacy of leaders are essential to legitimize changes, provide resources, and create expectations that changes will occur. As professional development designers plan teacher learning programs, it is critical for them to consider whether the leadership is in place to support the program and also if activities need to be initiated to strengthen the leadership.

> **Developing Leadership: Critical Reflection Questions**
>
> - Is leadership development a goal of the professional development program or initiative?
> - If developing leaders is important, what is meant by a leader, and what roles do leaders play?
> - What specific roles of teacher leaders are we interested in developing in science and mathematics education?
> - How can these leadership roles be developed?
> - Are there roles other leaders must play for professional development to be successful? If so, how can they be developed?

Is leadership development a goal of the professional development program or initiative?

Unless there is already a highly effective leadership corps in place, professional development designers will need to consider establishing goals and initiatives to build the leadership required to ensure that the program has a chance of success. Most major professional development programs or initiatives identify a goal for developing leadership as part of their plans based on the strong case made in the school improvement literature that leaders play a critical role in a school's ability to provide an effective science and mathematics education. St. John and Pratt (1997) found that in sites in which science and mathematics reforms were successful, one or more long-term, highly skilled leaders were involved. In recent years, hundreds of institutes and academies began to focus on the professional learning of leaders, from classroom teachers to principals and other administrators. The development of instructional coaches, mentors, and in-house professional development providers who provide the ongoing support and leadership needed for continuous improvement of teaching and learning is becoming more commonplace in schools across the nation. The key issue for professional developers designing programs is to ensure that their leadership development efforts are designed to inspire and engage leaders in meaningful ways around issues of teaching and learning and that they align well with and complement the entire design of the program.

If developing leaders is important, what is meant by a leader, and what roles do leaders play?

Effective leaders can be the teacher who asks the tough questions of her colleagues or the one who jumps in to lend a hand to the beginning teacher struggling to get his classroom organized. They are resource providers, problem solvers, content experts, cheerleaders, and critical friends. They are often connected to professional networks through which they gain access to resources and support for continuing the work of educational change. They primarily focus on issues of educational substance, such as supporting new curriculum and instructional and assessment practices, while remaining attuned to the politics and organizational and cultural issues that may thwart them (Kaser, Mundry, Stiles, & Loucks-Horsley, 2002). They see standards not as a lockstep formula to be followed but rather as guideposts to lead and direct efforts. These leaders anchor change efforts in a vision of effective learning and build support for the vision and the practices needed to support it. They continuously reflect on and inquire into teaching and learning and engage in professional discourse and use research-based models as a way of understanding and leading change (Anderson & Pratt, 1995). They have moral purpose, actively build relationships, create coherence, and encourage the creation and sharing of knowledge (Fullan, 2001).

Kouzes and Posner (2001) identify five practices exemplary leaders use:

1. *Challenging the process:* Searching for opportunities to change the status quo and innovative ways to improve

2. *Inspiring a shared vision:* Seeing the future and helping others create an ideal image of what the organization can become

3. *Enabling others to act:* Fostering collaboration and actively involving others

4. *Modeling the way:* Creating standards of excellence and leading by example

5. *Encouraging the heart:* Recognizing the many contributions that individuals make, sharing in the rewards of their efforts, and celebrating accomplishments

All leaders—teachers, principals, district administrators, policymakers, and other educators involved in science and mathematics education—need to develop the knowledge, skills, and abilities identified.

Leaders play different roles at different times. Leadership implies that there are others to lead and, thus, a leader must have authority whether it is vested in the position itself; in the personality, character, or expertise of the person; or in the vision that is espoused. They recognize and accept the responsibilities of leadership. Teacher leaders and administrators alike share leadership roles by advocating for science and mathematics education with families and the community. Although the specific roles that leaders play vary, for change to be successful, everyone must be ready to be a leader (Fullan, 1993; Lieberman & Miller, 2004).

What specific roles of teacher leaders are we interested in developing in science and mathematics education?

Increasingly, teachers are taking on formal and informal roles as educational leaders (Killion & Harrison, 2006). Through the National Academy for Science and Mathematics Education Leadership at WestEd, the authors have seen firsthand the passion and power of talented teacher leaders when they take responsibility for changing the quality of teaching and learning in their schools and districts. Using data to guide them, they become superb diagnosticians focusing in on what needs to be done, who needs to be involved, and where to start.

New forms of teacher leadership are bubbling up as teachers are empowered to take action to improve their schools. As Crowther, Kagan, Ferguson, and Hann (2002) write: "Ultimately, teacher leadership, as we intend it, is about action that transforms teaching and learning in a school, that ties school and community together on behalf of learning, and that advances social sustainability and quality of life for a community" (p. xvii). In an insightful essay written on the success of teacher leadership in the National Writing Project, Barbara Heenan (2009) explores the nature, purposes, and support of teacher leadership. The essay reveals that teacher leadership may develop from "genuine, rigorous, and compelling" (p. 8) learning experiences focused on the content teachers teach. In this case, the teacher engaged deeply with the discipline of writing himself, deepening his knowledge of the discipline, and later made connections to how his students think, which awakened an appreciation for his students' unique perspectives. The experiences brought about rethinking of the teacher's role and how to teach and a desire to share his experience and the transformation he made in his practice with other teachers through mentoring and collaboration.

Like the teacher in this case, many teachers have had the opportunity to deepen their content and pedagogical content knowledge and were inspired to take on key leadership roles in supporting the learning of their colleagues:

- *Teacher development.* More and more teacher leaders are providing professional development for their colleagues. They coteach content courses with local university faculty and lead informal sessions to share "best practices" they use in their own teaching. Teachers are serving as instructional coaches and facilitators of various kinds of professional learning experiences, such as study groups, case discussions, or demonstration lessons. As professional development opportunities continue to shift from one-shot workshops offered by external experts to more ongoing, job-embedded forms rooted in teaching practice, teachers' ability to guide these efforts is increasingly important.

- *Curriculum, instruction, and assessment.* As an extension of their involvement in professional development, teachers become leaders in changing curriculum, instruction, and assessment practices. Teachers play key leading roles as members of school and district committees that select or write curriculum, adopt textbooks and other instructional materials, select or develop assessments, and respond to new initiatives, for example, establishing partnerships with mathematics and science faculty to improve the preparation of teachers. Through such a partnership in Massachusetts, teacher leaders are coteaching rigorous mathematics content courses and building a video library of classroom teaching that other teachers can view and discuss to enrich their own practice.

- *School improvement.* Teachers are serving as leaders well beyond their own classrooms or departments by facilitating communication among teachers schoolwide to strengthen the school's culture for learning, sitting on school leadership or management councils, and addressing political problems with administrators and community members that relate to new ways of teaching and learning science and mathematics (Ferrini-Mundy, 1997). They also participate in or facilitate networks within or across schools, both in person and online.

Leadership roles provide teachers with numerous benefits, both personally and professionally. As Roland Barth (2001) states,

Teachers win something important. They experience a reduction in isolation; the personal and professional satisfaction that comes from improving their schools; a sense of instrumentality, investment, and membership in the school community; and new learning about schools, about the process of change, and about themselves. All of these positive experiences spill over into their classroom teaching. These teachers become owners and investors in the school, rather than mere tenants. They become professionals. (p. 449)

How can these leadership roles be developed?

Experienced teachers require development opportunities to effectively take on roles of leadership (Ball & Cohen, 1999; Darling-Hammond & McLaughlin, 1999; Friel & Danielson, 1997; Grady, 1997; Katzenmeyer & Moller, 1996). Leaders need to possess an in-depth understanding of science and mathematics content; a thorough knowledge of the best practices in teaching, learning, and school organization; self-awareness and an ability to be self-critical; willingness to learn from mistakes and successes; knowledge of schools, both the learning and teaching processes and the political structures and culture; knowledge of how adults learn; and an understanding of the process of implementing and evaluating changes. Leaders who serve as professional developers must also be skillful organizers and coordinators, networkers and relationship builders, and fundraisers. They value the knowledge adults bring to their learning experiences and are willing to take risks and experiment with new approaches and ideas.

They also need skills in decision making, building and managing teams, conflict resolution, using data as a guide to instructional improvement, problem solving, vision building, communicating, and managing diversity. They need to be astute about how to operate as leaders among their peers. Especially in the absence of a professional culture, teacher leaders can become targets and find that their colleagues are reluctant to accept them in their new roles.

This large skill set and knowledge base does not develop overnight. It develops through a combination of deepening one's own content knowledge and transforming ideas about teaching and learning, on-the-job experiences, reflection on practice, leadership coaching, and leadership development programs. For example, for the Massachusetts Intel Mathematics Initiative (MIMI), teacher leaders receive year-long development in how to lead mathematics learning communities in their sites, including learning the mathematics content involved and developing facilitation and mathematical discourse skills. They grapple with their own understanding of mathematics in preparation for helping other teachers come to new understandings. Throughout the year, they lead their own mathematics learning communities in local sites, get feedback from experienced facilitators, and document their results through a portfolio. Another example, the Learning to Lead Mathematics program at WestEd (Carroll & Mumme, 2007), provides rich videotaped case discussions that afford leaders the opportunity to learn content-specific facilitation skills and norms for mathematical discourse. Other leadership development programs include leadership academies or institutes that convene cohorts of new leaders over time to delve into and develop their understanding of the skill sets and knowledge of leaders. A hallmark of these programs is that learning is grounded in the leaders' real work, and they include opportunities to demonstrate new leadership knowledge by carrying out projects in their local sites and sharing the results with their leadership academy peers.

Developing leadership does not stop with learning new knowledge and skills. As in any other professional development, teachers learning to be leaders require ongoing support and opportunities to learn over time and to experiment with some of their new skills and strategies, receive feedback from more experienced leaders, discuss problems that arise, and make appropriate changes. Professional development designers have found it useful to structure regular meetings of teacher leaders for these and other purposes (see especially "Professional Development Case C" on the Mathematics Renaissance and "Professional Development Case E" on the Cambridge school district in Chapter 6).

Are there roles other leaders must play for professional development to be successful? If so, how can they be developed?

Administrator leadership is required for professional development to promote learning and changes in classroom practices. Principals, for example, support changes in school mathematics and science through such roles as advocate, facilitator of curriculum selection, provider of funds and other resources such as time to meet, broker of professional development and other support, monitor of progress, and troubleshooter. They also must understand their role in supporting teachers by learning to anticipate how teachers will feel and behave as they change their practices; what help teachers are apt to need and when; what materials, other supplies, and support staff are required; and what outcomes they can expect from the changes teachers are implementing. In addition, principals need to be instructional leaders themselves and therefore must develop their own in-depth understanding of science and mathematics standards, instructional strategies, professional development, the change process, assessment, and curriculum (Fullan, 2000, 2002; Institute for Educational Leadership, 2000). Their own professional development, in fact, mirrors effective professional development for teachers: It should be long-term and planned, focused on student achievement, job-embedded, and supportive of reflective practice and should provide opportunities to work, discuss, and problem solve with peers (Drago-Severson, 2004; Educational Research Service, 1999).

All these leadership activities and experiences reinforce the importance of building a learning community around new ways of learning and teaching and of working together to change perspectives and expectations. Learning together, when it is done in an open and trusting environment, can build respect for different roles and relationships that help school personnel weather the difficulties associated with making significant changes in practice.

Leadership is required for professional development to make its impact felt in schools and classrooms. Professional development programs can address this by building the leadership knowledge, skills, and dispositions of participating mathematics and science teachers, as well as administrators, at all levels of the education system.

ENSURING EQUITY

Ensuring equity in a diverse society has become extremely important as science and mathematics education has shifted from producing a relatively few highly skilled scientists and mathematicians to promoting literacy for every citizen. There is underrepresentation of some populations—such as persons of color, individuals from low socioeconomic groups, persons with disabilities, and women—in various areas of science and mathematics, including careers, higher-level coursework, and opportunities to learn from adequately prepared teachers. The inadequacies of curriculum materials and instructional approaches for such a diverse population are often cited as problems, particularly with the movement to build new learning based on the learner's experiences and context. Widespread strategies such as tracking have come under attack as obstructing access to mathematics and science learning for a large portion of the student population. For example, Oakes (2005) reports that students of color are disproportionately represented in lower-level classes and underrepresented in higher-level classes. African American students are more likely to be overrepresented in special education, and the literature cites several causes, including testing bias, economic disadvantage, and a cultural mismatch between students of color and their teachers (Blanchett, Mumford, & Beachum, 2005; Skiba et al., 2008). Males are underrepresented in gifted and talented programs and are less likely to enroll in advanced courses (Ford, Grantham & Whiting, 2008). The achievement gap between African American, Latino, Asian American, White, Native American, and other student populations continues to widen. In some cases, this gap is the result of "negative assumptions about what children of color, students with exceptional needs, or students living in poverty are capable of learning and achieving" (Love et al., 2008, p. 24) that influence the way in which students are educated.

Clearly, students in our schools are receiving inequitable opportunities for high-quality learning and, as an educational system, we are failing a large proportion of our students. But how does equity relate to a discussion of effective professional development in science and mathematics? The answer is, How could it not? The purpose of professional development is to enhance teachers' knowledge and skills to address every students' learning needs, and that cannot happen without attention to ensuring equity.

There are several issues regarding equity that play out in professional development. The first, and perhaps most critical, issue is whether the professional learning experiences include opportunities for teachers to examine and challenge their beliefs about who can learn and how diverse groups of students learn best. Professional development is designed to enhance quality teaching,

> ## Ensuring Equity: Critical Reflection Questions
>
> - Does the content of the professional development experience include opportunities for teachers to examine and challenge their beliefs about who can learn and how diverse groups of students best learn?
> - Does the content of the professional development experience include the issues of equitable opportunity for all students to learn science and mathematics and participate in careers in science and mathematics?
> - Is access to the professional development experience equitable? Is this opportunity available to all, or does it favor people in certain locations, with certain lifestyles, and from certain cultural, gender, or racial groups?
> - Does the design of the professional development invite full engagement and learning by participants?

and without an exploration of the ways in which teachers' beliefs influence their instructional approaches, quality teaching cannot be achieved. A second issue also relates directly to students: ensuring that what teachers learn in professional development provides them with the skills, resources, and sensitivities necessary to help a diverse student body gain literacy in science and mathematics. The third issue relates to equitable access for every teacher to quality professional development, and the fourth issue concerns whether the design of learning sessions invites full engagement and learning by every participant. Thus, the issues relate to both the content and the design of professional development. The discussion here is organized around these four areas and proposes questions that professional developers can ask about their programs.

Does the content of the professional development experience include opportunities for teachers to examine and challenge their beliefs about who can learn and how diverse groups of students best learn?

Too often, we hear complaints that teachers are required to attend districtwide presentations on being culturally sensitive and attentive to diverse learners' needs. While these awareness sessions might be effective in initiating some action, helping teachers explore their beliefs about who can learn goes much deeper than attending one workshop. Rather, the conversations should be embedded within their professional learning experiences and authentic in nature. For example, examining student work or student learning data is often a catalyst for what Glenn Singleton and Curtis Linton call "courageous conversations" (2006). When teachers see for themselves that certain students are not learning at the same levels as other students, the context is ripe for exploring the reasons why. The discussions should steer clear of blaming students, their families, their home environments, or their cultural backgrounds and instead focus on what is happening in the classroom that is not supporting these students to learn.

Facilitators need to have their own professional development to learn to facilitate these challenging conversations and to learn to look for the "teachable moments" in professional development sessions. One way to both prepare facilitators and embed equity as "content" within professional development is to engage learners in exploring cultural proficiency— "honoring the differences among cultures, seeing diversity as a benefit, and interacting knowledgably and respectfully among a variety of cultural groups" (Lindsey, Roberts, et al., 2005, p. 54). Lindsey and his colleagues have several resources that help educators explore the cultural proficiency continuum, and in the authors' work on engaging school teams in data-driven dialogue, we have found these experiences invaluable. (For more information and resources for introducing these tools see *The Data Coach's Guide to Improving Learning for All Students* by Love et al., 2008.)

In addition to preparing facilitators, it is important for designers to deliberately plan for these conversations: It is not enough to assume they will happen on their own. For example, when conducting case discussions, designers can include cases that raise the issue of equitable opportunities for every student to learn science or mathematics. Issues of equity are also a frequent focus for teachers' investigation through action research.

The key is to ensure that dialogue about equity and cultural proficiency are part of teachers' professional learning experiences. The conversations will inevitably arise, and designers need to anticipate and plan for these conversations, as well as prepare facilitators to lead constructive dialogue with their peers.

Does the content of the professional development experience include the issues of equitable opportunity for all students to learn science and mathematics and participate in careers in science and mathematics?

The goal of equitable science and mathematics education is to ensure successful outcomes for all students regardless of their race, ethnic heritage, gender, educational abilities, socioeconomic class, or learning style. How can professional development help teachers improve their strategies for reaching all students with effective science and mathematics education? One way is to introduce tools that assess student progress and allow teachers to identify the differential impact on groups of students; areas of identified weakness can be the focus of professional development. Research on equity, motivation, and achievement among children of color and females can be included in professional development. Schools can carefully examine their student learning data and data on structures, such as tracking, to identify imbalances in equitable opportunities for student learning. They can examine which teachers are teaching which courses, grades, and students to see whether certain students are being taught by less qualified teachers. Some research indicates that there is inequitable distribution of highly qualified teachers in low-income and high-minority schools (Goe, 2007). Professional developers can help teachers examine school data to identify whether these inequities exist and develop plans to address them. Study groups of teachers and staff can explore equity through reading and discussing research and cases. Researchers argue that schools and programs must be structured for effective use of formative assessments and support small groups of teachers collaborating to focus on teaching and learning (Frances, Rivera, Lesaux, Kieffer, & Rivera, 2006; Gersten et al., 2007). All of these approaches to professional learning can enhance teachers' ability to reach every student.

In addition, research increasingly shows that "the professional development that makes a difference for students of color is professional development that deepens teachers' knowledge of the curriculum they are teaching, helps them find or create effective lessons, and enables them to assess and respond to student performance" (Haycock & Robinson, 2001, p. 18). In other words, *effective* professional development—professional learning opportunities that embody the characteristics of practice-based learning for teachers—leads to enhanced learning for *every* student. The content of professional development should focus squarely on the practice of teaching and learning; that focus in and of itself can enhance equitable learning for students. For example, data from the National Association of Education Progress (NAEP) indicate that schools and districts that are closing achievement gaps are using their local assessments and data to make improvements in their curriculum and instruction (Perie, Moran, & Lutkus, 2005). These data are further evidence that teachers' focus on their practices and how to improve instruction can lead to enhanced student learning.

Issues of equity in mathematics and science education reveal themselves in many elements of education; opportunities for educators to become aware of this critical issue and ways to think about change are very appropriate as content for professional development. Exploration of how students best learn challenging content in a second language, the impact of tracking on opportunities to learn, cooperative learning as an alternative pedagogical approach, and family and community collaboration are all important issues that can be part of professional development programs in mathematics and science for teachers, administrators, and other educators.

Numerous programs have been developed in recent years to specifically address equity in teaching, learning, and schools, including the work of the Education Trust (www.edtrust.org), the Dana Center's Advanced Placement Equity Initiative (www.utdanacenter.org), and TERC's Weaving Gender Equity Into Math Reform (http://wge.terc.edu) and the Using Data Project (http://using data.terc.edu). Many Web sites, books, and journals, including publications by the National Council of Teachers of Mathematics (NCTM, www.nctm.org) and the National Staff Development Council (NSDC, www.nsdc.org), are now devoted specifically to the topics of equity and diversity.

In addition, Weissglass's (1996, 1997) seminal work in mathematics education remains a good example of addressing the issues of equity for both education in general and professional development specifically. His work suggests the need to make equity the central focus of educational change efforts. His professional development goal is to help educators understand the relationship between mathematics and culture and to increase their capacity to provide mathematical experiences that meet both the needs of a diverse student population and the NCTM standards. Through reading, discussion, and observation, educators in Weissglass's programs explore how cultural values and ways of understanding can affect mathematics learning and teaching; understand the culture of mathematics and the value of building classroom mathematics on children's own experiences; examine instructional materials though an "equity filter"; and experience the application of mathematics to understanding important social issues, such as hunger, poverty, and teen pregnancy. These kinds of experiences help educators to better understand the issues of equity as part of their own professional development.

Is access to the professional development experience equitable? Is this opportunity available to all, or does it favor people in certain locations, with certain lifestyles, and from certain cultural, gender, or racial groups?

Access is a simple concept, but it is often ignored by professional development designers who are not aware of the inequities that can be created when opportunities are offered to teachers. They may think they offer the same chance to everyone to participate in professional development, but many factors, some of which are in their control, inhibit participation. Some of these factors include scheduling, distance, and resources required to use what is learned. For example, there are many opportunities for teachers to participate in multiday immersion experiences and institutes during the summer, but these opportunities are not always accessible to all teachers. Many teachers have summer jobs, and others have family obligations that prohibit them from enrolling in an intensive professional development program that will keep them away from home for multiple days or weeks. When only some teachers are able to participate in this kind of professional development, it is imperative that designers include alternative options for teachers who are unable to attend, such as study groups that explore the content provided in the institute over time during the academic year.

States with many rural schools struggle with providing quality professional development for every teacher in all schools. Many districts, regions, and states have addressed this issue by instituting online professional learning and networking opportunities for teachers. For example, programs provide in-person learning sessions complemented by online study groups, book study discussions, and electronic networking, thus ensuring that teachers in the most remote regions, often serving the poorest of students, have access to professional development. In other instances, videoconferencing allows isolated teachers to participate in common learning experiences even when they are dispersed throughout a region.

Inequitable policies and practices in school funding can create unequal opportunities for professional development. Just examining the variation in how professional development funds are distributed and then used in different schools, districts, and states is enlightening. Resource-rich schools, which often do not serve underrepresented student populations, usually have professional development programs, while other schools struggle to find funds to just purchase lab equipment, books, and other materials. Designers are attentive to these inequitable circumstances and strive to make professional learning opportunities available for every teacher.

Does the design of the professional development invite full engagement and learning by participants?

Making professional development accessible is a necessary first step, but the design will determine whether it is truly equitable. Professional development strategies should be chosen to meet the diverse needs and learning styles of participating teachers. Unfortunately, professional development planners are not always aware of the characteristics of programs that could be problematic. For instance, cultural norms may create barriers to some professional development activities, such as modeling and giving critical feedback. Or programs that expect participants to learn mainly from reading materials do not serve auditory and kinesthetic learners well.

Demonstrating equity in the design of professional development programs also involves who is chosen to play leadership roles. The designation of leaders sends a strong message about the priority of equity and its role in what and how educators learn. Schools need to select professional development leaders who represent the diversity in both the teacher and student population, understand and value equity and diversity, and proactively involve teachers in professional development efforts who are from underrepresented groups or who teach underrepresented students.

WestEd staff Carne Barnett-Clarke and Alma Ramirez have actively recruited and supported teacher leadership development among African American, Latino, Native American, and other underrepresented groups through their work with teachers using mathematics cases. In the initial stages of the project, they found relatively few minority teachers volunteering to participate in the professional development sessions that use mathematics case discussions to enhance teachers' pedagogical content knowledge. Since one of the explicit goals of their work is to reach a diverse audience of teachers and to develop a diverse group of teacher leaders as case facilitators, Barnett-Clarke examined the ways in which teachers were recruited and invited to participate. She found that the practice of contacting schools and sending out fliers resulted in recruitment of the "usual suspects"—the most active, frequently engaged teachers were the ones who attended or were nominated by their principals but were most often not representative of a diverse group of teachers. For example, Barnett-Clarke found that in the initial case discussions most teachers were White, shared a common pedagogy and philosophy of teaching and learning, and were more experienced teachers. There were few teachers of color and no new and inexperienced teachers, and there was a lack of diverse perspectives about teaching.

To address the lack of diversity among participating teachers and the resulting pool of people to develop into case facilitators, Barnett-Clarke and her colleagues began to personally invite teachers from more diverse backgrounds, contact previous case discussants asking them to nominate teachers, and encourage and support leadership among diverse participants. Case discussions were also designed to help teachers move from low-risk engagement to higher-risk participation, such as sharing the facts and details of the case before critically examining the teaching beliefs or behaviors of the case teacher. These strategies resulted in case discussions characterized by diverse perspectives, confident case discussants, and case facilitators who represent varied cultural backgrounds and experiences (see Barnett-Clarke & Ramirez, 2009, for more information on their approaches).

BUILDING A PROFESSIONAL LEARNING CULTURE

The culture of a school contributes to the learning of all within its walls. As described in Chapter 3, a school that embodies a collaborative culture and professional learning community is characterized by a strong vision of learning, is focused on continuous learning, promotes a community of learners who all take responsibility for learning, "deprivatizes" teaching through collaborative and collegial interactions, and routinely supports and engages teachers in collaborative inquiry and dialogue (DuFour & Eaker, 1998; Fullan, 2001; Hord & Sommers, 2008; Love et al., 2008; McLaughlin & Talbert, 2007).

Professional learning communities are associated with both changed teacher practices and changed professional culture by embedding continuous teacher learning into the culture (Andrew & Lewis, 2002; Louis & Marks, 1998; Supovitz, 2002). Without a supportive culture, however, professional learning of teachers has little chance of survival as teachers' newly gained knowledge and skills fail to have a lasting impact on their practice. What can professional developers who aim to help teachers foster improved learning of science and mathematics do to strengthen or build a strong professional learning culture? Especially in instances in which the professional development opportunity is neither inside the school nor connected with the school or district in any way, professional developers have special challenges for nourishing professional cultures. The first step in that direction, however, is to understand what is known about professional culture and why it is important.

Rosenholtz (1991) aptly coined the terms *learning enriched* and *learning impoverished* to describe elementary schools in which students, teachers, and other members of the school community either learned and grew in an exciting, supportive environment or languished with none of the expectations, norms, and rich learning experiences to help them grow. Little's (1982) early work on professional development pointed out differences between schools in which teachers talked continuously about their teaching and their students, experimenting with new strategies and sharing successes and failures, and those in which teachers were isolated, private, and not prone to innovation. Both researchers found student learning differences that favored schools in which teachers also learned.

In their studies of teachers' workplace settings, McLaughlin and Talbert (2001, 2007) determined that strong professional cultures are essential to changing norms of practice and pedagogy. This happens when teachers examine assumptions, focus their collective experience on solutions, and support efforts on the part of everyone to grow professionally. Professional communities with norms of privacy and unchallenged sacred principles or personal beliefs breed embittered, frustrated teachers. Interestingly, departments within a single high school can have such different professional cultures that the influence of school leadership seems much less important.

Researchers with the Qualitative Understanding: Amplifying Student Achievement and Reasoning (QUASAR) project examined teacher development and change in middle schools through a "community of practice" framework (Stein, Silver, & Smith, 1998), which was originally developed by Lave and Wenger (1991). The notion of a community of practice helps describe how teacher learning occurs in collaborative, school-based communities. For example, in looking at ways in which "newcomers" (p. 37) to a school were participating in the community, the QUASAR project found that simply being a "member of a community of practitioners provides meaning and context to newcomers' learning experiences" (Stein et al., 1998, p. 37). The community provided opportunities to observe teaching strategies in action, to hear stories about the process of changing, and to become immersed in the "language" of reform. Rather than teacher collaboration being simply a contextual variable that enhances individual change and growth, it also nurtures and supports learning and change in the community. It is the culture of the community itself that contributes to both individual and group changes and learning.

> **Building a Professional Learning Culture: Critical Reflection Questions**
>
> - What is a good starting place for building a professional learning culture?
> - What can professional developers specifically do to build professional communities among teachers?

These findings about the power of professional community cut across levels of schooling. They provide clues to what professional developers working with teachers of science and mathematics can do to foster deeper learning and development. The following paragraphs provide questions that professional developers can ask themselves to improve the impact of their programs by building professional culture.

What is a good starting place for building a professional learning culture?

Professional developers have used three strategies to build professional communities. First, they have increasingly required teacher participants to bring colleagues and principals with them to share in learning. For example, teachers are asked to participate in pairs or teams with an administrator. Having an administrator present can be important in creating both the culture and the structures to support implementation of learning and professional community back at the school. In particular, administrators can provide needed resources, allocate time for professional development, and serve as advocates for professional development when interacting with district administrators and families. In other cases, the professional development is for the whole department (as in high schools and some middle schools), whole school, or even whole district so that an entire staff learns together.

A second strategy is for professional developers to build their own professional communities outside the boundaries of departments, schools, or districts. The professional networks described in Chapter 5 provide examples. The professional developers supporting these networks take pains to build relationships among their members that lack only the physical proximity of an intact teaching staff. A critical ingredient of what some call "temporary systems" is that they continue over time, purposely nurturing the relationships between their members in an ongoing way rather than severing them after a "main event," such as an institute or workshop experience.

A third strategy that professional developers have used to nurture professional community is to work with individual participants to equip them with ways to build their own professional communities "back home." This is not the "each one, teach one" strategy that some use, largely unsuccessfully, in which teachers learn new skills and strategies and are expected to return to their schools and teach others the same skills and strategies. In the case of developing a professional community, professional developers suggest and encourage sharing of strategies for teachers to use in their schools to (a) initiate and sustain dialogue about what they have learned, (b) work with their administrators to build realistic expectations and garner support, and (c) encourage others to participate in similar, complementary learning experiences. For example, teachers may return home with study guides for examining articles or videos that engage others in what they are learning. They practice "reentry" behaviors that keep them from becoming isolated by virtue of their changing beliefs and values and enthusiasm for new ideas and approaches and that allow them to respond constructively to questions and issues raised by others. Instructional coaches and teacher leaders may also learn how to work collegially with peer teachers and prospective teachers who are placed with them for practice teaching to strengthen the school culture. Sergiovanni (2007) suggests that coaches need to be prepared to raise questions about the school culture, such as "What changes will we need to make in the norms [and] systems of our schools? What will be the accepted ways we do things? How will our purposes, values, and commitments be used to point the way to evaluate our work?" (p. 65). These kinds of strategies help teachers make inroads in building or strengthening their own professional communities. A central focus of this work is on articulating the goals, values, and beliefs that will guide the learning culture (Love et al., 2008).

What can professional developers specifically do to build professional communities among teachers?

Research indicates that professional communities thrive where collaboration, experimentation, and challenging discourse are possible and welcome (Elmore & Burney, 1999; Fullan, 2001; Hord & Boyd, 1995; Little, 1993; McLaughlin & Talbert, 2007; Norris, 1994; Sparks, 2002; St. John & Pratt, 1997). Collaboration is fostered through finding time for professional learning (see "Making Time for Professional Development" in this chapter). Also, collaboration must meet the needs of participants; there must be something in it for each of them, and it must have a purpose that is better served by collective rather than individual work or expertise. The purpose of collaboration must be improving student learning; clear goals for students coupled with use of student learning data, including student work, help teachers to maintain that focus.

Effective collaboration requires special skills—in communication, "data-driven dialogue" (Love et al., 2008; Wellman & Lipton, 2004), decision making, problem solving, and managing effective meetings. Finally, collaboration requires a genuine caring about others that can be strengthened through opportunities to do constructive work together and to share interesting and stimulating experiences. Professional developers can foster collaborative communities through structuring experiences of shared learning and skill development in these areas.

It is important to note that collaboration as a vehicle for learning and community building can be a negative as well as a positive force. Fullan and Hargreaves (1991) point out that "contrived collegiality" can take teachers away from valuable time with students, and "groupthink" can stifle rather than stimulate innovation and imaginative solutions (p. 7). As pointed out by Mundry and Stiles (2009), poor implementation of the professional learning communities model can result in teachers being locked into stifling conversations guided by narrowly focused protocols. Instead, professional learning cultures must work to build teachers' capacity and professional judgment to effectively engage in inquiry into student learning and needed changes in practice. McLaughlin's (1993) research has found collegiality can focus on being critical of students and reinforcing norms of mediocrity. The chances of collaboration taking a more learning-enriched path are increased when it is accompanied by the establishment of respect for teachers and students, experimentation, and challenging discourse.

Developing respect for teachers involves examining beliefs about the roles of teachers and their status as professionals and developing their capacity to use evidence and research, as well as knowledge grounded in teaching experience, to inform decisions. Effective collaborative cultures also build a strong commitment to student learning and believe in students' capacity to be successful. As discussed in this chapter, ensuring equity for students requires teachers to develop their own cultural competence and to strive to provide excellence for every student.

Experimentation requires skills and dispositions toward inquiry, norms that recognize and support failure, and ideas with which to experiment. Although this does not refer specifically to formal action research, insights into fostering inquiry are provided in the discussion of action research as a professional development strategy in Chapter 5. Professional development programs can be sources of new ideas and practices with which to experiment and can assist teachers to do so in ways that increase their potential for learning. More difficult is the issue of making it okay to fail. Teachers have traditionally been expected to be the source of knowledge; it is understandable why some struggle with the perception that they must always have the right answers. Learning to accept and learn from trial and error is harder for some than others. It can be enhanced by having a community of people who value trying new approaches, a structured way to reflect on both successes and failures, and a clear picture of which situations are low stakes and which are high—that is, the ability to analyze the consequences of failure for different situations.

Finally, challenging discourse is not very common among teachers. Often, teachers equate critical reflection on practice with criticism of personal performance. Building professional cultures, however, by the very definition of the word *professional,* carries with it a commitment to effective practice in oneself and in others who share the profession. Desiring high-quality teaching for every student requires teachers to challenge their own practices and the practices of others to improve the learning opportunities for all. Teachers need skills and practice in applying standards of effectiveness to their and others' practice; in gathering, analyzing, and explaining the evidence for their convictions; and in communicating criticisms to each other. It cannot be otherwise because the science and mathematics teaching promoted by the standards requires challenging what the learner thinks he or she knows to reorganize or deepen understanding. What we want for students, we should want for ourselves as learners. Often, difficult discussions are the ones we learn from most.

Professional developers can purposely build structures that promote a positive professional culture by breaking down isolation through strategies such as study groups, coaching, mentoring, lesson study, examining student work, professional networks, and case discussions (see Chapter 5). They can use the strategy of curriculum topic study (Keeley, 2005) to build teachers' ability to apply research and standards to their decision making. They can help teachers and facilitators learn the processes of quality discourse that are essential for professional learning communities, such as carefully listening to the meanings of statements, probing and inquiring to promote reflection, and persistently focusing on teaching and learning (Oehrtman, Carlson, & Vasquez, 2009). Also, they can prepare teachers to use the skills of collaboration, problem solving, and inquiry (Garmston & Wellman, 2009; Love et al., 2008) that will equip them with tools and techniques to build and maintain supportive, professional communities in their schools.

GARNERING PUBLIC SUPPORT

Constantly shrinking resources are a sign of the times, and nowhere is it felt more keenly than when the public scrutinizes an education budget. What stays and what goes is based on what is valued. Making time and funding for professional development in the budget requires public support.

Public support for professional development is needed at times other than when budgets are being determined. When substitute teachers are in classrooms, school is out because of professional days, or teachers are attending a conference far from home, the public needs to voice its support for ongoing teacher learning and know the benefit it has on student achievement.

Public support for professional development is intimately related to public support for science and mathematics education. A public that values quality science and mathematics learning for all children knows that teachers need opportunities to continually update their knowledge and skills to support students. Such supporters acknowledge and commit to playing an ongoing role of advocacy and support for science and mathematics education over time.

Professional developers can address the dual purpose of garnering public support for science and mathematics education reform and for teacher professional development. They can do so by paying attention to two areas: (1) increasing awareness of the importance of science and mathematics education as well as

> **Garnering Public Support: Critical Reflection Questions**
>
> - How can professional developers build awareness of the importance of mathematics and science education and of effective professional development?
> - How can professional developers engage the public in improving mathematics and science teaching and learning?

effective professional development and what they entail and (2) engaging the public in improving science and mathematics teaching and learning.

How can professional developers build awareness of the importance of mathematics and science education and of effective professional development?

The first step is to clarify why science and mathematics education and the public's support for it are essential. There are several reasons; many relate directly to families, who are an important segment of "the public." The reasons include the following:

- Families and the general public can benefit from a better understanding of science and mathematics—for example, they can see how it is used to understand and propose solutions to everyday problems and to better understand technological developments happening all around us.
- Families can help by supporting their children to learn in new ways—for example, they can help their children use inquiry and problem solving by asking and investigating questions that arise in everyday life.
- Schools can benefit from the contributions of committed families and community members, such as scientists and mathematicians, who have expertise to contribute. In addition, generating their interest could increase the resources available to the school.
- An informed public will be more skeptical about and able to address misinformation about science and mathematics education—for example, be able to address issues that arise in the media regarding the

teaching of evolution in science or problem solving and computation skills in mathematics.

- Authentic partnerships between schools and families and the community benefit students' learning.

Mathematics and science educators are clear about the need for public engagement around the future of science and mathematics education. For example, in its charge to groups writing the *National Science Education Standards,* the NRC (1996) stated the following:

> The traditions and values of science and the history of science curriculum reforms . . . argue for a large critique and consensus effort. Science is tested knowledge; therefore, no matter how broadly based the perspective of the developers, their judgment must be informed by others' responses . . . particularly teachers, policymakers, and the customers of education systems—students, parents, business, employers, taxpayers. One of several reasons for the limited impact of past reform efforts was the weakness of their consensus building activities. (p. 2)

Professional developers can help teachers and other educators understand the importance of improved mathematics and science teaching and learning and, more important, become articulate about it. They can help educators communicate with families and the public about the benefits of a mathematically and scientifically informed populace. In addition, sharing data and research with the public regarding the impact of their support on student learning can go a long way toward garnering their involvement. For example, studies have found that when families are involved in their students' education, there is improved academic achievement for all ages of students (Epstein et al., 2009; Henderson & Mapp, 2002; Sheldon, 2003).

Mathematics and science educators have found that family involvement is essential in their educational change initiatives. Many schools conduct science and mathematics family events where student work and projects are shared, families engage in exploratory activities with their children, and information is shared about the science or mathematics program. However, one study found that elementary schools reported more family involvement than did middle or high school and that they more frequently and consistently offered opportunities and programs for involvement (Hutchins, Sheldon, & Epstein, 2009). Clearly, as a K–12 education issue, more emphasis on building these relationships at the secondary level is called for since family involvement activities go a long way toward building awareness, support, and ultimately, improved student learning.

Educators have also learned that when they do not have public support, there are severe ramifications for science and mathematics education improvement efforts. For example, parents and the public have been activated to oppose some mathematics and science teaching because it was not understood or perceived as lacking rigor or in conflict with certain religious beliefs such as the opposition to some mathematics curricula and the debate about how to teach the concept of evolution. These examples point to the critical need to provide the public with information to help raise awareness and understanding of the content and processes for teaching science and mathematics that are advocated for in national standards and supported in scientific educational research.

Providing information, however, is only one step in the process toward developing authentic relationships and partnerships with families who can be strong advocates for science and mathematics education. Schools must develop a broader conception of what "family involvement" means and expand the roles of parents beyond volunteering for field trips or helping out in classrooms. If families are viewed as true partners in children's education, the National Network of Partnership Schools at Johns Hopkins University (n.d.) recommends that their involvement include activities such as participating in school planning and governance, engaging in decision-making processes regarding the ways structures and policies influence students' learning, examining their child's work with the teacher to better understand what the child is learning, and participating in science or mathematics "curriculum and concept awareness" activities to enhance their understanding of the instruction their students receive. Numerous schools and districts have found that when families are truly engaged as partners in children's learning, they are advocates for the school and the ways in which their students learn. (See Chapter 3 for more on "Families and Communities" and their roles as partners.)

In addition to awareness of effective mathematics and science education, the public must have awareness of the importance and nature of effective professional development. It helps to state how little education systems invest in their employees compared with corporations. Again, clear articulation of what professional development is for, what it entails, and what its benefits are can help to increase the public's support. Linking professional development to student learning—as in the statement, "the more teachers know and are able to do, the more students can learn"—is an effective motivator for family and community support. Sharing recent research and literature on the relationship between teacher professional learning and student learning can also increase the community's understanding of and support for teachers' learning. More important, local school or district data on the ways in which students' learning is increasing in science or mathematics and the relationships to their teachers' professional learning can "convince" and motivate the community to support time and resources for teacher professional development.

How can professional developers engage the public in improving mathematics and science teaching and learning?

Another strategy for garnering public support is by actually engaging people from the community in mathematics and science education. This can be done in several ways. First, families and community members can be invited into the professional development experiences as learners; for example, they may join teams from schools or districts for professional development during summer institutes. In other cases, families and community members can collaborate together in learning experiences, such as study groups to examine and understand national or state standards. Second, they can be invited in as "teachers," working with students in classrooms and teachers in professional development settings. This is of particular benefit when they have science or mathematics expertise and experiences to share. (See "Making Time for Professional Development" in this chapter for specific examples.)

As noted in the introduction to this chapter, the critical issues are ones that designers "ignore at their own peril," and not attending early in the planning and implementation of a program to garnering public support can have a negative impact on science and mathematics education and professional development. The research and suggestions in this section provide ideas to help designers initiate steps as they plan their programs to involve the public.

SCALING UP

Scaling up becomes an area of great concern as schools and districts implement new standards-based science and mathematics teaching and learning strategies. Often, it is the "early adopters" who quickly translate their new learning into practice in their classrooms. However, after this first wave of users, designers are faced with bringing the rest of the teachers on board, which can often be a challenge. In early reform efforts in science and mathematics education, leaders sometimes took the attitude that the "resisters" could be left behind. Today, educators and leaders cannot afford to take this stance—if educators are to reach *every* child, then *every* teacher also needs to implement the approaches. As Krajcik writes, "Scaling up matters because it does no good if the ideas work only in a few classrooms with the very best teachers" (as cited in Roop & Best, 2005, p. 13).

At state and regional levels, there are some districts or schools that have benefited from educational changes while others have been untouched. There is a need to scale up to reach those that have not been served. Since there are about 100,000 schools and more than 3 million educators in this country, the challenge of reaching these large numbers is daunting. A 2004 report from RAND Education, *Expanding the Reach of Education Reforms: Perspectives from Leaders in the Scale-Up of Educational Interventions,* acknowledges the daunting task and recommends that scale-up efforts must involve district administrators, school leaders, and teachers in "aligning policies and infrastructure in coherent ways to sustain practice" if scale-up is to be successful (Glennan, Bodilly, Galegher, & Kerr, 2004, p. 648).

The particular challenge for many professional developers is how to design programs and initiatives so that they are able to reach a significant number of teachers. Institutes and workshops are strategies that are one solution, but we know from research that these approaches alone will not impact teachers' practice and student learning. In-depth learning with fewer teachers over longer periods of time does result in changes, but only in a few classrooms, and we cannot afford to create "pockets of innovation" where only some students are afforded access to high-quality teaching and learning.

How can professional developers address this need to reach large numbers of teachers with quality, long-term, practice-based professional development? To scale up from a few teachers to every teacher? Although there is no single answer to this question, several factors, discussed in this section, can contribute to success.

> **Scaling Up: Critical Reflection Questions**
>
> - Is the innovation clearly defined and based on a sound foundation?
> - How do you provide professional development opportunities to large numbers of people?
> - Does each teacher have sufficient support to change his or her practice?
> - What mechanisms are in place for quality control of the professional development for all?
> - Is there a plan at each unit of implementation (department, school, district, state, etc.) for ongoing use, support, and institutionalization?

Is the innovation clearly defined and based on a sound foundation?

The *innovation* refers to a program or practice that is new to teachers and that deviates from current practice (Hall & Hord, 2006). For an innovation to be scaled up, it is imperative to articulate what the change is supposed to look like when it is being practiced: what teachers and students are doing (and not doing) and what one would see in classrooms and schools if the program was working well (Hall & Hord). This does not necessarily imply a highly prescriptive set of teaching behaviors and materials, although it could; even the national standards for science and mathematics are specific enough to reveal themselves in teachers' practices and students' responses. One knows them when one sees them.

Therefore, clarity is important but so are utility and practicality, because unless a change seems possible, it will not be attempted. There must be evidence that it does not require superhuman efforts, skills that few have or can develop, exotic equipment, or special classroom or school situations (e.g., extra staff), or that it does not rely on a specific teacher or a unique situation. Finally, the change must be credible and backed by evidence that if this change were to occur, clear benefits would ensue for teachers, students, and schools. These attributes of a change make it better able to be shared from one place to another, to be picked up by larger numbers of people, and to be communicated to those whose support is needed for it to become common practice (Fullan, 1991).

How do you provide professional development opportunities to large numbers of people?

This is a particularly difficult question to address. Rarely does professional development succeed when it is "delivered en masse" because it usually lacks attention to individual needs, person-to-person interaction, and opportunity for in-depth study and experimentation. Several strategies, however, are being used to reach large numbers. One is online professional development (as discussed in Chapter 5). Online learning enables teachers from throughout the country to engage in ongoing professional development with other teachers, facilitators, scientists and mathematicians. In some instances, such as a Webinar, there is no limit to how many people can participate, especially when combined with smaller group learning strategies, such as online book study or online study groups. Other means of providing online professional development, as noted in Chapter 5, have limitations similar to other in-person professional learning strategies: They are limited by how many participants a single moderator or instructor can respond to and engage in learning.

Another strategy is to use a *multiplier,* which is referred to by many names, including *certified trainers, teacher leadership cadres,* or *teachers on special assignment.* This strategy is discussed in the cases in Chapter 6 and in this chapter in the "Developing Leadership" section. In the context of scaling up, a cadre of teacher leaders or other educators learn science or mathematics content and pedagogy, master the new practice(s) in their own classrooms, and are prepared to work with adult learners and are given time to do so. This can have a multiplier effect, enabling larger numbers of teachers to be reached.

Reaching large numbers is not about everyone having the same experience and having that experience in a constrained period of time. Professional development is not "one size fits all" but rather should be a combination of strategies. For example, teachers can learn new teaching practices through workshops, institutes, coaching, study groups, case discussions, and immersion experiences. When teachers are offered a variety of strategies from which to learn, and these are offered over an extended period of time, many people can be reached. Here, the issue may be one of focus. When schools or districts decide to focus their professional development resources on one particular change or area of change, teachers have the opportunity to learn fewer new practices more in-depth (Bennett & Green, 1995; Elmore, 1996). They can be engaged intellectually, rather than superficially, in the change (Klein, McArthur, & Stecher, 1995).

Does each teacher have sufficient support to change his or her practice?

Although it may be economical to supply teachers with materials in large numbers, such as in the use of science kits in elementary schools, it is still the case that each teacher needs professional development, follow-up support, time to learn and experiment, and ways to assess results with students. Scale-up cannot occur if teachers lack what they need to change. Furthermore, it may take increasingly more resources, largely in the form of time and energy on the part of "change agents," to reach those who come to a change at the end of the line—that is, the "late adopters." These schools or individuals may require more evidence to be motivated or convinced of the value of the changes.

Cohen and Ball (2006) suggest that scaffolding is one approach to addressing quality implementation when scaling up, especially when working with "late adopters." They state, "Innovations can be implemented only as they are apprehended and used by teachers and learners. The more innovations depart from conventional practice, the more new ideas, beliefs, norms, and practices teachers and students would have to learn, and the more implementation would depend on that learning" (p. 26). Scaffolding "would improve implementation by providing more opportunities for adopters to learn how to use the innovation" (p. 27). They also note, however, that more scaffolding also "takes more time, forethought, and money, and increases work, time, and costs" (p. 27).

These are all issues that need to be anticipated and planned for all those who will ultimately be involved. Curriculum and assessment practices, school administration and policies, school structures (including time, materials support, and teaching assignments), and other change initiatives must be coordinated and focused for scale-up to succeed. The support plan must accurately estimate and ensure provision of the resources that are necessary to reach everyone.

What mechanisms are in place for quality control of the professional development for all?

This is a particularly important issue, especially where a multiplier strategy is being used. When a particular change has been chosen that promises certain outcomes if all of its critical elements are in use, it is important that all who are involved in the initiative learn and implement those elements well. This requires that professional developers have the knowledge and skills to transfer their understanding of the changes to the teachers they work with and support their implementation of the innovation. In cases where teachers are not provided with support to implement new learning, the learning is either not put into practice or is implemented without fidelity to the original intent of the innovation. Quality control requires intense attention to developing professional developers, coaching them to develop their content and professional development skills, and supporting them over time as they work with increasing numbers of teachers.

Other quality control mechanisms include clear expectations for the roles of professional developers, written guidelines for professional development activities (e.g., workshop plans and materials, cases and facilitator notes, coaching guides, and immersion activities), and tools for monitoring and evaluating the work of professional developers.

Is there a plan at each unit of implementation (department, school, district, state, etc.) for ongoing use, support, and institutionalization?

Plans at each level acknowledge that successful change is simultaneously top down and bottom up (Fullan, 1991). Individual progress in learning and changing can be anticipated (Hall & Hord, 2006) as can the management and policy moves that each unit of the organization will need to make to support increasing numbers of people involved in the change. Institutionalization, the stage at which a change becomes "how we do things around here," requires attention to such issues as routine professional development for new teachers or those who change grade levels; support networks; routine ordering of required materials and equipment; continuous reflection, monitoring, evaluation, and commitment to changes based on what is learned.

Scaling up is a challenge that every professional development designers faces at some point during the planning or implementation of the program. Attending to the scale-up issues early in the program enables designers to be better situated for expanding the program to reach every teacher.

The seven critical issues discussed in this chapter are all essential considerations for professional development design. Expert professional developers intentionally think through each one and make sure that their goals, plans, and programs are designed to address each as needed in any particular context. If the leadership is not in place, that will influence the design. If the school lacks certain capacity such as clear goals and program coherence, that needs to go on the "to do" list for the program. If there has been little work to develop cultural proficiency and attention to equity, that focus is woven into the overall tapestry of the program.

Professional developers also continually assess and think about each one of these issues as the program plays out. For example, they evaluate the extent to which the professional learning culture is building and what conditions threaten its success. They watch out for discontent among families and the public or turnover in leadership that could impede continued support for mathematics and science education, and stand ready to take action as new issues emerge.

5

Strategies for Professional Learning

Figure 5.1 Professional Development Design Framework

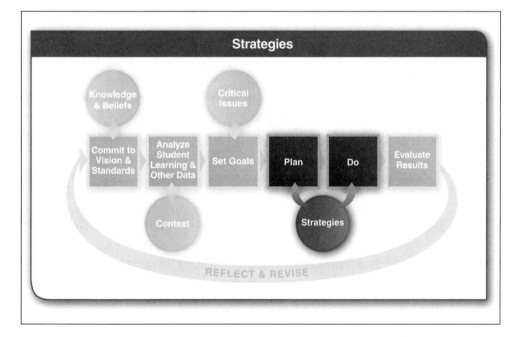

The decision about which strategies for professional learning to include in your design is informed by all other inputs into the process of designing (see Figure 5.1). In fact, this is the point in designing when your reflection on the design processes (committing to a vision and standards, analyzing student learning and other data, and setting goals) and inputs (knowledge and beliefs, context, and critical issues) come to fruition in the form of a plan that you will implement and evaluate. For example, the goals you set for the professional development program—which were informed by the vision and standards and your analysis of student learning and other data—drive the selection of specific strategies. Strategy choices are also informed by the knowledge base and beliefs the designers hold about the change process, teaching, learning, professional development, and the nature of science and mathematics. The context within which the strategies will be implemented shapes the selection, combination, and sequence of the learning opportunities that will be provided. The critical issues that influence the implementation and outcomes of any professional development program play a role in determining the selection of strategies. Deciding how to evaluate the results of the professional development as well as the quality of the teachers' learning opportunities is an important step in the design process. Given the goals and the strategies chosen, designers consider what will be assessed (e.g., changes in teachers' content knowledge or increased use of certain instructional practices) and how these outcomes will be assessed (e.g., pre- and postassessments, observations, or teachers' self-report). Information from the ongoing evaluation provides continuous feedback to designers to inform revisions to the professional development program.

The design framework in Figure 5.1 is intended to remind professional developers that good teacher learning programs require a lot more thinking and design than simply grabbing and implementing the latest strategy. We have seen this playing out recently with the wave of interest in professional learning communities (PLCs). Principals and teachers tell us they are "doing PLCs this year." In some cases, little thought has gone into what the goals are for the PLC, and the context has not been primed for this strategy (e.g., Have teachers learned to use student data effectively to address achievement gaps? Have they developed norms of collaborations and team skills that will support them?). A word of caution—implementing strategies in isolation and without clear goals does not constitute effective professional development. This book emphasizes why designers and planners of teacher learning programs need to carefully consider the different strategies and make choices that align with their different contexts, goals and purposes, and circumstances. Every program, initiative, and professional development plan relies on a variety of strategies in combination to form a unique design. Each strategy is one piece of the puzzle, and how a designer fits strategies together to assemble a combination of learning activities depends on the intricate interplay of all components of the design framework that are used to inform the selection of strategies for teachers' professional learning.

SELECTING STRATEGIES FOR A PROFESSIONAL DEVELOPMENT PLAN

In the first two editions of this book (1998, 2003), we described several constructs to guide designers through the process of selecting and combining strategies, from clusters of strategies that shared common underlying assumptions, to frameworks that identified purposes of individual strategies, to models describing the developmental stages of teachers' needs, to frameworks depicting the sequential support of teachers' learning. In the last 11 years, new research, emerging best practices, changes in the field of school improvement, and our experiences with professional developers, leaders, and teachers engaged in the hard work of designing have contributed to an evolving understanding of how to select and implement strategies for professional learning. We have arrived at three overall questions to use as one selects strategies for a professional development plan:

1. What do we want to achieve?

2. What is our cycle of implementation?

3. What are the factors that guide and inform the selection and combination of strategies?

What do we want to achieve?

In the 11 years since the publication of the first edition, the field of professional development has increasingly emphasized the ultimate outcome of teachers' professional learning: increasing student learning (National Council of Teachers of Mathematics [NCTM], 2000, 2003b; National Science Teachers Association [NSTA], 2006; National Staff Development Council [NSDC], 2009; Sparks, 2005). Professional development is no longer simply seen as a way to comply with policies or only to enhance teachers' knowledge. Rather, professional learning is increasingly focused on developing teachers' professional skills and abilities to recognize and correct student learning problems and to enhance students' learning. For example, in your analysis of student learning data, you may have discovered that students lacked the knowledge and ability to effectively design and conduct investigations that included controlling variables. With this explicitly identified student learning need, the question is, "What do our teachers need to know and do in order to support students to conduct high-quality investigations?" For some teachers, it may be the need to enhance their own content understanding of inquiry processes, and for others, it may be the need to learn effective instructional strategies to support student learning. In both cases, there is an identified focus for teachers' professional learning that is in direct support of student learning.

Having such an identified focus for professional development helps to avoid the lack of coherence that has plagued many teacher learning programs. One way to think about ensuring a coherent approach is to focus professional development on what actually happens in classrooms. Judith Mumme and Nanette Seago (2002) have adapted the work of Deborah Ball and David Cohen (2000) to reflect what they propose as the main content for professional learning—to study and understand classroom interactions (see Figure 5.2). Mumme and Seago define teaching as "a set of relationships

Figure 5.2   Teaching Interactions

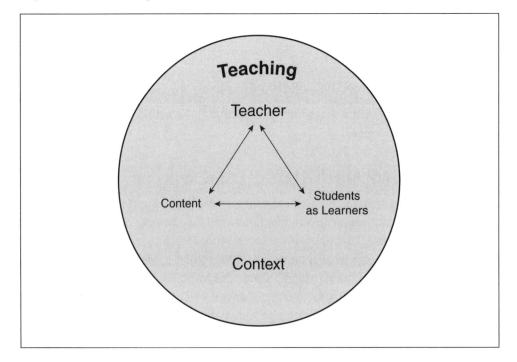

Source: Mumme, J., and Seago, N. (2002, April). *Issues and challenges in facilitating videocases for mathematics professional development.* Paper presented at the annual meeting of the American Education Research Association. Used with permission.

between teacher and student, student and content, and teacher and content" (p. 3). Teachers must have an in-depth understanding of the science or mathematics content, knowledge of their students' needs and prior experiences and how students learn the content, and the teaching strategies and activities that will lead to student learning. Effective professional development designs include a combination of strategies that engage teachers in examining each component of the classroom interaction model in order to address specific student learning needs.

Since it is not practical to offer unique professional development programs on every conceivable student learning problem, professional development needs to provide teachers with the professional expertise, tools, and skills to spot student learning difficulties and decide on a course of action. This requires adequate content knowledge and the use of quality teaching strategies. In addition, schools need the leadership and the culture to support ongoing improvement in student learning.

Four *interconnected* outcomes support the goal of enhanced student learning and can form the basis for most professional development plans:

1. *Enhancing teachers' knowledge,* including teachers' deep understanding of science and mathematics content and in-depth understanding of the ways in which students learn the content, the alternate conceptions students have of the concepts within the content, and instructional approaches that facilitate learning of the concepts (pedagogical content knowledge) (see Chapter 2 for a more in-depth discussion of teachers' content knowledge)

2. *Enhancing quality teaching,* including opportunities to translate new knowledge into practice and to practice teaching with an understanding of the standards and research that guide effective instructional approaches (see Chapters 2 and 3 for a more in-depth discussion of quality teaching)

3. *Developing leadership capacity,* including an emphasis on building capacity through the development of teacher leaders and professional developers (see Chapters 3 and 4 for a more in-depth discussion of developing leadership)

4. *Building professional learning communities,* including opportunities for teachers to engage in continuous learning and sustained improvement in a collegial culture (see Chapters 3 and 4 for a more in-depth discussion of professional learning communities and cultures)

Four *interconnected* outcomes support the goal of enhanced student learning and can form the basis for most professional development plans:

1. Enhancing teachers' knowledge

2. Enhancing quality teaching

3. Developing leadership capacity

4. Building professional learning communities

When professional development plans are designed to promote these four outcomes—in the service of increasing student learning—it is easy to see that one strategy will not be sufficient. Instead, the designer combines different strategies to address the different outcomes, with some strategies addressing more than one outcome. Increasing teachers' content knowledge is often best accomplished by immersing teachers in content as learners themselves. But learning content alone will not lead to quality teaching, so designers must build in opportunities for teachers to put the content they learn into the context of teaching and provide opportunities to develop pedagogical content knowledge. Some more experienced teachers may translate their learning into practice, but more commonly, teachers need opportunities to reflect on what they have learned and to practice effective instructional approaches. When teachers put their new knowledge to work and make changes in their teaching practices, then we can expect to see changes in student learning (Banilower et al., 2006; Borko, 2004; Blank, de las Alas, & Smith, 2008; Fishman et al., 2003; Supovitz & Turner, 2000; Yoon et al., 2007).

Yet, teachers need help and encouragement as they apply new behaviors in the classroom. That is why professional development programs also consider how to develop school-based leadership to support ongoing improvements in classroom practice. Developing leadership capacity is often achieved through providing opportunities for teachers to take on roles as facilitators of other teachers' learning, such as coaches, mentors, and facilitators of professional development. Finally, just as we know that plants can only thrive in nutritious soil, good teaching practice can only thrive in cultures that support growth and change. Schools often need to make changes in the culture to better support collegial learning versus isolation, adoption of best practices versus adherence to the status quo, the development of collective responsibility versus hierarchy, and a commitment to learning for all. Engaging in collegial learning opportunities contributes to this culture and the fourth outcome—building a professional learning community. Implementing strategies that are designed to achieve the first three outcomes can also contribute to creating schools as communities of rigorous and ongoing learning that, ultimately, achieve increased student learning.

What is our cycle of implementation?

The second important question to consider is what your implementation cycle is and where your teachers are currently in the cycle. The idea of a cycle of implementation refers to the way in which teachers' learning is sequenced over time. The research on change that describes and anticipates how teachers' needs change over time is helpful to guide the cycle of professional development implementation (Hall & Hord, 2006). Different strategies can be more appropriate for people depending on where they are in the change process. For example, at the beginning of the process, teachers may need concrete information first about what they will learn and its purpose. As they learn, they want more how-to advice and images of what the practices look like in real classrooms. Later, they want ways to collaborate with others on the use of the practice and to assess impact on students (Hall & Hord, 2006).

The Concerns-Based Adoption Model (CBAM), discussed in Chapter 2, describes the emerging questions or concerns that teachers have as they are introduced to and take on new programs, practices, or processes (Hall & Hord, 2006). These concerns develop from questions that are more self-oriented (e.g., "What is it?" "How will it affect me?" and "What will I have to do?") to those that are task-oriented (e.g., "How can I get more organized?" "Why is it taking so much time?" and "How can I best manage the materials and schedules?"), and finally, when these concerns begin to be resolved, to more impact-oriented concerns (e.g., "How is this affecting students?" and "How can I improve what I'm doing so all students can learn?").

This model suggests that teacher concerns can guide the selection of strategies for professional development and provide insight into the content of the strategies in order to adequately address teachers' needs and concerns as they go through the change process. For example, if the goal of the professional development is to increase teachers' content knowledge so they can provide more inquiry or problem solving approaches in science or mathematics classes, the designer might choose to first offer teachers' an immersion experience in science or mathematics and then workshops that help raise teachers' awareness of what new teaching practices look (and feel) like in action. They learn the content through the immersion experiences and get a sense of new roles teachers must play through the workshops such as the use of a learning cycle for inquiry, how to use higher-order questioning, how to select students' mathematics or science work to show in the classroom, and the flow of instruction.

Another approach for the same goal might be to use new curriculum or textbooks as the basis for teacher learning. As teachers experience some of the lessons in the new curriculum they are expected to use with their students, they gain understanding of what the new material is, how it is organized, and what the learning sequence is. As they engage as learners, they develop content knowledge from the materials and become aware of the instructional strategies that are used in the curriculum materials. This experience guides their planning for how they will use the materials and may offer time-management and classroom-management techniques. Such strategies can help teachers translate what they are learning into their practice and engage teachers in drawing on their knowledge base to plan instruction and improve their teaching. As they practice new moves in their classrooms, they need opportunities to meet with other teachers to discuss what is working and how to make refinements. Through this, they increase their understanding and their skills.

Teachers' more impact-oriented questions can be addressed through opportunities for them to examine student work or to conduct action research into their own questions about student learning. During these latter stages of learning, teachers are often engaged in examining their experiences in the classroom, assessing the impact of the changes they have made on their students, and thinking about ways to improve. At this point in their learning, teachers also reflect on others' practice, relating it to their own and generating ideas for improvement.

What are the factors that guide and inform the selection and combination of strategies?

As a designer, it is important to keep the goals of the professional development firmly in the foreground while planning as well as to consider the cycle of implementation when sequencing teachers' learning experiences. As you engage in the planning stage, there are four factors that can facilitate your decisions about which strategies to select and in what sequence:

1. *Individual teachers will have different, and often multiple, learning needs, will be in different learning stages, at different points along the professional continuum, and this will be true at every point during the implementation of your plan.* Often, designers create a professional development plan that anticipates teachers' initial learning needs and stages of learning but then fails to anticipate the arrival of teachers new to the school or district or that teachers' learning needs will evolve over time. It is also important to consider the professional development continuum that suggests teachers need different supports at different points in their career. Beginning teachers may need opportunities to learn content and be inducted into the school culture.

For example, new teachers need opportunities to learn the curriculum they will teach and can benefit from support of mentors or coaches. As teachers grow and become more experienced, it is critical to continue to support their learning through strategies that engage them in examination of their practices. And as teachers look for opportunities to develop outside of their classrooms and take on roles to support other teachers' learning—roles such as facilitators of study groups or lesson study, or leaders of demonstration lessons—it is important to provide experiences that enhance those roles. The lesson learned is that ongoing, sustained professional development that supports a community of learners includes strategies that address all teachers' needs at every point in their careers.

2. *No one or two strategies can effectively result in achievement of the four interconnected goals and increased student learning.* Rather, it is the combination of multiple strategies, offered at different points in teachers' careers, which will contribute to the achievement of the goals. An effective professional development plan includes a balance of strategies that support the four goals. It is also important to keep in mind what we know from research and best practice—that it is when teachers make changes in their instructional approaches that we see concurrent changes in student learning. Teachers enact changes in their practices as the result of reflecting on their learning and learning how to apply their new knowledge, and as designers, you will need to include strategies that contribute to both outcomes.

3. *Some strategies may be more appropriate at certain times, whereas others become a permanent practice in the school.* For example, you might consider periodically offering specialized learning experiences like weeklong inquiry institutes or immersion in content through courses, since the structure and purpose of these strategies is primarily focused on increased content knowledge. Other strategies, such as examining student work, demonstration lessons, mentoring, coaching, and lesson study, are ones that you might consider institutionalizing in the school's culture as the ongoing ways teachers work together. These strategies support teachers' continuous improvement and are often used by schools that operate as professional learning communities.

4. *Strategies are led by professionals who have the requisite expertise to facilitate adult learning in the subject area.* All professional learning experiences for teachers require facilitation by people who understand both the structure of the strategy itself and have in-depth content

Four factors facilitate designers' decisions about which strategies to select and in what sequence:

1. Individual teachers will have different, and often multiple, learning needs, will be in different learning stages, at different points along the professional continuum, and this will be true at every point during the implementation of your plan.

2. No one or two strategies can effectively result in achievement of the four interconnected goals and increased student learning.

3. Some strategies may be more appropriate at certain times, whereas others become a permanent practice in the school.

4. Strategies are led by professionals who have the requisite expertise to facilitate adult learning in the subject area.

knowledge, pedagogical content knowledge, and an understanding of adult learning theory and instructional practices. Part of the designers' job is to make sure the leaders of learning have the requisite expertise and are provided with opportunities to reflect on feedback from teachers they work with to make improvements and to engage in activities to continue to enhance their own learning.

As a designer of professional learning experiences for teachers—whether you are a professional developer at the district or state level, a coach or mentor, a school-based administrator, or a teacher leader—the process of developing your plan involves selecting a balance of strategies that address the desired outcomes and match the developmental level of the participants. At any point in the implementation of the plan, you should be able to answer the question, "How are my actions supporting the outcomes and goals of the professional development plan and addressing the needs and concerns of my diverse audience of teachers?"

A REPERTOIRE OF STRATEGIES FOR PROFESSIONAL LEARNING

The remainder of this chapter describes 16 specific professional development strategies that support the teaching and learning of science and mathematics. The 16 strategies are grouped into four clusters: (1) immersion in content, standards, and research, (2) examining teaching and learning, (3) aligning and implementing curriculum, and (4) professional development structures (see Figure 5.3).

The strategies within the first three clusters share a common focus for teacher learning that is reflected in the title of the cluster. For example, the

Figure 5.3   Strategies for Professional Learning

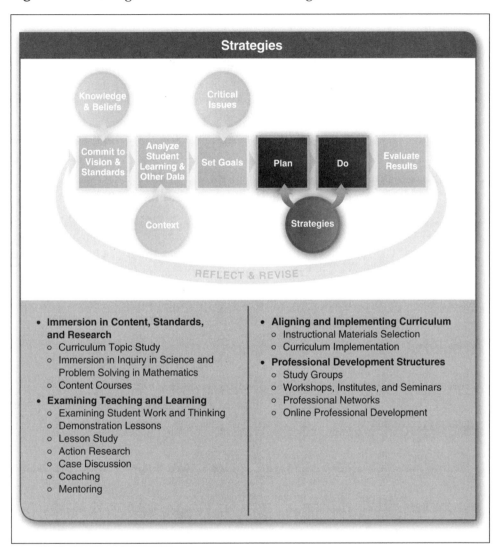

three strategies within the immersion in content, standards, and research cluster focus on enhancing teachers' in-depth understanding of and engagement with science and mathematics content and processes, the standards and research that guide and inform the content to be taught, how students learn the content, and the science and mathematics pedagogical content knowledge needed to teach the disciplines.

The six strategies within the cluster examining teaching and learning emphasize teachers engaging in collaborative learning experiences to reflect on their teaching practices and their students' learning. These six strategies are practice-based and engage teachers in grappling with authentic issues encountered in their classrooms. The two strategies within the cluster aligning and implementing curriculum are focused on curriculum as the catalyst for teacher learning. In both strategies, teachers' learning is focused on learning about, trying, reflecting on, and sharing information about teaching and learning in the context of selecting or implementing new curriculum.

The fourth cluster, professional development structures, includes four strategies that are used as structures into which the other strategies are often embedded. For example, within a study group, teachers often engage in case discussions or examination of student work.

We invite professional developers to become familiar with the 16 strategies for teacher learning in this chapter and to reflect on how to best combine them to address local goals, needs, and other contextual factors. The remainder of this chapter describes the four clusters and the strategies within each cluster, starting with the underlying assumptions and implementation requirements for a cluster of strategies. Each individual strategy is then described and discussed following a common structure that includes:

- *Opening Vignette.* A brief practice-based illustration of the strategy in action and, often, in combination with other strategies.
- *Key Elements.* A description of the characteristics specific to the strategy.
- *Intended Outcomes.* A discussion of why the strategy supports one, or more, of the four interconnected goals.
- *Combining Strategies.* A discussion that explores how the strategy often combines with other strategies.
- *Issues to Consider.* A discussion of some of the issues to consider when selecting and implementing the strategy.
- *Resources.* A listing of resources for learning more about the strategy.

As you explore the 16 strategies in this chapter, you may decide to read the chapter from beginning to end. You might also want to consider learning about the clusters and the strategies within them in an order that best meets your own interests and needs. Once you have explored the strategies, we encourage you to read Chapter 6, which provides examples of how various professional development programs identified and combined strategies to achieve specific outcomes within different contexts.

Immersion in Content, Standards, and Research

Figure 5.4   Strategies for Professional Learning: Immersion in Content, Standards, and Research

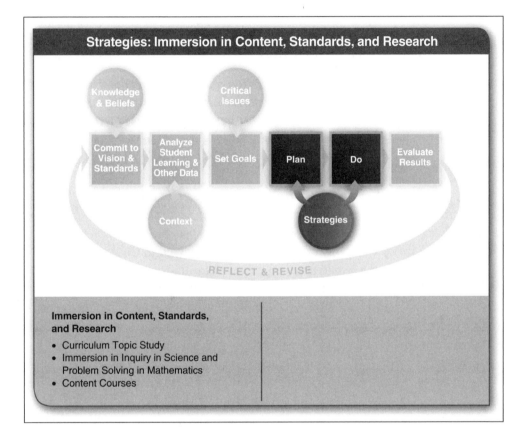

The three professional learning strategies described in this section reflect approaches to teacher learning that engage teachers in deepening their science and mathematics content and pedagogical content knowledge and their understanding of standards and research. These strategies are curriculum topic study, immersion in inquiry in science and problem solving in mathematics, and content courses (see Figure 5.4). All three strategies are grounded in research indicating that teachers' learning is enhanced through direct experience with science and mathematics content and the processes of inquiry and problem solving, and that teachers' need to understand the progression of content knowledge from grade to grade and recognize what content is difficult for students and commonly held conceptions that may impede learning (American Association for the Advancement of Science [AAAS], 2001, 2007; Bransford et al., 1999; NCTM, 2003a; National Research Council [NRC], 1996).

Immersion experiences for teachers of science and mathematics are based on several assumptions about the disciplines of science and mathematics, teachers, learning, and professional development. These assumptions form the foundation for the design and implementation of the three strategies in this cluster.

Underlying Assumptions

Science and mathematics comprise process and content. The content of science and mathematics is the understandings, meanings, and models that have been created and continue to be created by scientists and mathematicians. Science and mathematics as inquiry and problem solving encompass the methodologies used to develop scientific and mathematics knowledge and understanding.

Teachers benefit from learning experiences that are based on the same principles that they are expected to implement with students, as well as from opportunities to learn what content and instructional approaches are recommended by standards and research. As discussed in Chapter 2, the principles of human learning apply equally well to adults and children; they both learn through direct experience and by constructing their own meanings from those experiences using previous knowledge. Immersion in content experiences provides opportunities for teachers to learn science and mathematics content and processes at their own level of learning. In the case of the curriculum topic study strategy, teachers gain a set of tools they can turn to whenever they encounter a content question or wish to learn more about the research on how students learn science or mathematics.

Teachers must have an in-depth understanding of science and mathematics content and processes. Through immersion in scientific inquiry or mathematical problem solving, teachers necessarily learn both content and the requisite skills for investigating and learning the science or mathematics. This is necessary for teachers to provide students with in-depth learning of science and mathematics content and processes. For example, a teacher with an understanding of the interconnected concepts of buoyancy and density is better able to guide students' learning during inquiry-based activities when students ask, "Why does the cork float and the marble sink?" By engaging in curriculum topic study, teachers gain an understanding of what ideas related to buoyancy and density are developed at each grade level and what makes this topic difficult for students to understand. In mathematics, a teacher who has a firm understanding of fractions would "hear a student's comment that 'the larger the number on the bottom, the smaller the fraction'" as being "true only when the numerator remains constant (1/5 is less than 1/3, but 3/5 is not less than 2/4)" and would be able to provide additional problem-solving experiences to help the student refine his or her understanding (Cohen & Ball, 1999, p. 8).

Teachers must have an in-depth understanding of the science and mathematics standards and related research that guide teaching and learning of the content. Studying the standards and research on how people learn specific concepts and topics within science and mathematics contributes to teachers' effectiveness. Through a rigorous process of study, teachers explore connections across topics, clarify central concepts, and enhance their skills in facilitating students' conceptual understanding of the content.

Implementation Requirements

Qualified Facilitators

Guiding teachers through the inquiry process, solving challenging mathematical problems, and investigating standards and research must be a specified goal of the professional learning experience and one that is carried out by someone with expertise in content and process. Often, immersion experiences are cofacilitated by scientists or mathematicians and professional developers who can, in collaboration, support teachers' learning of the content and the process of the disciplines.

Long-Term Experiences

Immersion in content, standards, and research experiences require in-depth, learning over time. They often occur within a one-week (or longer) institute or a semester-long course.

Access to Resources

Teachers need access to standards and research books and articles, as well as physical materials as they engage in immersion in inquiry and problem solving.

Administrative Support

Administrators provide time and incentives for teachers to participate, ensure access to resources and experts, and offer opportunities to share their learning with other teachers and implement that learning in their classrooms.

CURRICULUM TOPIC STUDY

A group of Grade 5 through 8 teachers and the district math coordinator attended a two-day program on how to use research on learning mathematics and the national standards to enhance the teaching of mathematics and promote greater alignment of what mathematics is taught across the middle grades. They practiced using the six different sections of Curriculum Topic Study (CTS) (Keeley & Rose, 2006). Working in groups of two, the teachers each explored CTS Sections I through IV focused on two algebra topics: expressions and equations, and variables. Later they would work together on Section V since it is the one focused on articulation across the grade levels.

The teachers who were immersed in Section I reported out what all high school graduates should know and understand about these topics and reported that they were surprised to learn what the standards consider basic adult literacy in these topics. They admitted that they did not even understand some of the content that the standards say all high school graduates should know. They shared a few areas where they want to get more information on the content. The team who read CTS Section II reported that this section helps teachers understand the instructional implications for teaching the topics to students at different grade levels. They shared that they learned that we have to be thinking about laying the groundwork for algebra much earlier than they thought. They reported that the fifth-grade students could be using patterns and models to write and solve simple equations and graph their equations (NCTM, 2006). The Section III group reported out their discovery of what students should learn at each grade level and connected their reading to what the Section II group reported, saying that they could see why it was important for the fifth-grade students to begin to write and solve simple equations, because in sixth grade, students solve one-step equations and develop understanding of the need to have equality on both sides of an equation (NCTM, 2006).

The teacher teams started seeing many connections between what other teams had read and what they read as well as some of the logical connections and progression of learning from grade to grade. One teacher suddenly said, "I can see why anyone trying to reduce redundancy and promote coherence in the curriculum would start by reading this research!"

The team that read Section IV discovered the difficulties students sometimes encounter as they make sense of what variables represent. They reported that the research says students view variables as abbreviations or labels and not as a representation of quantity (Stephens, 2005). They went on to say that before teaching students to start plugging in numbers and solving the equations, they needed to make sure they were building an understanding of what a variable is.

The teachers reflected on what they learned from the readings, and together they all reviewed the readings to Section V to discuss what the research and standards suggest about sequencing learning across the grade levels. Their overall purpose was to discover how the mathematics topics they were teaching in Grades 5 through 8 were aligned with what the research and standards say students need to know and understand in algebra and what is needed to help them think algebraically. Through the different sections of CTS, the teachers learned what all literate adults should understand, what students at different grade levels can learn so that they are ready for algebra in the higher elementary and middle grades and the common misconceptions and difficulties students face in understanding variables and what they represent, and the concept of equality. The teachers came back together again later to explore how what they learned from CTS would inform their sequencing of learning activities in Grades 5 through 8.

Curriculum topic study (CTS) is a unique professional development strategy on its own and a valuable supplement to many other professional development strategies. CTS is basically a rigorous, methodical study process that leads teachers to develop their understanding of the key curriculum topics in science and mathematics that are found in national standards. *Science Curriculum Topic Study* (Keeley, 2005) provides 147 different one-page study guides, and *Mathematics Curriculum Topic Study* (Keeley & Rose, 2006) provides 92 different one-page study guides that teachers can use to explore science and mathematics topics. Each one-page study guide includes Sections I–VI:

Section I: What should all twelfth-grade graduates know about the topic?

Section II: What are the instructional implications for teaching the topic?

Section III: What are the specific ideas or concepts that should be learned at each grade span?

Section IV: What is the research on learning this topic and what misconceptions should teachers be aware of?

Section V: How do the concepts and ideas of this topic develop coherently over the grades (K–12)?

Section VI: What do our local and state standards say about teaching and learning this topic?

The CTS approach was adapted from the American Association for the Advancement of Science's (AAAS) Project 2061 study of a benchmark by professional developers at the Maine Mathematics and Science Alliance. The CTS project developed a procedure similar to Project 2061's study of a benchmark to examine teaching and learning at the larger grain size of a curricular topic.

KEY ELEMENTS

CTS uses a rigorous, methodical study process. Through CTS, teachers engage in true study of a topic. They read text, from standards documents and science and mathematics trade publications that have been pre-vetted to ensure alignment with the topic of study. Teachers reflect on the reading and make connections to their own practice and may set goals for additional learning around content that is still unclear.

> **KEY ELEMENTS FOR CURRICULUM TOPIC STUDY**
>
> - CTS uses a rigorous, methodical study process.
> - The CTS study guide is used to facilitate learning.
> - Access to resource books is essential.
> - Teachers engage in "CTS talk."
> - Teachers engage with the CTS learning cycle.

The CTS study guide is used to facilitate learning. Teachers use a CTS study guide that directs them to a set of readings for the topic they are studying and refers them to a Web site for supplemental readings. This takes the guesswork out of trying to find the right section or the right resource to read on any given topic. There are two sets of study guides, one for mathematics, *Mathematics Curriculum Topic Study,* and one for science, *Science Curriculum Topic Study.*

Access to resource books is essential. At the heart of CTS is a set of resource books that are used with the CTS study guide to locate vetted readings within each of the six sections of study. The resources include the four books from AAAS's Project 2061, including *Science for All Americans, Benchmarks for Science Literacy,* and the *Atlas of Science Literacy, Volumes 1 and 2;* two books from the National Council of Teachers of Mathematics, *Principles and Standards for School Mathematics* and *Research Companion to Principles and Standards for School Mathematics;* the National Research Council's *National Science Education Standards;* a set of adult science and mathematics trade books, *Science Matters* and *Beyond Numeracy;* and the collection of research on students' science ideas, *Making Sense of Secondary Science.* (See "Resources" at the end of the discussion of CTS for citation information on each CTS resource book.)

Teachers engage in "CTS talk." Teachers learn to use CTS talk, which involves citing the evidence in the readings to make any claims and to report out findings.

Teachers engage with the CTS learning cycle. Most CTS professional development sessions are designed around the CTS learning cycle (Keeley, 2005). The cycle involves the following stages: engagement, elicitation, exploration, development, application, and reflection. By engaging in each stage, teachers assess what they know and what they learned, apply what they learned to teaching, and reflect on how they will use what they learn.

INTENDED OUTCOMES

Depending on the use of CTS, there can be different outcomes. Some of the most common goals served by this strategy are to create awareness of the mathematics and science content needed for basic adult literacy and to set goals for deepening content knowledge in areas that are weak; to understand what research suggests about teaching different science and mathematics topics; to become facile at identifying the recommended grade spans for teaching certain mathematics and science content; to become aware of common misconceptions students' hold and gain insight into how to spot them; and to better understand how science and mathematics ideas develop across Grades K–12.

One of the powerful uses of CTS is to *develop leaders* for mathematics and science education. Leaders such as university scientists or mathematics professors working with teachers, teacher leaders who are supporting a wide range of grade levels or professional developers may all have excellent background in the science or mathematics they know, but may not have a deep understanding of what content is appropriate at what grade levels, how concepts are nested and build on one another, nor what common difficulties and misconceptions students have when learning the content. CTS helps leaders fill the gaps in their knowledge so they can be better informed leaders. Whether you are in a coach role or you are a professor leading a content institute, conducting a CTS study on the topics of your work can broaden your knowledge to support you to design more effective experiences for teachers and provide more research and standards-based feedback and input.

COMBINING STRATEGIES

While CTS can be used on its own to explore the research and standards on a single mathematics or science topic or on many topics, it is often used in combination with other professional development strategies. For example, when educators are engaging in strategies to examine teaching and learning such as lesson study, demonstration lessons, or case discussions, it is advisable to use CTS prior to observing lessons or cases to inform the analysis. Teachers would then ask, "If this lesson or case reflected the research what would we see?" They would develop a summary of the readings for the topic and grade level of the lesson or case and use that to inform the discussion and analysis. Likewise, when mentors or coaches are working with novice teachers they might include CTS as a process for deepening teachers' knowledge and understanding. Together, the coach or mentor and novice teacher would do the CTS readings and discuss how they influence the teaching of the topic. Then they might use what they learned to design or modify a lesson plan. Designs for using CTS and embedding it into many other professional development designs can be found in *A Leader's Guide to Science Curriculum Topic Study* (Mundry, Keeley & Landel, 2009) and *A Leader's Guide to Mathematics Curriculum Topic Study* (Mundry, Keeley, Rose, & Carroll, forthcoming).

> **Curriculum topic study in science and mathematics combines well with other strategies:**
>
> - Study groups
> - Demonstration lessons
> - Coaching
> - Mentoring
> - Action research
> - Examining student work and thinking
> - Lesson study
> - Curriculum implementation

Issues to Consider

The CTS process is rigorous and involves significant reading and processing of readings. Teachers may encounter content that is very new to them and may become frustrated. It is very important that the facilitators provide a safe environment where teachers can surface questions about content they do not understand so they can get additional help. In addition, the CTS process asks teachers to engage in behaviors that may not be routine—they must speak from the evidence of research and standards and not simply refer to what they do in their classroom or school. Developing and keeping to this norm is hard, and teachers need to be reminded to "stick to the facts" in the readings and avoid inferences and connections until they have a deeper understanding.

Obtaining the resources needed to engage in CTS presents a challenge to anyone with little or no access to the required books and materials. While many of the resources are available online, many CTS users find they prefer to have their own copy of each of the resource books. This will require a considerable investment. An alternative is to buy just those resources that are not available online and print copies of the online books, or buy used copies that are usually readily available.

Resources

Curriculum Topic Study Web site: www.curriculumtopicstudy.org

Keeley, P. (2005). *Science curriculum topic study: Bridging the gap between standards and practice.* Thousand Oaks, CA: Corwin.

Keeley, P., & Rose, C. M. (2006). *Mathematics curriculum topic study: Bridging the gap between standards and practice.* Thousand Oaks, CA: Corwin.

Mundry, S., Keeley, P., Rose, C., & Carroll, C. (forthcoming). *A leader's guide to mathematics curriculum topic study.* Thousand Oaks, CA: Corwin.

Mundry, S., Keeley, P., & Landel, C. (2009). *A leader's guide to science curriculum topic study.* Thousand Oaks, CA: Corwin.

Science Curriculum Topic Study Resource Books

American Association for the Advancement of Science. (1989). *Science for all Americans.* New York: Oxford University Press.

American Association for the Advancement of Science. (1993). *Benchmarks for science literacy.* New York: Oxford University Press.

American Association for the Advancement of Science. (2001, 2007). *Atlas of science literacy* (Vols. 1–2). Washington, DC: Author.

Driver, R., Squires, A., Rushworth, P., & Wood-Robinson, V. (1994). *Making sense of secondary science.* London: Routledge.

Hazen, R., & Trefil, J. (1991). *Science matters: Achieving scientific literacy.* New York: Anchor Books.

National Research Council. (1996). *National science education standards.* Washington, DC: National Academy Press.

Mathematics Curriculum Topic Study Resource Books

American Association for the Advancement of Science. (1989). *Science for all Americans.* New York: Oxford University Press.

American Association for the Advancement of Science. (1993). *Benchmarks for science literacy.* New York: Oxford University Press.

American Association for the Advancement of Science. (2001, 2007). *Atlas of science literacy* (Vols. 1–2). Washington, DC: Author.

National Council of Teachers of Mathematics. (2000). *Principles and standards for school mathematics.* Reston, VA: Author.

National Council of Teachers of Mathematics. (2003a). *A research companion to principles and standards for school mathematics.* Reston, VA: Author.

Paulos, J. A. (1992). *Beyond numeracy.* New York: Vintage Books.

IMMERSION IN INQUIRY IN SCIENCE AND PROBLEM SOLVING IN MATHEMATICS

Elaine, Teri, Kevin, and Shelly, mathematics teacher colleagues at Riverside School, were attending a weeklong immersion institute. As a prelude to a discussion on open-ended investigations, the institute facilitator presented the teachers with a mathematics problem and asked them to explore it: How many 1 ft. × 1 ft. square floor tiles would you need to make a border on the floor around the edge of a rectangular room? The group began by trying to decide what the smallest room could be that would have a tile border as described. After some discussion of the meaning of "border," they agreed that a 3 ft. × 3 ft. room would be the smallest and that it would have one tile in the interior. The group proceeded to build a model of the situation and concluded that the border would require eight tiles. At this point, Teri suggested that they look at a room that was 7 ft. × 8 ft. (She had drawn a sketch of the tile border for a 7 ft. × 8 ft. room while the other three members of the group were determining the smallest case.) Kevin suggested that they subtract the area of a 6 ft. × 5 ft. rectangle from the area of the 7 ft. × 8 ft. rectangle because this difference would result in the number of tiles on the border of the 7 ft. × 8 ft. rectangle. He used Teri's diagram to explain this solution method to the members of the group.

> The teachers continued to explore different cases and to make conjectures regarding the number of square tiles in the borders of rooms with different dimensions. After much discussion and exploration, Kevin suggested an approach that seemed to "work" for rooms of any dimension. They then tested the suggested generalization and concluded that it did indeed work for any case.
>
> Once the facilitator reconvened the large group, Kevin shared his small group's solution and illustrated their approach using the materials. The facilitator asked probing questions to further explore the group's solution, and other participants joined the discussion, raising their own questions. At several points in the discussion, the facilitator invited a participant to "test" an idea using the tiles.

Immersion in inquiry in science or problem solving in mathematics is the structured opportunity to experience, firsthand, science or mathematics content and processes. By becoming a learner of the content, teachers broaden their own understanding and knowledge of the content that they are addressing with their students. By learning through inquiry and problem solving—putting the principles of science or mathematics teaching and learning into practice and experiencing the processes for themselves—teachers are better prepared to implement the practices in their classrooms. The goal is to help teachers become competent in their content and reflective about how to best teach it. Immersion experiences are guided by knowledgeable and experienced facilitators with expertise in science or mathematics. The curriculum is designed specifically to highlight the processes of scientific inquiry and mathematical problem-solving approaches to learning mathematics and science content.

Often, immersion experiences are conducted during multiday institutes held during the summer months when teachers from multiple schools are available to participate, or are offered by organizations outside of the district, such as universities and colleges or science and mathematics education organizations. In some cases, teachers have opportunities to strengthen their knowledge base in content areas by becoming active participants in a mathematics or scientific community. The setting for this approach to immersion in content is usually a research environment, such as a scientific laboratory or a mathematics research group or a museum research department. In other words, teachers are immersed in scientists' or mathematicians' environments and teachers join them in their work and fully participate in research activities. The purpose of this approach to immersion is for teachers to learn science and mathematics content; to learn elements of the research process, such as designing experiments, creating mathematical models, and collecting, analyzing, and synthesizing data; and to develop a broader and increased understanding of the scientific and mathematics approaches to building knowledge and solving problems.

KEY ELEMENTS

Teachers are immersed in an intensive learning experience. Teachers are immersed in an intensive experience in which they focus on learning science or mathematics and are able to pursue content in-depth. In science, they participate fully in the generation of investigable questions, plan and conduct investigations that allow them to make

> ### KEY ELEMENTS FOR IMMERSION IN INQUIRY IN SCIENCE AND PROBLEM SOLVING IN MATHEMATICS
>
> - Teachers are immersed in an intensive learning experience.
> - One goal is learning how students learn science and mathematics.
> - Teachers' conceptions about science, mathematics, and teaching change.

meaning out of the inquiry activities, collect and organize data, make predictions, and gain a broader view of the science concepts they are investigating. In mathematics, they "generate compelling questions, conduct investigations to make meaning out of mathematical activities, collect and organize data, make predictions, measure and graph, and gain a broader view of the mathematics concepts they are investigating" (Eisenhower National Clearinghouse, 1998, p. 11).

One goal is learning how students learn science and mathematics. One goal of these experiences is to engage teachers in firsthand learning of what they are expected to practice in their classrooms—guiding students through inquiry-based science or mathematical problem solving.

Teachers' conceptions about science, mathematics, and teaching change. One outcome from in-depth immersion in the processes of learning science and mathematics is a change in teachers' conceptions of the nature of science or mathematics learning and teaching. For example, as teachers begin to see science or mathematics teaching as less a matter of knowledge transfer and more an activity in which knowledge is generated through making sense of or understanding the content, they begin to see their own role as teacher changing from a direct conveyor of knowledge to a guide helping students develop their own meaning from experiences. As Schmidt (2001) proposes, "A teacher's understanding and conception of subject matter is one of the major aspects that defines teacher quality. The key is that the conceptual problem-solving aspect, together with the attendant pedagogical approaches, must be embedded in real science content" (p. 162).

INTENDED OUTCOMES

The primary outcome of immersion in inquiry and problem solving is *enhancing teachers' knowledge.* The very nature of the strategy is focused on science and mathematics content and the processes of the disciplines. A secondary outcome is *enhancing quality teaching,* which is achieved by supporting teachers to implement their new knowledge in their teaching practices.

As noted in the key elements for this strategy, qualified and experienced facilitators are essential for this immersion strategy, a role that teacher leaders and professional developers often play. This strategy lends itself well to *preparing teacher leaders* and professional developers to serve in those roles by enhancing their own content knowledge. Additionally, coaches and mentors benefit from immersion in science and mathematics content to enhance their support of other teachers. In essence, the strategy is an effective one for enhancing the content knowledge of all leaders who directly support other teachers' learning.

COMBINING STRATEGIES

Immersing teachers in deepening their science and mathematics content knowledge is supported by participation in various other strategies that enable teachers to translate their knowledge into practice. For example, a strategy such as action research during which teachers might study the ways in which their own enhanced content knowledge influences their use of questioning strategies or how they engage students with the content. Teachers would also benefit from bringing their enhanced content understanding to the examination of student work and thinking, as well as participating in lesson study, giving them the opportunity to use their knowledge to enhance specific science or mathematics lessons. The strategy might also be implemented in combination with curriculum implementation to extend teachers' content understanding of the concepts included in the new curriculum.

Immersion in inquiry in science and problem solving in mathematics combines well with other strategies:

- Action research
- Examining student work and thinking
- Lesson study
- Curriculum implementation

ISSUES TO CONSIDER

Even with extensive coursework in their preservice programs, many teachers come to the teaching of science or mathematics without having had opportunities to engage in science inquiry or mathematical problem solving. An immersion strategy can provide an opportunity to help teachers address this gap in their learning. Immersion experiences are beneficial, but they have their drawbacks as well. Teachers with limited time and programs with limited resources may not be able to afford the time required for in-depth investigation and may opt for shorter-term experiences.

Another issue is where immersion in science inquiry or problem solving in mathematics best fits into a teacher's learning sequence. For example, at the City College Workshop Center in New York (see Chapter 6), Hubert Dyasi used immersion in science inquiry to initiate teachers into a new view of science. Others may choose immersion as a more in-depth enrichment, once teachers learn to use and are comfortable with a set of materials for their students. They then gain a better understanding of how to help students explore important ideas, follow their own lines of investigation, generate alternative solutions to problems, or all three. For example, teachers implementing new standards-based mathematics programs often experience the need to increase their own content knowledge through immersion experiences.

One additional issue related to immersion experiences is the critical need to directly connect teacher learning of science and mathematics to what is taught in the classroom. For example, although an elementary school teacher might personally benefit from learning calculus, unless there is an emphasis in the immersion experience to help teachers translate the new knowledge into direct application in the classroom, the professional development aspect of the experience may be lost.

RESOURCES

Biological Sciences Curriculum Study. (n.d). *BSCS science institutes.* Retrieved August 17, 2009, from http://bscs.org/professionaldevelopment/pdservices/scienceinstitutes

Exploratorium. (n.d.). *Institute for inquiry.* Retrieved August 17, 2009, from www.exploratorium.edu/IFI

WestEd & WGBH Educational Foundation. (2003). *Teachers as learners: A multimedia kit for professional development in science and mathematics.* Thousand Oaks, CA: Corwin. (See Tape 4, Program 4, "Immersion in Biotechnology," Biological Sciences Curriculum Study, Colorado Springs, CO; Tape 3, Program 1, "Scientific Inquiry," Institute for Inquiry at the Exploratorium, San Francisco; Tape 4, Program 3, "Immersion in Number Theory," PROMYS, Boston University, Boston; and Tape 2, Program 4, "Immersion in Spatial Reasoning," San Diego State University, San Diego, CA.)

CONTENT COURSES

In preparation for the coming school year, Terrence reviewed his folder on revisions he needed to make to some of his middle school science courses. He remembered that he had analyzed his students pre- and postassessments for the force and motion module, and the data indicated that students did not fully understand the concepts. Terrence knew that his own understanding was not as strong as it needed to be in order to facilitate his students' learning. He talked with some of the other teachers and the department chair to learn more about his options for enhancing his own content understanding. One of the other science teachers had taken an online course that she highly recommended, and Terrence got information from her about the background of the organization offering the course, the quality of the instructor, and whether he could obtain graduate credit for taking the course. He then enrolled in the course and was excited about the structure of the course as well as the in-depth content he would be learning. Through pre-readings and facilitated discussions, the syllabi noted the topics for learning, including speed, velocity, acceleration, force, mass, weight, Newton's laws of motion, and the applications of the concepts. A few weeks into the course, Terrence was really beginning to more fully understand the physical science concepts, and the 90-minute online sessions included both presentations and discussions that enabled him to fully participate in exploring questions and ideas. Terrence was keeping notes during the course on the specific changes he wanted to make in the force and motion module he would teach in the fall and how he would engage students in exploring the concepts in more depth.

Content courses provide opportunities for teachers to focus intensely on topics they teach for an extended period of time. Most often, courses are facilitated by an external expert (e.g., university professor, scientist, or mathematician) who has in-depth understanding of the topic. Content courses designed for educators also have the added benefit of an expert facilitator with a foundational knowledge of the education environment and how the specific content is translated into classroom instruction. Sometimes, such courses are cotaught by an educator and a content specialist. As the opening vignette illustrates, content courses offered online or through hybrid or blended models (i.e., partly in person and partly online) are becoming more and more prevalent. The content organizations (e.g., NSTA and NCTM) either offer these courses or provide links to other organizations or universities where educators can enroll in courses.

In many cases, content courses serve as an entry experience into a series of professional learning opportunities. For example, a teacher might enroll in a content course, followed by a video case discussion or demonstration lesson where the content is being taught with a group of students. Since content courses are frequently professional learning experiences that teachers embark upon individually, ensuring concurrent or follow-up opportunities to apply the learning to teaching is critical.

Effective courses for educators attend to and reflect the principles of effective professional development and adult learning. For example, "sit-and-get" learning is not the model, but rather, the learner engages in reading, explorations, investigations, problem solving, and discussions to make meaning of the content and has opportunities to reflect on the learning and the application of that learning.

KEY ELEMENTS

Courses are facilitated or taught by a content expert. Since the intent of this professional learning strategy is to deepen teachers' content knowledge, the leader of the course needs to have extensive understanding of the content. Ideally, the facilitator is also able to connect the content that is the focus of the course to other topics and concepts within the discipline.

> ### KEY ELEMENTS FOR CONTENT COURSES
>
> - Courses are facilitated or taught by a content expert.
> - Courses are aligned with the content that teachers teach.
> - Access to the curriculum or syllabus is provided prior to enrollment.

Courses are aligned with the content that teachers teach. Although teachers may have an interest in learning new content, it is important that the specific topic or concepts that are the focus of the course are in alignment with the content the teacher teaches. The purpose of this strategy is to enhance teachers' ability to apply strong content knowledge to strengthen teaching and learning in classrooms, and therefore, the content should be grade-level appropriate and standards-driven.

Access to the curriculum or syllabus is provided prior to enrollment. To make informed decisions about the appropriateness of the course, individual teachers need access to the specific information about the content that will be addressed during the course.

INTENDED OUTCOMES

The primary outcome of content courses is *enhancing teachers' knowledge.* The very nature of the strategy is focused on science and mathematics content and the processes of the disciplines. A secondary outcome is *enhancing quality teaching,* since the purpose for participating in a course is to deepen knowledge of the content the teacher teaches. However, transferring the new learning into practice needs to be supported through engagement in other strategies that help teachers apply their learning.

As noted in the key elements for this strategy, qualified and experienced facilitators are essential, and this strategy lends itself to achieving the third outcome, *developing leadership capacity.* Teacher leaders, coaches, and professional developers who possess the necessary depth of content knowledge are ideal candidates for leading content courses, and they often collaborate with professors from a local college to offer a course. Additionally, content courses lend themselves well to helping teacher leaders and professional developers enhance their knowledge to serve in those roles. Like other strategies in this cluster, content courses are effective for enhancing the content knowledge of all leaders who directly support other teachers' learning.

COMBINING STRATEGIES

As noted above, supporting teachers to enhance their science and mathematics content knowledge is supported by participation in various other strategies that enable teachers to translate their knowledge into practice. For example, bringing enhanced content knowledge to the process of lesson study increases the quality of the lesson as well as provides an opportunity for teachers to apply what they have learned. Similarly, curriculum implementation is supported when teachers also increase their content understanding, since they are better able to facilitate students' learning of the content in the curriculum. This strategy might also be used in combination with instructional materials selection, where teachers' in-depth content knowledge would help them assess the quality and sequence of the content in the materials.

> **Content courses combine well with other strategies:**
>
> - Lesson study
> - Curriculum implementation
> - Instructional materials selection

ISSUES TO CONSIDER

Often, content courses as a professional learning strategy are thought to be most appropriate for elementary teachers since their preservice coursework usually does not include many content courses within a discipline. However, many middle and high school teachers can also benefit from further enhancing their knowledge of science or mathematics, and this strategy can be appropriate for any teacher who has an identified need to enhance his or her knowledge of the content. It is an appropriate strategy for a teacher to include in his or her own portfolio of professional learning experiences.

Although it is essential for teachers to enhance their content knowledge when needed, this strategy is not sufficient to ensure changes in teaching practice. Teachers also need opportunities that help them to translate their learning into practice (e.g., by implementing the curriculum), to actually use their new knowledge (e.g., through improving lessons or asking better questions in the classroom), and to reflect on their learning and practice (e.g., with support from a coach). It is the combined and sequenced learning opportunities that can best support teachers' learning and teaching.

Another issue is the quality of the course that is offered and the expertise of the instructor. In this age of technology-delivered professional learning opportunities, there is a plethora of available content courses from which to select. However, not all courses are of the same quality, and teachers need to fully investigate the credibility of the organization as well as the reputation of the instructors. Equally important is the need for teachers to investigate the format of the course and to select one that best fits their needs. For example, courses are offered through colleges and universities, as well as other organizations and programs that require in-person attendance at all sessions. In some cases, a course may be offered within the school district for all teachers who wish to take it. This format makes courses easily accessible. Other courses employ a hybrid or blended format, requiring some in-person class time as well as online learning between the in-person sessions. Given the diversity of formats, teachers are well positioned to find options that best fit their personal and professional needs.

If schools, districts, or programs are considering content courses as one component of teachers' professional learning, attention needs to be given to ensuring equitable access to the courses. For example, if enhancing content knowledge is a "requirement" of a program, all teachers need options for exploring courses with different ranges of costs, that provide credit toward advanced degrees or promotions, and that can be taken in person or online to accommodate individual needs.

RESOURCES

Massachusetts Department of Elementary and Secondary Education. (2009). *The Massachusetts Intel Mathematics Initiative (MIMI).* Available from www.doe.mass.edu/omste/news07/mimi.html (MIMI is an 80-hour mathematics content course.)

National Council of Teachers of Mathematics Web site: http://nctm.org (NCTM offers online courses, seminars, and workshops.)

National Science Teachers Association Web site: http://learningcenter.nsta.org/?lid=lnavhp (NSTA offers online short courses.)

Public Broadcasting System Web site: www.pbs.org/teacherline (Public Broadcasting System offers online content courses through PBS TeacherLine.)

TERC Web site: www.terc.edu/ (TERC offers mathematics and science online courses.)

Examining Teaching and Learning

Figure 5.5   Strategies for Professional Learning: Examining Teaching and Learning

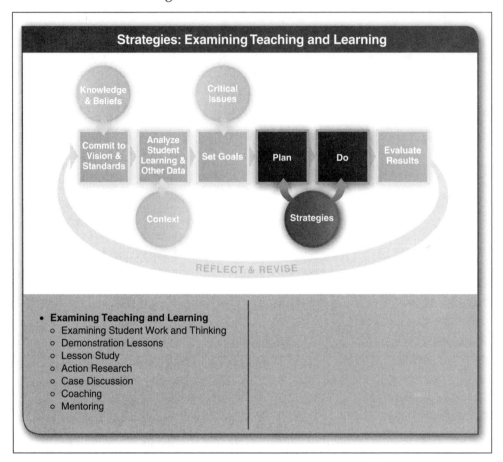

The seven strategies described in this section emphasize teachers engaging in professional learning experiences to examine their teaching practices and their students' learning (see Figure 5.5). The seven strategies are: (1) examining student work and thinking, (2) demonstration lessons, (3) lesson study, (4) action research, (5) case discussion, (6) coaching, and (7) mentoring.

These strategies provide opportunities for *practice-based* learning—the opportunity to solve and grapple with authentic issues encountered in classrooms and schools (Hawley & Valli, 2000; Mumme & Seago, 2002). Many professionals use "practice sessions" as a means to enhance their knowledge, skills, and performance. For example, musicians, lawyers, athletes, and medical personnel are called on to practice through demonstration and gain tips and feedback from colleagues and coaches.

Practice-based professional development allows teachers to examine the "artifacts" of their work (Ball & Cohen, 1999; Driscoll, 2001). For example, by watching videos or observing in classrooms, teachers are able to examine and reflect on their and others' teaching practices; examining student work and thinking provides an opportunity to explore what students are and are not understanding in science and mathematics; and by uncovering the conceptual development addressed in instructional materials and designing lessons to enhance that development, teachers increase their own science and mathematics content and pedagogical knowledge. In addition, discussion of other forms of artifacts, such as cases or actual observations of classroom-based experiences, provides an opportunity to engage in in-depth analysis and reflection on answering some of the most critical questions that teachers face in their work: "What is good teaching?" "What concepts in science and mathematics are difficult for students to understand?"

The seven strategies described in this section are grounded in several assumptions about teaching, learning, and professional development.

Underlying Assumptions

Teachers are competent professionals whose experience, expertise, and observations are valuable sources of knowledge, skill development, and inspiration for other teachers. This is an assumption professional developers must subscribe to in order to effectively use the strategies in this cluster. Some people believe that what science and mathematics teachers need is assistance from an outside expert. The critical and specialized knowledge that experienced teachers have—pedagogical content knowledge (Shulman, 1986)—is sometimes not acknowledged as valuable or worth sharing. It is this very knowledge, however, that helps teachers understand what their students need, how they come to understand and apply mathematics and science content, and what they need to increase that understanding.

Stepping outside of the teaching moment is a valuable way of examining teaching and learning. When teachers are engaged in interactions with students in their classrooms, they are constantly making decisions, gauging the appropriate next steps, and anticipating questions to ask of students. Being in the "teaching moment" does not provide an opportunity for teachers to reflect on their teaching decisions and "moves" or students' interactions. It is a valuable experience for teachers to observe other teachers with the explicit purpose of examining instructional strategies, listening to student ideas, and seeing a lesson in action.

When teachers observe examples of practice showing learning results with students, they are more likely to implement and sustain changes in their own teaching. For most teachers, it is seeing enhanced student learning that leads to a commitment to teaching in new ways or using new instructional materials. Observing others teach a lesson with students allows teachers to carefully attend to the questions students ask, the struggles they have with understanding the content, and the ways in which they interact with each other and the demonstration teacher. When student learning is evident, observing teachers are more likely to see the value of the strategies used and be willing to try them in their own classrooms. Observing examples of practice also enables teachers to see when student learning is not the result of a lesson or certain instructional approach. These instances provide teachers with opportunities to explore alternative approaches that address aspects of the lesson or practice that need to be changed to facilitate greater student learning.

Translating new learning into practice is best accomplished in collaboration rather than in isolation. These strategies provide an opportunity for teachers to work together as they practice and apply new strategies in their teaching, reflect on results, and make continuous improvements. The strategies support teachers to engage in transformational learning, rather than just additive learning (Thompson & Zeuli, 1999), and this type of learning occurs when learners reject deeply held ideas, reorganize what they know, and restructure and question their basic assumptions and frameworks for learning (Mezirow, 1991, 1997). Community-centered environments that nurture learning communities characterized by collaboration, collegial interaction, and reflection (Bransford et al., 1999) support teachers' to make these transformational changes that are not achieved when teachers work in isolation.

The opportunity to carefully observe and analyze actual teaching and learning situations leads to changes in teachers' beliefs, attitudes, convictions, and ultimately, practice. Advocates of practice-based professional development that focuses on examining teaching and learning believe that teachers need to examine both their practices and beliefs about teaching and learning that undergird their current practices. Examining teaching and learning raises teachers' awareness of important issues, such as the expectations teachers hold for students, and may cause them to confront and possibly rethink their beliefs about how to teach and who can learn. As Thompson and Zeuli (1999) advocate, providing an experience that creates "disequilibrium" for teachers can be a catalyst for transformational thinking. For example, seeing the achievement gaps that might exist for students based on standards and current student performance by examining student work or engaging in lesson study can demonstrate to teachers discrepancies between what they believed they were teaching and what students appear to have learned (Driscoll & Bryant, 1998).

The learning of all students is a shared responsibility of all teachers. In schools bringing examination of teaching and learning strategies to the repertoire of teachers' learning, it is imperative that all involved believe that teaching students is a process that is enhanced through a collaborative endeavor and not one that is achieved in isolation. It is this belief in a shared responsibility that contributes to and characterizes professional learning communities.

Improving teaching and learning is a long-term, gradual process. Too often, the educational system seeks quick fixes to solve deep-seated, complicated problems. At the core of examining teaching and learning is the belief that change takes time and improving student and teacher learning is an evolving process. These strategies are characterized by engaging in collaborative examination of practice over time and will require a shift in the educational system's approach to and perceptions of what is involved in improving teaching and learning, moving away from short-term fixes to long-term continuous improvement.

Implementation Requirements

Focused Time for Collaboration, Engagement, Discussion, and Reflection

These strategies require focused periods of time outside of instructional time, without distraction, to examine and observe teaching practice, explore student learning, and engage in dialogue with colleagues and coaches or mentors.

Critical Reflection in a Risk-Free Environment

For many teachers, it can be intimidating to have others observe their teaching and to then engage in critical reflection on what was observed. It is essential for these strategies that teachers feel comfortable with each other and have experience critiquing teaching practices in a nonthreatening environment. These strategies require an attitude of self-reflection on the part of all involved with the goal of improving each teacher's understanding and practice.

Skills of Facilitators

Facilitators must have an understanding of the science or mathematics being taught and must have the skills and experience to manage discussions that are intellectually stimulating, challenging, and supportive. Facilitators need to know about and be able to use processes and protocols specific to many of the strategies in this cluster, such as protocols for examining student work and pre- and postconferencing protocols for coaching. They need their own professional learning experiences to develop the knowledge, skills, and abilities to facilitate other teachers' learning, especially in the case of coaching and mentoring.

EXAMINING STUDENT WORK AND THINKING

Teachers from a middle school were concerned because their students did not do well on the most recent common formative assessment in the area of inquiry process skills. Wanting to help them do better, the teachers decided to look carefully at their students' work to uncover where the problems might lie. They selected 10 students in different classrooms and then gathered and studied the students' portfolios, scoring sheets, and other records. Following a protocol familiar to all of the teachers, they first completed the assessment tasks themselves and explored several questions: "What were the tasks asking?" "How were the responses scored?" "What does one need to know and be able to do to complete the task?" "How did the students interpret and approach the task?" They then examined the student work samples, and as a result of their discussions, the teachers were better able to "see" the students' work and understand their thinking. They listed the kinds of understandings that the assessment measured, what students seemed to know, and the areas of difficulty they saw in their students' work. They noted that students seemed to do well interpreting data tables that were similar to what students included in their science notebooks. Yet, students seemed to be lacking understanding of concepts the teachers thought they would know, such as the importance of controlling variables and what would constitute fair tests. This guided subsequent discussions of how they could help students improve their understanding and application of these science inquiry skills.

Examining student work and thinking as a strategy for professional learning has exponentially grown in the educational community. Numerous articles have been written describing the process as it is carried out in schools throughout the country; there are Web sites devoted to looking at student work, and many organizations have developed protocols and guidelines for helping teachers look at student work in meaningful ways.

As teachers and entire faculties turn to examining student work as a means of enhancing their own and their students' learning, collaborative learning communities are developing, and teachers are becoming more reflective of their practice. The benefits that are emerging from this approach to professional learning are being studied and documented. Many programs and projects embed the examination of student work as a core process within their larger initiatives, such as looking at student learning data to inform instructional improvements (Love et al., 2008) or analyzing student responses to teacher questioning approaches as a means of improving lessons (DiRanna et al., 2008).

Although there are numerous protocols and guidelines for examining student work and thinking, they reflect a similar structured format. This format includes the following:

- *Identification of a focus or goal by answering the questions:* "What do we want to learn from the student work?" "What outcomes do we expect from the process?" "What data do we have to support our goal?" "How is our goal related to student performance and schoolwide goals and standards?"
- *Selection of student work that relates directly to the identified goal and outcomes.* It is important that documentation be brought to the session that provides information on the objectives of the task the student responded to, the learning strategy associated with the student work, and any other information that helps all participants better understand the context within which the student completed the work. Who brings student work to the sessions varies according to the goals, but most groups rotate among the teachers, asking each to share responsibility for bringing student work for all to examine. Many projects refer to this teacher as the "presenting teacher," and there are specific roles in the discussions for the presenting teacher.
- *Facilitation of discussions that guide participants' interpretations and understanding of the student work samples.* This facilitation varies among groups of teachers who engage with this strategy, but most emphasize that it is critical to have a facilitator guide the discussions in order to focus on what students know and understand and how to build on that, versus only focusing on deficiencies and to ensure in-depth analysis of student learning and its relationship to teacher practice. Often, this facilitation rotates among the teachers. The facilitation can be more effective if the teachers use protocols and have some training in how to facilitate discussions.
- *Reflection on the implications and applications of what is learned to teaching.* This facilitated discussion highlights the ways in which the teachers can enhance their teaching based on what they have learned about student understanding of important concepts.

KEY ELEMENTS

Collaborative experiences are guided by an experienced content expert. Although an individual teacher can certainly examine student work or reflect on student thinking in isolation, there is power in examining student work as a team. Together, teachers can begin to develop shared ideas and standards that can guide their collective

KEY ELEMENTS FOR EXAMINING STUDENT WORK AND THINKING

- Collaborative experiences are guided by an experienced content expert.
- Engagement in examining what teachers have plenty of, student work, is fundamental.
- Discussion and examination of student work has a focused goal and purpose.
- Structured protocols enhance the learning experience for participating teachers.

efforts to improve student learning. Creating a supportive environment in which teachers can work with each other and examine their own values about teaching and learning enhances the process. Delving deeply into understanding what students are thinking by analyzing their written work or responses on assessments requires substantial knowledge of the science or mathematics content and, in the case of examining assessments, a facilitator with expertise in assessment is helpful.

Engagement in examining what teachers have plenty of, student work, is fundamental. The richest discussions are stimulated by work samples that are varied in their nature and quality, require more than short answers, and include students' explanations of their thinking (e.g., why they answered the way they did and what made them do what they did). Student work can include written responses, drawings, graphs, journals, portfolios, or videotapes of interviews with students. Facilitators of examining student work sessions suggest various collections of student work, including work generated by one student in response to one assignment or task, several samples of work from one student generated from multiple assignments or tasks, or samples from each student in the class in response to one assignment (National School Reform Faculty, n.d.a). Other facilitators suggest examining student work that teachers are wondering about or that raises a dilemma about teaching or learning (National School Reform Faculty, n.d.b). The type of student work and the collection gathered to examine should depend on the goals and intended outcomes of the process of looking at the work.

Discussion and examination of student work has a focused goal and purpose. The focus of discussion may vary. In the opening vignette, for example, teachers had a compelling reason to examine student assessments and did so using the actual assessment that had been given. At other times, teachers might bring to discussion groups examples of student work that puzzle them. In some situations, teachers may begin with a rubric supplied by others to apply to a set of student work (e.g., the contents of portfolios or the results of performance tasks) or may take the opportunity to develop their own rubric through examining student work. Also, the focus for a discussion may be a videotape of children's explanations of their understanding of a problem or situation.

Structured protocols enhance the learning experience for participating teachers. Numerous protocols and guidelines have been developed that describe focusing questions to guide teachers as they look at student work or assessment responses, and most describe processes for looking for evidence of learning in the student work, listening to colleagues' thinking and perceptions, reflecting on individual thinking, and applying what is learned and discussed to teaching practices.

INTENDED OUTCOMES

As is true for the majority of the strategies within this cluster, the primary outcome of examining student work and thinking is *enhancing quality teaching*. As teachers explore students' thinking in relationship to science and mathematics concepts, they identify areas in need of improvement and take action to enhance their instructional approaches. Often, focusing on students' learning needs helps teachers identify their own needs for *enhancing their content knowledge,* and they can then engage in other strategies to deepen their own understanding. Since this strategy is best enacted in a collaborative setting, it works well within learning communities, while at the same time, teachers' engagement in the strategy contributes to *building professional learning communities* focused on improving student learning.

Developing leadership capacity is achieved by preparing facilitators for leading teachers' examination of student work and thinking. For example, engaging a group of teacher leaders in examination of student work with the explicit purpose of learning to facilitate the protocols and processes enhances their ability to use those skills when leading groups of teachers. In some cases, this strategy also lends itself to developing administrators' awareness of the kinds of student thinking advocated in the science and mathematics education standards.

COMBINING STRATEGIES

Since the focus of this strategy is on the artifacts of teachers' practice, it combines well with most other professional learning strategies. For example, teachers can benefit from examining student work as they implement new curriculum or engage in lesson study since this helps to pinpoint concepts that students are finding difficult and may uncover areas of the curriculum or the lesson that are not yet being fully implemented or need revision. When combined with curriculum topic study, teachers learn about common student conceptions of a topic and can then examine their own students' work looking for evidence of those same conceptions. In mentoring relationships, student work can serve as the catalyst for dialogue and reflection on both teaching practices and student learning. Case discussions can (and often do) relate to student work, discussing in some depth what students did and what teachers can learn from that. In their action research, teachers can pay

> **Examining student work and thinking combines well with other strategies:**
>
> - Curriculum implementation
> - Lesson study
> - Curriculum topic study
> - Mentoring
> - Case discussion
> - Action research

special attention to students who are talking to each other or working on problems or investigations and teachers can question students about what they are doing and why. Video cases of teaching can be accompanied by the student work produced during the lesson so that teachers viewing and discussing them can get a clearer picture of what students are learning.

ISSUES TO CONSIDER

There are many who see this strategy as the most powerful way to help teachers improve their practice. Clearly, it is totally "authentic" in that teachers work with products of student thinking and study closely the very thing they are responsible for improving. As professional development becomes more results oriented, there is no better way to focus on learning.

When looking at student work that is the result of assessments, teachers benefit from collaborating to develop a common rubric for scoring the assessments. They review standards and come to consensus about how they will score student work or assessment items. They practice scoring to obtain inter-rater reliability and discuss why they scored individual items on assessments in certain ways. This leads them to a shared view of the standards for students' learning.

As noted in the "Key Elements," it is important to have a skilled content expert to contribute to the examination of student work. Equally important is a facilitator who has the skills and abilities to navigate through the "difficult conversations" that can emerge from examining student work. For example, if teachers have lower expectations for some students' learning, this belief will influence their interpretations of the specific students' work. For example, some teachers might want to disregard written samples from students who are recently learning the English language and who may not clearly communicate their ideas in writing. Teachers might state that they do not know what the student intends and therefore cannot interpret what the student has learned. It is important in situations such as this one for the facilitator to probe more deeply into the beliefs that underlie the teachers' comments and to inquire into what can, in fact, be learned from the students' work.

In other instances, if teachers are aware of which students generated each sample of work, they can bring their own biases—both negative and positive—to their interpretations of the work. For example, if teachers know that a highly achieving student is the author of a sample of work that lacks clarity, they might adjust their interpretations based on knowledge of the student, rather than solely on the ideas that are communicated in the sample. Although it can be important to know which students generated which student work samples in some cases, when this is the case, facilitators need to be prepared to help teachers focus only on what is communicated in the sample. One strategy for facilitators is to ask teachers to provide evidence seen in the student work sample that results in their interpretations. This approach can support teachers to focus on what is observed in the sample, rather than bringing their own biases to the table.

With a skilled facilitator, examining student work and thinking can be a strategy that has great impact on teachers' understanding of the content students are struggling with and ways that they, the teachers, can help. Pedagogical content knowledge—that special province of excellent teachers—is absolutely necessary for teachers to maximize their learning as they examine and discuss what students demonstrate they know and do not know. The strategy can also be a catalyst for probing into teachers' knowledge and beliefs about learners and learning, contributing to more equitable opportunities for all students to learn.

RESOURCES

Education Development Center's Schools Around the World Web site: www.edc.org/CCT/saw2000

Education Trust. (n.d.). *Standards in practice (SIP): Professional development model.* Retrieved August 18, 2009, from www2.edtrust.org/EdTrust/SIP+ Professional+Development

Looking at Student Work Web site: www.lasw.org

Love, N., Stiles, K. E., Mundry, S., & DiRanna, K. (2008). *The data coach's guide to improving learning for all students: Unleashing the power of collaborative inquiry.* Thousand Oaks, CA: Corwin.

National School Reform Faculty, Harmony Education Center Web site: www.nsrfharmony.org/protocol/learning_from_student_work.html

WestEd & WGBH Educational Foundation. (2003). *Teachers as learners: A multimedia kit for professional development in science and mathematics.* Thousand Oaks, CA: Corwin. (See Tape 3, Program 3, "Assessing Student Work," Arizona State University East, Mesa, AZ, and Tape 4, Program 5, "Examining Content and Student Thinking," Urban Calculus Initiative, TERC, Cambridge, MA.)

DEMONSTRATION LESSONS

Kendra, a second-grade teacher, and Jamika, a third-grade teacher, are participating in a demonstration lesson group as part of their district's approach to supporting teachers as they implement the new mathematics curriculum. They are both experienced teachers but are new to the curriculum being introduced. They request that the demonstration lesson group spend some time looking at how the curriculum in second grade supports the content in third grade. In response to their request, the teachers in the group, all second- and third-grade teachers, decide to observe the teacher leader who has been working with them all year coteach lessons in two classrooms. During the preobservation conference, they discuss their questions about how the lesson in second grade and its underlying concepts can be built on in the lesson being taught in third grade. They also decide that they want to make sure to watch for how the teacher leader asks questions to probe for student thinking. They note that during the postobservation conference they want to discuss the "teaching decisions" the teacher leader makes based on what he thinks students understand during the lesson.

After observing both lessons, the teachers gather for the postobservation conference. Kendra starts the conversation by noting, "I really saw how the mathematical concepts in my class are transferred to third grade." The discussion quickly moves into sharing how they think the curriculum aligns with the school goals and what they know from their student data about the gaps in students' mathematical learning and understanding. They raise and discuss in-depth such questions as "How do I address errors in thinking when I notice them?" "What are the concepts behind each of the activities in the curriculum in second and third grades?" "What are the mathematical ideas that are built on from first through fifth grades?" The teacher leader provides great insight for the other teachers by sharing his own thinking about the specific teaching moves and the minute-by-minute decisions that he made during the demonstration lesson based on his understanding of the purpose and learning intent of the lesson. In particular, hearing the reasons why the teacher leader chose the strategies he did helps the other teachers to become more conscious of the need to connect teaching moves to the learning objectives. By the end of the conference, more questions than answers have been raised, but all of the teachers are ready for their next demonstration lesson and the chance to continue to become more purposeful in their use of the new curriculum lessons.

Demonstration lessons are professional learning opportunities that are situated in classroom practice and provide an opportunity to enhance teacher practice and reflection. The learning is grounded in teachers' daily work and directly connected to the content and curriculum that they teach in their classrooms. Teachers' expertise and knowledge are brought to the learning situation, and through collegial reflection, their perceptions and understandings are increased.

Many school districts have been using demonstration lessons as a key strategy for supporting teacher growth and reflection on the design and implementation of instruction. Groups of teachers meet to discuss the goals for observing one teacher in the group conduct a classroom lesson. All others in the group observe the lesson and then debrief their experience. Often, the process of teaching and observing a lesson is done by having the demonstration teacher videotape the lesson, which groups of teachers then convene to observe and discuss. For example, the Northern New England Co-Mentoring Group had teachers bring the videos from their applications to become board certified teachers to a group for discussion and used those videos for demonstration lessons. Unlike lesson study that is focused on fine-tuning a lesson, demonstration lessons aim to help teachers actually see what it looks like to teach certain content in particular ways. They may focus on how the teacher identifies and addresses students' prior conceptions or on the questions a teacher asks of students as they explain how they solved a mathematics problem.

Effective teachers have an in-depth understanding of the science or mathematics content, knowledge of their students' needs and prior experiences and how students learn the content, and the teaching strategies and activities that will lead to student learning. In demonstration lessons, observing teachers often identify this interactive relationship as the focus of their observations, attending to the ways in which the demonstration teacher guides and facilitates learning based on knowledge and understanding of the content, students, and teaching strategies. Through postobservation discussions, observing teachers can further question the demonstration teacher to surface thinking about how the lesson was approached and why certain activities, behaviors, or questioning were used at specific times during the lesson.

In addition, by focusing on the dynamic interactions in teaching, demonstration lessons raise the level of in-depth discussions and learning. For example, during the postobservation discussion, the focus stays on understanding what the students learned and understood, why the teacher asked certain questions or guided the students in certain directions, and what was significant about the content being presented. Keeping the observations and discussions focused on these interactions helps avoid discussions that emphasize only the most obvious actions and behaviors in a classroom, such as the ways in which students are grouped or the hands-on activity itself. Rather, the increased learning comes from examining the thoughts and perceptions regarding *why* students were grouped the way they were or what content was learned by engaging in the hands-on activity.

The purpose of demonstration lessons is to use a *prelesson discussion, classroom demonstration lesson observation,* and *postlesson debrief* cycle as a catalyst for this kind of in-depth reflection on science and mathematics teaching and learning. In the same way that teachers use student work as a means for increasing their understanding of student understanding, teacher work—in this case, classroom teaching—is used as a means for increasing understanding of teaching practices specific to mathematics and science education.

For example, in the opening vignette, the demonstration lesson observation and accompanying pre- and postlesson discussions focused on enhancing second- and third-grade teachers' implementation of a mathematics curriculum and understanding the mathematical concepts common to both second- and third-grade student learning. The teachers were all either second- or third-grade teachers, and the explicit purpose of the demonstration lesson and discussion was increasing understanding of the concepts addressed at each grade and enhancing implementation of the curriculum. The new learning in this vignette does not come from the observation alone. The prelesson and postlesson discussions are critical in raising the teachers' awareness of the larger mathematical concepts, increasing their understanding of the overall curriculum, and providing them with specific "teaching moves" related to implementing the lessons in the curriculum. In addition, their discussions highlight several issues frequently asked by science and mathematics teachers, including "How do I know whether the students are learning?" and "What are the key concepts behind the activities?" Through collegial discussion they share their ideas and develop greater understanding.

KEY ELEMENTS FOR DEMONSTRATION LESSONS

- Teachers need time and structure.
- Groups of teachers observe each other.
- There is a cycle of prediscussion, observation, and postdiscussion.
- Observations and discussions are facilitated.

KEY ELEMENTS

Teachers need time and structure. As with all professional learning strategies, but especially those that are embedded in teachers' practice and occur during the school day, teachers need protected time to interact with each other. Demonstration lessons necessarily include numerous teachers being released from their classrooms to observe lessons being taught and to reflect on their observations.

Groups of teachers observe each other. Unlike coaching or mentoring—that can occur in one-on-one situations—demonstration lessons usually involve groups of teachers working together. For example, groups can be grade-level teams, novice teachers in induction programs, study groups, and whole-school faculty implementing new curriculum. One of the underlying principles girding the strategy is that the interactions of a group of teachers lead to more diverse discussions, bring varied perspectives to the discussions, and provide an opportunity to observe different teaching approaches. Together, they develop a shared vision of what they want teaching and learning to look like in their school.

There is a cycle of prediscussion, observation, and postdiscussion. During the prediscussion, teachers learn about the goals and purposes of the specific lesson they will observe, become familiar with the instructional materials used in the lesson, and hear from the teacher whose classroom the lesson will be taught in about what students have done prior to this lesson to build conceptual understanding of the content. The lesson is then taught by a teacher leader in one of the teacher's classrooms, cotaught by the teacher leader and teacher, or taught by the teacher himself or herself with his or her own students. The observing teachers take notes, script the teacher and student interactions during the lesson or videotape the lesson, attending to specific classroom practices identified during the prediscussion. The post-discussion engages teachers in a dialogue regarding what was observed—usually after the demonstration teacher reflects on what he or she experienced and perceived—and the facilitator raises issues related to content, pedagogy, instruction, or assessment that were related to the teaching of the lesson. Many groups also ask teachers to reflect in a journal at the end of the postdiscussion on their insights or perceptions.

Observations and discussions are facilitated. Although demonstration lessons can be conducted without a "trained expert," it is essential that the prediscussion, the demonstration lesson itself, the teachers' observations, and the postdiscussion are facilitated by an experienced teacher or leader. The teachers as a group need a clear focus and purpose for their discussions and observations, and a facilitator enhances the dialogue among the teachers, raising important issues in science and mathematics content and teaching. Based on their prediscussion, many demonstration groups develop a protocol to guide their observations and postdiscussion conversations.

Intended Outcomes

Enhancing quality teaching is the primary outcome of demonstration lessons. Teachers are focused on specific classroom practices during the lesson and their dialogue during the pre- and postdiscussions engages them in reflection on ways to improve teaching and learning. During their discussions, they also explore their own *content and pedagogical content knowledge* and, with the guidance of a skilled facilitator, can increase their knowledge. And as is the case with other strategies within this cluster, teachers' dedicated time and focus on improving practice both contributes to and results in *building a professional learning community.* Demonstration lessons also contribute to *developing leadership capacity,* since more experienced teacher leaders are often ideal candidates for conducting the lessons and, when fully prepared through their own professional development, for facilitating the pre- and postdiscussions.

Combining Strategies

Demonstration lessons are often used as a strategy in combination with other professional learning strategies, such as with curriculum implementation, curriculum topic study, study groups, or case discussions. As the opening vignette illustrated, demonstration lessons can provide a vision of learning and teaching associated with the implementation of a set of instructional materials for numerous teachers within one school. Teachers might use curriculum topic study prior to observing lessons to inform their analysis. Teachers would then ask, "If this lesson reflected the research, what would we see?" They would develop a summary of the readings for the topic and grade level of the lesson and use that to inform the discussion and analysis. In other cases, teachers who are participating in a study group or case discussion might decide to use demonstration lessons to enhance their understanding of an instructional strategy they are studying or have read about in a case, such as questioning strategies that lead to increased student understanding of science or mathematics concepts. Demonstration lessons—whether implemented alone or in combination with other strategies—are an effective way to increase collegial and reflective interactions on science and mathematics teaching and learning.

> **Demonstration lessons combine well with other strategies:**
>
> - Curriculum implementation
> - Curriculum topic study
> - Study groups
> - Case discussion

ISSUES TO CONSIDER

As noted previously, one of the changes in professional development has been an increased focus on embedding teachers' learning in their practice. Demonstration lessons are an example of such practice-based learning. For example, the focus for learning and observations during the teaching of a demonstration lesson is often on the interaction between the science or mathematics content, the students, and the teacher. Judith Mumme and Nanette Seago (2002) have adapted the work of Deborah Ball and David Cohen (2000) to reflect this interaction. Mumme and Seago define teaching as "a set of relationships between teacher and student, student and content, and teacher and content" (p. 3). (See the introduction to Chapter 5 for a discussion of this relationship.) In demonstration lessons, teachers have opportunities to explore those relationships and the interactions among them. When facilitators support teachers to attend to one or more of these interactions during the preobservation and demonstration lesson, the dialogue during the postobservation is more focused and beneficial for teachers.

One of the issues to keep in mind with this strategy relates to one of the implementation requirements for this cluster of strategies: *critical reflection in a risk-free environment.* Although this requirement is true of many other professional learning strategies, it is especially important for teachers engaged in demonstration lessons since they are observing and critiquing each other's practice. Teachers need to be firmly committed to the belief that the purpose of this strategy is to enhance student learning through improved teaching practices. Such a belief is nurtured through a culture that emphasizes the values inherent in a professional learning community and is essential for the success of this strategy.

Because demonstration lessons require administrative support and structural changes in teachers' daily schedules, a school that routinely uses demonstration lessons as a strategy for teachers' learning embodies one of the principles of effective professional development: lifelong learning for teachers within a professional learning community. Continuous improvement in knowledge, skills, and understandings is key to lifelong teacher learning; and demonstration lessons provide teachers with a model for examining their own and others' practice and a structure for collaborating with each other in the process. Supporting teachers' engagement in demonstration lessons conveys the message that reflection on teaching and learning is important.

RESOURCES

Manno, C., & Firestone, W. (2007). Content is the subject: How teacher leaders with different subject knowledge interact with teachers. In M. M. Mangin & S. R. Stoelinga (Eds.), *Effective teacher leadership: Using research to inform and reform* (pp. 36–54). New York: Teachers College Press.

Math and Science Partnership Knowledge Management and Dissemination Project. (n.d.). *Teacher leaders providing classroom support to teachers through demonstration lessons/modeling.* Retrieved August 17, 2009, from www.mspkmd.net/index.php?page=03_1a

WestEd & WGBH Educational Foundation. (2003). *Teachers as learners: A multimedia kit for professional development in science and mathematics.* Thousand Oaks, CA: Corwin. (See Tape 2, Program 5, "Observing Mathematics Teaching," Clark County Schools, Las Vegas, NV; and Tape 3, Program 2, "Observing Science Teaching," Clark County Schools, Las Vegas, NV.)

LESSON STUDY

Katie, Aiden, and Leah, three third-grade teachers, wanted to start lesson study as a professional learning strategy in their school. They, and almost all of the other teachers and the principal, were already conducting cross-grade and content-alike study groups, had an effective mentoring program in place for new and experienced teachers, and spent numerous hours weekly examining their students' work and thinking to better meet the learning needs of all students. Given the diversity of learning experiences at the school and the collegial culture in place, they believed they were ready—as individuals and a faculty—to embark on lesson study.

They started by first learning more about lesson study by reading *The Teaching Gap* (Stigler & Hiebert, 1999) and better understanding the contextual issues that influenced the success of lesson study in Japan. They also read numerous articles and studies done by researchers and visited a myriad of Web sites on lesson study. By the end of the semester, they felt ready to try lesson study.

Katie took the lead on compiling the data they had from their classrooms and from the state test in mathematics to help them identify specific learning goals that needed to be addressed. After they analyzed the data and saw patterns in their students' ability to reason and problem solve, they decided to focus their first lesson on improving their students' abilities in these areas. Throughout the year, and into the next year, Katie, Aiden, and Leah studied the NCTM standards and the Third International Mathematics and Science Study (TIMSS) mathematics videos and developed a lesson aimed at increasing students' ability to use proportional reasoning. They followed the eight-step structural design for lesson study as outlined in The Teaching Gap, including defining the problem, planning the lesson, teaching the lesson, evaluating the lesson and reflecting on its effect, revising the lesson, teaching the revised lesson, evaluating and reflecting again, and sharing the results. They identified a terrific mathematics educator from the local state college who provided feedback and helped them think through why some parts of the lesson were not effective. During the next two years, additional teachers joined Katie, Aiden, and Leah, and a group of four teachers decided to begin focusing their lesson study experiences on science lessons.

The Trends in International Mathematics and Science Study (TIMSS) has shed light on the extent to which education in the United States supports the learning of all students, provides teachers with opportunities for professional development, and translates national standards into policy and practice. TIMSS data continue to provoke discussions about how curriculum and instruction in the U.S. can be improved to support students in achieving at the highest levels, internationally. For example, the recent report, *Professional Learning in the Learning Profession: A Status Report on Teacher Development in the United States and Abroad* (Wei et al., 2009), highlights the persistent need to provide teachers with collaborative learning opportunities that are focused on designing curriculum and sharing practices.

"Originating in Japan, lesson study is a cycle of instructional improvement focused on planning, observing, and discussing research lessons and drawing out their implications for teaching and learning" (Lewis, 2008, p. 175). In Japan, lesson study is a structured process through which teachers' develop lessons to enhance student learning in all subject areas. Use of lesson study results in teachers developing a thorough understanding of how a particular lesson should be conducted and why. Groups of teachers meet regularly over long periods of time (e.g., several months to several years) to work on the design, implementation, testing, and improvement of one or several lessons (Stigler & Hiebert, 1999). Research lessons are at the core of lesson study—groups of teachers discussing, teaching, observing, and revising specific lessons that are designed to enhance student learning of specific concepts and content. Lesson study and the accompanying research lessons are supported and advocated by all educators and seen as an inherent part of being a teacher. As one Japanese teacher noted, "Why do we do research lessons? I don't think there are any laws [requiring it]. But if we didn't do research lessons, we wouldn't be teachers" (Lewis, 2002b, p. 60).

In the United States, lesson study has been implemented in hundreds of schools and districts, and there are numerous research studies being conducted to determine the effectiveness of translating the Japanese model into the cultures and contexts of American schools. Most variations of the Japanese model, however, include the elements described next in the "Key Elements" section.

KEY ELEMENTS

Teachers collaborate on the development and refinement of lessons. In lesson study, teachers collaborate with each other in every aspect of the teaching process, from planning lessons to assessing student outcomes. Engaging in lesson study requires that teachers voluntarily participate with a motivation to learn from each other toward the goal of improving student learning. Inherent in the process of researching a lesson is the belief that discussing others' points of view enhances the learning process and the final product, the lesson itself.

> **KEY ELEMENTS FOR LESSON STUDY**
>
> - Teachers collaborate on the development and refinement of lessons.
> - The results of lesson study benefit all teachers and students.
> - The focus of the lesson studied is researched and directly related to standards and school goals.
> - Critical feedback is on the effectiveness of the lesson and not the teachers' performance while teaching.
> - There is a structured process for guiding the lesson study.
> - Administrators provide support and access to resources and knowledgeable others.

In addition, teachers' reflection on their own teaching practices and their students' learning comprises a major emphasis of the lesson study process. Engaging in lesson study presumes that participating teachers have the desire to enhance their own learning and their students' learning through interactions with their colleagues and self-reflection.

The results of lesson study benefit all teachers and students. Not only does engagement in researching lessons result in the individual learning and growth of teachers, but also the product developed enhances the learning of students in participating teachers' classrooms. The concrete product of lesson study is well researched, conceptually grounded lessons that promote students' learning of science or mathematics concepts. The participating teachers incorporate the lessons into their overall curriculum, and often, the new lessons are shared with teachers at other schools, or even, with teachers in schools across the world via Web sites devoted to sharing lessons. In this way, the benefits extend to numerous teachers and students.

The focus of the lesson studied is researched and directly related to standards and school goals. To benefit students and teachers beyond those directly involved in the lesson study experience, the themes or concepts being addressed in the lessons must be a reflection of school, district, or national standards and goals for student learning in science or mathematics. In addition, identifying the concepts to explore through lesson study should be based on data that indicate there is a need for improvement in current student achievement or learning, as well as on an examination of the standards and research to thoroughly understand the key concepts that should be taught. It is also important that teachers explore what is known in the research about effective instructional approaches for teaching the concepts and the common student conceptions of the content that need to be addressed in the lesson.

Critical feedback is on the effectiveness of the lesson and not the teachers' performance while teaching. Although this is a subtle distinction, it is a critical one. The focus of lesson study is on the lessons and the ways in which the teaching and learning strategies enhance student learning. The individual teacher conducting the lessons, who is observed by the other teachers, is not at the center of improvement. Individual teachers do, however, often relate that they gain immense knowledge about ways in which to improve their teaching through reflecting on the feedback from their peers. Keeping the critical feedback discussions focused on the lessons and the student learning that results enhances teachers' comfort level with engaging in a discussion of the strengths and weaknesses of the collaboratively designed lessons.

There is a structured process for guiding the lesson study. Numerous resources have been published describing varied approaches to conducting lesson study, both as it occurs within schools in Japan and how it has been adapted to meet the cultural and contextual issues within schools in the United States (see "Resources"). Most researchers and educators, however, outline a similar process (Lewis, 2002a, 2008; Stigler & Hiebert, 1999), which includes the following:

- *Defining the theme or concept to guide the lesson study.* The theme, topic, or concept to be studied should be based on data indicating a need to improve student learning as determined by local, state, or national standards and goals.
- *Designing the lesson.* Teachers research the topic or concept of the study, including examining what the research says about how students learn the concept and what common alternate conceptions students hold. They often examine existing instructional materials and use these as a starting point, or in the absence of appropriate lessons, they collaborate to develop a lesson plan. The lesson plan is then shared with a larger group of teachers for additional feedback and revision. Although individual lessons are developed and studied, several lessons relating to the defined concept or goal are designed and

studied over time. As Catherine Lewis notes, "Lesson study focuses on specific content goals and also broad, long-term goals for student development [and] team members need to consider both types of goals as they shape their lesson study work" (Lewis, 2008, p. 176). Before moving onto the next step, teachers often complete the activity embedded within the lesson themselves and identify "expected student responses" (ESRs) (DiRanna et al., 2008). The student responses then become one of the foci for data collected when the lesson is taught.

- *Teaching the lesson.* One teacher teaches the lesson, although all teachers participate in the preparation of the lesson, and sometimes, teachers role-play the lesson prior to teaching it in the classroom with students.

- *Observing the lesson.* While the lesson is being taught, the other teachers observe and take notes on what the students and presenting teacher do and say, following the "storyline" of the lesson, and document the questions the presenting teacher asks and the student responses. In some cases, such as WestEd K–12 Alliance's Teaching-Learning Collaborative approach to lesson study, a facilitator scripts the lesson. What is critical is that data are collected during the lesson, including a script, notes, or videotape, student work, and other artifacts from the lesson.

- *Reflecting and evaluating.* Critical, in-depth discussions focus on what was observed during the teaching of the lesson. Teachers refer to the data that were collected during the lesson and use them to inform their decisions about the effectiveness of the lesson and to identify specific changes that are needed.

- *Revising the lesson.* Based on their reflections and evaluation, the lesson is collaboratively revised. Teachers take into account the conceptual flow of the lesson, student engagement through active learning, teacher questioning strategies, and the extent of student learning as they make informed decisions and refinements.

- *Teaching the revised lesson.* The revised lesson is taught and observed; the same teacher may teach the lesson again to either the same or a different group of students, or another teacher may conduct the lesson, and often, additional faculty members are invited to observe when the revised lesson is taught.

- *Reflecting and evaluating.* This second debriefing is attended not only by the lesson study teachers but also by a larger group of the faculty, the principal, and a "knowledgeable other"—a content expert, university faculty, or other outside professional. As Stigler and Hiebert (1999) note, the discussions in this second debriefing often extend to larger issues: "Not only is the lesson discussed with respect to what these students learned and understood, but also with respect to more general issues raised by the hypothesis that guided the design of the research lesson. What about teaching and learning, more generally, was learned from the lesson and its implementation?" (p. 115).

- *Sharing the results.* The lesson that has been researched and developed is shared with a broader audience of teachers and other educators. Articles might be published, and many schools and districts have established Web sites to share lessons that result from the process.

Administrators provide support and access to resources and knowledgeable others. As is evident from the procedure outlined above, lesson study can involve all teachers in the school, as well as teachers from other schools and knowledgeable others, and building supervisors must support the intense process of lesson study and structure the school day in ways that provide opportunities for teachers to plan, design, teach, and reflect together. In addition, lesson study teachers need readily available access to the resources required to study and research the theme or concept that they are exploring through the research lesson and have appropriate resource people who can serve in the "knowledgeable other" role.

INTENDED OUTCOMES

Lesson study is an example of a professional learning strategy that aims to achieve all four of the outcomes: *enhancing teachers' knowledge, enhancing quality teaching, developing leadership capacity,* and *building professional learning communities.* The strategy requires that teachers delve deeply into science or mathematics content embedded within the lesson, study the standards and research to identify grade-appropriate pedagogical and instructional approaches, develop facilitators and leaders of the lesson development, and do so within a culture that promotes collaborative learning focused on improving teaching and learning.

COMBINING STRATEGIES

Lesson study combines well with other strategies:

- Curriculum topic study
- Examining student work and thinking
- Action research

Although lesson study is a robust, coherent, and comprehensive approach to enhancing teachers' professional learning, it also complements teachers' engagement with other strategies, such as curriculum topic study where teachers have opportunities to focus on their knowledge, research and standards, students' conceptions of science and mathematics, and instructional strategies. Inherent in the lesson study approach is examining student work and thinking, which are data that inform the effectiveness of the revised lesson. Teachers can also extend lesson study by conducting action research to explore the effectiveness of revised lessons in diverse classroom settings.

ISSUES TO CONSIDER

It is tempting to jump on the bandwagon and import a strategy that clearly works so effectively in one setting into another setting. Several issues arise, however, when schools consider using lesson study as a strategy for professional development. First, as noted previously, the contextual and cultural environments differ vastly between Japanese and American schools as well as within American schools. For example, in Japan there is a national course of study that determines the content to be taught at each grade level, and the curriculum addresses a few conceptual topics each year. In the United States, there are local, state, and national standards in science and mathematics, and the curriculum addresses numerous topics each year. In fact, TIMSS revealed that for eighth-grade mathematics, the Japanese curriculum focuses on only eight topics while U.S. curriculum includes more than 65 topics (Schmidt et al., 2001). This difference between the two countries has implications for how teachers spend their valuable time. In Japan, they do not need to examine standards, translate those standards into curriculum, or select instructional materials to address the different concepts included in the curriculum. Rather, they can focus on enhancing the individual lessons they teach in their classrooms, with lesson study being the strategy to guide their planning and designing. In the United States, on the other hand, teachers often do not have the opportunity or time to focus on the lessons they teach; they are often overwhelmed by testing schedules, an overly exhaustive curriculum, and limited opportunities within the school day to focus on their own teaching and learning. However, with careful attention to their contexts and cultures of learning, more and more schools are implementing lesson study and using the model to enhance teachers' knowledge and improve teaching and learning.

Lesson study is much more involved than simply organizing and conducting demonstration lessons with observation. The eight-step process of lesson study distinguishes it from this, and it requires real collaboration among teachers and ideally with external resources—people and research—to expand views. Furthermore, lesson study must be an ongoing process and should be approached this way as one considers it as part of the professional development design for a school or district. It involves more than the study of just one lesson.

In fact, lesson study can be a catalyst for schoolwide reflection on the goals and vision for developing a more collegial faculty and encourage teachers and administrators to take steps toward achieving those goals.

U.S. educators and policymakers often turn to quick fixes to solve the educational system's complex problems. Lesson study is based on the assumption that learning and change are gradual and intensive endeavors. As Stigler and Hiebert (1999) state, "Lesson study is a process of improvement that is expected to produce small, incremental improvements in teaching over long periods of time" (p. 121). This assumption is echoed by Catherine Lewis (2008) when she writes, "Lesson study is a way for teachers to help one another slow down the act of teaching in order to learn more about students, subject matter, and their own teaching" (p. 183). Teachers and schools must necessarily consider the political climate that most directly influences their school and the parental and community perceptions of what reforming and changing teaching should entail. If the beliefs inherent in lesson study conflict with those critical factors, it is important to address them prior to implementing lesson study.

Finally, there is the overarching issue of how professional development is viewed. Although there have been significant shifts in recent years away from the view of professional development as one-shot, short-term experiences disconnected from student learning, many educators still do not conceive of professional learning experiences, such as those described in this book, as effective strategies. Strategies like lesson study require a paradigm shift in thinking about what best-practice professional development looks like and is an issue that should be addressed prior to implementing a long-term, practice-based, job-embedded learning experience for teachers.

Catherine Lewis (2002a) has written extensively about lesson study in Japan and the United States. She raises several additional questions regarding the transfer of lesson study into schools in the United States, which schools can, and should, consider when exploring lesson study as an option for teachers' professional learning, including the following:

- What are the essential features of lesson study that must be honored when lesson study is conducted in the United States (and what are the nonessential features that can be changed)?
- How do educators improve instruction through lesson study?
- What supports will be needed for lesson study in the United States, given its educational system and culture? (pp. 6–7)

Current research and ongoing experience with implementing lesson study in this country have greatly enhanced the education community's ability to answer the questions Lewis raises and contributed to the effectiveness of this strategy in the United States. There are schools that have successfully adapted lesson study to meet their specific school cultures and contexts. It is crucial to consider the specific contexts within a school before moving forward toward implementing lesson study. For example, teachers and administrators need to ask themselves: "Does our learning culture support collaborative learning?" "How will we restructure time constraints to provide the necessary learning opportunities for teachers?" "Will the parents and community support this long-term, gradual approach to improving science and mathematics teaching and learning?" Reflecting on these and other questions can guide a school or district to determine whether and when lesson study is the best strategy for teacher learning in their site.

RESOURCES

Global Education Resources Web site: www.globaledresources.com

Education Development Center's Lesson Study Communities Project in Secondary Mathematics Web site: www2.edc.org/lessonstudy

Lesson Study Group at Mills College Web site: www.lessonresearch.net/index.html

Lesson Study Research Group, Teachers College, Columbia University Web site: www.teacherscollege.edu/lessonstudy

Lewis, C. (2002). *Lesson study: A handbook of teacher-led instructional improvement.* Philadelphia: Research for Better Schools.

Northwest Regional Education Laboratory (NWREL), Center for Classroom Teaching & Learning. (n.d.). *Lesson study.* Retrieved August 17, 2009, from www.nwrel.org/lessonstudy

Research for Better Schools. (n.d.). *Lesson study.* Retrieved August 17, 2009, from www.rbs.org/lesson_study

Stepanek, J., Appel, G., Leong, M., Turner Mangan, M., & Mitchell, M. (2007). *Leading lesson study: A practical guide for teachers and facilitators.* Thousand Oaks, CA: Corwin.

Stigler, J.W., & Hiebert, J. (1999). *The teaching gap: Best ideas from the world's teachers for improving education in the classroom.* New York: Free Press.

WestEd K–12 Alliance Teaching-Learning Collaborative Web site: www.wested.org/cs/we/view/serv/71

The Teaching Gap Web site: www.lessonlab.com/teaching-gap/index.htm

ACTION RESEARCH

After attending a workshop on equity issues in the classroom, Pat and Linda, two tenth-grade geometry teachers, were inspired to examine whether they treated boys and girls differently during their classes. In particular, they decided to focus on how many times they called on boys versus girls to answer questions and whether they responded differently to answers offered by boys versus girls. In addition, they wanted to examine the types of questions that they asked all students: "To what extent are we asking procedural questions or higher-order questions that promote reflection and discussion?" After reading some additional research on gender issues and consulting their school's psychologist, Pat and Linda developed their research design, which included audiotaping several of their classes and keeping running logs of how many boys versus girls were called on during those lessons and documenting the types of questions they asked. Analyzing the audiotapes proved to be a significant challenge for the teachers, but after discussions with an educational researcher from a local college they developed a coding scheme that allowed them to characterize four different types of teacher responses to student comments and to apply a rubric to their questioning strategies.

As they had suspected at the start of the project, they discovered a fair amount of gender bias in their approaches to teaching geometry and that they frequently asked more procedural questions than reflective questions. Through discussing the audiotapes and observing each other's teaching, they were able to work at increasing their awareness of gender equity and develop strategies to address it in their classrooms. One of those strategies was to strive to ask all students probing, reflective questions. As a result of sharing their research findings with other mathematics teachers in their department, three other teachers joined Pat and Linda to form an ongoing action research group, which continued to conduct classroom research on issues and concerns relevant to mathematics teaching and learning.

Action research has a long and varied history. First introduced by Kurt Lewin in the 1940s, action research has evolved in the education community into an ongoing process of systematic study in which teachers examine their own teaching and students' learning through descriptive reporting, purposeful conversation, collegial sharing, and critical reflection for the purpose of improving classroom practice (Miller & Pine, 1990). Action research is also emerging as a form of whole-school collaborative inquiry into improving student learning in science and mathematics, where "collective responsibility for student learning, commitment to equity, and trust is the foundation for collaborative inquiry" (Love et al., 2008, p. 6).

Through action research, teachers reflect on their practices and student results by studying teaching and learning. When teachers conduct action research, the emphasis is on practice-based professional inquiry. "Teachers are at the center of this work—their thinking, their questions, their desire to improve" (Caro-Bruce, 2008, p. 64). Its main tenet is that practical reasoning and problem solving are adequate for generating scientific knowledge, and the natural language of practitioners is just as suitable for creating scientific understanding as empirically derived statements framed in technical language (Duckworth, 1986). This form of knowing comes from experience and direct interaction with students.

The strength of action research as a professional development strategy is that teachers either define the research questions or contribute to their definition in a meaningful way. Therefore, they have ownership over the process and are committed to promoting changes in practice indicated by the findings.

The form of the action research can vary, with teachers working together in collaborative teams of inquiry or with other researchers who are often from universities or research centers. Individual teachers may also pursue their own research studies, with opportunities to discuss their progress and findings with fellow teachers or researchers. In another variation, teachers examine relevant research, which is then used as a basis for collecting and analyzing data from their own classrooms (Loucks-Horsley et al., 1987).

The characteristics of any particular action research project will depend on the goals emphasized, the degree of collaboration between teachers and outside researchers, the process used in carrying out the research, the relationship of the project to the school, and the project outcomes. For example, in some action research projects, the goal is to improve teaching through teacher-led research and reflection on teaching and other classroom strategies. If outside researchers are involved, their role is to help build teachers' skills in research methodology and pedagogical content knowledge and guide teachers in the reflective process.

In some instances of action research, the goal is to not only contribute to teachers' professional growth but also add to the education knowledge base. In these projects, teachers engage in the action and reflection process on a practical issue of classroom teaching, and their findings also contribute to answering larger questions that may be under investigation by the school district, a university, or another research organization.

In still other instances of action research, whole schools engage in collaborative inquiry into improving science or mathematics teaching and learning. At the core of these efforts is teachers and administrators using data collected about their schools to inquire into how to improve student learning. As Love et al. (2008) state, "Collaborative inquiry—a process where teachers construct their understanding of student learning problems and invent and test out solutions together through rigorous and frequent use of data and reflective dialogue—unleashes the resourcefulness and creativity to continuously improve instruction and student learning (p. 5)."

Whichever goal is being pursued, action research supports teachers to examine their teaching practices in a systematic, ongoing way with the purpose of changing those practices. It is not simply about identifying a problem to be solved but rather is more a process based on a vision of creating "learner-centered classrooms and building knowledge through inquiry" (Watkins, 1992, p. 4). Although this can apply to any area of education, it is especially relevant to mathematics and science, whose national standards encourage this vision explicitly. Although the national standards advocate for this type of learner-centered environment, a recent study of professional learning in the United States and other countries found that "the U.S. appears to be significantly behind [other countries] in providing certain kinds of professional learning opportunities" such as "collaborative action research and regularly scheduled collaboration among teachers on issues of instruction" (Wei et al., 2009, p. 59). Action research as a strategy for inquiry into teaching and learning in science and mathematics is a professional learning strategy that can contribute to ongoing changes in our country's professional development.

KEY ELEMENTS FOR ACTION RESEARCH

- Teachers contribute to or formulate their own questions and collect the data to answer these questions.
- Teachers use an action research cycle.
- Teachers are linked with sources of knowledge and stimulation from outside their schools.
- Teachers work collaboratively.
- Learning from research is documented and shared.

KEY ELEMENTS

Teachers contribute to or formulate their own questions and collect the data to answer these questions. Educational research has typically been done "on" or "to" teachers and not "with" or "by" them. Researchers have assumed that research relevant to teachers would be picked up by them and used. The action research strategy assumes that a more intense teacher involvement with research will increase the likelihood that they will learn from their practice and use research results, thus contributing to their growth as teachers. It assumes that meaning can be constructed through action and reflection. It gives teachers the power to make decisions and puts teachers in the position of accepting responsibility for their own professional growth (Caro-Bruce, 2008; Fichtman Dana & Yendol-Hoppey, 2003; Sagor, 2005). Several researchers have studied the ways in which teachers' practices, beliefs, perceptions, and knowledge change as a result of engaging in action research. For example, Koba, Clarke, and Mitchell (2000) found that after one year of facilitated action research, teachers in Omaha, Nebraska, school districts changed their perceptions of students, themselves as teachers, and their conceptions of teaching and learning. The changes were the result of "reflection that promoted shifts in belief systems about teachers and learning; collaborative relationships with teachers and students that evolved when teachers listened to student voice; and the knowledge necessary to implement effective change and to empower both students and teachers" (pp. 99–100).

Teachers use an action research cycle. Action research involves a cycle of planning, acting, observing, and reflecting. Teachers identify a subject of research and develop a plan of action, often in collaboration with others. The questions pursued through action research are usually focused on the behaviors and processes of teaching and learning, although they can also focus on schoolwide systems or structures, the culture or climate of the school, or family and community. Data are collected by observation, anecdotal records, checklists, videotaping, collections of students' work, interviewing, and surveying, among other techniques. Data are analyzed, reflected upon, and used to inform further planning and subsequent action.

Teachers are linked with sources of knowledge and stimulation from outside their schools. Action research projects are often informed by others' research and resources. Although the question for inquiry relates to teachers' own practices and the culture of their learning environments, effective projects draw on available knowledge and build on it rather than re-create it. For example, action researchers often consult research syntheses on effective instructional practices and standards documents to help them frame questions for classroom inquiry. Furthermore, individuals and resources that offer expertise on research methodology often help teachers to ensure the quality of their methods (Glanz, 2003).

Teachers work collaboratively. Action researchers typically work together on all aspects of the project—setting common goals, mutually planning the research design, collecting and analyzing data, and reporting the results. The collaborative nature of the interactions allows for mutual understanding and democratic decision making and requires all participants to communicate openly and freely. For all participants, this requires an openness to discussing problems and limitations, to the ideas of others, and to learning new skills and behaviors needed for the research process (Oja & Smulyan, 1989).

Learning from research is documented and shared. Sharing learning and results from action research can make a significant contribution to professional development. Opportunities to write about a project and submit articles to journals, share results through in-house publications or Web sites, present findings at professional conferences and workshops, participate in discussions of the implications of findings for teaching and schools, and to develop materials that other teachers can use are just some of the ways that teachers can increase their skills and knowledge beyond what they learn from their own action research. For example, a group of teachers in Maine produced monographs of their action research projects and disseminated the findings through a bound volume (Tugel, 2008), and thousands of teachers document their findings on Web sites devoted specifically to sharing action research results (see "Resources").

INTENDED OUTCOMES

Similar to lesson study, action research is a professional learning strategy that is designed to help educators achieve all four of the outcomes for teachers: *enhancing teachers' knowledge, enhancing quality teaching, developing leadership capacity, and building professional learning communities.* For example, through action research teachers deepen their knowledge of the science or mathematics content they teach, explore effectiveness of instructional practices, engage as teacher leaders in the process of conducting research, and collaborate with other teachers, experts, and content specialists. Additionally, it is a strategy that lends itself to teacher leaders, such as coaches and mentors, investigating their own practices as facilitators of other teachers' learning.

COMBINING STRATEGIES

Because action research is intended to achieve all four of the outcomes of professional learning experiences, it combines well with almost all of the other professional development strategies. For example, combining action research with curriculum topic study enables teachers to deepen their "understanding of commonly held student ideas and implications for curriculum and instruction, [and] generate and share CTS and new knowledge with colleagues" (Keeley, 2008, p. ii). Action research also combines well with examining student work and thinking, since these artifacts are often the data collected through the process of investigating teaching and learning. It can also serve as a focusing activity for collegial learning between mentors and their colleagues.

> **Action research combines well with other strategies:**
>
> - Curriculum topic study
> - Examining student work and thinking
> - Mentoring

ISSUES TO CONSIDER

Science and mathematics teachers interested in continuous assessment and improvement can benefit greatly from action research projects. Benefits are generated by both the process and the products of the action research. For example, in the process of conducting an action research project, teachers gain knowledge and skill in research methods and applications (Lieberman, 1986; Miller & Pine, 1990; Oja & Smulyan, 1989). They can become more flexible in their thinking, more receptive to new ideas, and better able to solve problems as they arise. They can change their definitions of professional skills and roles, feel more valued and confident, increase their awareness of classroom issues, become more reflective, change educational beliefs and align their theories and practice, and broaden their views of teaching and learning. Teachers gain new knowledge that helps them solve immediate problems, broaden their knowledge base, and learn skills that can be applied to future interests and concerns (Koba et al., 2000; Oja & Smulyan, 1989).

Action research can also support overall change efforts in schools because findings can help prepare the school staff for needed improvements (Love et al., 2008). The school culture can also shift positively. The action research team unites teachers and encourages collegial interaction. The collaborative nature of action research has the potential to encourage greater professional talk and action related to teaching, learning, and school problems. In addition, a collaborative team provides possibilities for teachers to assume new roles and exhibit leadership, with feelings of powerlessness transformed into a greater sense of empowerment (Lieberman, 1986).

Another benefit of action research is its contribution to narrowing the gap between research and practice. This occurs when researchers work closely with teachers to define and conduct research. New educational theory and knowledge are generated. As a result of learning more about research and research methods, teachers make more informed decisions about when and how to apply the research findings of others.

With its many benefits, action research can be a powerful strategy for professional learning. As teachers and schools engage in action research, however, some of the requirements for effectively implementing this strategy are not addressed; some issues often arise:

- *Time.* Action research requires a great deal of time and focus. Research involves many steps, and it takes time to observe how different strategies work with different students and in different circumstances. Teachers should be recognized for the time spent in action research projects and have it count toward district or state professional development or recertification credit. Teachers and administrators can examine the school schedule to find common time, during the day if possible, for teachers to work together on a research project.
- *Legitimacy of the action research.* Often, professional development that is not in the form of institutes or workshops does not receive legitimate recognition in schools. This calls for both administrators and participating teachers to communicate more frequently and publicly acknowledge the value of the research. Teachers can help convey the importance of action research by providing regular updates and presentations of findings to all staff, resulting in other teachers' awareness of the purpose of the action research project and how its findings could be used to benefit all teachers.
- *Readiness of action research participants.* This approach for professional development may not be for all teachers at the same time. Teachers differ widely in their priorities and interests, and these change over time. Teachers who are struggling to get new practices working may not be ready to collect data and then step back and reflect on the data. Teachers who are less concerned with trying to master new practices in the classroom and more concerned about the effectiveness of their teaching and its impact on student learning may be in the best position to benefit from action research projects.

Resources

Anderson, G., Herr, K., & Sigrid Nihlen, A. (2007). *Studying your own school: An educator's guide to practitioner action research* (2nd ed.). Thousand Oaks, CA: Corwin.

George Mason University, Graduate School of Education, Teacher Research Web site: http://gse.gmu.edu/research/tr

Madison Metropolitan School District, Classroom Action Research Web site: http://oldweb.madison.k12.wi.us/sod/car/carhomepage.html

Sagor, R. (2005). *The action research guidebook: A four-step process for educators and school teams.* Thousand Oaks, CA: Corwin.

Tugel, J. (Ed.). (2008). *Notes from the field: Teaching for conceptual change: Uncovering student thinking in science through action research.* Augusta: Maine Mathematics and Science Alliance. (available for download at www.mmsa.org/docs/SC4monograph.pdf)

CASE DISCUSSION

Sharon Friedman is a fourth-grade teacher, case writer, case discussion facilitator, and researcher involved with the Mathematics Case Methods Project. In her reflections on her involvement in case discussions, she writes the following (Barnett & Friedman, 1997):

When I first participated in a math case discussion, I thought that I would be examining instructional practice. I thought that I would share what I do in the classroom and hear about alternatives, which would lead to better informed decisions for my mathematics program. I was right, except for my understanding of what it means to "examine" instructional practice. I quickly learned that the "examination" entailed more than merely acquainting myself with various instructional methods. Through the discussions we looked deeply into the way instructional practice influenced and responded to student thinking. Any teaching practice, it seemed, had a consequence in terms of its effect on student thinking. Some curricula even led to confusion. We delved into the thoughts and misconceptions that students carry with them to our math classes, derived from past instruction, experience, and intuition. Good instructional practice, I was to discover, is an interaction between what the teacher says and the experiences he or she provides, and what the students do with it. Good practice is not, as teachers are often led to believe, a preset formula that does what it is supposed to do because the curriculum writers say so. I learned the importance of focusing the impact of my words and actions on children, on framing instruction that could anticipate student thinking as much as possible, and on responding effectively to the results. In planning, I learned to consider an interaction rather than simply a teaching method that does not take student thinking into account. (p. 383)

Case discussions offer teachers the opportunity to reflect on teaching and learning by examining narrative stories or videotapes that depict school, classroom, teaching, or learning situations. Cases are narratives (whether in print form or on videotape) that offer a picture of a teaching or learning event and are specifically designed to provoke discussion and reflection. They are not simply stories about teaching or learning but are, as Shulman (1992) notes, focused on events such as a teaching dilemma, students engaged in mathematics or science investigations, images of student thought processes, or teaching strategies in action.

Case discussions are used in a variety of ways with different goals and purposes. For example, educators and researchers promote the use of case discussions to examine student thinking and learning as a means of professional development. In these instances, cases are used as a window into children's thinking within a specific context. Teachers listen to students' ideas about mathematics and science and examine students' responses. By analyzing children's thinking and how their ideas are developing and by identifying what they understand and where their confusions lie, teachers become aware of how children construct their mathematical and scientific ideas. Being able to see mathematics and science through students' eyes helps teachers know and anticipate how students may misunderstand certain concepts and enables them to choose instructional experiences that can capitalize on the children's thinking. Teachers develop a greater recognition that student misunderstandings can be a valuable teaching tool and can inform teachers about what to do next with their instruction. Case discussions promote professional learning when they cause teachers to reexamine their perceptions of students' capabilities and their own assumptions about what understanding mathematics and science really means (Schifter, Russell, & Bastable, 1999).

The process of reflecting on students' thinking and learning through case discussions often results in teachers "trying out" the ideas or activities contained in the cases in their own classrooms (Barnett, 1991; Davenport & Sassi, 1995; Schifter, 1994). The powerful images of students in the cases prompt teachers to wonder about the thinking of their own students, how they might pose similar problems in their classes, and what might happen as a consequence. Teachers discover that they are better able to provide their students with experiences to help them articulate their confusion and with activities that help them resolve those confusions.

In addition, when teachers confront mathematics and science issues through the lens of students' perspectives, they often increase their own mathematics and science knowledge (Heller et al., 2001; Schifter & Bastable, 1995). As teachers reflect on students' thinking and approaches to solving problems, and assess the reasoning of students' responses, they begin to think through the mathematics or science again for themselves, often seeing new aspects of familiar content and expanding their own understanding (Russell et al., 1995). Case discussions can also be a powerful tool for helping teachers examine their own teaching practices. In these instances, cases typically convey a contextual problem, dilemma, or issue in teaching as well as the thoughts, feelings, and internal struggles of the case teacher (Schifter, 1996b).

Cases can present "whole stories" that include an ending describing how the case teacher addressed the dilemma (Shifter, 1996b). Others stop short of describing how the case teacher handled the problem and instead end with a series of open-ended questions to be addressed by the case discussants. Some are "packed full" of information to convey the complexity of teaching (Merseth, 1991), whereas others focus on discrete instances of teaching. Finally, some cases are grouped into clusters based on cases that have one or two similar dominant themes or that illustrate different aspects of the same principle. Examining clusters of cases requires teachers to retrieve, understand, and grapple with the domain or theme in different contexts and under different conditions (Barnett & Friedman, 1997).

Whatever the focus of a case, case discussions share common goals: to "motivate inquiry and support critical analysis" (Barnett-Clarke & Ramirez, 2008, p. 88); increase and enrich teachers' fundamental beliefs and understanding about teaching and learning; provide opportunities for teachers to become involved in critical discussions of actual teaching situations; and encourage teachers to become problem solvers who pose questions, explore multiple perspectives, and examine alternative solutions (Barnett & Sather, 1992; Shulman & Kepner, 1994).

While many case discussion sessions use published cases or commercial videos, teachers can also write their own cases. Usually, teacher writers follow a structured case development process that progresses from identifying a topic or issue of concern to collaborating with an editor or facilitator who helps turn the narrative into a case that has benefits for a larger audience. Most teachers who have written cases report that the process has a strong impact on their professional life, how they think about their teaching and students, their strategies and modes of instruction, and the ways in which they interact with colleagues regarding their experiences (Shulman & Kepner, 1994).

KEY ELEMENTS FOR CASE DISCUSSION

- Case materials present a focused view of a specific aspect of teaching or learning.
- Case materials illustrate theory in practice.
- Case materials can provide images of standards-based mathematics and science teaching and learning.
- Teachers interact and learn through discussions.
- Cases are facilitated by a knowledgeable and experienced facilitator who promotes reflection by case discussants.
- Cases are relevant and recognizable.

KEY ELEMENTS

Case materials present a focused view of a specific aspect of teaching or learning. Often, observers in a classroom focus on management behaviors and miss opportunities to examine specific teaching or learning episodes. By using cases, all participants are examining the same experience of the case teacher and students and have the immediate opportunity to reflect on those experiences during the case discussion.

Case materials illustrate theory in practice. Case discussions create a context for teachers to integrate their research-based knowledge into their view of students' learning and their own teaching and to apply this to their instructional practice. In some case discussions sessions, teachers read short research summaries prior to reviewing the case to inform their analysis and discussion. Vivid descriptions of classroom process provide grounding for theoretical principles where contexts for interpreting these abstractions are lacking (Schifter, 1994) and help teachers tie abstract learning to the complexities of real world application (Filby, 1995).

Case materials can provide images of standards-based mathematics and science teaching and learning. Standards-based teaching in mathematics and science may require teachers to change their beliefs about the nature of knowledge and learning and how knowledge is derived, increase their knowledge of content, and reinvent their classroom practice (Nelson, 1995). Translating the ideals of these ways of teaching and learning into actual classroom practice, however, is often the most complex and challenging task teachers face. Some cases offer an image of what effective learning environments look like and how teachers implement best practice. Far from being examples of the "unattainable," teachers have found that they can identify with many of the struggles faced by teachers and students in the cases and have found them motivating and inspiring (Schifter, 1996b).

Teachers interact and learn through discussions. Through verbalization and interaction, teachers formulate ideas, learn from each other, become aware of alternative strategies and perspectives, internalize theory, critique their own and others' ideas, become aware of their own assumptions and beliefs, increase their pedagogical content knowledge, and "develop a common language for discussing classroom instruction and for beginning the process of connecting ideas learning in the case discussions to teachers' day-to-day practice" (Stein, Smith, Henningsen, & Silver, 2009, p. 26).

When reflecting on cases that promote discussion about teacher actions, discussants may focus on what they think the case teacher should do next or evaluate the action that was taken. This process engages teachers in an analysis of why and how to use certain teaching strategies, challenges some of their assumptions and beliefs about the appropriate use of strategies, and broadens their repertoire of strategies for planning and implementing instruction (Shulman & Kepner, 1994). A goal of case discussions is to develop an attitude of inquiry toward and strategies for inquiring about classroom practice.

Cases are facilitated by a knowledgeable and experienced facilitator who promotes reflection by case discussants. Using the facilitator guidelines that accompany most published case materials, the facilitator helps participants tease out the facts of the case, identify and understand the problem or issues it raises, inquire into the approach taken or examine the source of students' confusion, discuss alternative actions, and reflect on the theoretical underpinnings of the action taken and discuss the consequences for learning. The facilitator helps the case discussion group establish norms for interaction and ground rules that enhance an atmosphere of learning and trust (Barnett-Clarke & Ramirez, 2008). They attend to teachers' levels of engagement during discussions and use various strategies to encourage and support all teachers to contribute to the analysis and discussion of the case.

Cases are relevant and recognizable. Although some cases depict teaching or learning situations that reflect the "ideal image" of what teaching and learning can look like, teachers need, at least initially, to be able to identify aspects of their own teaching within a case. Ideally, teachers encounter situations similar to the cases in their own teaching and can draw on their experiences during the discussion. Once teachers feel a sense of connection with a case, they can delve deeper into how the case is either similar or dissimilar to their own teaching approaches and beliefs. For example, some cases will parallel a teacher's own approaches or philosophy and can provide opportunities to examine and evaluate the consequences of specific decisions based on those ideas. Other cases will present notions that conflict with the beliefs of the teachers and can provoke critical analysis of the perspectives presented; "wrestling with the resulting disequilibrium" is what leads to changes in teachers' thinking about teaching and learning (Barnett & Sather, 1992; Thompson & Zeuli, 1999).

Intended Outcomes

Enhancing quality teaching is the primary outcome of case discussion. Teachers are focused on specific cases of teaching and learning, and their dialogue about the case engages them in reflection on ways to improve their practice. During their discussions, they may also explore their own science or mathematics content knowledge, and these discussions provide an opportunity to *enhance teachers' knowledge* of specific concepts as they arise as a result of the case discussion. For example, in cases that focus on teachers leading classroom lessons, facilitators often invite case discussants to complete any mathematics or science task that is in the case lesson prior to reading about or viewing the case. Completing the task in advance gives the discussants an opportunity to explore the content on their own so that when they read or view the case, they can focus on how students or teachers approach the task, rather than on trying to solve the task themselves. This type of precase exploration of content can provide an opportunity to help teachers examine their own understanding of the content.

In addition, this strategy lends itself to *developing leadership capacity* both through the development of teachers as facilitators of cases and through using cases that have images of teacher leadership practices as their content. In the latter instance, teacher leaders can explore the issues and challenges related to their roles, and their dialogue contributes to building their capacity to lead and facilitate other's learning. And, finally, this strategy contributes to *building professional learning communities.* A key feature of PLCs is the continuous focus and reflection on ways to improve teaching and learning, and case discussion provides a structured opportunity for these types of dialogue.

COMBINING STRATEGIES

There are numerous strategies that combine well with case discussion, since one of the purposes of this strategy is to enhance quality teaching. For example, case discussions can support teachers as they implement new curriculum when the case provides images of the new curriculum in classrooms. In other instances, teachers might decide to use cases to extend their learning about instructional strategies they are observing during demonstration lessons. Engaging teachers in curriculum topic study prior to a case discussion can be an ideal way to deepen knowledge and enhance reflection on practice. For example, based on learning through CTS, teachers might ask, "If this case reflected the research on student misconceptions, what would we see?" They would develop a summary of the readings for the topic and grade level of the case and use that to inform the discussion and analysis. Since case discussions can (and often do) relate to student work, teachers can continue to reflect on lessons learned from the case by examining their own students' work and thinking or by conducting action research to examine students' ideas in the case.

Cases also provide an excellent approach for helping coaches and mentors focus on the issues and challenges they face in their roles as teacher leaders. As these examples illustrate, case discussions work well with many other strategies, and it is the designers' task to clarify the purposes for teachers' learning to determine which strategies are best combined with case discussion.

> **Case discussion combines well with other strategies:**
>
> - Curriculum implementation
> - Demonstration lessons
> - Curriculum topic study
> - Examining student work and thinking
> - Action research
> - Coaching
> - Mentoring

ISSUES TO CONSIDER

Case discussions create a stimulating environment in which teachers use their expertise and professional judgment to consider underlying assumptions, analyze situations, and draw conclusions about teaching and learning. As a professional development strategy, it has many benefits. Teachers' ideas and insights are valued and challenged, leading them to reflect on and change their beliefs about how children learn and how and what they teach. Case discussions lead to increased teachers' content knowledge when teachers explore the science and mathematics content in the case. They also situate learning in actual practice and draw upon teachers' expertise. They provide teachers with opportunities to have in-depth conversations about teaching and learning.

Several issues surround the use of case discussions as a professional development strategy. For example, one issue is whether case discussions must be conducted face-to-face or whether they can be facilitated online. Bank Street College has conducted very successful electronic case discussions as part of its online courses. Outside evaluations have shown this approach to be highly valued by and beneficial to participants. There is good reason to argue, however, that because they often challenge teachers' deeply held beliefs about teaching and learning, case discussions are best conducted in person. The interpersonal, face-to-face dimension can be critical to establishing rapport and trust and to communicating disagreements in respectful and constructive ways. Preserving these benefits from the interpersonal dimension via electronic means presents a considerable challenge. Successful online case discussion facilitators are well versed in the strategies that build online communities and relationships over time. The decision about whether to conduct case discussions in person or online will depend on each group's specific context and teachers' needs, and the designer's role is to assess those needs to make an informed choice.

Another similar issue that has been raised is whether teachers can benefit from reading cases on their own and addressing key issues in solitary reflection. Because a serious time commitment may be required to be part of a case discussion group, it is sometimes tempting for teachers to cut the recommended corners and read about, rather than participate in, case discussions. Although teachers can certainly learn many things from reading cases, the real benefits of this strategy derive from the group process itself. It is difficult, if not impossible, to throw oneself into the kind of disequilibrium that Thompson and Zeuli (1999) have shown to be the essential step in changing beliefs and practices without some opportunity to process ideas and assumptions with other teachers. In addition, the diverse contributions of the group are what determine the unique nature of each case discussion and even cause discussions of the same case to have a distinctive character.

The question of whether unfacilitated discussions are as effective as those that are facilitated is at the heart of another issue. A small group of teachers who are committed to using this approach or who are reluctant to designate a facilitator may still benefit from case discussions, but they would need very effective communication skills and would need to have at least some organized method of recording and tracking the group's progress.

The role of the facilitator in many case approaches is more than that of a guide. Particularly in those instances where the approach includes published case facilitation guides or notes, the facilitator can be responsible for encouraging the group to address certain issues raised in the guides and be the content expert who helps teachers understand the mathematics or science ideas embedded in the case. Without a facilitator, some of these issues might be left unexamined. Another danger inherent in unfacilitated case discussions is that they may become more like informal discussions and lose the essence that characterizes case discussions as a professional development strategy.

RESOURCES

Annenberg Media Web site: www.learner.org/index.html (Provides access to teacher professional development and resources and classroom video for case discussions.)

Barnett, C., & Friedman, S. (1997). Mathematics case discussions: Nothing is sacred. In E. Fennema and B. Scott-Nelson (Eds.), *Mathematics teachers in transition.* (pp. 381–399). Hillsdale, NJ: Lawrence Erlbaum.

Barnett, C., Goldstein, D., & Jackson, B. (Eds.). (1994). *Mathematics teaching cases: Fractions, decimals, ratios, and percents: Hard to teach and hard to learn? Facilitator's discussion guide.* Portsmouth, NH: Heinemann.

Barnett, C., Goldstein, D., & Jackson, B. (1994). *Mathematics teaching cases: Fractions, decimals, ratios and percents: Hard to teach and hard to learn?* Portsmouth, NH: Heinemann.

Barnett, C., & Ramirez, A. (1996). Fostering critical analysis and reflection through mathematics case discussions. In J. Colbert, P. Desberg, & K. Trimble (Eds.), *The case for education: Contemporary approaches for using case methods* (pp. 1–13). Boston: Allyn & Bacon.

Barnett, C., & Tyson, P. (1994). *Enhancing mathematics teaching through case discussions.* San Francisco: WestEd.

Barnett-Clarke, C., & Ramirez, A. C. (Eds.). (2003). *Number sense and operations in the primary grades.* Portsmouth, NH: Heinemann.

Carroll, C., & Mumme, J. (2007). *Learning to lead mathematics professional development.* Thousand Oaks, CA: Corwin & San Francisco: WestEd. (videocase-based leadership development materials)

Madfes, T. D., & Shulman, J. H. (Eds.). (2000). *Dilemmas in professional development: A case-based approach to improving practice.* San Francisco: WestEd.

Merseth, K. (Ed.). (2003). *Windows on teaching: Cases of middle and secondary mathematics classrooms.* New York: Teachers College Press.

Miller, B., & Kantrov, I. (1998). *A guide to facilitating cases in education.* Portsmouth, NH: Heinemann.

Miller, B., Moon, J., & Elko, S. (2000). *Teacher leadership in mathematics and science: Case book and facilitator's guide.* Portsmouth, NH: Heinemann.

Pace University, School of Education, Center for Case Studies in Education Web site: www.pace.edu/page.cfm?doc_id=8912

Seago, N., Mumme, J., & Branca, N. (2004). *Learning and teaching linear functions: Video cases for mathematics professional development, 6–10, facilitator's guide.* Portsmouth, NH: Heinemann.

Shulman, J., & Mesa-Bains, A. (1993). *Diversity in the classroom: A casebook for teachers and teacher educators.* San Francisco: WestEd.

Shulman, J. H., & Sato, M. (Eds.). (2006). *Mentoring teachers toward excellence: Supporting and developing highly qualified teachers.* San Francisco: WestEd & Jossey-Bass.

Shulman, J., Whittaker, A., & Lew, M. (2002). *Using assessment to teach for understanding: A casebook for educators.* New York: Teachers College Press.

Stein, M. K., Smith, M. S., Henningsen, M. A., & Silver, E. A. (2009). *Implementing standards-based mathematics instruction: A casebook for professional development* (2nd ed.). New York: Teachers College Press & Reston, VA: National Council of Teachers of Mathematics.

WestEd Eisenhower Regional Consortium for Science and Mathematics Education and Distance Learning Resource network. (1996). *Tales from the electronic frontier.* San Francisco: WestEd.

WestEd & WGBH Educational Foundation. (2003). *Teachers as learners: A multimedia kit for professional development in science and mathematics.* Thousand Oaks, CA: Corwin. (See Tape 3, Program 4, "Exploring Science Through Cases," WestEd, Oakland, CA; Tape 2, Program 1, "Exploring Mathematics Through Cases I," Mt. Holyoke College, South Hadley, MA; and Tape 2, Program 2, "Exploring Mathematics Through Cases II," WestEd, Oakland, CA.)

COACHING

Steve is reflecting on his most recent observation and conversations with Renata, whom he is coaching this year. They started the year by agreeing to focus on Renata's use of probing and inquiry-oriented questioning of students. Since Renata is teaching the eighth-grade chemical changes module this semester, their focus is on her use of questioning during the teaching of the module. Steve observed Renata teaching early in the year so that he had a better sense of her strengths and areas in need of improvement. During the observation, Steve scripted Renata's questions and students' responses, which they analyzed and discussed during the postconference. Renata noted that the majority of her questions were lower-level ones that did not promote student thinking or reflection. Steve helped Renata reflect on why she often resorted to lower-level questions and Renata communicated that she was unsure of her own scientific understanding of the content and was "afraid" she wouldn't be able to provide answers to students' questions that could potentially diverge from the teachers' guide.

Steve thought that Renata could benefit from engaging in curriculum topic study to deepen her own knowledge as well as to enhance her understanding of how students learn the content and what they find difficult. Rather than conduct the topic study only with Renata, Steve invited the two other eighth-grade teachers to join them. The addition of these teachers definitely contributed to the depth and breadth of the discussions they had about chemical changes. After the session, Renata decided to try some of the questioning strategies they had learned about in the research when she taught the module. Steve and Renata discussed the lesson prior to her teaching it, and Steve again scripted her questions and students' responses. During the postconference, the analysis of the data revealed some changes in Renata's questioning. For example, they noted that she more frequently asked questions such as "Can you tell me more about the evidence you have to support your conclusion?" and "What other solutions did you explore and why did you reject them?" Renata still asked some lower-level questions during the lesson, and she and Steve developed plans for further reading they would do to help expand Renata's repertoire of instructional questioning strategies.

Coaching is a professional development strategy that provides one-on-one learning opportunities for teachers focused on improving science and mathematics teaching by reflecting on one's own or another's practice. It takes advantage of the knowledge and skills of experienced teachers, giving them and those with less experience opportunities to learn from each other.

Over the years, particular forms of coaching have emerged with different purposes and correspondingly different techniques, as suggested by the labels of *technical coaching, collegial coaching, challenge coaching, team coaching, cognitive coaching, linguistic coaching,* and *peer coaching* (Acheson & Gall, 1987; Caccia, 1996; Costa & Garmston, 2002; Garmston, 1987; Saphier & Gower, 1997). All incorporate a model focused on classroom observations and use a preconference-observation-postconference cycle. More recently, coaching as a form of collaborative peer learning has emerged, and districts across the country have developed content coaching models. In this model, the goal of coaching is to enhance the learning of both the coach and the teacher being coached and to improve classroom practice, and the role is characterized by facilitation of learning and not on evaluation of practice. Content coaches engage in supporting teachers through numerous activities, including conducting demonstration lessons, team-teaching lessons, examining student work, coplanning and designing lessons, critical friend inquiry and reflection on practice, and studying research and standards. In these roles, content coaches help teachers extend their understanding of the content, instructional strategies, and ways to assess student thinking and develop effective lessons (Noyce Foundation, 2007).

Coaching is most effective when the coach is able to match the coaching style with the level of structure needed by the teacher being coached. For example, teachers who are just learning a new curriculum model have a high need for structure. In these cases, the coach may use a *direct informational style of coaching* where the coach directs the conversation by providing pertinent information. When the teacher has a low need for structure and needs to "talk through" which of several strategies he or she might use in the classroom, a *nondirect style* of coaching is most appropriate. When using a nondirect style, coaches listen, clarify, and encourage the other teacher to present their ideas. A *collaborative style* of coaching is one where the coach and the teacher engage in a collegial exchange of ideas, coplan, and problem solve. When teachers have a moderate need for structure, that is, they have some ideas and some challenges to work through, this approach works best.

KEY ELEMENTS OF COACHING

- Teachers focus on learning or improvement.
- A climate of trust, collegiality, and continuous growth is cultivated.
- Coaches are well prepared with in-depth content knowledge and adult learning skills.
- Mechanisms for observing practice and providing feedback are critical.
- Opportunities for interaction are provided.

Key Elements

Teachers focus on learning or improvement. Coaching is most successful when teachers agree that they will work on examining particular teaching techniques, student interactions, perplexing problems, or learning strategies. Sometimes, this is as focused as tallying the number and kinds of questions teachers ask of different students to understand any gender or cultural biases, which is of great importance in teaching science and mathematics. Other times, it is more general, such as gaining feedback on their techniques used to manage materials. What is critical is that coaches and teachers establish agreement on the areas of instruction they will focus on and set realistic goals for improvement.

A climate of trust, collegiality, and continuous growth is cultivated. Coaching relationships are strengthened by a willingness to take risks and learn from failures, acknowledgment of strengths and weaknesses, and a desire to build improvement strategies, welcoming the role of a critical friend (Costa & Kallick, 1993), and accepting learning as a continuous process. Teachers in coaching relationships also must build an understanding about what each knows about teaching, learning, and content. As this understanding increases, they become more helpful to each other. This can happen only if their interaction occurs with some regularity, so suggestions and insights can be tried and reflections on their impact shared.

Coaches are well prepared with in-depth content knowledge and adult learning skills. The more a coach understands about the content being taught and knows from experience how students learn it (and how to teach it), the better. Good coaches help teachers become more reflective in their practice and better inquirers into problems and dilemmas of teaching. They can be of much greater assistance when they know the specific science or mathematics content being taught by the teachers with whom they are working.

In addition to content and pedagogical content knowledge, coaching requires special skills in communication (e.g., clarifying, paraphrasing, conflict management, and listening), observation, and giving feedback. Coaches need their own professional development to learn how best to translate their own knowledge and experience to others (see "Resources"). Coaches also benefit from understanding principles of adult learning and the change process (see Chapter 2).

Mechanisms for observing practice and providing feedback are critical. For classroom observations, preconferences typically are opportunities for the coach and the teacher being observed to agree on the focus and set ground rules about the kind of feedback that will be helpful. Postconferences, then, are guided by these agreements. Different approaches to coaching suggest different forms of sharing and feedback, some structured by classroom observation instruments and others as open as sharing detailed, but unstructured, observations of the flow of the lesson. Likewise, forms of feedback vary from simple description to particular forms of questioning. Critical feedback provided in a nonthreatening manner is essential in all reflective sessions. Teachers often are not experienced in challenging each other's ideas, and in a coaching relationship it is essential that both participants be willing to be a critical friend, which involves direct yet supportive feedback that addresses what worked well as well as what areas could be enhanced (Costa & Kallick, 1993).

Opportunities for interaction are provided. It almost goes without saying that for coaching to be successful, the coaches and teachers need opportunities to interact with each other. For example, just having time for classroom observations without protected time to talk before and after defeats the purpose of careful and shared examination and understanding of teaching practice. Although a novice teacher may pick up some tips from sitting in on a lesson taught by a more experienced teacher, a follow-up discussion of what was done, why, and with what impact is critical to understanding teaching.

INTENDED OUTCOMES

Since the focus of coaching is to support teachers' knowledge and practice in a professional relationship with a teacher leader, this strategy is designed to achieve all four of the outcomes: *enhancing teachers' knowledge, enhancing quality teaching, developing leadership capacity,* and *building professional learning communities.* The focus on teaching and learning provides the "content" for the coaching relationship and coaches engage teachers in deepening their content knowledge and reflecting on their practice through many of the other strategies described in this book (see "Combining Strategies"). In some states and districts, coaching is being used as a model to support administrators' growth and learning, pairing experienced school leaders with novice leaders, which expands the use of this strategy to develop schoolwide leadership capacity.

COMBINING STRATEGIES

Coaching is a strategy that supports teachers' use of specific curriculum, instructional materials, or teaching strategies. For example, some school districts combine the use of coaching with science or mathematics curriculum implementation. Teachers new to the science or mathematics curriculum have a coach who helps them understand the conceptual ideas in the lessons and who provides feedback on their teaching. Coaching also combines well with many of the other strategies focused on supporting teachers to examine and reflect on their practice, including examining student work and thinking, demonstration lessons, and action research, and those focused on deepening understanding of standards and research through strategies such as curriculum topic study.

Coaching combines well with other strategies:

- Curriculum implementation
- Examining student work and thinking
- Demonstration lessons
- Action research
- Curriculum topic study

ISSUES TO CONSIDER

Coaching is a powerful strategy that, in combination with other professional learning strategies, contributes to enhancing teachers' science and mathematics knowledge and teaching practices. The focus on examining practice through dialogue and observations grounds this strategy in teachers' real work. However, several issues can arise when coaching is introduced to teachers, whether in a department, as a schoolwide effort, or as a part of a professional development program or initiative. First, norms of isolation and privacy work against many teachers' willingness to open their classrooms and their teaching to observation and scrutiny. Going slowly, developing trust, building relationships before classroom observations occur, and having a very specific focus that is nonthreatening but challenging are some ways to overcome teachers' hesitancy. Additionally, it is imperative to ensure that the coaching relationship is focused on collaborative efforts to improve practice and not on supervisory or remedial efforts.

Finding time for conducting and discussing classroom observations is a challenge within a typical school schedule. Creative solutions include rearranging planning times, using team teaching, and having substitutes and volunteers work with students on independent projects during observation time. It is also critical to develop administrative support. Administrators must recognize and communicate the importance of coaching relationships, allocate or reallocate time in ways that pairs have time to observe each other and work together, and nurture and support the building of a learning community in the school that has these teacher partnerships at its core (Garmston, 1987; Showers & Joyce, 1996).

Before coaching is initiated, it is important for schools or districts to choose and communicate the coaching methods that will be used and the plans for the professional development of coaches. As noted at the beginning of this section, not only does coaching have many labels, but also each type has a different purpose, technique, and outcome. Being clear about the intentions and approach to coaching can build commitment to the coaching program. Studying and then learning the techniques, through reading or focused professional development, can maximize the impact of coaching as a professional learning strategy.

RESOURCES

Costa, A., & Garmston, R. (2002). *Cognitive coaching: A foundation for renaissance schools* (2nd ed.). Norwood, MA: Christopher-Gordon.

Dunne, K., & Villani, S. (2007). *Mentoring new teachers through collaborative coaching: Linking teacher and student learning.* San Francisco: WestEd.

Fichtman Dana, N., & Yendol-Hoppey, D. (2008). *The reflective educator's guide to professional development: Coaching inquiry-oriented learning communities.* Thousand Oaks, CA: Corwin & Oxford, OH: National Staff Development Council.

National School Reform Faculty, Harmony Education Center, Critical Friends Groups Web site: www.nsrfharmony.org/faq.html

Noyce Foundation Silicon Valley Mathematics Initiative: Content Coaching Web site: www.noycefdn.org/svmi.php

WestEd & WGBH Educational Foundation. (2003). *Teachers as learners: A multimedia kit for professional development in science and mathematics.* Thousand Oaks, CA: Corwin. (See Tape 4, Program 2, "Content-Based Coaching," Belmont Public Schools, Belmont, MA; and Tape 4, Program 1, "Curriculum-Focused Coaching," City On A Hill Charter School, Boston.)

MENTORING

> Jacob was anxious about starting his first week as a fifth-grade teacher at the local elementary school. He had done his student teaching and practicum experiences in elementary schools and had some sense of what to expect but was not sure about how he would be received by the other teachers. Some of his anxiety was lessened by the summer meetings he had with his mentor, Wesley. They met for coffee a few times and spent a day at the school helping Jacob learn his way around. It was a relief just to know where his classroom and the supply closet were located!
>
> When Jacob arrived at school on Monday morning, Wesley was already waiting for him in Jacob's classroom. The students weren't scheduled to start school for another three days, so Jacob knew he had some time to adjust. Wesley welcomed him and let him know that they would spend the day together walking through the school to meet all of the other teachers, reviewing the curriculum and lessons Jacob would teach his first few weeks, and working with Elisabeth, the technology specialist, to orient him to the computers in his classroom and the school networking system.
>
> At the end of the day, Jacob was feeling welcomed and more comfortable about joining an already cohesive faculty; they had organized a pitch-in lunch to give him a chance to be with the entire faculty and the principal in an informal setting. He admired the friendly and collegial interactions and knew he would have several "mentor buddies" in addition to Wesley. Before Jacob left for the day, he met with Wesley to debrief on how the day went and to discuss any unanswered questions. They reviewed the schedule for the next day when Jacob would meet with teachers from other grades to discuss the mathematics curriculum and with the school's instructional leadership team to discuss some schoolwide issues, such as "What is expected of us here at this school?" "How are we evaluated?" "How do we know whether students are learning what we are teaching?" Wesley assured Jacob that this was not going to be a crash course in teaching, but only the beginning to his immersion into teaching.

Mentoring is a teacher-to-teacher professional development strategy that sustains a system of long-term, ongoing professional learning embedded within the school culture. Mentoring usually occurs between a teacher new to the field and a more experienced teacher or an experienced teacher taking on a new role or new teaching approach.

In mentoring programs, a primary purpose is to provide support for the new teacher and to enhance the leadership roles of the mentor. A mentor is an experienced teacher who serves as a content specialist, as well as a "collegial guide, helping to orient and acclimate the new teacher to the culture of the school; a consultant who actively supports the new teacher in identifying strategies for managing and resolving struggles; a seasoned teacher, who shares wisdom and practical knowledge; and coach, who leads the new teacher through a process of collaborative inquiry that expands and improves the new teachers' instructional repertoire" (Dunne & Villani, 2007, p. 30). Mentors in science and mathematics programs are typically teachers with more content knowledge or experience in using a particular curricular program or teaching practices. Sometimes, scientists and mathematicians are mentors for teachers, helping them to develop an increased understanding of the content they are teaching and to incorporate discussions of real-world applications in their teaching of science or mathematics content. They also take on the role of "problem solvers for instructional dilemmas" to help teachers address many of the challenges in their first years of teaching (Robbins, 1999, p. 40).

Mentoring as a strategy for professional learning has expanded in recent years to focus on the retention of practicing teachers and, specifically, the support of new teachers in their first years. Of new teachers, 30% to 50% leave the profession during their first few years of teaching with the highest attrition rates occurring in urban settings (Ingersoll & Kralik, 2004; National Center for Education Statistics, 2001; National Commission on Teaching and America's Future, 1996). Some studies report that effective mentoring programs have shown a significant increase in teacher retention ranging from 85% to 90% (Newton et al., 1994; Villani, 2002; Wong, 2004), while others indicate no changes in retention after one year of participation in a comprehensive mentoring program (Glazerman et al., 2008). Ongoing investigation through research continues to enhance the education communities' understanding of both the short-term and long-term impacts of mentoring programs.

Many states and school districts have implemented mentoring programs for new teachers to support their induction into the teaching profession. Some of those states and districts have expanded the notion of induction to include "far more than the mere orientation of beginning teachers at the start of the school year or the provision of ongoing practical support throughout the school year . . . to recognize that even fully prepared beginning teachers need to learn more about teaching" (Britton, Paine, Pimm, & Raizen, 2003, p. 1).

In addition, demanding standards and changing demographics present challenges for both novice and experienced teachers. Educating highly diverse students to meet much higher science and mathematics standards requires tremendous skills on the part of teachers. Teachers need to provide a wide range of learning experiences connected to what a diverse student body knows, how they learn, and the content and structure of the disciplines (Ball & Cohen, 1999; Darling-Hammond & McLaughlin, 1999; Partnership for 21st Century Skills, 2008). Teachers need opportunities to deepen their understanding of how children learn science and mathematics and to stay abreast of emerging research. Veteran and novice teachers alike need collegial arrangements, like mentoring, that provide a structure through which they continually develop their expertise as teachers (Bransford, Brown, & Cocking, 1999).

KEY ELEMENTS FOR MENTORING
• Mentors have extensive knowledge and skills.
• The mentoring relationship focuses on science and mathematics content and pedagogical content knowledge.
• New teachers and mentors have valuable expertise to share with each other.
• It is essential to have mutual agreement and understanding on the goal and purpose of the mentoring relationship.

KEY ELEMENTS

Mentors have extensive knowledge and skills. Mentors need their own professional development and orientation to their roles. Although a mentor may have extensive experience as a teacher of students, mentoring adults requires additional knowledge, skills, and abilities including the following:

- *Knowing how to establish a climate of peer support.* Mentors need to know how to nurture a supportive environment and relationship with the new teacher by communicating an attitude of support rather than one of an expert with all of the answers (Denmark & Podsen, 2000).
- *Able to model reflective teaching practices.* One of the most valuable aspects of mentoring relationships is the opportunity for the new teacher to learn about the ways in which the mentor thinks about teaching and learning—"getting inside the mentor's head." In addition, by modeling reflection, mentors provide new teachers with a valuable skill and attitude for continuous learning that is part of the teaching profession. "Mentors can assist novices in translating content knowledge and skills into successful instructional behaviors . . . by demonstrating a reflective approach to teaching, self-evaluation, and implementation of new ideas" (Denmark & Podsen, 2000, p. 21).
- *Staying current on research.* Mentors can model best practice professional learning by reading recent research and sharing articles, books, and other resources with novice teachers. Accompanying discussions and reflections enhance the learning of both.

The mentoring relationship focuses on science and mathematics content and pedagogical content knowledge. While it is important for mentors to help new teachers with generic teaching strategies and classroom management techniques, they must also focus on ensuring that new teachers have the science or mathematics content knowledge needed to implement effective instruction. Mentors need in-depth science or mathematics content and pedagogical content knowledge to provide the most effective help to new teachers who are learning to teach or use new strategies.

New teachers and mentors have valuable expertise to share with each other. Although the intent of mentoring relationships is for the mentor to enhance the learning and growth of the new teacher, teachers new to teaching bring their own level of expertise and learning to the relationship. For example, new teachers often have a wealth of information on new research and learning in their content area, how students learn the content, and awareness of curricular goals and standards. The mentor's role is to facilitate the translation of the new teachers' knowledge into classroom practices. When working with experienced teachers, mentors can help them build on their existing expertise and knowledge as they, for example, try new teaching strategies or implement a new curriculum. Likewise, new teachers provoke learning in the mentor teachers when they ask them to reflect on why they do what they do in the classroom, evoking insights and making implicit knowledge more explicit to both the mentor and the mentee.

It is essential to have mutual agreement and understanding on the goal and purpose of the mentoring relationship. For individuals pursuing mentoring as a structure for continual learning, both the new teacher and the mentor must have common goals and intended outcomes. One of the first conversations between mentors and mentees should focus on what each person brings to the relationship and what each one wishes to learn. Through the discussion, these professionals should arrive at goals that are aligned with the school goals (e.g., orientation and comfort with implementing the school's curriculum, making instructional improvements, or contributing to a positive school culture).

Intended Outcomes

The primary outcome of the mentoring strategy is *enhancing quality teaching,* while also *enhancing teachers' knowledge.* As noted in the next section on combining strategies, the mentoring relationship relies on examining practice and exploring content through various professional learning experiences. It is this focus on practice that contributes to teachers' achievement of the intended outcomes. Additionally, through the mentor relationship, both the mentor and the novice teacher are part of *building professional learning communities,* and mentors who participate in their own professional learning contribute to *developing the leadership capacity* within the school and sustaining a focus on continuous improvement.

Combining Strategies

There are numerous strategies that combine well with mentoring, since the focus of the mentoring relationship is on supporting new teachers to enhance

> **Mentoring combines well with other strategies:**
>
> - Examining student work and thinking
> - Demonstration lessons
> - Study groups
> - Action research
> - Curriculum topic study
> - Professional networks

their knowledge and teaching practices. For example, mentors often facilitate the examination of student work and thinking, conduct demonstration lessons, and participate with novice teachers in study groups and collaborative action research. Mentors are ideal candidates for facilitating curriculum topic study with their colleagues, as well as participating in their own professional networks to support their work as teacher leaders.

ISSUES TO CONSIDER

In recent years, mentoring as a formal structure for providing professional learning has grown into a strategy used with novice teachers, experienced teachers, principals, and administrators. As mentoring becomes more prevalent, there are, however, issues that impact the successful implementation of formal structures for mentoring. First, many schools and districts are learning that simply matching any mentor with a new teacher is often not successful. Careful consideration and thought must go into pairing teachers in a mentoring relationship. For example, practitioners suggest that mentors volunteer to serve in mentor roles, be committed to the time and interpersonal requirements of the role, and recognize that they too can benefit from the relationship. In addition, structures need to be put in place that allow mentors and new teachers to "select" alternate partners should there be major obstacles to an effective relationship. Some schools and districts anticipate the critical need for the "authentic" development of a mentoring relationship and pair teachers with a team of mentors, resulting in relationships that can more naturally develop between individuals, developing at a more authentic level.

Second, it is essential for the school culture to support collegial interactions among teachers. Given the interpersonal nature of mentoring relationships, it is critical that the mentor and new teacher develop a collaborative, mutually rewarding environment for learning. Instituting a mentoring program in a school in which time is not provided for collegial interactions or in which teachers' continual learning is not valued often results in failure of the mentoring program. Time must be allocated to building the mentoring relationship, for observing in classrooms, and for informal and formal interactions. Not only is structured daily or weekly time essential, the mentoring relationship necessarily evolves over time and often requires several years to develop its full benefits for the mentor, the novice teacher, and the students in both teachers' classrooms.

A related issue is ensuring that the goals and intended outcomes of the individual mentoring relationships align with the overall school goals. For example, one initial activity for a newly developing mentoring relationship is to examine the school vision and mission concerning science and mathematics teaching and learning and identify specific teaching practices (e.g., implementing a specific set of instructional materials designed to address specific student learning goals) to focus on in the mentoring situation. It is also important to balance the individual needs of the new teacher with the goals of the mentor and the school's goals.

It is imperative that mentors receive their own professional learning opportunities to support them to develop knowledge and skills over time. For example, one project in the New England region developed a tiered program over a three-year period to allow mentors the necessary time and commitment to support several teachers. In the first year, mentors focus in-depth on developing their own mentoring and leadership skills and knowledge and working with one new teacher, helping him or her problem solve their most immediate needs as a new teacher. In the second year, mentors continued their own learning and began to address the needs of teachers entering their second year of teaching—implementing strategies for curriculum, instruction, and assessment that are standards based. In the third year, mentors add another new teacher to work with while decreasing the dependence of their first-year teachers by helping them focus on their own self-assessment, reflection, and teaching. This scaffolded approach to preparing mentors attends to their own professional learning needs and growth over time.

Resources

Association for Supervision and Curriculum Development, Mentoring Leadership & Resource Network Web site: www.mentors.net

Dunne, K., & Villani, S. (2007). *Mentoring new teachers through collaborative coaching: Linking teacher and student learning.* San Francisco: WestEd.

Johnson, S. M., & The Project on the Next Generation of Teachers. (2007). *Finders and keepers: Helping new teachers survive and thrive in our schools.* San Francisco: Jossey-Bass.

Lipton, L., & Wellman, B. (with Humbard, C.). (2001). *Mentoring matters: A practical guide to learning-focused relationships.* Sherman, CT: Mira Via.

Newton, A., Bergstrom, K., Brennan, N., Dunne, K., Gilbert, C., Ibarguen, N., et al. (1994). *Mentoring: A resource and training guide for educators.* Andover, MA: Regional Laboratory for Educational Improvement of the Northeast and Islands.

Shulman, J. H., & Colbert, J. A. (Eds.). (1987). *The mentor teacher casebook.* Eugene, OR: ERIC Clearinghouse on Educational Management & San Francisco: Far West Laboratory for Educational Research and Development.

Villani, S. (2002). *Mentoring programs for new teachers: Models of induction and support.* Thousand Oaks, CA: Corwin.

Aligning and Implementing Curriculum

Figure 5.6 Strategies for Professional Learning: Aligning and
Implementing Curriculum

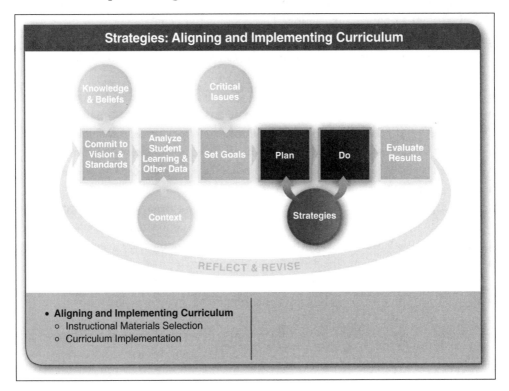

The two strategies described in this section (see Figure 5.6) emphasize using quality mathematics or science curriculum as the focus for teachers' professional learning—instructional materials selection and curriculum implementation. In districts across the country, curriculum selection, adoption, and implementation are such common practices in science and mathematics that focusing teachers' professional learning around the curriculum is a great way to embed professional development within the real work of teachers. In fact, more and more curriculum developers are writing curriculum with the explicit purpose of promoting teacher learning as well as student learning. Often referred to as "educative curriculum materials" (Ball & Cohen, 1996; Davis & Krajcik, 2005; Schneider & Krajcik, 2002), the materials go beyond simply providing teachers with guidelines for teaching the lessons by supporting teachers' learning of the content, exploring students' conceptions of the content, and discussing instructional approaches aligned with the way in which students learn the content. Whether traditional or educative, curriculum materials provide opportunities for teachers' professional learning.

This section describes two strategies that link curriculum improvements and professional learning opportunities for science and mathematics teachers. Both of the strategies are based on several underlying assumptions about teaching, learning, and professional development.

Underlying Assumptions

Quality curriculum materials are designed to support students' learning of concepts and content as identified in the national science and mathematics standards. In an era of standards- and research-based teaching and learning, educators are acutely aware of the need and the mandate to provide quality learning opportunities for all students. In many cases, states have developed state content standards aligned with the national standards, and often, school districts create their own district standards and pacing guides. These adaptations and interpretations of the national standards vary greatly in their quality. It is critical that those involved in curriculum-based professional development develop an understanding of the national standards and other research that documents what content students should learn and how they can best learn it. They need to consider the extent to which any state's or district's standards align with national standards and the extent to which the curriculum they use provides opportunities for all students to develop the skills, knowledge, and abilities articulated in the national standards.

Teachers become clearer about the goals for student learning and increase their own understanding of the subject matter by learning to use quality curriculum materials. For teachers, going through the process of selecting and implementing new curriculum that is standards based, well organized, and accurate can clarify (a) the nature of the content itself and assumptions about what students bring to the content, (b) how the content can be taught (e.g., what is hard and what is easy for students to learn as provided in the curriculum and as determined by the teacher's use of the curriculum), and (c) the nature of student knowledge—how students work and talk—and the nature of the discourse that teachers orchestrate to give them access to information about what and how students are learning.

Supporting teachers to learn science and mathematics content and pedagogical content knowledge that is directly connected to their curriculum materials increases the likelihood of changes in classroom teaching. Numerous studies report that when teachers engage in professional development that is directly connected to curriculum materials, teaching behaviors change. For example, Cohen and Hill (1998) conducted a study of mathematics teachers in California, studying the effects of varied professional development experiences on teaching and student learning. They found that "student curriculum-centered learning opportunities seem to increase Framework practice and to decrease conventional practice. Teachers did not just add new practices to a conventional core, but also changed that core" (pp. 5–6).

Teachers who experience new ways of teaching and have opportunities to reflect on and enhance their use increase their abilities to implement and develop a commitment to the new approaches. Using new approaches to teaching (e.g., inquiry) and curriculum materials designed to support such approaches provides teachers with experiences that often raise many questions. Reflecting on and analyzing what they are experiencing in their classrooms and talking with other teachers about what they are learning enhances teachers' understanding of how to best teach the curriculum. Professional development that supports teachers to use the curriculum is an optimal way to help teachers learn content and new ways of teaching. Structured discussion following their use of the curriculum allows teachers to reflect on and analyze their own classroom performance. They can articulate their experiences, receive reinforcement for successes and help in understanding and addressing their problems, and then work through challenges.

Implementation Requirements

District or School Administrative Support

Administrators encourage the process, provide time and incentives for teachers to participate, ensure access to resources and experts, and support ongoing, long-term improvement of the curriculum and instructional materials that are ultimately implemented.

Process for Selection or Alignment of Curriculum Including Rubrics, Tools, and Forms for Tracking What Was Piloted and Its Results

When the focus is on trying out curriculum for the purpose of selecting one for full implementation, it is essential that the process be clear to everyone involved. Using resources such as those listed later in this section keeps the teachers involved and on track and helps document what was done and why.

Time

Teachers have protected and structured time to learn about the curriculum, try it in their classrooms, observe other teachers using the curriculum, and reflect with colleagues on their experiences and those of their students.

Teacher Development Opportunities

Teachers are oriented to the curriculum, learn its contents, get support in using and managing materials in the classroom, learn any new science or mathematics content, teach the curriculum, and assess both their own and their students' learning.

Policies

The school and district anticipate and plan for institutionalization by ensuring that structures are in place for the continued use of the curriculum after the initial phases and ongoing professional development for all teachers and that the curriculum is part of the overall school and district goals and policy.

Ongoing Commitment and Support

Teachers and school administrators support the curriculum implementation and accompanying professional development over time (i.e., not just for one year) and avoid becoming distracted by other innovations and competing priorities.

Mechanisms for Assessment and Evaluation

Teachers have routine meetings and interactions with other teachers to critique and process what and how they are teaching and data are collected to assess the extent of implementation and the interim results from the curriculum.

INSTRUCTIONAL MATERIALS SELECTION

At the request of the superintendent, a group of teachers from four schools and their principals and the science curriculum specialist formed a committee to coordinate selection of instructional materials. Following a process called analyzing instructional materials (AIM), developed by K–12 Alliance at WestEd, their first step was to come to consensus on the criteria they would use to select from among the many science texts and kit-based materials available. They each took responsibility for using curriculum topic study (CTS) as a guide for learning more about research, practices, and standards in science education and shared findings with each other. They also carefully studied and discussed the expectations for students reflected in their district, state, and national standards. They identified criteria for the content, student engagement, assessment, and instructional approaches, and from this they created a rubric for scoring the different elementary science materials they were considering. The rubric would help them measure the extent to which the curriculum materials reflected the content in the standards; engaged students in the kind of work, learning, and assessment activities recommended by research; and were developmentally appropriate. The engagement with CTS and development of the AIM rubric resulted in substantial learning among the participants. They learned the content of the standards as well as research on children's ideas in science and developed a shared vision of what the elementary science program for the district needed to include.

The committee obtained copies of commercially available materials to review for consideration, examining the extent to which each set of materials addressed appropriate science content, the intended learning goals for all students, and strategies for teaching, learning, and assessment. They narrowed their choice down to two different products that the committee scored the highest using their rubric. They enlisted teacher leaders at each elementary grade level throughout the district to pilot test the two different sets of instructional materials in their classrooms. During pilot testing, teachers engaged in weekly study group sessions to reflect on what they did in their classrooms and examine the students' work to better understand what the students were learning and how the instructional materials supported learning. Pilot-testing teachers also met monthly with the curriculum committee to share what they, as teachers implementing the new materials, needed to enhance their ability to use the materials effectively, including science content knowledge and better understanding of inquiry-based learning. The curriculum committee responded to these needs during the pilot testing and used what they had learned to inform plans for large-scale professional development.

Based on the results, the committee and pilot-testing teachers selected one of the instructional materials for use in the coming school year and developed a long-term plan for implementing the new instructional materials.

In many districts, the process of selecting instructional materials has been simply to pick something popular with a few teachers or, worse, have teachers all use their own materials with little coordination. Increasingly, districts are engaging in more thoughtful analysis of the curriculum and its alignment with local and national standards. They use this curriculum analysis in combination with a deliberate materials selection process to select a coherent and focused program for all students. In addition, many districts are capitalizing on this process as an opportunity for teacher learning. The strategy of instructional materials selection develops teachers' understanding of effective curriculum, science and mathematics education standards, content, pedagogy, and assessment.

As the above vignette illustrates, the selection committee engaged in various activities to increase teachers' knowledge including the following:

- Studying the local and national standards to identify the meaning and intent of student learning goals
- Developing a clear picture of what curriculum was needed based on the standards and student learning goals and how concepts and skills would develop in a coherent fashion through the grades
- Developing a common vision of standards-based teaching and learning
- Identifying local needs based on analysis of student learning and other data
- Using a process for selecting instructional materials that was guided by a systematic approach to gathering evidence
- Selecting the materials, pilot testing them, and developing a plan for implementation

KEY ELEMENTS

Teachers are essential participants in the process of aligning, selecting, and implementing instructional materials. Many districts appoint a selection committee composed of content area coordinators and classroom teachers to conduct the initial identification of curriculum to consider for adoption. The involvement of teachers, however, often ends once the instructional

> **KEY ELEMENTS OF INSTRUCTIONAL MATERIALS SELECTION**
>
> - Teachers are essential participants in the process of aligning, selecting, and implementing instructional materials.
> - Selecting instructional materials requires a clearly articulated procedure that addresses all aspects of the process.
> - Instructional materials selection is a collaborative activity.

materials are adopted and added to the approved district or state list. For this strategy to maximize professional learning, teachers need to stay involved throughout the whole process—from establishing learning goals to implementing instructional materials. Their involvement in studying standards, learning new content, and setting learning goals increases their understanding of the relationship between the curriculum and the learning goals or standards, giving them insight into the intent of the curriculum. Their active participation in pilot testing the instructional materials helps them see how the curriculum works with children, and this can inform the professional development needed to support the implementation of the materials by other teachers. Helping to shape professional development plans and monitor and support implementation is another learning opportunity for teachers.

Selecting instructional materials requires a clearly articulated procedure that addresses all aspects of the process. There are numerous tools and guidelines available for curriculum selection (see "Resources"). No matter which process is selected, it is critical that the following components be included:

- The formation of a team or committee includes representation from teachers at the appropriate grade levels and content areas, different school sites, and administrators.
- Select tools and a comprehensive process to guide the examination of national and local standards, analysis of current performance levels in the appropriate grade levels and content areas, development of a content matrix that identifies student learning goals across grade levels, and the selection of the instructional materials.
- Instructional materials selection should include an analysis of the content, student learning activities, teaching activities, teacher content information, and assessment strategies. These components should be evaluated based on rubrics developed or adapted by the committee members to meet their local contexts and goals.

In addition to the components noted above, the selection of instructional materials should include a prescreening process to narrow the choices of instructional materials; a paper screen process to gather and analyze evidence from the materials to determine whether they meet the established criteria and standards, using a rubric or other scoring device; pilot testing of the materials in classrooms to gather and analyze student work and other data from the classroom; selection of the final instructional materials; and full-scale implementation of the materials with accompanying professional development.

Instructional materials selection is a collaborative activity. The process of collaborating with other teachers and curriculum experts enriches the professional development opportunities. Through analysis of curriculum and discussion, teachers build their own knowledge of the content, curriculum organization and design, and content-specific pedagogy. They begin to identify content that they do not understand and plan together to address such gaps in knowledge. Often, as teachers examine the curriculum and see how and why different concepts and lessons are organized the way they are, their attitudes about what constitutes effective science or mathematics teaching and learning change. They return to their classrooms with new views. For example, they might have a greater appreciation for how content that they teach helps prepare students to better understand content that is covered at the next grade level. Also, by collaborating with others, teachers become less isolated in their individual classrooms and develop a broader perspective of science or mathematics education.

INTENDED OUTCOMES

Selecting instructional materials as a professional learning strategy is largely targeted toward achieving the second of the four interconnected outcomes, *enhancing quality teaching.* The materials that are ultimately selected are designed to enhance teaching and learning, and through the selection and trial process teachers learn the strategies embedded in the materials. However, the strategy also supports the first outcome, *enhancing teachers' knowledge,* since the process of selecting the materials involves deepening teachers' understanding of the content, how students learn the content, and examining student work for evidence of student learning.

This strategy also lends itself well to *developing teacher leaders* who serve in various roles during the selection of instructional materials. For example, in the opening vignette, teachers were members of the selection committee, which is a role often played by teacher leaders. In addition, teacher leaders in each elementary school were identified to pilot test the instructional materials. However, what is not conveyed in the vignette is the professional development that would have been required to orient the teacher leaders to the new materials and support the teachers to implement them in their classrooms. The teacher leaders might have participated in an orientation workshop, followed by demonstration lessons to experience the materials before using them in their classrooms. The vignette also identified another role for the teacher leaders—participating in the identification of the content and instructional approaches that other teachers would need to learn in order to implement the new instructional materials, resulting in the identification of specific learning goals to guide the professional development. In each case, developing teacher leaders to be involved in and guide the selection of instructional materials contributes to the school's capacity by investing in teachers who can facilitate and lead professional learning experiences for other teachers.

COMBINING STRATEGIES

The opening vignette includes examples of several strategies that are often combined with selecting instructional materials: curriculum topic study, study groups, and examining student work and thinking. In combination, the strategies support teachers' learning and instructional practice. Through engagement in curriculum topic study, the teachers deepened their understanding of the standards and research, how students learn the content, and effective instructional practices. During the study group sessions, teachers in the vignette reflected on how the instructional materials influenced their teaching practices, and they examined student work to gather evidence of the impact on student learning. In addition to the strategies noted in the vignette, selecting instructional materials also combines well with demonstration lessons. For example, teachers with more experience using the instructional strategies embedded within the new materials might teach a lesson from the materials under consideration while other teachers observed the lesson. The lesson would be followed by a discussion during which teachers reflect on the effectiveness of the instructional materials to guide how materials are managed, how students are organized and grouped, how teacher questioning strategies contributed to student understanding, and the overall contribution to student learning.

Instructional materials selection combines well with other strategies:

- Curriculum topic study
- Study groups
- Examining student work and thinking
- Demonstration lessons

ISSUES TO CONSIDER

Many of the benefits of using instructional materials selection for professional development of science and mathematics teachers have previously been identified in this section. As with any professional development strategy, however, there are challenges and issues to consider.

It is difficult for teachers to find the time to devote to the intensive process of examining curriculum and selecting instructional materials. Frequently, teachers are available only after school or during the summer months to devote time to this intensive effort. It is imperative that teachers who volunteer for curriculum committees are given adequate time and support for their efforts, such as reduction of class load or some other duties in exchange for their participation on the committee. It is also critical that administrators recognize that this is a long-term process and necessarily engages teachers for more than one academic year.

As noted previously, numerous documents, guidelines, and procedures are available to guide the instructional materials selection processes. It is important to keep in mind that the main purpose of these processes is the professional learning and growth of the teachers involved—both those on the committee and the pilot teachers—and ultimately the selection of curriculum materials that will improve student learning. Both goals can be accomplished if care is taken in the identification of the guidelines used to facilitate the processes. In some districts, multiple-year efforts may not be feasible and shorter alignment and selection procedures may need to be identified.

RESOURCES

American Association for the Advancement of Science. (n.d.). *The Project 2061 analysis procedure for mathematics curriculum materials.* Retrieved August 17, 2009, from www.project2061.org/publications/textbook/algebra/report/analysis.htm

Burns, R. (2001). *A leader's guide to curriculum mapping and alignment.* Charleston, WV: Appalachia Educational Laboratory.

Carr, J. F., & Harris, D. E. (2001). *Succeeding with standards: Linking curriculum, assessment, and action planning.* Alexandria, VA: Association for Supervision and Curriculum Development.

Drake, S. (2007). *Creating standards-based integrated curriculum: Aligning curriculum, content, assessment, and instruction.* Thousand Oaks, CA: Corwin.

English, F. W. (2000). *Deciding what to teach and test: Developing, aligning, and auditing the curriculum.* Thousand Oaks, CA: Corwin.

National Research Council. (1999a). *Designing mathematics or science curriculum programs: A guide for using mathematics and science education standards.* Washington, DC: National Academy Press.

National Research Council. (1999b). *Selecting instructional materials: A guide for K–12 science.* Washington, DC: National Academy Press.

Penuel, W., Fishman, B., Yamaguchi, R., & Gallager, L. (2007). What makes professional development effective? Strategies that foster curriculum implementation. *American Educational Research Journal, 44*(4), 921–958.

Posner, G. J. (2004). *Analyzing the curriculum.* New York: McGraw-Hill.

CURRICULUM IMPLEMENTATION

Sarah Johnson is a sixth-grade teacher in a district that has three middle schools, each with approximately 600 students, Grades 6 through 8. The school board has just voted to implement a new mathematics curriculum. Sarah participated with other teachers in a preliminary meeting during the spring that provided an overview of this new curriculum, but she really has little understanding of the total program or of what it will mean for her to actually use it.

The middle school coordinator has asked Sarah to join her, one seventh- and one eighth-grade teacher, and the principal from her school, along with similar teams from each of the other two middle schools in the district to participate in a one-week residential professional development institute that will introduce them to the curriculum. At the institute, she finds 18 other middle-grades teachers and their administrators from two other districts. This will be a good opportunity to learn with teachers who are from very different districts.

At the beginning of the institute, an overview of the structure and organization of the curriculum is provided. Very quickly, the leader moves to engaging participants in doing actual activities from the first module they will teach. Sarah jumps right in, as do the rest of her team members, and they work through the various math problems. Sarah is particularly attentive to some of the teaching strategies that the leader is using. In particular, she likes the way the leader expects different groups to take responsibility for initiating summary discussions about problems that have been investigated. She also notes that the leader makes a point of highlighting particular learning strategies as a way of pointing out the interaction of the teaching methods used and ways to promote student engagement and problem solving.

That night, participants are given homework problems to complete for the next day. Sarah and her team meet to work together on the problems; they are challenged as they solve problems and talk about the implications for use with their students. When they arrive at the workshop the next day, the leader designates various teams to take responsibility for presenting their solutions, providing a model for a strategy that Sarah plans to use as part of her classroom structure for the next year.

As the week progresses, the participants begin to understand the structure of the curriculum and how to use it with their students. The leader makes building a community of learning seem easy; Sarah wonders how she will develop such a community with her own students but is filled with enthusiasm. As the week draws to a close, the leader focuses on planning to use the curriculum. Using the school calendar and the pacing guide provided with the curriculum, teachers from the same grade levels team up and lay out a schedule to implement the first module. Sarah feels confident about the detail provided in the teacher support materials, particularly because the curriculum has actually been field tested at a number of different sites. There are many things planned when Sarah returns to her district. She knows that the middle school coordinator is counting on her and the other teachers in her district to use the new curriculum in their classrooms this year and then to help introduce the curriculum to other teachers in their schools the following year. The principals and the middle school coordinator intend to be quite proactive in their efforts to support the teachers in developing learning communities that are oriented toward problem solving, and they will provide the teachers with opportunities for peer coaching and support group meetings. Two more one-day workshops are scheduled throughout the year with the institute leader both to provide time for discussion and to gain an understanding of other modules that will be used at each grade level. Also, the institute leader will return to the school district in the spring to conduct several one-day sessions for the other teachers in the schools.

For right now, Sarah is focused on what will happen with her students. For the first time in a long time, Sarah finds she is very excited about teaching mathematics and that the curriculum seems to reflect her beliefs about what constitutes good teaching and learning.

The implementation of new curricula in the classroom can serve as a powerful learning experience for teachers. For curriculum implementation to support professional development, plans must be designed that enable teachers to learn about, try, reflect on, and share information about teaching and learning in the context of implementing the curriculum with their colleagues. Through using curriculum in their classrooms, reporting on what happens, and reflecting with others on the strengths and weakness of different ideas and activities, teachers learn about their own teaching and their students' learning.

Curriculum implementation involves using a set of materials that includes both content and instructional guidelines. The "set" of materials may be from one publisher or developer, or it may have been selected from a variety of quality materials available and organized by the school or district for use at particular grade levels in the development of specific concepts. For curriculum implementation to serve as an effective professional development activity, it is important that the curriculum selected or organized for implementation meets quality standards for content and for appropriate teaching strategies.

Curriculum implementation that is designed for professional development focuses teachers on learning about the new curriculum and how to use it and on implementing it—not on researching, designing, testing, or revising curriculum. The teachers' time is devoted to learning the science or mathematics content necessary to teach the new curriculum, learning how to conduct the activities, learning how students learn the new material, and incorporating the new curriculum into their long-term instruction. The goal of this professional development strategy is not only for teachers to implement a new curriculum but also for them to strengthen their knowledge of the content and pedagogy in the curriculum.

KEY ELEMENTS

Quality curriculum materials are based on standards. Curriculum is the way content is designed and delivered. It includes the structure, organization, balance, and presentation of the content in the classroom (National Research Council, 1996). Curriculum and instruc-

> **KEY ELEMENTS FOR CURRICULUM IMPLEMENTATION**
>
> - Quality curriculum materials are based on standards.
> - Teachers learn about the curriculum by teaching it and reflecting on it.
> - Implementation is supported by a plan.

tional materials structure and organize the content and lend support for the teaching strategies and learning environments used by teachers to help their students learn. The curriculum implementation strategy relies on quality curriculum materials carefully developed by people with expertise in content and pedagogy and sufficiently tested for use in diverse classrooms.

Teachers learn about the curriculum by teaching it and reflecting on it. As teachers become familiar with the curriculum and go through the materials as learners, they see the various teaching strategies they will use with their students. Specific attention is paid to helping teachers translate their own learning experiences into those that are appropriate for their students. Teachers then try the new instructional materials and teaching practices in their classrooms and continuously assess and discuss their results and progress with colleagues.

A variation of the curriculum implementation strategy, implementing curriculum replacement units, focuses explicitly on the key element of engaging teachers in teaching units and reflecting on their experiences. In this case, the purpose is not to fully implement a new curriculum, but to use new curriculum to introduce teachers to new instructional approaches. In other words, the replacement units themselves are the content of the professional development. Through the experience of teaching the units, teachers change how they think about teaching and embrace new approaches to facilitating student learning. Through reflection and collegial discussion, teachers are then supported to translate their learning and apply the new approaches to the ways in which they teach all of the curriculum.

Implementation is supported by a plan. A plan contains the structure and timeline of the curriculum implementation. Teachers and professional developers work together to decide how and when the curriculum will be implemented and the milestones that will be met at different points in the implementation process. Usually, curriculum implementation involves using an entire curriculum for all grades in the school that covers all topics of the content area instead of only one topic or one grade level. The implementation process spread over time, however, may introduce units at one grade level at a time or introduce one unit at a time at each grade level. As the curriculum is introduced over a period of time, teachers are given different kinds of support that are tailored to their changing needs. Teachers share ideas and insights with one another as they implement the new curriculum. They also coach one another and conduct classroom visits to support implementation.

Intended Outcomes

Similar to selecting instructional materials, the primary intended outcome of curriculum implementation is *enhancing quality teaching* by providing all teachers with access to high-quality curriculum and materials. Additional professional development strategies that are necessarily embedded within the implementation of curriculum contributes to *enhancing teachers' knowledge, developing leadership capacity, and building professional learning communities.* In the opening vignette, Sarah's experiences supported her as a classroom teacher as well as introduced her to her role as a teacher leader. Had we visited Sarah a year later, we might see her serving in roles such as coach, case discussion facilitator, or presenter at workshops or institutes. Since implementing curriculum is a fairly comprehensive professional learning strategy, it serves as a natural way in which to develop leaders throughout the system, from district coaches to teacher leaders who facilitate others' learning and reflection on practice. What is critical is that teacher leaders receive their own professional development to strengthen their knowledge and skills related to leading adult learning before taking on the leadership demands.

As noted throughout this section, simply implementing new curriculum is not the vehicle for professional learning. Rather, it is teachers' engagement in strategies such as intensive institutes to learn the content in the new curriculum, curriculum topic study, study groups, or demonstration lessons that provide opportunities for teachers to enhance their content knowledge, practice their instructional approaches, and collaborate with other teachers as they implement the curriculum over time.

Combining Strategies

Several strategies that work well with curriculum implementation have already been mentioned in this section, including an institute that included immersion in problem solving, curriculum topic study, study groups, and demonstration lessons. In addition, examining student work and thinking and case discussions support teachers as they implement new curriculum. In essence, strategies that immerse teachers in content, standards, and research and engage them in examining teaching and learning all combine well throughout the entire process of teachers' using new curriculum in their classrooms.

> **Curriculum implementation combines well with other strategies:**
>
> - Immersion in inquiry in science and problem solving in mathematics
> - Curriculum topic study
> - Study groups
> - Demonstration lessons
> - Examining student work and thinking
> - Case discussion

ISSUES TO CONSIDER

Although virtually all schools implement new curricula at some time, often they do not organize the implementation process around professional development that provides opportunities for teachers to reflect on and learn from their experiences over time.

There are several benefits to using curriculum implementation as a structure for professional development. First, such an initiative aligns professional development with the three major dimensions of effective educational systems—the curriculum as written, the curriculum as taught (instructional practices), and the curriculum as assessed—all of which are firmly grounded in and guided by standards (English, 2000). (See Figure 5.7.) This avoids what is an all too common practice in many districts: professional development that is disconnected from and unrelated to the curriculum that teachers teach. A second and related benefit is the efficiency of teachers learning exactly what they need to teach. This contrasts with the situation in which teachers learn content and teaching strategies, but have no ready-made vehicle to put these together in their classrooms. Finally, curriculum implementation is beneficial because it provides a focus for teacher reflection. Teachers can share issues, concerns, and students' work in the context of discussing the new curriculum.

In addition to its benefits, there are also pitfalls of the curriculum implementation strategy. First, there is a tension between the "mandates" to implement a new curriculum with fidelity and teacher creativity and independence. It is important for teachers to know how much adaptation they can make and still implement the curriculum effectively. Some changes in the new curriculum (e.g., finding and developing appropriate connections to other subject areas) can enhance the materials' effectiveness. Others can be

Figure 5.7   Effective Education Systems

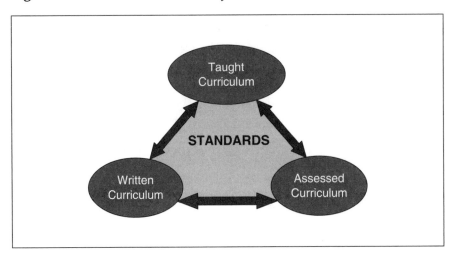

Source: Adapted from Fenwick W. English, *Deciding What to Teach and Test: Developing, Aligning, and Auditing the Curriculum, Millennium Edition,* 2000, p. 13. Thousand Oaks, CA: Corwin. Used with permission.

harmful (e.g., when science teachers decide that live organisms are too difficult to manage or that demonstrations work better than each student doing his or her own investigations). The nature of acceptable adaptations requires early and ongoing negotiation.

Schools can ensure continual use of the curriculum by proactively supporting all teachers and providing orientation for new teachers or teachers who change grades. The needs of teachers change over time. Initially, teachers may be focused on the "how-to's" for using the new curriculum. Given the nature of problem-centered and inquiry-based curricula, this focus could span the first few years of implementation. Once teachers are comfortable with the tasks, they often become concerned with the impact of the curriculum on students' understanding. At this stage, broader considerations of the nature of the mathematics or science content being addressed and how best to understand students' thinking may surface, requiring a different orientation to professional development. Eventually, teachers may find themselves at points at which they want to "fine-tune" or make modifications in the use of the curriculum to better meet the needs of their students. This sequence of learning opportunities to support teachers' emerging needs reflects the cycle of implementation discussed in the introduction to this chapter.

A final caveat: With this approach, there is a real danger that professional development support will stop once (or before) the curriculum is fully in place. This disregards the need for continuously increasing teacher knowledge and skills. The mechanisms for teacher reflection, sharing, assessment, and adjustment should become part of the overall school routine. As teachers become more sophisticated in curriculum use, they will want to assess the impact on student learning. Professional development can help them learn about effective ways of gathering and analyzing student learning data.

RESOURCES

Biological Sciences Curriculum Study. (n.d.). *BSCS National Academy for Curriculum Leadership.* Retrieved August 17, 2009, from www.bscs.org/professional development/nacl

Education Development Center, The K–12 Mathematics Curriculum Center Web site: www2.edc.org/mcc/default.asp

National Science Resources Center, Leadership and Assistance for Science Education Reform (LASER) Center Web site: www.nsrconline.org/school_district_resources/index.html

WestEd & WGBH Educational Foundation. (2003). *Teachers as learners: A multimedia kit for professional development in science and mathematics.* Thousand Oaks, CA: Corwin. (See "Standards-Based Curriculum Implementation: Mathematics Curriculum Workshop," Clark County Schools, Las Vegas, NV.)

Professional Development Structures

Figure 5.8   Strategies for Professional Learning: Professional Development Structures

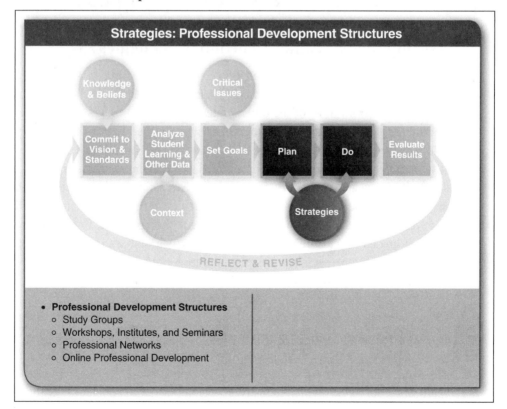

The four professional development strategies described in this section are grouped together because they are structures through which many different professional learning activities can be organized and carried out (see Figure 5.8). These four structures are: (1) study groups, (2) workshops, institutes, and seminars, (3) professional networks, and (4) online professional development. These strategies differ from the others described in this chapter because they do not usually have a particular focus or a set process; they are simply a generic way to organize content for teacher learning.

Study groups, for example, can be used for many different teacher learning activities, such as examining student work or conducting action research. Workshops, institutes, and seminars can focus on immersing teachers in content or inquiry and problem solving or can serve the purpose of orienting teachers to the new curriculum that they will implement. Online professional development can have a wide range of learning goals, such as deepening content knowledge, engaging in case discussions, or conducting lesson study across schools, districts, and even states or nations. Professional networks are a mechanism for convening teachers and teacher leaders who share a common interest and goal and are seeking professional relationships that extend beyond the school.

The strategies in this cluster are not grounded in a common set of assumptions that unite them. Rather, there are several assumptions that professional development designers need to keep in mind as they decide whether to include these strategies in teachers' overall professional learning plans.

Assumptions to Guide Selection of Strategies

Goals and purposes for the content to be embedded within the strategy are clearly established. Since these strategies lend themselves to including content and processes from most of the other strategies described in this chapter, it is important to ensure that there is alignment between the intent of the strategy selected to include and the structure of these strategies. For example, if the goal is to immerse teachers in science or mathematics content, a short-term workshop will not be appropriate. However, a multiday institute is more effective in providing the time for teachers to engage in inquiry or problem solving as well as to reflect on the application of their learning to their practice. If teachers are eager to engage in curriculum topic study, they can embark on this learning experience through a seminar or study group. Online professional development aligns well with teachers' needs to deepen their content knowledge through courses but does not facilitate teachers to observe in each others' classrooms. What is essential is that, as a designer, you identify content, processes, and goals that align with the structure of the strategy.

Establish coherence with teachers' and schools' needs and goals, avoiding "one-shot" learning experiences. Teachers have experienced far too many one-shot workshops in their lives! It is important to consider how these strategies align with teachers' overall learning needs and ensure that there is a coherent repertoire of learning opportunities from which teachers can select. Just as each of the clusters of strategies described in this book serve different purposes and result in different outcomes, the strategies in this cluster are best implemented in support of, or as a follow-up to, teachers' engagement in other learning opportunities. For example, teachers might attend a workshop to become oriented to a new curriculum, followed by demonstration lessons and case discussions to gain a better understanding of what the curriculum looks like when implemented. In another case, teacher leaders who serve as coaches or mentors might participate in a professional network to support their continuous learning and reflection on practice through dialogue with others in their same roles. Here again, the important idea is to create a coherent and continuous learning plan for teachers, rather than isolated and disconnected experiences.

Balance internal and external expertise when identifying facilitators. Educators must constantly expand their knowledge of both their teaching fields and how to teach them. The strategies described in this section provide teachers with opportunities to connect with outside sources of knowledge in a focused, direct, and intense way. For example, national experts are often called on to facilitate local workshops, or teachers attend institutes offered by national organizations. Local scientists or mathematicians often participate in study groups to support teachers' content learning. However, there is a wealth of expertise that resides within schools and districts, and professional development designers need to build leadership capacity within their own systems as well as bring in credible experts. Developing teacher leaders who can facilitate study groups, lead workshops, or copresent with experts during institutes contribute to leadership capacity.

Implementation Requirements

Time to Participate

Like all other strategies for professional learning, participation in these strategies requires time to participate and focus on learning and to do so over a period of time. Even when teachers embark on learning through these strategies on their own, they need to balance the requirements for engaged learning time with other demands in their lives.

Support From Administrators

The school or district provides support by paying for substitutes and offering incentives and stipends for teachers to participate, especially when strategies such as workshops or institutes are offered during nonteaching time (e.g., summer, evenings, or weekends). Since these professional learning experiences should not be extraneous to teachers' ongoing learning, teachers need opportunities to share with others what they are learning and the "authority" to implement new learning in their teaching practices.

Expert Knowledge and Facilitation Skills

Knowledgeable people must be available to provide or facilitate access to the knowledge that learners will gain during the sessions. These experts need science or mathematics content and pedagogical content knowledge, as well as the skills and abilities to facilitate adult learning. In some cases, the experts may reside within the school—teacher leaders who have been prepared to lead professional learning with their colleagues—or external to the school—scientists or mathematicians from the community or national experts. Often a study group will invite a local science faculty member to work with the group to provide this expertise.

Clear Focus of Activity That Is Connected to Teachers' Learning

It is essential that teachers' participation in these strategies contributes to a cohesive plan for enhancing knowledge and practice. They are not "add-ons" to teachers' learning and work, but rather, should complement teachers' overall professional learning plans. There should be a clearly articulated purpose, goal, and intended outcome for participating.

STUDY GROUPS

After several years focused on implementing a new mathematics curriculum, the teachers at State Middle School were still fine-tuning their practice. Their curriculum was sound, they had developed teacher leaders who supported all teachers' learning, and they had a firmly established professional learning community. However, even though students' mathematical learning was improving, their common formative assessments indicated that students struggled with some concepts. Their analysis of the data led them to consider the quality of the instructional tasks they were using in their classrooms. In particular, they thought that their instructional approaches did not always seem to play out in the ways they intended. They had attended a session at a recent NCTM conference in which a framework was presented that described the cognitive demands of mathematical tasks. The teachers wanted to explore this framework further to determine whether it might offer some insight into how and why their lessons sometimes did not seem to deliver to their potential.

They decided to meet as a group biweekly after school to study videotapes of their own teaching and use the framework to reflect on whether or not the cognitively demanding tasks that they set up in their lessons were indeed being carried out by students in such a way that reduced their cognitive demands (e.g., not showing their mathematical reasoning). Each week, a teacher volunteered to show a 20- to 30-minute clip of instruction that would then be discussed using the framework as a guide. One of the teachers commented later that year, "This sustained attention to practice was absolutely what was needed to take us over the top." Another commented that the regular group sessions were the motivating force that pushed everyone to be more critical and reflective.

Study groups are collegial, collaborative groups of problem solvers who convene to mutually examine issues of teaching and learning. They are conducted within a safe, nonjudgmental environment in which all participants engage in reflection and learning and develop a common language and vision of science and mathematics education. Study groups are not teachers gathering for informal, social, or unstructured discussions. Rather, study groups offer teachers the opportunity to come together to focus on issues of teaching and learning. The topics addressed in these groups vary from current issues in mathematics and science education to achievement of whole-school goals. Groups may be composed of small numbers of teachers interested in pursuing a topic together or subgroups of the entire school faculty addressing whole-school educational issues. They can also be composed of teachers across schools or even across districts. Regardless of the topic or issue being addressed, study groups provide a forum in which teachers can be inquirers and ask questions that matter to them, and are based on improving student learning, over a period of time, and in a collaborative and supportive environment.

Teachers should join and form study groups voluntarily and determine their own focus for learning and the format for the sessions. Although teachers' professional learning is the goal of study groups, increasing student learning is the end result of teachers' collaboratively examining their own knowledge, skills, and abilities. Carlene Murphy and Dale Lick (2001) suggest a problem-solving cycle that can help teachers effectively structure their study groups around specific goals and needs for student achievement:

- *Data analysis.* Analyze a wide range of data and indicators describing the status of student learning and the conditions of the learning environment.
- *Student needs.* From the data, generate a list of student needs.
- *Categorize and set priorities.* Categorize student needs and prioritize categories or clusters, stating what the "problem" is.
- *Organization.* Organize study groups around the prioritized needs and specify the intended results that will indicate that the problem is lessened or solved.
- *Plan of action.* Create a study group plan of action that includes specific activities or strategies to implement that will reach the intended results.

- *Implementation.* Implement the study group action plan, including data collection and tracking changes through logs or journals, and specify procedures for organizing and sustaining the group.
- *Evaluation.* Evaluate the impact of the study group effort on student performance and teacher learning, and determine plans for institutionalizing the changes.

KEY ELEMENTS OF STUDY GROUPS

- Study groups are organized around a specific topic or issues of importance to the participants and are related to teaching and learning goals.
- Study group activities are coherent and planned.
- Study group teams need group interaction skills.
- Study groups have varied structures.
- The formation and success of study groups require direct support from school administrators.

Key Elements

Study groups are organized around a specific topic or issues of importance to the participants and are related to teaching and learning goals. One of the primary elements of this strategy is that groups are organized around a specific topic or issue of importance to the participating teachers. Participating teachers identify a topic or issue that is "complex, rigorous, and substantive enough to keep all members of the group engaged and immersed in the learning process" (Murphy & Lick, 2001, p. 184). In addition, if the topic selected is too narrow or can be addressed in a very few sessions, the group may find itself moving from topic to topic without really reflecting on what they are learning. These topics range from school-based concerns to curriculum and instructional issues. For example, grade-level teachers might form a study group to learn more about assessing their students' understanding of science concepts. Over a period of time, they might meet to study research and standards, share examples of assessments and critique the appropriateness of the assessments, or invite school or district personnel to join the group to discuss other assessment requirements and how these influence classroom practice. Other study groups might be composed of entire school faculties or departments that focus on, for example, "supporting the implementation of curricular and instructional initiatives, integrating and giving coherence to a school's instructional programs and practices, or targeting a schoolwide instructional need" (Murphy & Lick, 2001, p. 18). Still other study groups might be composed of teachers from different schools who convene to analyze student learning data and share best practices that contribute to improved student learning.

Study group activities are coherent and planned. Study group participants identify a process for how to address the issues or topics. Most study groups use a variety of activities including reading, examining school data, viewing videotapes, observing in each others' classrooms, examining student work, and studying research and standards; learning about new teaching and learning approaches through reading, attending workshops or other sessions, or inviting experts to work with the group; and implementing new practices in their classrooms and using the study group time to reflect on and analyze the experience both for themselves and their students. In fact, many of the other professional development strategies described in this book are often combined with study groups: examining student work and thinking, examining standards to inform curriculum alignment and selection of instructional materials, conducting action research, and engaging in case discussions.

Study group teams need group interaction skills. As with other strategies that rely on teacher collaboration, group interaction skills are critical. Successful groups have members who share a common goal and are committed to accomplishing the goal, work to create an environment of trust and openness and foster communication, believe that diversity is an asset and that each member brings something unique to the group, value risk taking and creativity, are able to plan and implement strategies, share leadership and facilitation of group processes, are comfortable with consensus decision-making procedures, and are committed to building a team that reflects deeply on their learning.

Study groups have varied structures. Depending on the nature of topics discussed or issues addressed, the form study groups take varies. Makibbin and Sprague (1991) suggest four models for structuring study groups. The implementation model is designed to support teachers' implementation of strategies recently learned in workshops or other short-term sessions. The goal is to provide teachers with an ongoing system for discussing, reflecting on, and analyzing their implementation of strategies after the workshop has concluded. The institutionalization model is used once teachers have already implemented new practices in the classroom and want to continue refining and improving these practices. Research-sharing groups are organized around discussions of recent research and how it relates to classroom practice. Investigation study groups are a way for teachers to identify a topic or practice about which they would like to learn. In this model, teachers read about, discuss, and implement new strategies that are relevant in their own contexts—their teaching practices and their students' learning. These models have been successfully implemented by teachers of mathematics and science as they investigate content, instructional practices, and student learning.

The formation and success of study groups require direct support from school administrators. Administrative support is critical not only for the time for the group to meet but also for support for the endeavor itself. Administrators send a clear message of the importance of professional development for teachers if time is set aside during the school day for study groups to convene. In most cases, study groups meet frequently and over a long period of time; some suggest a minimum of at least once a week over a period of several months (LaBonte, Leighty, Mills, & True, 1995; Murphy, 1995; Murphy & Lick, 2001). Regardless of how frequently the group meets, it is critical that groups maintain a regular schedule of consistent contact with the expectation that their work is ongoing. Administrators can also offer support by providing access to resources, technology, or experts when teachers request assistance in meeting their goals. In instances where whole-faculty study groups are formed, administrator support and participation are critical.

INTENDED OUTCOMES

Because of the flexibility of the specific content that can be embedded within study groups, given the group's focus there is the potential to achieve any, or all, of the four outcomes for professional learning. For example, if teachers are focused on immersion in content, standards, and research strategies, the outcome will be on *enhancing content knowledge.* If, however, teachers are focused on examining their teaching and learning, an expected outcome would be *enhancing quality teaching* practices. No matter the content, though, participation in a study group contributes to *developing the leadership capacity* and *building professional learning communities.*

COMBINING STRATEGIES

The very nature of a study group's structure and purpose enables it to be combined with other professional learning strategies. As noted throughout this discussion on study groups, almost any of the other strategies can be the focus of the work of study group members—such as curriculum topic study, examining student work and thinking, demonstration lessons, lesson study, action research, or case discussion—as well as supporting teachers engagement in other strategies—such as ongoing reflection after attending a workshop or institute, frequent reflections on practice as teachers implement curriculum, or as they pilot instructional materials. The options for combining with other strategies are limited only by the purposes, goals, and needs of the participating teachers.

> **Study groups combine well with other strategies within *all* of the clusters:**
>
> - Immersion in content, standards, and research strategies
> - Examining teaching and learning strategies
> - Aligning and implementing curriculum strategies
> - Professional development structures, such as workshops, institutes, and seminars

Issues to Consider

Study groups require the participation of teachers who are committed to reflecting on their work and taking initiative for their own learning. It is not a strategy that lends itself to raising awareness about a topic in a short period of time but rather one that encourages teachers to "go deep" and question and reflect on their practices and their students' learning.

Because study groups necessarily involve teachers in reflection outside of the classroom, it is difficult to sustain study groups in traditional school cultures. Although they may be slow to get started in such environments, once study groups "take hold" in a school, teachers enthusiastically support their continuation. Often, administrators come to recognize their benefit and realize that study groups lend themselves well to investigations and inquiries into numerous topics and issues of concern to both teachers and the entire school community. For example, study groups concerned with finding time for professional development, using national and state standards to improve teaching and learning, or developing community support for science or mathematics improvement, can benefit teachers and students while building ownership and commitment by a broader school community.

Resources

Murphy, C., & Murphy, M. (2008). Study groups. In L. B. Easton (Ed.), *Powerful designs for professional learning* (2nd ed., pp. 243–258). Oxford, OH: National Staff Development Council.

Murphy, C. U., & Lick, D. W. (2001). *Whole-faculty study groups: Creating student-based professional development* (2nd ed.). Thousand Oaks, CA: Corwin.

Murphy's Whole-Faculty Study Groups Web site: www.murphyswfsg.org

---

WORKSHOPS, INSTITUTES, AND SEMINARS

Tony Sanchez and the other mathematics teachers at his school participated in a two-week summer institute held at the school. The institute was intended to help them develop their knowledge of algebra. The instructor, in this case a teacher educator who would be available to teachers during the following school year, regularly used the algebra pieces, which were available in each algebra classroom, to engage teachers in exploration of traditional algebraic concepts and procedures from new perspectives. The teachers often worked in small groups and then shared their solution strategies with the whole group. Following an activity, the instructor and teachers would discuss both what the teachers had done and what the instructor had done to support their learning. They would talk about how the algebra pieces had been used, the kinds of questions that arose, and the decisions the instructor had made.

Workshops, institutes, and seminars are structured opportunities for educators to learn from facilitators or leaders with specialized expertise as well as from peers. They bring together educators from the same school or district or from different locations in a region or the country for common experiences and learning. They provide opportunities for participants to focus intensely on topics of interest for weeks (e.g., institutes) or for shorter periods of time (e.g., seminars and workshops). Workshops tend to address more discrete learning goals, such as learning to use a particular set of lessons or a new assessment strategy. Institutes typically include more immersion experiences and experiential or hands-on activities through which participants engage in-depth with new ideas and materials. Seminars tend to be more oriented to sharing knowledge and experiences through discussions and reactions to others' practice or studying books, research, and standards. Depending on the learning goals for a particular group, a professional developer might choose to combine one or more of these strategies, such as combining a multiweek institute with a quarterly seminar series.

Whether implementing a workshop, institute, or seminar, it is critical that each be designed to include principles of effective professional development. Too often, they are characterized by passive learning or sit-and-get approaches that do not meet the needs or the interests of the participants. In the book *Designing Successful Professional Meetings and Conferences in Education* (Mundry, Britton, Raizen, & Loucks-Horsley, 2000, pp. 6–8), the authors identify features of effective workshops, institutes, and seminars:

- *Clear purpose and outcomes.* Participants know the goals, expectations, purposes, and benefits of the session(s).
- *Value.* The session offers value to the participants by addressing their goals for learning and growth.
- *Variety.* A variety of learning activities are combined that engage participants and appeal to different learning styles.
- *Networking.* Sessions provide time for participants to interact with each other and build relationships with new colleagues.
- *Effective use of time.* Effective sessions make "every minute count." For example, lunch discussions can be tailored to help participants process the content of the morning and to network.
- *Quality of leaders and facilitators.* The facilitators know their content well and are skilled in effective adult learning methods. They understand and respond to the goals of the participants.
- *Ongoing evaluation.* Sessions are evaluated and feedback is used to make adjustments and enhance future sessions.
- *Quality of content and design.* The content is "credible, sound, current, and interesting."

- *Resources.* Participants get access to print or electronic resources that extend their learning and provide them with reference material to use in the future.
- *Products.* Participants are guided to develop artifacts or products that reflect what they are learning. These include plans, conceptual frameworks, assessments, or maps of their progress or thinking.
- *Right audience.* The session communicates clearly about its goals and purposes to target the right people for participation.

Optimal workshops, institutes, and seminars also reflect what is known about effective adult learning (Bransford et al., 1999; Mundry, 2003; Regional Educational Laboratories, 1995), including the following:

- Opportunities for learners to provide input to the content of the workshop, institute, or seminar and understand the purpose for learning the content that will be addressed
- Time for reflection, predictions, and explorations
- Multiple modes of presentations and information processing and opportunity to address real problems or challenges
- A respect for the expertise adults bring and activities that encourage all to share their knowledge
- Support and feedback from people with expertise
- Connections between new concepts and information and current knowledge and experience
- A safe environment to try new ideas and approaches

Designers should keep these features, as well as the principles of effective professional development discussed in Chapter 2, in mind as they develop workshops, institutes, and seminars that meet the intended goals and learning needs of the participants.

KEY ELEMENTS

Clearly stated goals are communicated to the participants. Leaders of effective workshops, institutes, and seminars communicate with participants about the goals of the learning experience prior to and during the sessions. They receive input from learners before setting goals so that the learning experience addresses the learners' needs.

> **KEY ELEMENTS FOR WORKSHOPS, INSTITUTES, AND SEMINARS**
>
> - Clearly stated goals are communicated to the participants.
> - A leader or facilitator guides the participants' learning.
> - Group structures necessitate a collegial learning environment.

A leader or facilitator guides the participants' learning. The leader or facilitator also guides and supports the participants' learning, often by being a primary source of expertise or bringing in other information through readings, consultants, the participants' experiences and knowledge, and structured experiences.

Group structures necessitate a collegial learning environment. Because these strategies are intended for groups of people, the learning environment should be designed so that it is collegial for participants to learn from one another and from the leader of the session. Often disparaged as the "traditional form of professional development," workshops, institutes, and seminars, like other professional development strategies, can range in quality, depending on the extent to which they reflect the principles of effective professional development and incorporate effective adult learning strategies. At their best, they provide adult learners with important and relevant new knowledge and opportunities to try new ideas, practice new behaviors, and interact with others as they learn. The following paragraphs describe what these strategies look like "at their best."

Workshops, institutes, and seminars can use the "training" model, which helps teachers learn new behaviors that contribute to improved student learning (Joyce & Showers, 1988). This model includes the following steps: explanation of theory, demonstration or modeling of a skill, practice of the skill under simulated conditions, feedback about performance, and coaching in the workplace. An example of the application of this model would be training in cooperative learning strategies for use in science and mathematics teaching.

These structures also lend themselves to using a teaching or learning model for developing conceptual understandings, such as those on which many science curricula are based. For example, a model developed by the National Center for Improving Science Education (NCISE) suggests the following four stages: invite, explore, explain, and apply (Loucks-Horsley et al., 1990). These stages can help structure a multiday institute or a workshop or seminar series. Table 5.1 indicates how professional developers can structure appropriate activities at each stage. For example, during a five-day professional development institute on inquiry in environmental education, participants might engage in a two-day inquiry into participant-generated questions about a beach area (invite); two days of analysis and limited tryout of activities from different environmental education curriculum materials (explore); discussion of that analysis with regard to questions of congruence with the *National Science Education Standards* (National Research Council, 1996), clarification of the scientific concepts and processes embedded in the activities, and an opportunity to share insights and conclusions (explain); planning for tryout in participant classrooms (apply); and follow up, in-classroom coaching and support group meetings to review, revise, and retry (apply and recycle).

Table 5.1   Professional Development Learning Model: What the Professional Developer Does

Stage	Consistent With the Model	Inconsistent With the Model
Invitation	• Creates interest • Generates curiosity • Stimulates dialogue • Raises questions • Elicits responses that uncover what the teachers/learners know or think about the concepts/topics	• Explains concepts • Provides definitions and answers • States conclusions • Provides closure • Lectures
Exploration, discovery, and creativity	• Encourages the teachers/learners to work together without direct instruction from the professional developer • Provides or stimulates multiple opportunities or experiences to explore an idea, strategy, or concept • Observes and listens to the teachers/learners as they interact • Asks probing questions to redirect teachers'/learners' investigations and dialogues when necessary • Provides time for teachers/learners to grapple with problems and challenges • Acts as a consultant to teachers/learners	• Provides answers • Tells or explains how to work through the problem • Provides closure • Tells the teachers/learners that they are wrong • Gives information or facts that solve the problem • Leads teachers/learners step by step to solutions
Proposing explanations and solutions	• Encourages teachers/learners to explain concepts and definitions in their own words • Asks for justification (evidence) and clarification from teachers/learners • Formally provides definitions, explanations, and new labels (e.g., through lectures) • Uses teachers'/learners' previous experience as the basis for explaining concepts	• Accepts explanations that have no justification • Neglects to solicit teachers'/learners' explanations • Introduces unrelated concepts or skills

Source: Loucks-Horsley (1996, p. 88). Adapted from the National Center for Improving Science Education, *The High Stakes of High School Science*, 1991.

Another conceptual model for learning goals, the "5 E Model" (Bybee, 1997), reflects a similar flow of learning phases that includes engagement, exploration, explanation, elaboration, and evaluation. Either the NCISE or 5 E Model can be used by professional developers to guide the design and implementation of effective sessions that incorporate what is known from research and practice about effective workshops, institutes, and seminars as strategies for adult learning.

The best workshops, institutes, and seminars are designed to include a variety of modes through which learners can process information. These include journal writing, analysis of case studies and video examples, studying research and standards, role playing, small group discussions, modeling lessons, engaging in problem solving, and exploring questions. Learners have ample time for follow-up opportunities to discuss the application of their learning, solve problems, and generate new ideas for teaching.

In addition, the most effective workshops, institutes, and seminars are designed to include a variety of learning and engaging activities. As Mundry et al. (2000, pp. 29–40) describe, there are diverse learning activities that engage participants in active learning, including break-out sessions, carousel brainstorming, commitment statements, consensus decision making, demonstration, dialogue and discussion, ground rules, fishbowl, group reflection, ice breakers, interviews, observers, panel presentations, poster sessions or exhibits, product development, questionnaires, readings, review or reflection worksheets, "seasonal partners," simulations, small group activities or exercises, speeches or formal presentations, video viewing, and writing a "think piece."

Intended Outcomes

Depending on the goals and purposes as well as the specific structure for professional learning (i.e., workshop, institute, or seminar), these strategies can result in the achievement of any of the four outcomes for teachers' learning. For example, during a workshop, teachers might learn about the new curriculum and instructional materials that will be used in the coming year and then engage in a case discussion to explore the instructional approaches aligned with the new curriculum. During an institute, teachers might deepen their adult-level content understanding of science or mathematics and then have opportunities to engage in lesson study to apply that new learning. During a seminar, teachers might engage with curriculum topic study and discuss the implications for instruction.

Combining Strategies

Workshops, institutes, and seminars can be combined with almost any of the other strategies described in this chapter. The critical issue is to ensure that the content embedded within workshops, institutes, or seminars addresses teachers' learning needs and contributes to the achievement of one or more of the intended outcomes or that the structure is used to support or follow up on teachers' learning through other strategies.

ISSUES TO CONSIDER

Workshops, institutes, and seminars have the potential to reach larger numbers of teachers, unlike some of the other school-based strategies described in this chapter. As Weiss and Pasley (2009) note, "These venues bring teachers together from various sites to focus on a particular topic [and] the advantages of this approach include maintaining quality control and establishing a shared experience for teachers" (p. 17). However, even when designed well and implemented with high quality, one-time learning experiences are unlikely to result in significant, long-term changes in teacher practice, especially since we know from research that close to 50 hours or more of professional learning experiences are required to impact teaching practices and student learning (Blank, de las Alas, & Smith, 2008; Elmore, 2002; Garet et al., 2001; Supovitz & Christman, 2003; Wei et al., 2009).

> **Workshops, institutes, and seminars combine well with other strategies within *all* of the clusters:**
>
> - Immersion in content, standards, and research strategies
> - Examining teaching and learning strategies
> - Aligning and implementing curriculum strategies
> - Professional development structures, such as study groups, professional networks, and online professional development

Changing practice and beliefs requires multiple opportunities to learn, apply, and reinforce the use of new behaviors. As stand-alone strategies, workshops, institutes, and seminars may fall short of providing a well-rounded professional development experience. It is wiser to combine these strategies with other strategies to enhance the learning experiences of the participants. For example, one workshop on mathematical pedagogy is insufficient for teachers to alter their practices. They also need opportunities that help them to translate their learning into practice (e.g., by observing and discussing a demonstration lesson), to actually use their new knowledge (e.g., with support from coaching), and to reflect on their practices (e.g., through examining student work resulting from the use of the new practices). When the principles of effective professional development are incorporated into the design of workshops, institutes, and seminars and are then combined with other strategies, they yield greater benefits. For this reason, workshops, institutes, and seminars should not be "stand-alone" strategies but should be implemented in combination with other strategies that support teachers' learning and practice over time.

These learning sessions should incorporate opportunities for teachers to surface and challenge their existing beliefs and assumptions and resolve conflicts that result when new ideas and practices do not fit with existing beliefs. Too often workshops, institutes, and seminars focus only on adding new skills and methods without helping teachers to understand underlying beliefs that support their use or help them know what practices they should discard as they take on new approaches. Although a single workshop may be a good kick-off for learning and can result in new knowledge or awareness on the part of participants, additional opportunities are needed for producing meaningful change in beliefs and teaching behaviors.

RESOURCES

Garmston, R. J., & Wellman, B. M. (2009). *The adaptive school: A sourcebook for developing collaborative groups* (2nd ed.). Norwood, MA: Christopher-Gordon.

Mundry, S. (2003). Honoring adult learners: Adult learning theories and implications for professional development. In J. Rhoten & P. Bowers (Eds.), *Science teacher retention: Mentoring and renewal* (pp. 123–132). Arlington, VA: National Science Teachers Association & National Science Education Leadership Association.

Mundry, S., Britton, E., Raizen, S., & Loucks-Horsley, S. (2000). *Designing successful professional meetings and conferences in education: Planning, implementation, and evaluation.* Thousand Oaks, CA: Corwin.

Mundry, S., Keeley, P., Rose, C., & Carroll, C. (forthcoming). *A leaders' guide to mathematics curriculum topic study.* Thousand Oaks, CA: Corwin. (CTS seminars)

Mundry, S., Keeley, P., & Landel, C. (2010). *A leaders' guide to science curriculum topic study.* Thousand Oaks, CA: Corwin. (CTS seminars)

WestEd & WGBH Educational Foundation. (2003). *Teachers as learners: A multimedia kit for professional development in science and mathematics.* Thousand Oaks, CA: Corwin. (See Tape 4, Program 3, "Immersion in Number Theory," PROMYS, Boston University, Boston, and Tape 2, Program 4, "Immersion in Spatial Reasoning," San Diego State University, San Diego, CA.)

PROFESSIONAL NETWORKS

When Christine applied to be a coach for her state's new science and mathematics education initiative, she never dreamed how it would benefit her own teaching and increase her knowledge and skills. As a local coach, she became actively involved in two networks of teachers. The first was statewide and involved all of the 30 teachers who were selected as coaches. The second was the network of teachers Christine created in her own local district. The statewide network meets once every other month to demonstrate use of new classroom materials, discuss developments from research and practice in the fields of science and mathematics teaching, and respond to one another's questions and issues. Between meetings, the state network members keep in touch through e-mail and phone calls. Several times each month, Christine replicates the state network meetings with teachers in her own district. In afterschool meetings, teachers in her district demonstrate lessons, discuss student learning, and present issues and problems for discussion.

Christine has been amazed at the insight many of her district colleagues have offered, and she takes these ideas and information back to her state network for wider consumption. The district network teachers are working together on cross-grade projects and are generating enthusiasm among other teachers. All of the teachers participating in the network report changes in their teaching and greater comfort asking other teachers in their buildings for help and ideas.

A network is an organized professional community that has a common theme or purpose. Individuals join networks to share their own knowledge and experience with other network members and learn from other participants. They are also referred to as communities of practice (Wenger, 1998).

Networks appear through school-university collaborations; teacher-to-teacher or school-to-school linkages; partnerships with neighborhood organizations, teacher unions, or subject-matter associations; and local or national groups. These communities are often organized to improve teaching of a particular subject matter, to address pedagogy for teaching certain content or grade-level students, or in support of particular school initiatives.

Networks often articulate specific goals and purposes, recruit their members, and have scheduled activities, such as summer institutes, regular meetings, electronic discussions, newsletters, or chat rooms. In addition to drawing on the expertise of network members, many formal networks also involve individuals who are experts in areas of interest to the network participants. For example, many education organizations and foundations host "Web chats" where a national expert engages in dialogue with participants.

One of the most important elements of maintaining a network is to keep people engaged and connected; online communication helps with this enormously. Effective networks have means to update members when they miss a meeting or other networking event. Mechanisms such as a buddy system or publishing minutes of discussions help to ensure continuity among participants.

Not all networks are structured formally; informal networks can also provide opportunities for exchanging information and obtaining professional support. For example, teachers in a city or region involved in implementing an innovation such as a new curriculum or trying to create more student-centered instruction might decide to talk regularly to discuss what they are learning, share resources, and identify and solve problems. Likewise, physics teachers from a district or region, who are often alone in their schools, may, through an informal network, share teaching materials and ideas and information about resources or learning opportunities. These informal networks can often benefit from being recognized by the teachers' schools or districts as legitimate professional development activities since they contribute to teachers' learning goals.

KEY ELEMENTS OF PROFESSIONAL NETWORKS

- Members share a clearly defined purpose.
- Membership is voluntary.
- Interactions among members are ongoing.
- Effective communication is essential.
- Members' perspectives are broadened.
- Leadership and management are necessary.
- Monitoring progress and impact increases effectiveness.

KEY ELEMENTS

Members share a clearly defined purpose. As networks recruit participants, these new recruits need to know why they are joining and what they can expect from their investment of time. The focus of the network might be broadly defined at first giving members the opportunity to fine-tune the purpose to address their common interests and objectives. For example, a state's Presidential Awardee teachers might form a network to share effective practice. New interests and more complex relationships may emerge through networking; there is, however, a need to retain the initial focus or declare that the purpose is shifting in response to a new condition. If the intent of the network becomes unclear, there is a greater chance that the network will become irrelevant for many participants.

Membership is voluntary. Membership in most networks is voluntary. Members are committed to a new idea or philosophy and develop loyalty to each other. Networks maintain an atmosphere of openness and sharing that helps fellow members see each other as problem solvers. In creating this atmosphere, members demonstrate trust, flexibility, and informality in their contacts with other network members.

Interactions among members are ongoing. Interactions within a network are ongoing and are focused on a particular subject or purpose. Networks are "discourse communities" that enable teachers to meet regularly (either in person or online) to solve problems, consider new ideas, evaluate alternatives, or reflect on specific issues in science and mathematics (Lieberman & McLaughlin, 1992). Sometimes they are self-directed with the participants defining their own agendas; sometimes they are moderated by experienced facilitators who encourage the exchange of ideas within the community. Having a facilitator or moderator can increase the quality and participation levels of the network. In defining the focus, teachers build an agenda that is relevant for their contexts and concerns and commit themselves to goals that are broader and more inclusive than their initial concerns. Learning networks must have a high level of trust among participants so that people feel free to disclose information about what they think, how they teach, and what they need and to take personal risks, such as being a critical friend to other members. Achieving the level of trust needed to support direct communication takes time but is useful as a ground rule from the very beginning of the network.

Effective communication is essential. A network is not a network without ongoing communication. The more varied the interactions, the more likely the participants are to remain involved and committed to the effort. Good communications allow all network members to benefit from one another's input and create records that are accessible by members who may have missed a particular meeting or interaction or want to review information. Ground rules encourage everyone to participate equally and to respect the ideas of others.

Members' perspectives are broadened. Networks help members develop perspectives that stretch beyond the walls of their classroom or school. Through interactions in the network, teachers gain new knowledge and access to research-based resources beyond their schools or districts. Effective networks promote sharing of information and ideas with other professionals in different environments and help teachers broaden their perspective of and exposure to issues. Creating an essentially new structure for teachers' involvement and learning outside of their workplaces results in new norms of collegiality, a broadened view of leadership, enhanced perspectives on students' needs, opportunities to be both learners and partners in the construction of knowledge, and an authentic professional voice for teachers.

Leadership and management are necessary. Effective networks require the clear assignment of responsibility for managing the network, orchestrating its activities, brokering resources from diverse segments of the community, and promoting and sustaining the involvement of teachers and others. In some formal networks, the designated leader(s) may be in an organization that has funding for network support. In informal networks, leadership is more emergent, or it may rotate, but it is nonetheless critical to maintain momentum. Capable network leaders are visionary, effective in a variety of contexts (e.g., schools, universities, private sector, and community), comfortable with ambiguity and willing to be flexible, knowledgeable about the focus of the network and its communication mechanisms, organized, action oriented, and able to nurture leadership in participants.

Monitoring progress and impact increases effectiveness. Effective networks pay attention to how they meet the needs of members and how they can improve. They assign responsibility for monitoring the progress of the network. Because participants' needs change over time, it is important to keep tabs on whether the network is keeping pace. Asking members to comment regularly on their satisfaction with the network and suggest ideas for improvement can keep a network strong and vital.

INTENDED OUTCOMES

The primary outcomes of professional networks are *building professional learning communities* and *developing leadership capacity*. As the opening vignette illustrated, teacher leaders are often members of multiple professional networks that support their learning as leaders and provide them with a forum for reflecting on practice. Networks, by their nature, promote communities of learning and with the explosion of online access to national and international networks, these communities of practice are connecting teachers around the world.

COMBINING STRATEGIES

Professional networks combine with many other strategies to create a coherent repertoire of learning experiences. For example, networks can be used—either in person or online—as a follow-up to workshops, institutes, or seminars to provide an avenue for teachers' ongoing reflection and sharing of ideas. There are online communities that form networks focused specifically on looking at student work and sharing the products from lesson study and action research. In other cases, professional networks provide a vehicle for sharing resources, advice, and lessons learned during curriculum implementation and for coaches and mentors to interact with each other and reflect on practice. Similar to the other strategies in this cluster, most other strategies described in this book combine well with professional networks to support the outcomes for teachers' professional learning.

Professional networks combine well with other strategies:

- Workshops, institutes, and seminars
- Examining student work and thinking
- Lesson study
- Action research
- Curriculum implementation
- Coaching
- Mentoring

ISSUES TO CONSIDER

Professional networks can be successful strategies for providing professional development for individual teachers and are especially effective in reducing isolation among teachers. Frequently, networks provide a forum for interaction with peers from other parts of the community and throughout the country or internationally. In the process, individual teachers gain access to new resources and perspectives and become part of a collegial, cohesive professional community that examines and reflects on issues related to teaching and learning. In addition to engaging teachers in collective work on issues that emerge out of their own efforts, networks provide support, encouragement, motivation, and intellectual stimulation. For those involved in the process of change, networks provide a venue for teachers to recognize that they are part of a profession that is also in the process of change. This can help legitimize local education efforts and increase the communication between and among levels of the system.

Managing effective networks, however, can be difficult. The strength, endurance, and effectiveness of a network are often directly related to its lack of complexity and the low cost of active participation. Although some electronic networks may be able to handle large numbers of participants, networks that rely on in-person interactions and prompting from a trained facilitator must be a reasonable size to allow for adequate interaction among all participants. With adequate resources, strategies such as tiered or multiple leadership can allow for larger membership.

RESOURCES

Most education organizations offer their members access to online professional networks. For more information, visit your content-area organization's Web site:

National Science Teachers Association (http://www.nsta.org/)
National Council of Teachers of Mathematics (http://nctm.org/)

ONLINE PROFESSIONAL DEVELOPMENT

Jessica and Hannah, two teachers in a rural elementary school, had each read *How Students Learn* (Donovan & Bransford, 2005) and engaged in many afterschool discussions regarding the book. They were intrigued with the book's descriptions of how the principles and research on learning play out in mathematics and science classrooms. They wanted to connect with other teachers outside of their small school to learn more about how others were using the ideas in the book in their own classrooms. Through the district's e-mail and Listserv system, they started an online discussion to share their thoughts and questions with other teachers in the schools throughout the state. By the end of the semester, 15 additional teachers had read the book and were routinely discussing ideas and sharing experiences from their own classrooms. Jessica and Hannah rotated the role of facilitator for the threaded discussions, but realized that they needed more knowledge about effective online moderation. Through the state university—located 200 miles away—they were able to recruit a science educator with online experience to facilitate their online discussions.

By the end of the school year, the teachers, with the guidance of the university facilitator, had read and discussed several additional books and articles focused on examining student work and thinking to expand their understanding of the ways in which different teaching approaches impact student learning. This prompted Jessica to explore options for learning more about looking at student work.

Through an Internet search, Jessica learned about an online workshop offered by a national learning center for science teachers from around the world to examine student work. The rest of the teachers were eager to join the workshop, and they spent six weeks during the summer engaged in discussions with teachers from Japan, Australia, and throughout the United States. Each teacher posted a selection of student work on an online database and a description of the context (the students, the school, the curriculum), the assignment that resulted in the student work, and their own questions about the student thinking based on the work. For example, Hannah posted an assessment item from one of her students and posed the question, "How do I know whether the student's response reflects real understanding of the concept of electric circuitry or just rote memorization?" Her question elicited a response from a Japanese teacher who asked about how Hannah taught the content of electric circuits. Others joined in the analysis of the student's assessment response, and the dialogue focused on teaching strategies, student thinking, and assessment.

By the end of the six weeks, Hannah and Jessica decided to extend their examination of student work to include looking at mathematics with other teachers in their school. In the fall, many of the teachers in the school joined an in-person study group to focus on the mathematics concepts they taught across the grade levels. They continued their chat room discussions and added video footage of classrooms to their repertoire of online discussions.

Online professional development uses technology and the Internet as a means of communication, delivery, and support of teachers' learning. Online professional development has exponentially grown in the last decade as an option for teachers' professional learning (Dede, Breit, Ketelhut, McCloskey, & Whitehouse, 2005). There are literally thousands of options—online courses, chat rooms, cyber learning, virtual environments, discussion boards, blogs, Webinars, wikispaces, podcasts, microblogging or social bookmarking, digital video tools, video conferencing, and social networking sites. Without a working knowledge and lexicon of these terms, it is easy to get lost in the language and miss the opportunity to explore the diverse ways in which teachers have to connect and learn with each other and experts from around the world. Many of these online options are used instead of face-to-face interactions or to provide follow-up support after in-person learning events. Online options may be even more popular among younger teachers who are in the age group to be digital natives.

As is true with the use of any professional development strategy, to use an online option for teacher learning, a first step should be to clearly examine the purposes and goals to see whether an online solution will work. For example, if a mathematics teacher is searching for an avenue to communicate and learn with other mathematics teachers outside the district, accessing one of the various online networks may be a natural choice. If a school wants to provide an opportunity for the entire staff to participate in an awareness presentation being made off site, investigating the possibility of linking the school to the presenter through a videoconference may be the best choice. A small study group of elementary science teachers wanting to expand their knowledge might choose to enroll in an online course. Like all professional development, the goals and purposes should drive the selection of the strategy.

When carefully selected as the most appropriate strategy for professional learning, the benefits of using online options are numerous—opportunities for teachers to participate from home on one's own schedule, attend online workshops or courses from a university located across the country, engage in online networking with other teachers, or increase their content knowledge in science or mathematics through videoconference courses. In whatever ways online professional development formats are used, it is critical to keep the guiding principles of effective professional development (see Chapter 2) firmly in the foreground as professional developers design programs. It is equally important that using online professional development complements teachers' overall professional learning experiences and is used to create a coherent learning plan. It is tempting to think of online options as learning experiences that teachers explore on their own, but the key for designers is to help teachers identify appropriate ways to enhance the learning they are developing through other strategies.

KEY ELEMENTS

The number of participants aligns with the format of learning. The number of teachers involved plays a critical role in selecting online professional development. If the purpose is to reach a large number of teachers spread out over a great distance with access to information, then videoconferencing, online courses, Webinars, or online networks may be the most logical choice. Small groups of teachers at

> **KEY ELEMENTS FOR ONLINE PROFESSIONAL DEVELOPMENT**
>
> - The number of participants aligns with the format of learning.
> - Effectiveness is dependent on the quality of the available technology.
> - Learning to use interactive tools is vital.
> - Skilled facilitators or moderators are essential for learning.
> - The content connects with teachers' practice.
> - Mechanisms for reflection are established.

one school interested in examining their own teaching and their students' learning may want to access online video to use as the basis for analysis and discussions but meet in person for their discussions.

Effectiveness is dependent on the quality of the available technology. If the cameras and audio equipment used during a videoconference are of poor quality, the endeavor is rarely worth the effort. Like a live but poor presenter or instructor, participants are distracted from learning. Similarly, Internet connectivity that is unreliable or too slow undermines the advantage of easy, anytime access and frustrates communication. For teachers to benefit from online learning, the available tools must be of high enough quality to ensure that the investment of both money and time is beneficial for all involved.

Learning to use interactive tools is vital. Looking at videos or listening to podcasts of classroom activities or engaging in discussions during a video-conferencing session are rarely uncomfortable or difficult activities for the participants. However, if teachers are expected to access interactive Web environments, such as wikis, blogs, or virtual environments, they need opportunities to learn how to effectively use the tools to promote and support learning. Ongoing technical assistance is critical because it allows teachers who encounter difficulties to have access to help when they need it.

Skilled facilitators or moderators are essential for learning. Whether participating in an online course, or an in-person session, the skill of the moderator or facilitator can "make or break" the professional learning experience. Simply viewing and discussing videos is not necessarily a learning experience. Although "surfing the Internet" to obtain information or taking part in discussions on Webinars can be beneficial, for the use of online professional development to be effective, it is often the skill and expertise of the facilitator or moderator that can lead to deeper and more reflective learning on the part of the teachers. Facilitators of online courses or workshops include varied formats and structures for learning, including threaded discussions and streaming video or audio in addition to text-based content.

The content connects with teachers' practice. In addition to meeting standards for online professional development (International Society for Technology in Education, 2008; National Staff Development Council, 2001a; Southern Regional Education Board, 2004, 2006), this form of learning must also live up to the rigorous standards for effective, ongoing professional development. Implicit in that statement is that the learning is focused on increasing science and mathematics content knowledge and pedagogical content knowledge, deepening understanding of student thinking and learning, and enhancing teachers' use of varied teaching strategies.

Mechanisms for reflection are established. One potential drawback of online professional learning is that it can isolate participants and provide one-way learning. To successfully use this approach to professional development, the structure and format need to incorporate numerous opportunities for learners to reflect on their own and others' ideas and practices, including activities such as real-time discussions or reflective entries posted online.

INTENDED OUTCOMES

The primary outcomes of online professional development are *enhancing teachers' knowledge* and *building professional learning communities.* Teachers' knowledge of science and mathematics content, instructional approaches, and understanding of student learning can be enhanced through online courses, discussion boards, and Webinars. Through online communication and active interaction with others, teachers develop communities of learners beyond the walls of their schools.

COMBINING STRATEGIES

Through an online professional development structure, teachers can enroll in content courses, examine student work with teachers from across town or around the world, view other teachers' demonstration lessons, share the products of lesson study and action research, engage in case discussions and study groups, attend virtual workshops or institutes, and participate in professional networks. As the interactive Web tools continue to evolve, teachers' options will also evolve. For example, virtual environments are beginning to make their way into schools and districts and through these experiences, teachers currently can learn—through the interaction of avatars with each other and their virtual worlds—about developing leadership, and as these virtual worlds evolve, teachers' learning experiences will also expand.

> **Online professional development combines well with other strategies:**
>
> - Content courses
> - Examining student work and thinking
> - Demonstration lessons
> - Lesson study
> - Action research
> - Case discussion
> - Study groups
> - Workshops, institutes, and seminars
> - Professional networks

ISSUES TO CONSIDER

For many teachers, access to learning with others who are separated by distance is one of the greatest advantages of using this strategy to enhance professional learning. Teachers in separate schools or from throughout the country have access to each other and to resources not available locally. Teachers in isolated rural areas can enroll in courses given at a major university hundreds of miles away or enroll in one of the many virtual universities. One study found that "rural science teachers appear to be taking advantage of online professional development at a higher rate than their suburban and urban counterparts" (Asbell-Clarke & Rowe, 2007, p. 5). Scientists and mathematicians in universities or laboratories are accessible for sharing information, and presentations given in one city can be viewed in another. Online options have given teachers access to information and people that were previously unavailable to them.

Teachers have found that learning to use a certain Web tool, originally as a way of communicating with others regarding a topic of interest, acts as a catalyst to open the door to more extensive technology-based knowledge and use. Once teachers begin using these tools and sustain ongoing conversations, they feel less isolated and begin to create a community of learners committed to each other's growth. Many of the tools also help teachers move away from the traditional model of learning in which an expert presents information; instead, teachers begin to learn from each other, especially with the guidance of a skilled facilitator. It is also an opportunity for teachers to experience and learn to use online tools such as databases, simulations, and video that are applicable in their own teaching of students.

The use of online learning can be effective in providing follow-up or enhancing other professional learning experiences. Workshop attendees can create an online discussion to continue discussing the ideas and information shared during the workshop. They can develop online study groups to collectively examine student work and engage in threaded discussions. Viewing a videotape, or listening to a podcast of another teacher's practices before implementing the same practices in their classrooms can help expand teachers' perspectives on their own teaching and provide an example of the practice "in action."

Online communication has benefits for the professional developer as well. A facilitator or monitor of an online course or network can take advantage of built-in management functions, such as monitoring participation, collating answers, and posting assignments. Because communication is conducted electronically, there is a complete record of all interactions and exchanges.

There are also potential pitfalls to online professional learning. Lack of appropriate hardware, software, technology, or Internet access can impede teachers' engagement in online learning. This is an important equity issue. Although online learning improves access for those who are geographically dispersed, such as teachers in rural areas, the economically disadvantaged have less access than those with technology already in their homes and schools. This is no different from in-person professional development opportunities—those who are the "haves" receive more opportunities, whereas those who are the "have-nots" receive fewer opportunities.

For those teachers who "fall behind" in an online course, it is often more difficult to catch up without face-to-face interactions and guidance. For some teachers, online interaction is simply not an effective means of learning or communicating. They suffer from a lack of social and visual cues that normally accompany personal interactions, and this can interfere with their learning. In addition to anticipating teachers' individual learning styles, it is important to consider their individual perceptions. For example, the Professional Development Laboratory (PDL) at New York University's School of Education found that when it incorporated electronic networking into its mentoring program, the results were not as expected. The main reason for the lack of success was that "the project hadn't taken into account the teachers' feelings about technology, a fear of writing, or the pull of existing networks, such as school-based teacher communities or memberships in national organizations" (Goldenberg & Outsen, 2002, p. 29).

To address some of the disadvantages noted here, many programs have learned the value of combining online learning with in-person learning in which participants have the opportunity to develop relationships face-to-face, engage in activities and discussions at their leisure through online formats, and conduct collaborative study, such as examining student work in real-time, online formats.

For some forms of online learning, there is a limit to the number of people who can effectively interact at any one time. For example, many online courses have found that they must limit their course enrollment to 30 or fewer participants if both the participants and the facilitators are to benefit from the interactions. This can make it difficult to scale up online courses to reach more teachers. This is especially true when one of the main goals of an online professional learning experience is to develop a learning community with in-depth discussions.

Professional developers must think carefully about when and where online learning is most appropriate and how it can extend the ability to create effective professional learning experiences for teachers. Research into the impact of online professional development is currently underway to help designers make more informed decisions and find answers to questions such as "What is the impact on participant's learning when online professional development does and does not have a facilitator?" "What are the key elements and characteristics of effective online professional learning?" "What impact does online learning have on teachers' knowledge, classroom practice, and student learning?" (Dede et al., 2005). As the findings from studies are available, designers will have more information on this growing area of professional development.

RESOURCES

Universities and education organizations offer many online courses. The following sites offer resources for science and mathematics teachers.

Annenburg Media Learner.org (http://www.learner.org/index.html)
National Science Teachers Association (http://www.nsta.org/)
National Council of Teachers of Mathematics (http://nctm.org/)
Teachers Domain (http://www.teachersdomain.org/)

6

The Design Framework in Action

Figure 6.1 Professional Development Design Framework

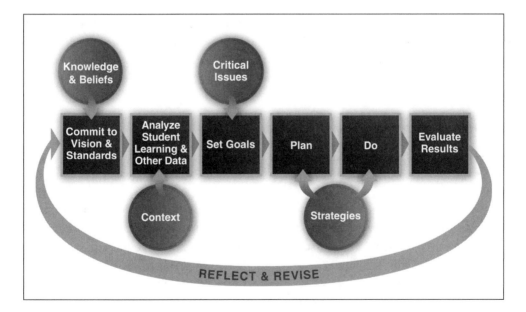

Why did professional development designers in Cambridge, Massachusetts, decide to implement a districtwide curriculum implementation strategy while the City College Workshop Center staff in Harlem, New York, opted for immersion? Why did a statewide kindergarten through sixth-grade mathematics education initiative in North Carolina choose curriculum implementation while California's middle school mathematics effort focused on curriculum implementation and networking? Why did a national high school science program go the route of curriculum development?

This chapter describes the professional development designs of five different programs, our collaborators on the development of the *professional development design framework,* and contributors to the first edition of this book. Throughout this chapter are woven quotations from interviews and personal communications with each collaborator, as well as excerpted text from their cases (see Professional Development Cases A through E at the end of this chapter). These professional development designers provide us with the rare opportunity to see the "artists" at work. We learn about more than their final products, if there ever are any *final* products. We learn how and why they and their colleagues made the decisions they did. We see the design framework (see Figure 6.1) come alive as these professional developers explain how knowledge and beliefs influenced the design of their programs, how they took into consideration features of the context, encountered critical issues, and how the planning cycle unfolded from committing to vision and standards to monitoring progress and evaluating results. And as we unravel the process, we learn more about the complexities and realities of planning for effective professional development not just in these five unique instances, but to the extent that they act as mirrors, in the readers' settings as well.

TAPPING THE KNOWLEDGE BASES, FRAMING BELIEFS: "WE STOOD ON THE SHOULDERS OF GIANTS"

When asked whether they consciously drew on the knowledge bases about learning, teaching, and professional development, the five designers unanimously replied, "Of course." "In the first year," said Judy Mumme of the Mathematics Renaissance program, "a team of professional development leaders came together and formulated a set of principles to guide our work. We were pretty conscious of the knowledge base we were drawing on all along the way" (personal communication, 1997). Susan Friel of Teach-Stat echoed Mumme's sentiments: "We stood on the shoulders of giants. Our definition grew directly out of the standards work" (personal communication, 1997).

Mumme's and Friel's responses were typical of the other designers. In every case, an important part of the planning process involved calling up the knowledge base and clarifying and articulating a set of beliefs, which influenced virtually every aspect of design. These professional developers could not imagine going about their design in any other way.

That did not mean that their beliefs were adhered to in practice 100% of the time. Inevitably, compromises had to be made. But the designers were aware of the tensions, knew that they were making compromises, and remained committed to having their professional development program reflect, as consistently as possible, the beliefs that they held most dear. As they carried out their work and reflected on it, the designers' own knowledge grew, and some early beliefs gradually changed. "Belief systems are not static," noted Mumme, "they have been subject to ongoing reflection and modification" (personal communication, 1997).

What was the particular set of knowledge and beliefs that drove the design process for the developers, and how did these influence their goals and plans? Some common themes cut across each of the five cases. All shared a similar view about the nature of mathematics and science learning, a belief that all students and all teachers can be successful learners, and a commitment to principles of effective professional development. Each of these themes and their influences on design are explored below.

KNOWLEDGE AND BELIEFS ABOUT THE NATURE OF LEARNING AND TEACHING MATHEMATICS AND SCIENCE

"How did we want students to engage in mathematics and the learning process? That guided how we went about our work with teachers," Mumme (personal communication, 1997) of Mathematics Renaissance stated. Each of the developers asked themselves the same question for mathematics or science. How they answered that question had a great deal to do with how their program took shape.

Susan Friel (1996) described the relationship between beliefs and program design for Teach-Stat as follows:

> We [developers] spent a number of sessions articulating our beliefs and then framing a coherent curriculum that supported teachers learning statistics in an environment that both modeled and encouraged teachers' eventual use of the key components of teaching as articulated by the Professional Standards for Teaching Mathematics (National Council of Teachers of Mathematics [NCTM], 1991). To do this, we worked to get past the notion of putting together a set of activities that addressed selected statistical concepts because developing a list of

activities did not address the process of teaching and learning that was believed central to the program. Two theoretical perspectives helped shape this direction. One was the conception of statistics as a process of statistical investigations and the articulation of the process by Graham (1987). The other was the introduction of the use of concept maps (Novak & Gowin, 1984) as a way of assessing what teachers knew about statistics prior to and following the institute. (p. 7)

For Hubert Dyasi and his colleagues at the Workshop Center, a passionate belief about the nature of science as inquiry led to their focus on "educating teachers to be confident science inquirers" (see "Professional Development Case A" at the end of this chapter) by immersing them in the investigation of familiar phenomena:

At the core of the Workshop Center's educational approach is the use of direct experience in learning through inquiry, generating science knowledge as a consequence, and the belief in each person's capability to inquire with meaning and understanding. In the center's view, science inquiry encompasses both content and approach. The content is derived from the common materials and phenomena learners encounter and from other sources. The approach is inquiry through which the learner is engaged in experiences, observations, and sense making in science. Learners gain scientific knowledge through a continual search for underlying commonalities in apparently disparate phenomena and refinement of their understanding by constructing and reconstructing what they know.

Direct experience with phenomena of nature helps learners to build connections among different phenomena on the one hand and between their conceptions of the world and actual events in the world on the other. (See "Professional Development Case A" at the end of this chapter.)

Dyasi and his colleagues believed that this approach to learning was as applicable to adults as it was to children:

Principles of human learning are not different between adults and children; they learn through direct experience and by constructing their own meanings from those experiences and from previous knowledge. Teacher education must faithfully reflect the way you want teachers to teach. They must themselves experience the ways they will guide children. (personal communication, 1997)

This belief was shared by other developers, who crafted professional development experiences that closely paralleled those to be used in the classroom. Judy Mumme has revised her thinking with respect to the idea that professional learning is similar to classroom learning. In a reflection on the Mathematics Renaissance case she contributed to this edition of the book, Mumme reveals her new thinking:

> Doing mathematics with teachers in professional development differs from what one does with students for several reasons. Teachers hold mathematical knowledge differently than students—teachers often already have some background experiences with the mathematical ideas they engage in professional development. They are not necessarily learning new mathematics, but expanding or deepening their understandings of the mathematics and learning the mathematics needed for teaching. Teachers' motivation for being in professional development is different from their students—teachers are there because they are learning about mathematics for teaching. Students, on the other hand, are not engaging in mathematics for the purpose of teaching it to their students. (See "Professional Development Case C" at the end of this chapter.)

EQUITY MATTERS: "ALL HUMANS ARE EDUCABLE"

We have to select strategies that give both students and teachers the opportunities to demonstrate their educability.

—Hubert Dyasi (personal communication, 1997)

Closely related to their understanding of the nature of mathematics and science learning were strong beliefs about the potential of all humans to master complex mathematical and scientific concepts and procedures. These permeated all the cases but played out in the design of professional development in different ways. For instance, at the heart of the Workshop Center's work was a commitment to the belief that "all humans are educable" (Dyasi, personal communication, 1997). "The ways we were doing education in schools masked that," commented former Center director Hubert Dyasi. "We were using strategies that were unidimensional. We had to select strategies that gave both students and teachers the opportunity to demonstrate their educability" (personal communication). This belief was another underpinning of the center's immersion strategy, which made deep understandings of science content and processes accessible to Harlem's diverse teacher and student populations.

Equity concerns influenced Melanie Barron, director of science in the Cambridge public schools, to choose a different strategy: curriculum implementation. She designed a centralized program to implement science inquiry-based units of study across the curriculum. Barron explained: "You need clear citywide goals, objectives and curriculum for what all children are to be taught. Then you need school-based technical assistance and support to the teachers" (personal communication, 1997). Karen Worth, who worked with the district from the Education Development Center (EDC), added: "If you don't require science from the center, not all teachers will teach it. If it is not mandated, some students won't get it" (personal communication, 1997). These beliefs determined Barron's decision to develop a team of science staff development teachers to provide ongoing support to teachers in every elementary school across the district. The combination of a mandate and a strong network of support, composed of both school and district-based staff developers, was Cambridge's approach to ensure that all students received quality instruction in science. (See "Professional Development Case E" at the end of this chapter.)

The mathematics education programs mirrored the science programs' commitment to excellence and equity. "None of it will matter unless it improves learning for all students, regardless of race, gender, or class," writes Judy Mumme from the Mathematics Renaissance (see "Professional Development Case C" at the end of this chapter). This belief strongly influenced the initial selection of the grade span for intervention, because the middle grades are often where decisions about a child's future are made. Furthermore, a concern with equity influenced both what strategy was chosen—curriculum implementation, using replacement units—and how it was implemented. Mumme stated,

> We used curriculum replacement units to surface issues about equity. Teachers were asked to try the units with all of their classes. We purposely asked teachers from different settings to describe their experience. They were surprised that kids from a learning disabled class and a gifted class were doing similar things. (personal communication, 1997)

A principle of the Mathematics Renaissance program was that "issues of equity must permeate the fabric of staff development" (see "Professional Development Case C" at the end of this chapter). Acquarelli and Mumme (1996) provide two examples of how that looked for participants at all levels of the program:

[Example 1] As uncomfortable as it often makes participants, meetings of teachers [and] cluster leaders . . . tackle issues of equity head on, sharing information, data and statistics about inequalities, confronting their own beliefs about tracking, or discussing examples of race, gender, and class discrimination in mathematics classrooms.

[Example 2] At a March cluster meeting one teacher reported, "ESL [English as a second language] students don't always have the words to write down but they definitely have the ideas. We let them talk about what they're going to write before they write it. Sometimes we let them dictate their words to someone else." Other teachers reacted to her comment, many nodding heads and taking notes. Teachers also learn to identify their own behaviors that can disadvantage females (e.g., calling on males more often and asking males probing questions). They may discuss the implications of the belief that "all children can learn," and probe the inconsistencies that exist between their beliefs and actions. (p. 481)

KNOWLEDGE AND BELIEFS ABOUT TEACHERS

Developers were inspired by teachers' capacity to learn, lead, and change. "We have strong beliefs that all kids are capable of engaging in quality mathematics," remarked Mumme. "But the temptation is to not believe that about teachers. We knew we could not write off any teachers" (personal communication, 1997).

An explicit principle of the Mathematics Renaissance program was that "all teachers are capable of making the changes." As a result, the program targeted all teachers at a school, not just the most innovative or eager. It also employed strategies and structures to remove, as much as possible, obstacles to teacher change. This was, in part, the thinking behind the choice of replacement units, which provided teachers with the concrete "stuff" to take back to their classrooms that they were clamoring for, and also worked as a catalyst for teachers to rethink their own practices and beliefs.

Similarly, the City College Workshop Center program was designed explicitly to contradict prevailing opinions that members of some populations, such as residents of Harlem, lack the intellectual capacity to understand science. Through its approach of firsthand inquiry, teachers generated investigable questions, planned and conducted investigations that sharpened direct observation, and made meaning out of inquiry experiences. As a result, they become inquirers into school science as well as into their own learning and teaching. These experiences prepared them to implement new approaches in their classrooms, improve their attitudes toward science, and lead professional development workshops for other teachers. "Of course, they can do this because they are humans. Teachers have been incapable only because they have not had the opportunity to do this," argues Dyasi (personal communication, 1997).

A strategy that relies on teachers to develop curriculum has to be rooted in respect for teachers' capabilities, an explicit belief of Global Systems Science (GSS). GSS brought teachers together to codevelop curriculum with staff of the Lawrence Hall of Science. Teachers field tested curriculum units first, before ever convening, and came to a summer institute to share their experiences and feedback on the curriculum. Then they created new activities and assessment instruments. "We have a strong belief in the importance of trusting teachers and respecting their craft knowledge. When we do that, we get the best product and the best performance from the teachers," commented developer Cary Sneider (personal communication, 1997).

While GSS relied on teachers as curriculum developers, other cases emphasized developing teachers as staff developers. Teach-Stat trained a cadre of 84 "statistics educators," teachers who served as resources to other teachers across North Carolina. Cambridge nurtured school-based liaisons, teachers who had a role supporting other teachers in their building in implementing the curriculum, as well as district-based staff developers, former teachers released full-time to provide training and technical assistance districtwide. Mathematics Renaissance was heavily focused on developing its 70 cluster leaders, who in turn, provided support to 350 schools. "Teachers are the best leaders of other teachers," Mumme (personal communication, 1997) stated, summarizing what each of the developers believe and exemplify in their goals and plans.

KNOWLEDGE OF EFFECTIVE PROFESSIONAL DEVELOPMENT

It is not hard to see how the designers drew heavily on what is known about effective professional development. Principles of effective professional development summarized in Chapter 2 are obvious aspects of all the programs. Clearly, each of the programs was driven by a well-defined image of effective classroom learning and teaching, provided teachers with opportunities to develop knowledge and skills to broaden their teaching approaches, were evaluated and improved, and prepared teachers for leadership roles. The Workshop Center designed a program that embraced the idea that teachers must experience science learning that reflects the national standards and provides opportunities for all students to learn challenging science content through inquiry. The GSS program grounded teacher learning in their own practice by supporting teachers to try out and reflect on their use of a new curriculum. The Cambridge program explicitly linked their efforts to the overall system by building support for improved science learning and support for adopting and implementing new curriculum. Each of the cases provides evidence of their commitment to building and strengthening the learning community through development of leaders, ongoing dialogue about what is working and why, and a zest for ongoing learning.

KNOWLEDGE OF THE CHANGE PROCESS

Each of the developers was well schooled in the knowledge base on change. Several reported studying and referring back to Michael Fullan's work like doctors use *Gray's Anatomy*. Knowledge of the change process served as an important touchstone for these developers. It shaped their initial designs, steeled them for the chaos and complexity they faced during implementation, and informed their daily "diagnosis" and problem solving.

Because these professional developers shared a common understanding of change, their program designs had common hallmarks. They were all long-term endeavors. They were clear about the changes they were making. They addressed change at many levels, from the individual to the organization. They had mechanisms in place for feedback and ongoing improvement. They provided different kinds of supports for learners over time as their needs evolved. However, exactly how the programs embodied a particular change principle varied widely.

Take, for example, the principle that as individuals go through a change process, their needs for support and assistance change (Hall & Hord, 2006). Each of the programs designed different learning experiences over time to address participants' changing concerns, questions, and experience. Most typically, programs began with some kind of knowledge-building experience like the summer institutes in Teach-Stat, Mathematics Renaissance, or the Workshop Center. These were followed by opportunities for planning for implementation, classroom practice with coaching and feedback, and reflection with colleagues.

GSS, however, approached that sequence of learning experiences differently. Participants' introduction to the program was not in a workshop, but in their own classrooms. Before ever coming to the summer curriculum development institute, teachers received the materials and taught units to their students. Then they gathered at Lawrence Hall of Science for a summer institute. The first phase of the institute was not knowledge building, but reflection on participants' experience teaching the program, which grounded the teacher learning in their own practice. Cary Sneider explained:

> We focused on experienced teachers and invited them to be creative, teach the material first, and then come back and talk about it. First they reflected with other teachers and gave us feedback on the

units. Then, after that, they were hungry for new knowledge. That's when they were most interested in seeing what earth scientists were doing and in gathering more information. Later, teachers were given the opportunity to plan for how they would adapt materials for use in their classroom when they used them again. (personal communication, 1997)

While staying true to the principle that professional development is "developmental," GSS's design capitalized on the questions and concerns teachers would bring to a workshop *after* experiencing a change in their classroom. The change literature, discussed more in Chapter 2, informs us that learners move through a predictable sequence of developmental stages in their feelings and actions as they engage with new approaches (Hall & Hord, 2006). Understanding this sequence of stages made the designers sensitive to teachers' needs and questions as they learned. Then, they found that the kinds of support teachers needed at each stage varied greatly, depending on experience level and the nature of the professional development program itself.

As much as their knowledge about change influenced their initial designs, it served another equally important purpose during implementation. It helped designers understand, cope with, and navigate through the resistance to change and the chaos they encountered as the change process unfolded. As Judy Mumme put it, "It gave us a language for what we were observing" (personal communication, 2007):

> We saw chaos in classrooms and schools. Teachers were struggling to make sense of what was happening. Change didn't come out in coherent ways. There was a lot of fumbling around. We came to understand this as our version of what Michael Fullan (1991) called "the implementation dip." I'll never forget one teacher who entered the process feeling that he was a good teacher. By all accounts, he was. But his world was being turned upside down. All that he had been doing was called into question. Before, he was clear in his mind what to do. Now it was fuzzy. He lost his sense of efficacy—his ability to say to himself, "I'm a good teacher!" (personal communication, 2007)

Without a framework or understanding the knowledge base on change for interpreting events like these, professional development designers could easily become discouraged. For Mumme and her staff (and each of the developers we interviewed), the change principles they had studied offered them perspective and reassurance. They were able to step back and look at what might seem like a setback as a natural part of the process and possibly a turning point if managed well. From initial design to daily problem solving, change theory was not "book knowledge," but a valued guide and partner in the designers' work.

The critical role of the school principal in sustaining educational change can be seen in the Cambridge example many years after their National Science Foundation project was completed. After several years of effective districtwide implementation of a common district science curriculum, a new superintendent turned control and decision making about curriculum back to the buildings. Worth and Barron reflected that in an atmosphere focused on meeting annual yearly progress and teaching mathematics and language arts, science suffered. They write, "The reality on the ground is that it is the decision of the principal or the teacher which, if any, of the units will be taught" (see "Professional Development Case E" at the end of this chapter), underscoring the need to work directly with principals to build support for science teaching and learning and establish that there is a connection between learning in science with achieving state standards in other subjects.

The knowledge bases that the professional developers brought to their programs were indeed important in their design work. However, two themes emerged as we heard their stories. First, their own experiences proved an important source of knowledge. And second, although they "knew" some things to be true, they were often called on to abandon that knowledge and make compromises. These themes are discussed below.

REFLECT AND REVISE: EXPERIENCE AS A SOURCE OF KNOWLEDGE

In addition to drawing on research and other literature, designers also tapped their own prior professional development experiences both as learners and designers. Hubert Dyasi described the process:

> You build a repertoire of experiences, which you bank. That is your database from which to select a strategy. You think, that approach worked because of this. That one didn't because of that. That takes you beyond guesswork to a more scientific, organized way of thinking. (personal communication, 1997)

Teach-Stat's decision to go with curriculum implementation, for example, was based, in part, on designers' analysis of why a previous effort at mathematics education reform they had been involved in had failed. Susan Friel's description reflects the designers' value placed on the process of using evaluation results from one set of professional development plans to inform next steps and revise designs:

> I had been involved in another effort where teachers were just trained in approaches to problem solving, but given no curriculum to

implement. The results were that teachers went back to a very structured, didactic textbook. They couldn't take what they had learned and translate it into changes in the classroom. That's why I have a bias now toward curriculum implementation. I think you can do a lot of workshops around problem solving. But if teachers don't have something to go back and work with, eventually it won't work. Teachers don't have the time to transform the curriculum. (personal communication, 1997)

GSS designers' experience as teachers trying to develop interdisciplinary curriculum was the impetus for the design for GSS, according to Cary Sneider (1995):

Each of us on staff at the GSS project had considered ourselves "innovative" teachers in the past, and we had all spent many years developing hands-on activities in astronomy, physics, chemistry, and biology. But we reeled from the disorientation of our first experiences in interdisciplinary teaching. Our need to prepare new lessons would take us to unfamiliar territories in libraries and bookstores.

We had to be ready to switch from physics to biology as we went from one chapter to the next, or from science to economics and politics, so that we could follow up the implications of an issue instead of going on to "cover" the next science topic. If that was challenging for us in the supportive environment of a science center like the Lawrence Hall of Science, we realized it would be even more difficult for many teachers in the context of local and state school systems where the resistance to change is likely to be far greater. (p. 5)

This reflection on what occurred in their own experiences informed GSS designers about what knowledge and skills teachers would need to implement an interdisciplinary program in their own classrooms. It also led to their choice of curriculum development as a professional development strategy. "We also hoped that involving teachers as codevelopers would engage their commitment to the new program, and help them acquire a deep understanding of the principles on which it is based," Sneider (1995, p. 5) continued.

Just as understanding the underlying principles of GSS was important to participating teachers, so was understanding the underlying principles of mathematics and science teaching and learning and professional development important to each of the professional development designers. They came to their "artist's palette" with knowledge of these principles as well as their own rich experiences as learners and professional developers. These gave rise to a set of beliefs that guided the moves and choices they made. However, staying true to those beliefs turned out to be more of a challenge than designers anticipated.

MAKING COMPROMISES

Tensions are inherent in the work. The challenge is how to make them live comfortably together.

—Karen Worth (personal communication, 1997)

The designers started out with clearly articulated knowledge and beliefs that influenced their goals and plans. But what happened when beliefs collided with reality, new knowledge, or even with each other? The creative tensions around these conflicts made for some interesting dynamics.

The conflict between a belief in inquiry and the necessity to jump-start a change effort quickly was an important one in Cambridge. Designers settled on implementing the same commercial units districtwide, not because they believed that these units represented inquiry at its purest and best; they were simply a good place to start. The considerations were more practical—providing teachers with good materials, coordinating the logistics of materials support, coordinating a support system. Science director Melanie Barron explained:

> What was missing in Cambridge was a curriculum. We needed a way to get teachers engaged in teaching science, to get the kids learning and the teachers teaching. Many of them hadn't been doing it. We didn't have time to immerse them in inquiry. We wanted to get them familiar with a unit and then build in more reflection, interaction, and autonomy over time. (personal communication, 1997)

Another compromise Barron made was to focus more strongly on leadership development rather than on broad-based teacher development. One can't do everything at the same time—even though there was a strong belief in developing teachers. Given the constraints of time and money, the Cambridge team decided to put the bulk of the resources into building the capacity of a smaller group—not all the teachers. The goal was to develop a structure to permanently sustain the program over time.

The Cambridge team members simultaneously grappled with the tension between their beliefs about teacher professionalism and their decision to mandate a curriculum. They knew the curriculum needed to be owned by the teachers. At the same time that they were telling the teachers, "We want you to own this curriculum," they were telling them that they had to do these three units.

Furthermore, Cambridge professional developers felt that the system needed to have a centralized system to handle logistics and to maintain the quality and rigor of science for all students. There was a definite tension between the two beliefs of teacher autonomy and centralized decision making. Barron was trying to balance them by supporting teacher initiative, encouraging their creativity, and providing professional development for teachers to develop their own strand of the curriculum. They were not mutually exclusive, but they were difficult to reconcile.

Similar conflicts characterized the design of the Mathematics Renaissance program. Regional director Kris Acquarelli and Renaissance director Judy Mumme (1996) describe the planning as a process of balancing "tensions that are inherent in our work" (p. 479). For example, the belief that change needs to be systemic and fundamental often collides with teachers' needs. As Mumme writes in her case later in this chapter (see "Professional Development Case C"):

> "I do not want to be gone from my classroom for days where I am not taught a specific unit that I can take back and use. My students lose every time I am gone." This teacher's comment is typical of many. How does one develop an in-depth understanding of the issues in mathematics education when teachers have a strong desire for things to take back—to add recipes to their files? Time spent exploring constructivism may not feel like a day well spent to some participating teachers. Short-term gains often limit long-term growth opportunities.

The decision to go with a curriculum implementation approach using replacement units grew out of this tension. Teachers would leave with "stuff" to try, not as an end but as a tool for their continuous learning. Like in Cambridge, Renaissance designers concede that they chose a strategy as a place to begin, not as their ultimate purpose.

Designers universally seemed to struggle with being true to their beliefs. "That's just part of the design process," remarked Karen Worth. "Beliefs can't get played out purely. You have to decide what gets into the foreground, what into the background, and sometimes, what is the most expedient" (personal communication, 1997). Balancing beliefs with expediency has a great deal to do with the unique circumstances of a particular program—the community, policies, resources, culture, structure, and history that surrounds it—what is called context in our design framework.

CONTEXT

Design always has to be tempered with reality. You want to both be realistic and push the system at the same time.

—Karen Worth (personal communication, 1997)

The context of the five cases varied widely—the state of California; Harlem, New York; multiple schools across the state of North Carolina; a national program based at the Lawrence Hall of Science in California; and Cambridge, Massachusetts, a small, urban school district. The different contexts helped to shape very different programs. But some common lessons emerged from their varied experiences: (1) Pay close attention to your context as you design, (2) watch for and respond to changes in context and needs as a program proceeds, and (3) help participants consider their own context as they implement changes. Each of these lessons is discussed in the sections that follow.

Pay Close Attention to Context as You Design

"Design always has to be tempered with reality. You want to both be realistic and push the system at the same time," explained Karen Worth (personal communication, 1997). For example, in Cambridge, science director Barron would have loved to have school-based liaisons freed up from classroom responsibilities full-time or more than five district-based science specialists. The resources just were not there. So working within the constraints of the resources available, she settled on two liaisons per school, who received stipends for their work and professional development time, but were not released from classroom responsibilities, and the five full-time district specialists. "Tempering design with reality" Cambridge ended up with a structure for developing teacher leadership and supporting curriculum implementation that was not perfect, but a real advance for the district nonetheless.

Context was not always constraining. In the case of Teach-Stat in North Carolina, designers were able to capitalize on preexisting infrastructure—the University of North Carolina's Mathematics and Science Education Network centers across the state housed at 10 of the state university system's campuses. Susan Friel explained how this contextual factor facilitated their design:

> The fact that these ten centers were available really influenced our design. The center's job was to be in touch with school districts in their geographic area. This was perfect for what we wanted to do— have university faculty help to prepare statistics educators who would in turn work with teachers in their districts. Using the structure of the centers, we were able to reach 450 teachers across the state and develop wonderful partnerships between teachers and university faculty. (personal communication, 1997)

The existence of the centers in North Carolina highlights how this feature of the context was readily apparent and drove the design from the beginning. This was also true for the Mathematics Renaissance program. As a statewide systemic initiative funded in part by the National Science Foundation (NSF), the Mathematics Renaissance program had a political context that could not be ignored—the expectation of the funding agency. Its charge was to institute a process that would not just make a difference in schools, but would have a ripple effect, impacting multiple levels of the educational system, including state policy.

Judy Mumme described how that charge propelled their design process:

> As we thought about design, we had to consider those expectations. We had to reach a large number of schools. We had to be visible. We had to be viewed as more than a project. These considerations influenced our decision to go with a large-scale effort.
>
> The theory was that if you get a critical mass of schools heading in a particular direction, that pushes on the system, informs legislators, informs CDE [California Department of Education], and influences policy—"inside-out" systemic reform. We needed a design that had the potential for influencing policy at various levels. That affected how we solicited schools for participation, how we worked through the state department, why we needed to remain neutral on issues around specific instructional materials, and lots of other features of our design. (personal communication, 1997)

In other cases, designers wished they had been more attuned initially to certain aspects of their context—particularly family and community concerns. Hubert Dyasi described how those concerns played out in Harlem:

> In our context, Harlem, parents thought that anything that looked different was discriminatory. What was this funny thing we were doing—inquiry science? Why were their kids the guinea pigs? Oppressed groups often want what oppressing groups have. We had to find ways of addressing their concerns. We had to bring parents into the discussion. (personal communication, 1997)

Mathematics Renaissance initiatives also met with parental objections:

> We had to redesign some of the focus of professional development. We paid more attention to helping teachers become more articulate about where basic skills were in the work they were doing. We made the false assumption that people would see that basic skills were getting taken care of. We also realized that our parent outreach component needed to be strengthened. We worked with each school to design activities to engage parents, including initiating Family Math. (personal communication, 1997)

While developers underscored the importance of being responsive to context, they also pointed out the danger of being too responsive. Judy Mumme offered an example from Mathematics Renaissance where designers' and teachers' needs were in conflict:

> Sometimes we found that what the schools wanted wasn't what we thought was in their best interests. That felt uncomfortable. What we heard was "just give us more curriculum units." We felt what was needed were more philosophical underpinnings. We couldn't be slaves to context. We had to take it into consideration, but also try to reshape it. (personal communication, 1997)

Scanning contextual factors such as teacher and student needs, political expectations, family and community concerns, policies, structures, and organizational culture helped designers ward off unexpected problems as well as take advantage of potential supports. But beware, our developers learned. Just when you think you understand your context, it changes!

Watch for and Respond to Changes in Context and Needs as the Program Proceeds

> *Productive educational change, at its core,*
> *is not the capacity to implement the latest*
> *policy, but rather the ability to survive the*
> *vicissitudes of planned and unplanned*
> *change while growing and developing.*
>
> —Michael Fullan (1993, p. 5)

Context is slippery. It is constantly changing, sometimes serendipitously, sometimes as a direct result of the professional development programs we design. What was right for one moment in time may not be right for another. The successful designers we talked to found that they had to constantly monitor and reflect on their context to discern changes that signaled the need for redesign. What happened with the emergence of teacher leadership in the Teach-Stat program illustrated the need to remain flexible and make changes:

> Originally, the pilot teachers were going to be available to help [with the workshop] but not to teach. However, by the second summer, faculty and teachers had developed such a good working relationship that the model of a "professional development team"—faculty and teachers coteaching—naturally emerged and was very successful.

This forced us to realize that you could back off and be flexible. (personal communication, 1997)

Cambridge science staff development teachers also found that teacher leaders' needs and capabilities changed over time. Melanie Barron explained:

The more experience the liaisons had, the more they became rigorous determiners of what they do next. They became more reflective and more autonomous and were looking for different kinds of support, like small study groups. We couldn't have started there. The context wouldn't permit it. But we had to be ready when they were. (personal communication, 1997)

Context could be as close to home as the individual teachers you were working with or as removed as the national education scene. Hubert Dyasi noted that the momentum for mathematics and science education changes nationally had a dramatic effect on the Workshop Center's approach. As the national movement developed, so did the Workshop Center's approach to inquiry:

What we are disseminating is not so strange now. Initially, we didn't want to scare people. Now we are more up-front. We have matured, too. Before, we were satisfied with having students uncover a phenomenon. We didn't push much on conceptualization. Now we are getting more to the heart of the matter . . . the real nature of doing science. People think that hands-on is science. It's not just a set of steps. Science is a great intellectual activity. Our work now is truer to that. (Dyasi, personal communication, 1997)

Other contextual changes were less intentional or desirable, such as the school personnel changes encountered in the Mathematics Renaissance program. "Superintendents left. Principals were transferred. Key people kept changing. We had to invest a lot more time in relationship building," commented Mumme (personal communication, 1997).

In addition, as California's state system discontinued its newly developed statewide assessment, the Mathematics Renaissance found itself missing one of the central elements it thought was in place to support changes. Mumme and her team were required once more to "regroup." Surviving the "vicissitudes of planned and unplanned change" (Fullan, 1993, p. 5) was an essential skill for these designers of professional development. It was also important for their teachers, who faced the challenge of implementing change in the context of their own classrooms and schools. The programs found ways to help teachers meet this challenge, as the following example illustrates.

Help Participants Consider Their Own Context as They Implement Changes

Any multischool or multidistrict effort can appreciate the design problem GSS faced. Participants in their national curriculum development institute came from all over the country. GSS literally had to consider as many different contexts as participants. How could GSS make the program as relevant as possible to a variety of contexts and help participants successfully implement the program? Designers had some creative answers to that question, as they write in their case later in this chapter (see "Professional Development Case D" at the end of this chapter).

Principal: Diane, I understand that you're excited about this new integrated program called Global Systems Science, but I'm concerned that some of our parents will worry that their children will do poorly on standardized tests if it replaces the usual science curriculum.

Diane: Then it's about time we educate some of our parents about the need for science literacy concerning environmental issues. National Science Education Standards and our State Science Framework say we should spend less time teaching science vocabulary and more time helping our students relate science to the real world.

Jim: I'm not convinced that students who take integrated science will miss out on chemistry, physics, and biology. We plan to present the same concepts we taught before, but in a meaningful context. Students will still have labs, but they'll also debate the social implications of science and technology.

Principal: Now I didn't say I was against it, but I'll be the one to take the heat if our community is not convinced it's a good idea. Are you willing to present your ideas at the Parent-Teacher Association next Thursday evening? (Sneider, 1995, p. 1)

The above conversation did not take place in a real principal's office. It was a role play from the GSS summer institute, where teachers thought about what might actually happen when they went back to their school districts to implement the GSS curriculum. At the GSS summer institute, participants did not just learn about the curriculum. They studied principles of change and thought about how the principles would apply to their own particular school context.

This was one of several ways that GSS honored participants' different contexts at the national institute, as former director Cary Sneider explained:

> Because we had as many contexts as school districts, we had to look at commonalities. We discovered that there were four different ways in which GSS was fitting into the schools. The implementation strategy depended on which one was at play. For some schools, the first year of science was wide open and GSS easily slid in. Other schools were starting it as an experimental program with the expectation that students would like it. Students demanding the program would bring about the change. In other districts, there was enough top-down pressure to have nontrack science, and they needed a program like GSS. At the other extreme, the teachers taught in a traditional school and they would sneak GSS into a traditional course. We addressed each of these realities at the institute. (personal communication, 1997)

Most important, participants came to the summer institute having already implemented units from the curriculum in their own classrooms. Discussions about GSS did not happen in a vacuum, but were grounded in the teachers' experiences. Participants gave feedback to the developers and designed their own activities and assessments based on what they knew from their experience would work best with their own students. In these ways, GSS was able to tailor their program to a diverse national audience.

The section above described how knowledge and beliefs, context, and reflection on results influenced the professional development design process. But many questions about professional development design remain unanswered. "What did that process look like?" "Who was sitting at the table?" "How much time did it take?" "What was the implementation of the program like?" "How did monitoring progress and reflection on evaluation results fuel revisions and redesign?" These are the focus of the next section, which takes a closer look at the steps involved in program design as they played out in the five cases.

THE PROFESSIONAL DEVELOPMENT DESIGN PROCESS

Commit to Vision and Standards

Each of these designs was motivated by a vision of mathematics and science teaching and learning based on national standards. Earlier in this chapter, we discussed how all the designers drew heavily on the multiple knowledge bases and worked with their colleagues to articulate and clarify the commitments and vision on which their programs rested. The designers were themselves pathfinders and visionaries, who strengthened and spread their vision through their professional development programs.

For example, Hubert Dyasi is sometimes called the "founding father of inquiry," so far ahead of his time was he in envisioning teachers and students as confident science inquirers and, with his collaborators, devising learning opportunities for teachers to achieve that end. In his case later in this chapter (see "Professional Development Case A"), he notes, "The present focus of the Workshop Center's work is on educating teachers to be confident science inquirers who understand the potential for science learning in the common everyday phenomena that capture children's interests." Many participants in the program came to embrace that vision as well. As one teacher wrote, "The center's modeling of what we were learning in the classes about classroom organization, social interaction, curricular inquiry, and observation gave me more confidence in the practicability of the ideas and allowed me to raise deeper questions about them and to try them in my classroom." (See Professional Development Case A.)

The Teach-Stat program was designed to enact the vision of statistics teaching articulated in the *Professional Standards for Teaching Mathematics.* One of the early projects in this particular strand of standards-based mathematics, Teach-Stat was committed to teachers' learning statistics through a process of investigation and relevant hands-on applications and activities. Its success served as proof-of-concept that when teachers learned statistics in these "new" ways, they deepened their content knowledge and changed their classroom practice.

Judy Mumme articulated the central commitment of the Mathematics Renaissance in this way: "At its core was the commitment to increase access and success for students historically underrepresented, while holding high expectations for improving performance for all students" (see "Professional Development Case C"). That commitment, along with a set of guiding principles, became the touchstone for all the design elements of the program and was ultimately realized in achievement gains for students.

Extending access and student success was also central to the vision of GSS. By engaging teachers as codevelopers of this science program, the project enlisted 125 teachers in its mission to "change the current emphasis of high school science departments from preparing a small segment of the population for college to providing all of the nation's students with the skills they will need to thrive in the modern world" (see "Professional Development Case D"). In the same vein, the Cambridge public schools initiative rested on its commitment to the *National Science Education Standards* and their local framework, based on the Massachusetts framework, for science in the elementary years. As teachers became involved in developing the local framework, implementing a standards-based curriculum, and leading the science education initiative, the commitment to this vision spread beyond the small cadre of project staff to many teachers throughout the elementary system.

Collect and Analyze Student Learning and Other Data

Each of these programs relied on analyses of students' and teachers' learning needs to frame program goals. For example, the Mathematics Renaissance made a decision to target middle school mathematics because of its role as the gatekeeper to high-level mathematics. They analyzed statewide demographic and student achievement data to document a compelling need for mathematics improvement at these grade levels. They also knew that "curriculum at this level was a wasteland, and this area seemed ripe for development and exploration" (see "Professional Development Case C").

National standards placed a new emphasis on statistics as a content strand for elementary mathematics. At the same time, students performed poorly in this strand on national, state, and local assessments. Many students were not being taught statistics at all, and teachers were often poorly prepared in this content strand. These factors were influential in establishing goals of the Teach-Stat program.

Set Goals

You've got to know what you are going to do, make a map, and define end points and mileposts along the way. Then you meander toward them.

—*Karen Worth (personal communication, 1997)*

Setting goals was an important launch point for the five programs, but not a process that bogged designers down. They agreed that without clear goals, they would have had no place to start and no reason to get involved. Also important was that goals were grounded in the expressed needs of participants and not just in the imagination of the designers. While all the designers engaged in some kind of process for figuring out what their vision was and then how to get from "here to there," they also warned against getting too caught up in the initial goal setting. As Cary Sneider explained, "You've got to start out with some goals. But goals evolve. The ones you start out with aren't the ones you end up with" (personal communication, 1997).

What was important for each of the five designers was aligning their goals with their teachers' and students' learning needs and designing plans for implementation based on achieving those goals.

Plan

While planning for each of the five programs looked very different, three common themes emerged. Planning was collaborative, time consuming and ongoing, and often involved the use of external consultants. These themes are elaborated below.

Collaborative

Each of the developers described a collaborative planning process with a small, clearly designated core group that expanded when necessary to take in more input. Developers consistently involved participants in the decision making.

Three professors at City College developed the idea for the immersion program. They immediately brought in school staff to see whether there was a possibility of doing something. From then on, "We shaped the program together" (Dyasi, personal communication, 1997).

The planning group for Mathematics Renaissance was the regional directors. Judy Mumme recalled:

> They came together in several meetings with staff development folks. The first year of the SSI [Statewide Systemic Initiative] we brought cluster leaders into the planning process. They put flesh on the model and advised us about what needed to happen. They were encouraged to talk to teachers about what they needed. It was an ongoing process of listening to teachers, administrators, and teacher leaders. (personal communication, 1997)

Melanie Barron reported that in the Cambridge public schools, the program began slowly:

> It was the decision to write a proposal that pushed the design process to the next stage. The original planning team was me, the director of science from the district, and the science staff development teachers, with assistance from consultants from EDC and others from MIT [Massachusetts Institute of Technology]. Once the proposal was funded and the liaison teachers became a reality, a number of them became involved with the ongoing planning. (personal communication, 1997)

Time-Consuming and Ongoing

Planning was time-consuming, sometimes painfully so. Susan Friel described the process for Teach-Stat:

> The first year was a planning year. We met as a group of five to seven in long sessions—two to three days. We drafted some material. I was intent on getting everyone's input. That was hard. I was criticized. People said I let things drag on too long. But it was worth it in the end, because we all "owned" the result. (personal communication, 1997)

Not only was planning time-consuming, it never stopped. Even when the programs were being implemented, they were simultaneously being revised and redesigned. Mathematics Renaissance is a good example of the iterative planning and refinement process. "The regional directors went out and did the work. Then we would debrief and figure out what to do next," Mumme (personal communication, 1997) explained. Similarly, in Cambridge, Barron added, "The detailed planning was a constant back and forth among the science staff development teachers, the liaisons, the EDC consultant, and others from MIT" (personal communication, 1997).

Involved External Consultants

In Cambridge, Melanie Barron was convinced of the need for external partners. She brought to the job in Cambridge years of experience in collaborative work and was convinced of its importance at the institutional level, the professional level, and the personal level as well. "You can't do it alone. You need expertise and support internally and externally. A system cannot close its doors to the outside world. Any project is a combination of building internal capacity and injecting external expertise" (personal communication, 1997). In the case of Cambridge, Barron developed a relationship with nearby MIT. She also contracted with EDC for technical assistance. The resulting partnership between Cambridge and EDC has been a critical component of the program.

Involving stakeholders, taking time, and bringing in outside expertise were important aspects of developing a well-conceived plan for staff development. While planning was an ongoing process that continued after the programs were implemented, the professional developers' focus eventually shifted from planning to doing. Designers settled on a plan and set it into motion. Their plans were now ready to meet the test of implementation.

Do

What happened to professional development plans as they were implemented, how they unfolded over time as programs matured, and what new decisions were made and why is as rich a story as the initial design process. In every case, programs looked very different two to five years (or in the case of the Workshop Center, 30 years) into their implementation than they did on the drawing board. Over the 30-year history of the Workshop Center, the approach to professional development changed dramatically as staff developed and refined their immersion approach and added significant, new components to the program. In Cambridge, the basic program components remained the same, but took on new qualities as the staff and program matured. Finally, as the Mathematics Renaissance scaled up from 78 to 420 schools in five years, some program elements stretched as the program grew while others, including replacement units, were abandoned as core strategies. The lives of these programs parallel survival in the natural world. Their capacity to reflect on their shifting contexts and emerging needs, and adapt and respond to change was their greatest asset, enabling them to weather the inevitable storms of implementation. Their evolution over time is traced in the section that follows, as professional development designers describe key elements of their programs' implementation.

Workshop Center: Immersion in Inquiry

The Workshop Center actually did not start off with what became its trademark—immersing teachers in scientific inquiry. It began in 1972 with Workshop Center staff engaging children in active learning strategies for language development in the corridors of Harlem's schools. The one condition center staff put on their work was that teachers keep the classroom doors open so other students and teachers could see what was going on in the hallways. The idea was that teachers would see change happening and want to try it themselves. It worked. Curiosity mounted as teachers heard children's busy chatter and saw the hallways cluttered with high-quality work. Many teachers were inspired and motivated to learn new strategies. But Workshop Center staff quickly learned that watching them work with children was not enough. Teachers needed experiences that would help them develop the capacity to do what they saw staff doing.

When the center moved into science education, center staff members drew on what they had learned—good and bad—from the early corridor program. Former Workshop Center director Hubert Dyasi elaborated:

> We knew we had to educate teachers directly to become inquirers. They would learn how to learn by using materials themselves at their own level. For a long time, that is what we did. After a while, however, we realized that teachers weren't implementing inquiry science in the ways they were experiencing it with us. They were tied to using the materials in exactly the ways we had used them. They

weren't really engaging students in asking their own questions. Their mind-set hadn't changed.

Then we remembered the corridor program. Teachers changed because they were following their kids. That's how they got won over. This led us to add a series of Saturday sessions during the academic year with children. Teachers taught sessions with support from center staff. Following that, we had the teacher study groups to talk about what was happening with their kids. (personal communication, 1997)

Recognizing that they were not having the intended impact on teachers' practice, they added two new strategies, teachers practicing with children and study groups, which helped the program in two ways. First, it offered the teachers important professional development experiences that they needed to successfully implement inquiry-based learning. They had the opportunity to practice new techniques with feedback from center staff and reflect on their practice and classroom experiences. Second, the addition of the practice and study groups gave center staff more information about what teachers were doing and thinking, so staff could become more effective at supporting teachers.

As center staff members observed and listened to teachers, they discovered another important stumbling block to successful implementation of inquiry science, which Dyasi stated as follows:

Teachers were often just giving the students materials and letting them go. They had difficulty raising questions that would draw children's curiosity to the important science. It seemed that the teachers weren't able to distinguish between what was valuable in the children's explorations and build on it and what was just play. Take the example of heating up water until it boils and then continuing to apply heat. That is trivial until you begin exploring what it really means. You keep on supplying heat but the temperature of the boiling water doesn't change. Why not? What does it mean to "supply heat"? Is it the same as providing energy? If yes, is energy then different from temperature? What else can we do to find out about heat and temperature? (personal communication, 1997)

Teachers themselves did not necessarily know the science content. And even if they did, the issue was not that they should tell it to the students, but rather that they should think about whether the students were ready to learn it. This observation led Workshop Center staff to another modification in the program—not a new strategy, but a change in how staff worked with teachers:

We needed to be more overt in pulling out what we were doing with the teachers. As we were doing the science with the teachers, we needed to say out loud, "The reason this is interesting is . . ." or to talk explicitly about the strands of inquiry from firsthand experience with phenomena, from asking questions, to collecting data, to making sense out of all this.

We also needed to help them see what the children were doing. For example, when children put materials in a certain way, we asked, "Why did you do that that way?" and refused the answer, "I was just doing it." Then we asked, "What did you see as a result?" Children often do not raise questions verbally; they act their questions out through what they do. The change for us was to be much more explicit about both the important science and the scientific process. When we did this, teachers began to open up about what their difficulties were. They started to raise questions about themselves. That's when we could open up the doors. (Dyasi, personal communication, 1997)

The Workshop Center opened up many doors for students and teachers over its long history. And it was not only teachers and students who were immersed in inquiry. It was the program staff members themselves who were engaged in investigating and improving their own practice. As they learned more about what it really takes to "change mind-sets," they moved from the corridors to the classrooms and to New York City's living laboratory, improving on their workshops and adding new strategies to their professional development program.

Cambridge: Building Leadership Capacity

The professional development program in Cambridge developed quite differently and over a much shorter period of time. In contrast to the Workshop Center, the basic strategy of the program remained the same—the development of local leadership through a structure of district-based staff developers and school-based liaisons. However, as these leaders developed, their needs changed and so did the nature of the support provided for them. Five years into the project, the EDC consultant to the project, Karen Worth reflected:

The five district-level staff developers' skills and knowledge have increased by leaps and bounds. We still meet once a week. But those meetings look very different now. I don't lead every meeting. The staff developers are more and more in charge of their own structure. Other kinds of interactions have been very important, like their intensive e-mail conversations. They are also more and more in charge of pieces of the program as a whole—the resource center, volunteers, the national gardening program, and the bilingual program. And they are doing all the staff development and training for teachers; we are using no more consultants. (personal communication, 1997)

It is no surprise that the character of the professional development for teachers changed as district-based staff developers took it over and made it their own:

The summer institute has been greatly enriched. Professional developers are not marching straight through the units now. As units are becoming more a part of the science program, staff developers are more interested in embellishing them. Every unit now has a field trip to a local resource. All the professional development is now delivered on site. (Worth, personal communication, 1997)

The school-based leaders and the liaisons also moved in the direction of taking more control over the design of their own learning experiences. They wanted less whole-group activity and more small, diversified groups based on their emerging interests and expertise. By the fourth year, they were pursuing an area of focus through four active study groups on assessment, how to pilot test units, "Cambridgizing" the units through use of local resources, and peer coaching. The annual liaison institute was scrapped, and the time and money were reallocated to group meetings and classroom visits throughout the school year.

It isn't that the topics the leaders were interested in changed over time. They just moved along a continuum from novice to expert in a whole variety of topics ranging from science content and pedagogy to leadership skills. As liaisons and district staff developers in Cambridge moved along that continuum, structures for their own learning changed to accommodate them, offering them increasingly more autonomy and choice.

Mathematics Renaissance: Scaling Up

Scaling up from 78 to 420 California schools over a five-year period brought about inevitable changes in strategy for the Mathematics Renaissance. Teacher academies, for instance, the initial foundation for the work, disappeared after the first year despite their apparent success. The academies brought teachers together from across the state to work with students in the morning and debrief the experience in the afternoon. The teachers involved were enthusiastic about the opportunity to experience new curriculum with their own students and receive direct support in the process. So why were they dropped? Judy Mumme explained:

They were a nightmare to administer. The first year, we involved 78 schools in eight to ten academies. The negotiations for stipends, time, and locations were monumental. When we grew to 210 schools, we knew that we couldn't pull it off. We continued to have academies whenever we could, but they were dropped as a primary strategy. Instead, we relied on two-week summer institutes and one- to two-day workshops during the school year. (personal communication, 1997)

Growing from 78 to 210 schools in one year resulted in other changes as well. The original support structure of seven regional directors (one for every 11 of the first cohort of schools) could not possibly meet the needs of an additional 132 schools. Three more regional directors were added in the second year. But even 10 regional directors could not make frequent enough visits to all the schools and build the necessary personal relationships with the teachers. So a whole new structure was instituted—the cluster leaders:

Out of the initial 78 schools, we took 57 promising teachers who showed leadership potential and created a cadre of cluster leaders. They were released from the classroom for 35 days to provide direct support for other teachers. That meant one cluster leader for every five schools. This move was based on the belief that personal relationships were critical. (Mumme, personal communication, 1997)

With the emergence of cluster leaders and the expansion of regional directors, another need arose, which helped to shape the program for the next four years:

The need for ongoing professional development for leaders cannot be understated. This is perhaps one of the central lessons we have learned thus far. Leaders must have opportunities to reflect on their work, learning from one another the crucial lessons of leadership for reform. They constantly need to be challenged as learners, expanding their own understanding of mathematics, teaching, and learning. The initial design of the Renaissance failed to take this into account and much of the statewide professional growth opportunities have been funded catch-as-catch-can. (Acquarelli & Mumme, 1996, p. 480)

In the third year, the project did not grow in numbers of schools (although the number of teachers involved doubled). It was an opportunity to refine the work and respond to problems that emerged:

One of the problems we observed was that much of teachers' time and attention was focused on management issues. This distracted them from getting at meatier issues about how kids were learning and experiencing mathematics. So we developed workshops on setting up classroom environment, cooperative learning, managing extended tasks, and writing in mathematics. We asked all continuing teachers, instead of doing new replacement units, to do the same unit, only this time to focus more on kids' learning. There was a lot of resistance to this. They wanted more replacement units. They wanted to cobble together a whole curriculum. Their intent was to permanently replace their curriculum. Our intent was to provide more in-depth professional development experiences. (Mumme, personal communication, 1997)

In the fourth year, the project grew in breadth and depth. As more schools were added and new teachers joined from participating schools, project staff had a pleasant surprise:

We thought new schools and new teachers from old schools were going to be less sophisticated and require more intensive work. That didn't bear out. The new teachers were quite sophisticated partly because of the spreading effect of our work beyond those who directly experienced it. (Mumme, personal communication, 1997)

By the fifth year, the Renaissance faced the monumental challenge of maintaining the quality of an effort that had grown to 420 schools—with about the same number of cluster leaders and regional directors. A key strategy was continuing to emphasize the professional development of the cluster leaders, despite their limited time on the project:

The professional development of the cluster leaders grew more important over time. It was critical that they had professional growth opportunities, which we continually had to balance with their classroom teacher role. They were now only released from their classrooms for 30 days because of concerns that they were away too much. We also realized that the coaching role was an important one, and provided more professional development for them in cognitive coaching. We asked the cluster leaders to play a coaching role with each other. Here again time got in the way. Because of that, it was the least uniformly effective strategy—one we wished we could have done better. Despite the difficulties of their role, over the life of the project, the cluster leaders grew into a remarkable group of people. (Mumme, personal communication, 1997)

The fifth year brought another major challenge to the project. The state of California adopted mathematics instructional materials, rendering the Renaissance's central strategy—the use of replacement units—irrelevant for adopting schools. In response to schools' changing and diverse needs, the Renaissance provided three choices for participation: (1) Schools that adopted instructional materials were clustered and provided with professional development in how to use them effectively; (2) schools that were still interested in replacement units continued with professional development related to their use; and (3) in schools that were interested in more site-based activities, cluster leaders focused on supporting a site-based facilitator, who took over some of the functions of the cluster leader.

Over the life of the Mathematics Renaissance, the project made several shifts in strategy. Due to the sheer logistics of scaling up, intensive summer teacher academies gave way to a focus on developing cluster leaders. As context and school needs changed, even the core strategy of the project—the use of replacement units—was replaced with a more flexible, multidimensional approach.

None of the changes in the programs described above would have happened without monitoring, evaluation, and reflection. While absorbed in the "doing," these staff developers were simultaneously able to step back, gather data, and learn from their experience. How some of them did so is the subject of the next section.

Evaluate Results, Reflect, and Revise

Each of the programs had multiple mechanisms—formal and informal— for gathering data about how the program was going, which fueled a process of continuous reflection and redesign. Formal mechanisms included evaluations of events, teacher and administrator interviews and surveys, classroom observations, and case studies. Some of the programs had a project evaluator to carry out some of this work.

However, it was often the less formal, more frequent means of monitoring and collecting data that had the biggest influence on program redesign— the "one-legged" chats in the hallway, the conversations in the teachers' room, or the visits to the classroom. Many of the programs had structures in place that allowed for a steady flow of information between the leadership and participating teachers. Karen Worth reported on how that worked in the Cambridge public schools:

Melanie relied on collective observation and the wisdom of the staff development team. She regularly went to the liaisons and asked them what they wanted, what they liked, what their impressions of the staff response were. The staff development teachers were quite rigorous in collecting information from the liaison teachers, who had regular conversations with teachers and were in their classrooms. There was a constant back and forth between the teachers and the liaisons and between the liaisons and the staff development team. (personal communication, 1997)

The Mathematics Renaissance's system of 70 cluster leaders helped to ensure that regional directors stayed in close touch with what was happening in the 350 participating schools. Cluster leaders were classroom teachers with experience and credibility among other teachers. They were released from the classroom 35 days during the academic year and worked five weeks during the summer to carry out their role as professional developers. Close to the schools and teachers, these leaders provided regular input to the regional directors about how the work was progressing. In turn, regional directors used their input to reflect and redesign as needed:

Regional directors meet monthly. Part of that meeting is an assessment of how things are going. We don't look at things at a macro level every time. But we do have an annual retreat for our cluster leaders, where we take stock. And we have a retreat just for regional directors. We also visit classrooms on a regular basis and debrief among ourselves. (Mumme, personal communication, 1997)

The Mathematics Renaissance also relied on continuous learning through reading and studying to help regional directors assess their work. Mumme elaborated:

We focused mostly on reading about change and the change process. A lot of what we read was validating of what we were observing, but gave us a language to talk about it. For example, Fullan's work on the implementation dip was reassuring. But we also made changes in our program as a result of outside reading. The literature was clear that peer coaching was important, but that was not part of our original design. We have now attempted to institute a cognitive coaching program. (personal communication, 1997)

Reflection often spurred developers to go back and redesign. This happened with the Teach-Stat workshops, as Susan Friel explained:

The first year, we led people through the curriculum. But our experience was that participants had very diverse understandings of statistics. The second year, we decided to do something different. We got a big problem from one of the modules. We found out what teachers' prior knowledge was of the mathematics involved. Then we designed the workshop experience to build on that knowledge. We had to find out more about where people were coming from first. (personal communication, 1997)

External evaluators collected valuable information about the quality and results of these programs, enabling the designers to make improvements and enhance program effectiveness along the way.

None of the programs discussed in this chapter moved neatly through the design process. They inevitably met up with the "vicissitudes of planned and unplanned change" (Fullan, 1993, p. 5), discovered design flaws, were temporarily out of synch with teachers' needs, or underestimated what it took to manage change. But two factors led to their eventual success. Because they went about the process systematically, they left the starting gate with good designs—programs that were grounded in sound principles of teaching, learning, and professional development, crafted from combinations of traditional and unconventional strategies, and tailored to their own unique contexts. And they never stopped trying to get better. They were able to "treat problems as their friends" (Fullan, p. 25), use data to inform decision making, learn from their mistakes, and improve their initial designs. They put the professional development design framework described in this book to work—not as a prescription, but as a map to help them navigate the chaos of improving mathematics and science education.

DESIGN FRAMEWORK IN ACTION: CASES

As mentioned several times in this book, the basis for the development of the professional development design framework came from work with five collaborators who conduct teacher learning programs in mathematics or science. The collaborators' complete cases of professional development design and implementation, which are referred to throughout this book, are included in the next section of this chapter. Most of the authors have provided a reflective update on their original cases, giving us a unique glimpse into where their projects are today as well as what they, as designers, have learned since writing their cases over a decade ago. That their original cases "hold up" over time—as illustrated in this chapter—is a testament to the design framework that each of these collaborators helped develop and continue to use as they embark on new science and mathematic initiatives.

A summary at the beginning of each case highlights the components of the professional development design framework that are addressed by the case. (See "Design at a Glance," Tables 6.1–6.5.)

Professional Development Case A

THE WORKSHOP CENTER AT CITY COLLEGE OF NEW YORK

Hubert M. Dyasi, Professor Emeritus, City College of the City University of New York

Rebecca E. Dyasi, Professor of Science Education, Long Island University, Brooklyn, New York

Table 6.1   Design at a Glance: Workshop Center

Level and content	Elementary science
Knowledge and beliefs	*National Science Education Standards*—Teachers learn science through inquiry and by constructing understanding through their own experiences; teachers learn in ways they can later use to engage students in science learning in the classroom
Context	University-based program working primarily with teachers, school administrators, and families in urban school districts
Goal	Educate teachers to be confident "scientific inquirers"
Primary strategies	Immersion in inquiry, workshops, institutes, partnerships
Critical issues	Ensuring equity, developing leadership, garnering public support

The Context

The Workshop Center is an academic unit at the City College, City University of New York. Its work is centered on the professional development of educators to make their classrooms rich and suitable contexts for science education in particular and for inquiry-based learning in general. A major portion of the center's work takes place in Harlem and in the school districts of New York City, drawing teachers from the city's boroughs. In the past, many minority children and teachers from these communities have been described as lacking understanding of science, even sometimes the capability to develop it. Staff members of the center do not accept that premise and assert the belief in the capacity of all children for active, quality learning and development. The center's activities are a testament of what it actually does to back up this belief—building teachers' understanding and acceptance that differences do not mean incapacity, educating teachers to acquire a deep understanding through their own experience of the process of science inquiry in the context of common phenomena of the world, and enhancing teachers' learning to engage students in learning science through inquiry.

The focus of the Workshop Center's work is on educating teachers to be confident science inquirers who understand the potential for science learning in the common everyday phenomena that capture children's interests. Three aspects of the focus are teachers learning (1) how to successfully conduct and make science sense from their inquiries into phenomena of nature, (2) how children construct their knowledge of science as a result of inquiry into everyday phenomena, and (3) how to successfully implement a science inquiry approach in their classrooms. The teacher is the principle agent in the introduction, guidance, and maintenance of children's many-layered inquiry. To play this role well, teachers need a science education that is faithful to the practice of scientific inquiry and to adult ways of learning and that gives them the reassurance that the physical reality of the world is a legitimate subject of scientific inquiry. They need extended opportunities for sustained engagement with phenomena to see how their own inquiries unfold and to revisit earlier observations and notions in light of their explorations and growing understandings of inquiry. Furthermore, they need to conceptualize the role materials, activity, interaction, and reflection play in the inquiry process. Most important, teachers themselves need to *experience* what they are trying to develop in children—a scientific understanding of phenomena and an experienced-based vision of how they learn.

As part of its work, the center also conducts workshops for school principals and for parents. Workshops for principals introduce them to constructive ways of supervising teachers who use the inquiry approach in their classrooms. Those for parents familiarize them with children's roles as first-hand learners in science inquiry so that they can better support their children's efforts.

The Workshop Center's Approach to Professional Education

At the core of the Workshop Center's educational approach is the use of direct experience in learning through inquiry, generating science knowledge as a consequence, and the belief in each person's capability to inquire with meaning and understanding. In the center's view, science inquiry encompasses both content and approach. The content is derived from the common materials and phenomena learners encounter and from other sources. The approach is inquiry through which the learner is engaged in experiences, observations, and sense making in science. Learners gain scientific knowledge through a continual search for underlying commonalities in apparently disparate phenomena and refinement of their understanding by constructing and reconstructing what they know.

Direct experience with phenomena of nature helps learners to build connections among different phenomena on the one hand and between their conceptions of the world and actual events in the world on the other. They refine their knowledge by asking more and better-focused questions that help them correct the limitations of their first understanding. Conceptual change and refinement by learners are common ingredients in elementary and middle school science practice; they have to be, because children's conceptions of the world undergo change as children grow and gain more direct experience with the physical world and with the worlds of symbols and ideas.

Framework of Professional Development

The Workshop Center's science education programs for middle and elementary school teachers educate teachers to be successful, confident, scientific inquirers in the world of school science. They enable teachers—through carrying out their own science inquiries—to become possessors and interpreters of significant science content and to be adept users of the requisite spoken and written language.

The educational practice adopted in the programs is based on four broad categories: (1) primary or firsthand inquiry, (2) representation, (3) abstraction, and (4) the "science research council conference" (Dyasi, 1990).

1. *Primary or firsthand experiential inquiry* involves noticing and exploring phenomena and raising questions that can be answered through scientific investigations. It also incorporates designing and carrying out investigations, collecting and organizing data in scientifically reliable ways, and formulating testable scientific conclusions based on evidence.

2. *Representation* occurs in all four categories, encompassing as it does both verbal and written descriptions. Depending on the kinds of investigations carried out, it also incorporates use of pictures (e.g., charts, diagrams, graphs, equations), numbers (measurements), and other suitable descriptive mechanisms.

3. Firsthand investigation and representation are necessary but not sufficient; teachers must also make scientific *abstractions* from data; that is, they should see testable patterns and generate possible scientific explanations consistent with evidence.

4. In a *science research council conference,* science inquiry teams or individual inquirers present comprehensive oral and written reports on their investigations to a critical but friendly community of peers. Reports include investigation question(s) raised and how they arose, designs followed (including equipment used, observations made, and the number of tests conducted), modifications made to the design along the way and why, data collected and scientific ideas they suggest, and unresolved questions. One of the peers or a staff member serves as moderator. After each report, the moderator highlights its scientific achievements, unresolved issues, and possible next steps.

By building teachers' understanding of science inquiry (how to raise questions that can be answered through scientific investigations, how to make meaning from inquiry experiences, and how that process is related to the acquisition of scientific concepts) and by building teachers' personal capacities to internalize the center's learning environments that helped them to develop and internalize scientific knowledge, the center's educational framework supports teachers to educate their students in a similar fashion and to create suitable rich learning environments for that to happen. The framework provides opportunities for teachers to see themselves as capable learners, mobilizing their capabilities, and succeeding in investigating and understanding what they had previously regarded as beyond their capacity.

Using the approach they experience in the Workshop Center programs, teachers also learn to work directly with children, observing and recording how they learn and responding positively to their inquiries and sense making. They leave the programs equipped with a rich repertoire of knowledge, practice, and resources necessary for an imaginative and educationally sound response to children's inquiries into natural phenomena.

In some of the programs, teachers also acquire knowledge and strategies for providing supportive leadership to their fellow teachers, thus creating communities of inquiring teachers in schools and in school districts.

In all programs, participants engage in science inquiry at their own level, often working in small groups and sometimes individually. Each participant maintains a written journal of his or her experience in the program. Since the journals include descriptions and reflections on the teachers' experiences in the workshop sessions, they facilitate recall and focus on participants' experiences and on special moments of the experiences that illuminate and further the teachers' investigative efforts. The journals also serve as a means of communication between each participant and the staff. They allow staff to revisit and "hold" for the teacher specific instances that illustrate their evolving understandings. As the staff learns directly from the teachers' journals what they choose to recapitulate and what meanings they attach to events, staff members are better able to confirm insights into what each teacher might use to further his or her efforts. With this process, they are increasingly able to identify problems that might impede growth. Participants also study, write summaries, and reflect on professional literature associated with the learner-focused approach used in the workshops. They relate the readings to possibilities of engaging children in their classes in practical science inquiry.

A very significant component of all the programs is the staff. Staff members model what they wish the teachers to learn in science inquiry, curricular inquiry, social interaction, and classroom organization. They use instructional strategies such as engaging teachers as learners in social contexts characterized by both learning and instruction. Participants and staff work with children and parents and examine and evaluate science curriculum resources.

Staff members work as an integrated unit composed of experienced science educators, scientists, and selected public school teachers with many years of experience at various educational levels. The integrated style of work is exhibited in observable ways: Participants observe faculty relate to other faculty in planning sessions in the morning, and they can "listen in" to faculty discussion in review sessions at the end of the day. They see faculty interaction in jointly led workshops and in response to a guest speaker, and they see in action how dialogue among colleagues occurs and what issues faculty continually think about. Participants also have the opportunity to relate to and see faculty members pursuing their own inquiries, and they share in the excitement of continuing professional development and learning. The way staff members interact with the teachers is based on the belief that the restoration of self-worth cannot be achieved through lectures and reasoned analysis, but through active engagement.

Illustrative Programs

The Lillian Weber Summer Institute

Open to college graduates regardless of field of study and to selected undergraduates, the Lillian Weber Summer Institute has been held annually since 1971. Its central feature is intensive immersion in a long-term investigation of a phenomenon over a four-week period to develop participants as competent inquirers and analytical students of their own individual learning. Selection of a phenomenon for investigation, the design of investigative activities, collection and organization of data, and construction of science knowledge from collected data are the responsibility of the participant in consultation with staff and with other participants.

During the introductory week, staff members highlight key elements that permeate successful inquiries, for example, an intense curiosity about a phenomenon, close observation and direct manipulation of the phenomenon, raising questions that increase a person's knowledge of the phenomenon, designing and carrying out ways to answer questions, formulation of some tentative generalizations that lead to further questions and perceptions of patterns, and generation of models demonstrating scientific understanding of phenomena. To give participants a general feeling for the elements of inquiry, staff members use a variety of mechanisms such as exploratory field trips on campus and in the neighboring park, visual exploration of portions of New York City from the top floor of one of the college buildings, and study of the total environment inside the Workshop Center. Inquiry activities that require participants to make general and specific observations of phenomena and report on them in small group sessions are assigned regularly, and assigned readings on the Workshop Center approach to inquiry in education, on issues in science learning and teaching, and on the nature of science are discussed.

In the second week, each participant selects an area of investigation, raises questions to pursue, and proceeds to design and to carry out investigations. Two- to three-hour blocks of time per day are devoted to these activities. Many selected areas of investigation are predictable (e.g., leaves, sound, or water), but others are more unusual (e.g., chewing gum or cracks on sidewalks). In addition to carrying out individual investigations, participants meet with staff in small advisory groups to share and discuss their individual investigations and to receive feedback from one another and from staff. Occasionally, invited specialists make presentations in general sessions involving all the participants, and at other times videos on specific aspects of science inquiry are shown and discussed. Also during this second week, a panel presentation by participants from previous summer institutes share their experiences and education they received when they were participants.

The third week is devoted to more intensive individual investigations and in the final week, each participant makes a professional presentation of her or his work during the institute. The audience of other participants contributes by raising questions and quite often by providing additional observations and data related to the investigations. Staff members also raise questions and make comments that highlight the scientific and educational significance of the work presented. At the end of the institute, each participant writes a reflective account of his or her institute experience.

Participants have had interesting reflections on their experiences in the institutes. For example, a former participant wrote, "As the staff talked about getting firsthand experience, I thought about the farm and all the things I had been fortunate enough to try firsthand . . . Whenever we went to the farm my cousins and I . . . captured frogs and tried to keep them alive, we looked at minnows in the fishpond along with dragonflies. For inner-city kids this was heaven! Little did I know that this was related to science."

Another stated her thoughts this way:

> I caught the vision that real learning about the natural world comes out of a combination of inspiration and technique. I saw how much more meaningful and helpful secondary sources are when they are used to support firsthand learning. I learned about myself and about my own learning style. I learned that I could move back and forth between rhythms of action and reflection, that I could take apart my darkest emotions and feelings of frustration, deal with them in the privacy of my thoughts, memories, and writing, and turn them into productive starting points. And perhaps most importantly, I learned how much more there is to learn, and . . . how capable I am of pursuing new knowledge.

Developing Teachers as Science Inquirers and Science Education Restructuring

Collaborative programs with Community School Districts 5 and 8 (Developing Teachers as Science Inquirers), and with Community School District 6 (School-Based Science Restructuring Program) in New York City, provided contexts for implementation of the Center's professional development model, approach, and practice. The model involves reflective teaching applied in a cyclical process, in which staff and teachers continually examined, adapted, and evaluated their practice (see Figures 6.2 and 6.3).

Figure 6.2   Fall Cycle of Activity

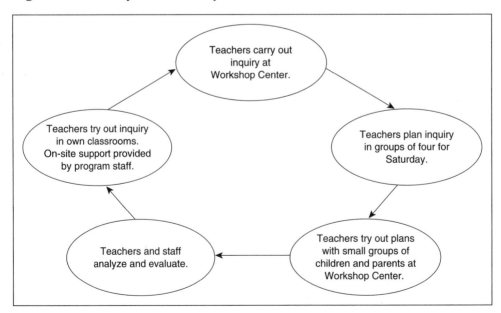

Figure 6.3   Spring Cycle of Activity

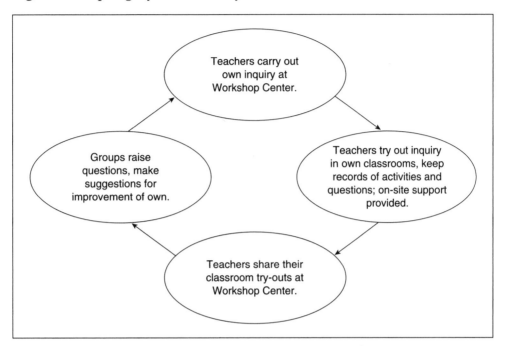

Each program was divided into five phases: (1) development of teachers as learners; (2) teachers' implementation of inquiry learning, first in a clinical setting and later in their own classrooms; (3) education of school principals and leader educators in the elements of science inquiry; (4) planning, implementation, and documentation of classroom inquiry experiences to be used by teachers and administrators; and (5) dissemination of program outcomes throughout the school district. Each phase of the program was planned and sometimes implemented in collaboration with districts' supervisory staff, school principals, and teachers; there was, therefore, a built-in element for enabling school districts to sustain the program with minimal outside assistance.

Each participant in the Districts 5 and 8 program spent two semesters to earn six graduate credits. The program deepened and increased participants' investigation skills, for example their ability to formulate researchable questions, carry out investigations directly, and collect, organize, and interpret data, while pursuing answers to their own questions about natural phenomena. The program created a critical mass of teachers who were educated in the implementation of inquiry approaches in the teaching and learning of science in the elementary school and in working with parents to support their children's inquiry activities at home.

To aid reflection on learning and teaching, each participant read and summarized science education readings that dealt with children's learning. The readings also provided guidelines for helping children to develop their capacities in planning investigations, developing observation skills, and constructing science knowledge commensurate with their stage of intellectual development. Some of the readings also dealt with the role of questions in stimulating children's thought and action, resources to encourage and engage children's inquiry, and the importance of children's communication in the learning process. In addition to the readings, each teacher kept a journal on workshop investigations, class discussions, and implementation of activities.

Program staff included a science educator, a scientist, a teacher who partnered with the science educator, a parent education specialist, a program evaluator, and on-site staff who worked as teachers' coprofessionals. The staff planned together, taught together in a seamless manner, and collaboratively reviewed teachers' work. Occasionally, a steering committee of university scientists, social scientists, science educators, public school personnel, and representatives of professional agencies provided advice and review of the program activities.

Saturday practicums with children facilitated and supported teachers' direct practice of skills acquired during the workshop sessions. Saturday workshops for parents ran concurrently with the teacher-children practicums; these workshops built the foundation for communication between parents and teachers and helped parents to understand how they could be helpful to their children's learning at home.

Teachers' Reflections on the Two-Semester Program

Reflecting on her own learning of science inquiry in the first part of the fall cycle of activities, a teacher participant wrote:

> I loved how our discussion about dry ice at the end of class honored the evidence we'd collected from one group to another, with the teacher helping us put vocabulary to the phenomena we observed rather than explaining the phenomena. This discussion often related back to the ideas that came out at the beginning of the activity, when we were brainstorming what we knew about matter, so that we could couch our new evidence in our already established ideas even as it stretched our understanding of those ideas. (Erika, 2nd grade)

Participant teachers made interesting observations and thoughtful reflections about their implementation of science inquiry in their classrooms. For example, a teacher participant reflected on his classroom implementation of what he had learned about science inquiry during his own learning phase:

> In working with my kindergarteners, I delivered a similar approach. . . .
> I found in doing this that it was quite a natural procedure to

incorporate. . . . The approach of assisting the children to build upon their observations worked very well when I made a chart of their ideas as a collective group and asked them a series of open-ended questions. Indeed they had a lot to say. (Jerome, kindergarten)

Another teacher highlighted her implementation of some of the essential components of science inquiry in the elementary school classroom:

This was a very meaningful activity for my students [scientific investigations of apples: what will happen to the apple if we put it in a bag and leave it outside in the classroom? What will happen to the apple if we put it in a bag inside the refrigerator? What will happen to the apple if we put it in a bag with water?]. . . . They learned about the process of planning, to work in groups, to work independently, to measure using a scale, to make detailed observations, to collect and organize data, to look at evidence and learn from the evidence. In the process they also used other skills such as reading a table to find information, writing observations using descriptive words and presenting information. (Naida, 1st and 2nd grades)

Teachers recognized the need to guide students to an acquisition of science subject matter and to go beyond mere observation to development of scientific ideas. For example, one teacher wrote:

The children were already somewhat familiar with color changes since they have had previous experience with mixing paints to create color change. However, although they expected changes to occur, they were very surprised and excited about the outcomes. I really felt that their efforts to understand the phenomena were overshadowed by their wanting to watch the changes that take place again, in this I mean they were just very excited to see that they had made the purple color disappear and had made the color pink appear. It didn't seem as if they were trying to understand why it occurred. They did seem somewhat aware of how it occurred as they recalled the items that were mixed to get a new color. (Dana, day care)

A teacher who had guided his students in carrying out investigations on different ways in which plants can propagate themselves made this observation:

By using their acquired knowledge concerning the function of the different plant parts . . . through observation [children] are able to see that there are various ways in which a new plant can form without seeds. . . . They also learned that the plant species played a role in whether certain ways worked. In order to have a new plant three parts must be present: roots, stem, and leaves. Also, it takes a while for a new plant to develop. (George, 4th grade)

From these examples it is clear that teachers can go beyond learning science inquiry at their own level; they can also successfully prepare inquiry-based science lessons and implement them in their classrooms. They also develop their capabilities to understand, interpret, and reflect and communicate their own and their students' science inquiry activities. However, to do so on a sustained basis they need strong, informed, and competent long-term support from education leaders in their schools and from experienced science teacher educators. Hence the academic year program incorporated education of leader teachers and school principals, and onsite support by science teacher educators.

Education of Leader Teachers and School Supervisors

The Community School District 6 program had an added component of educating lead teachers and teacher supervisors in science inquiry and in the education of other teachers; each lead teacher was in the program for two academic years and summers. It also substituted Saturday field trips for the Saturday practicums to help lead teachers generate inquiry ideas for their classrooms and for their work with other teachers. Other additional aspects of the program included workshops for school principals (see Figure 6.4) and the development of on-site instructional teams.

Figure 6.4   Cycle of Activities for Principals

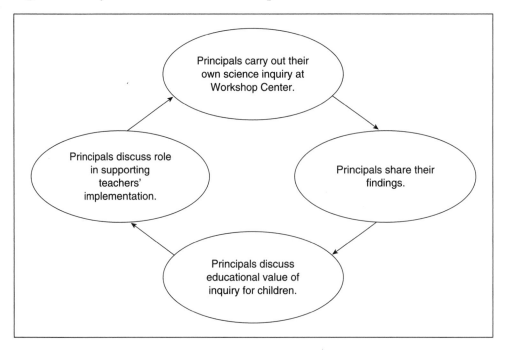

This component, together with the parents program described above, highlights the fact that no matter how well educated they are in science inquiry, without strong, sustained human and material support from the school and from the district, teachers cannot adequately implement science inquiry in their classrooms.

Excerpts From Teacher Leaders' Reflections on the Program

As customary, participants in the program wrote extensively describing and reflecting on the program's educational activities. These writings did not only sensitize participants to their own educational growth but were also data for assessing the impact of the program. One teacher leader wrote:

> I found the Workshop Center to be a very valuable experience. Too often teachers get caught in a tightly bound mind-set. The workshop can provide the teacher with a different way of looking at things. I also gained new insight into structures and how they are built. I hope to utilize the physical knowledge activities in the classroom. . . . The center is a marvelous experience for children. It was wonderful to see the kids looking at all the plants, animals, instruments, etc. around the center. A teacher can make the classroom the same sort of place on a smaller scale.

Another participant reflected:

> The center's modeling of what we were learning in classes about classroom organization, social interaction, curricular inquiry, and observation gave me more confidence in the practicability of the ideas and allowed me to raise deeper questions about them and to try them in my classroom. The Workshop Center is a place where I could "try" things I was unfamiliar with or uncertain of and where I could flounder a bit without the risks usually attendant on that. Experiencing the ups and downs of active learning gave me a more solid sense of confidence in my own ability to learn.

Reflections

In the past 10 years, most of the work we have described above has been implemented by an inquiry-based science education center directed by Professor Rebecca Dyasi at Long Island University, Brooklyn. That center has refined and highlighted all the program components, which have become major aspects of science education reform locally and nationally. For example, it has brought to the forefront the educational value of firsthand experience in the learning of all aspects of science inquiry to gain science content; pedagogical science content knowledge; on-site and in-classroom professional support of teachers from accomplished coprofessionals assisting them with implementation and with self-assessment of their own and of their students' performance; teachers' accurate understanding and interpretation of their students' engagement in all aspects of science inquiry; and the value of using science inquiry to enhance students' capacities in oral and written communication, in the use of science-related technology, and in self-confidence.

The impact of the program has been far reaching. Nearly half of New York City public schools have adopted an inquiry-based science teaching program or a combination of an inquiry-based science program with a science textbook program over a textbook-only program. The educational model and its associated practice have been adopted in several educational institutions around the country and modified to suit local circumstances. For example, the model was adopted, refined, and adapted by the San Francisco Exploratorium's Institute for Inquiry, the Teacher Educators' Network of the Association of Science-Technology Centers, and the Clark County (Nevada) School District. It has also been highlighted in national programs through the North Central Regional Education Laboratory in collaboration with the Public Broadcasting System, and through the Harvard-Smithsonian Center for Astrophysics and the Annenberg Corporation for Public Broadcasting programs.

The use of teacher and student journals (or notebooks), which were integral in the program from the beginning, has become a significant aspect of inquiry-based science education and in linking science and literacy. It is featured in several books including *Crossing Borders in Literacy and Science Instruction: Perspectives on Theory and Practice,* edited by Wendy Saul and published in 2004, and *Teaching Science in the 21st Century,* edited by Jack Rhoton and Patricia Shane and published by the National Association of Teachers in 2006.

Professional Development Case B

TEACH-STAT: A MODEL FOR PROFESSIONAL DEVELOPMENT IN DATA ANALYSIS AND STATISTICS FOR TEACHERS OF GRADES KINDERGARTEN THROUGH SIX

Susan N. Friel, School of Education, University of North Carolina at Chapel Hill

Table 6.2   Design at a Glance: Teach-Stat

Level and content	Elementary mathematics
Knowledge and beliefs	*Principles and Standards for School Mathematics—* focused on statistics
Context	Inputs considered included teacher knowledge and experience, state regional structure, availability of curriculum
Goals	Help teachers learn statistics and integrate it into their instruction and develop teacher leaders
Primary strategies	Workshops, institutes, and seminars; curriculum implementation; coaching; and mentoring
Critical issues	Developing leadership, building capacity for sustainability

The *Curriculum and Evaluation Standards for School Mathematics* (NCTM, 1989) identifies statistics and probability as a major strand across all grade levels. Since 1989, there has been growing interest in what to teach and how to teach with respect to statistics. Appropriate curricula for teaching statistics (e.g., *Used Numbers*[1] and *Quantitative Literacy Series*[2]) are available for use at the kindergarten though twelfth-grade levels.

Authors' Note: This case is a shortened version of a chapter by S. N. Friel and G. W. Bright: Friel, S. N., & Bright, G. W. (1998). Teach-Stat: A model for professional development in data analysis and statistics for teachers, K–6. In S. P. Lajoie (Ed.), *Reflections on statistics: Agendas for learning, teaching, and assessment in K–12.* Mahwah, NJ: Lawrence Erlbaum.

At the elementary level, available curricula are an essential ingredient in helping teachers find ways to integrate the teaching of statistics in a coherent and comprehensive manner. Curricula for use with students are not sufficient, however; using such curricula effectively requires a reasonable knowledge of statistics to pose tasks appropriately and promote and manage classroom discourse successfully. Elementary teachers are in need of professional development opportunities that will support their learning of content and promote the use of an inquiry orientation to help their students learn and use statistical concepts.

Teach-Stat: A Key to Better Mathematics (Friel & Joyner, 1991) was a project designed to plan and implement a program of professional development for elementary teachers, Grades 1 through 6, to help them learn more about statistics and integrate teaching about and teaching with statistics in their instruction. This project included the following three components:

1. The design of professional development curricula for use with teachers and with teacher leaders (here referenced as statistics educators)

2. A large-scale implementation program to provide professional development for both teachers and statistics educators using the professional development curricula

3. A program of research and evaluation to assess the impact of the project and to surface research questions related to the agenda of the project

Project Design

The project was funded by the NSF through the University of North Carolina Mathematics and Science Education Network (MSEN). MSEN consists of 10 centers throughout North Carolina housed at 10 of the state university system's campuses. Each center is directed by a faculty member in mathematics or science education; one of the main tasks for each center is providing professional development in mathematics or science or both for K–12 teachers in its service region. Because of its structure, MSEN is particularly well suited for supporting the implementation of large-scale, statewide projects.

The project involved 9 of the 10 MSEN centers; one faculty member (here referenced as site faculty leader) from each of the sites served as the local coordinator of the project. The nine site faculty leaders, with the addition of a few other university consultants, designed and implemented the Teach-Stat project. More than 450 teachers throughout North Carolina participated in the project, and of those, 84 received additional professional development to prepare them to be statistics educators.

The first fall and spring of the Teach-Stat project were used as a planning time to bring together the site faculty leaders and additional faculty consultants from across the state. This group met intensively for two- or three-day meetings several times during the first year. Their tasks were to design the draft of the professional development curriculum that would be used to teach teachers and then to jointly teach the first three-week summer institute.

The project was designed so that, during the first year, each site faculty leader selected six or seven teachers as a pilot team. The 57 teachers and nine site faculty leaders participated in a three-week summer institute, which was offered as a residential program at a central site. The faculty, working in teams of three, was responsible for various parts of the program. Throughout the following school year, each faculty site leader met with and visited the regional teacher team, jointly exploring with the teachers what it meant for them to teach statistics and integrate statistics with other subject areas.

In the second year, each of the nine sites offered a revised (nonresidential) version of the three-week professional development program to 24 new teachers. Each site faculty leader and the pilot team of six or seven teachers worked together to plan and provide the workshop. Originally, the pilot teachers were going to be available to help but not to teach. By the second summer, however, faculty and teachers had developed such a good working relationship that the model of a "professional development team" naturally emerged and was very successful. The second-year participants were able to hear from teachers who had spent the preceding year teaching statistics and had many actual examples to show them. The first-year pilot teachers received a great deal of support, informal "how to be a staff developer" training, and coaching and mentoring from their respective site faculty leaders.

In the third year, 84 teachers from either the first or second year were selected to become statistics educators to serve as resource people throughout North Carolina to provide professional development programs in statistics education for other elementary teachers. They participated (regionally at the nine sites) in the equivalent of a one-week seminar focused on the "how-to's and the why's" of staff development. The statistics educators at each site were responsible for developing and providing a two-week summer institute for an additional set of 24 new teachers at their site. As a result of this program, the statistics educators were equipped to offer the Teach-Stat professional development program to other elementary school teachers and to design variations of this program to meet the needs of the audience with which they happened to be dealing.

The documentation of the project includes the following various materials that permit others to replicate the program of professional development and implementation:

- *Teach-Stat for Teachers: Professional Development Manual* (Friel & Joyner, 1997) provides a how-to discussion for planning and implementing a three-week teacher education institute. It is written in a way that addresses teachers' needs for inservice education, and its audience is mainly those who provide professional development programs for elementary grade teachers.

- *Teach-Stat for Statistics Educators: Staff Developer's Manual* (Gleason, Vesilind, Friel, & Joyner, 1996) provides a how-to discussion for planning and implementing a one-week Statistics Educators Institute. This institute is designed for teachers who will serve as staff development resource people (statistics educators) who have participated in a three-week program in statistics education and have previously taught statistics to students.

- *Teach-Stat Activities: Statistics Investigations for Grades 1–3* (Joyner, Pfieffer, Friel, & Vesilind, 1997a) and *Teach-Stat Activities: Statistics Investigations for Grades 3–6* (Joyner, Pfieffer, Friel, & Vesilind, 1997b) provide how-to discussions of the planning and implementation of activities for elementary grade students that promote the learning of statistics using the process of statistical investigation.

Statistics Educators: Developing Leaders

The benefit of a structure such as MSEN is that it provides access to the state's school systems and assists in maintaining a consistent level of quality in the professional development programs it provides. North Carolina, however, still lacks the capacity to provide high-quality opportunities for the majority of elementary school teachers to increase their subject-matter knowledge and to continuously examine and modify their teaching practice. The Teach-Stat project sought to address the "capacity question" not only by providing professional development for a large number of teachers on a regional basis but also, more important, by developing teachers (statistics educators) who can work with other elementary school teachers in support of their learning statistics and how to teach statistics and teach using statistics. This is one of the elements needed in building an infrastructure for professional development.

The final teams of statistics educators varied in composition: Some teams included only first-year teachers, some included a balance of first- and second-year teachers, and some included a few or no first-year teachers with the preponderance of second-year teachers. They were selected based on their interest and on their potential ability to provide professional development to their peers. In cases in which first- and second-year teachers were balanced, it was found that teaming of a first-year teacher with a second-year teacher created a mentor-coach arrangement that seemed to support the second-year teachers in their initial experiences teaching other teachers. It was assumed that, in most cases, these teachers would work in teams of two statistics educators to provide such experiences for other teachers once they "graduated" as statistics educators.

Teachers selected for this opportunity participated in an additional week's professional development program that helped them explore staff development issues and ways to conduct a workshop. The Statistics Educators Institutes included content on adult learning, the change process, and statistics pedagogical content knowledge. Statistics educators completed three or four days of work prior to the Teach-Stat workshop they taught for third-year teachers; the remainder of the work was done as part of a "looking back" effort to reflect on what happened during the workshop.

As part of their participation, approximately half the statistics educators participated in a study (Frost, 1995) to investigate the effects of classroom teachers becoming Teach-Stat workshop leaders. They responded to three different instruments, and some also participated in interviews. These were completed at three different times: at the beginning and at the end of the Statistics Educators Institute and after teaching the third-year Teach-Stat summer workshops.

Frost's (1995) study is rich with information. For purposes here, the results suggest that staff development designs built on teachers becoming leaders should provide special assistance to help them develop in this role over time. The following are relevant:

- Opportunities to develop and demonstrate strong content knowledge in mathematics before becoming a workshop leader should be an important consideration in staff development.
- Teachers' classroom experiences are valuable assets to their work as workshop leaders. Classroom experiences using teaching activities like those presented in workshops provide the workshop leader with "personal memory tapes" of the practical, as well as the pedagogical, issues related to the activities.
- Teachers who become workshop leaders may need specialized assistance in conceptualizing effective staff development. The study suggests that workshop leaders progress through stages of growth in their conceptions about effective staff development; such stages can be used as "benchmarks" to assess readiness or potential of the teacher to serve as a workshop leader.
- Teachers who become workshop leaders need opportunities to develop their own understanding of the nature of adult learners and creating a climate conducive for adult learning. Furthermore, there is a need to help workshop leaders explore pedagogical content knowledge related to teaching adults.

What We Learned

When the study of statistics is framed within the context of a process of statistical investigation and involves the use of relevant hands-on applications and activities, teachers and students quickly become engaged. Unlike much of traditional elementary school mathematics, teaching statistics within this framework provides for a much more open learning environment. No longer is there only "one right way" to do mathematics, and questioning and exploration are encouraged and promoted. Professional development experiences that model such learning environments can be successful in helping teachers bring similar excitement and engagement in learning to their students. Overall, individuals at all levels of involvement, primary grade teachers to college teachers of statistics, learned from their Teach-Stat experiences and described these experiences as having influenced change in their respective classrooms.

Notes

1. *Used Numbers: Real Data in the Classroom*, is a set of six units of study for K–6 students, published by Addison-Wesley Publishing, Co. (Palo Alto, CA).

2. *Quantitative Literacy Series,* is a set of four units of study for students in Grades 8 through 12 and is published by Dale Seymour Publications (Palo Alto, CA).

Professional Development Case C

THE CALIFORNIA MIDDLE GRADES
MATHEMATICS RENAISSANCE

Judy Mumme, Principal Investigator, Learning to Lead
Mathematics Professional Development, WestEd

Table 6.3   Design at a Glance: Mathematics Renaissance

Level and content	Middle school mathematics
Knowledge and beliefs	*Principles and Standards for School Mathematics*, actively engaged learning, understanding of the change process, equitable access to high-quality teaching and learning
Context	Teachers' knowledge and experience in mathematics, current practices, student learning levels, state and local policies
Goals	Increase access and success of all students in mathematics, build teacher leadership
Primary strategies	Curriculum implementation using replacement units, professional networks, institutes
Critical issues	Ensuring equity, developing leadership, building capacity for sustainability, garnering public support

Reflection and Project Update

The Middle Grades Mathematics Renaissance project ended in 1997. Building on the work at the middle grades, the Mathematics Renaissance K–12 extended the work at many of the middle schools to create a series of K–12 articulated networks in 28 districts across the state. This project, funded by the National Science Foundation from 1997 through 2002, worked to establish coherence across the K–12 continuum. At its core was the commitment to increase access and success for students historically underrepresented, while holding high expectations for improving performance for all students. The Renaissance received recognition from the U.S. Department of Education as an exemplary mathematics professional development program.

It was identified by the National Staff Development Council as meeting the stringent criteria as a model staff development program that increased student achievement.

As an outgrowth of the two Renaissance efforts, the Mathematics Leadership Alliance was funded by the California Department of Education Eisenhower Program in 2002. It was designed to help districts build and sustain the leadership capacity and build an infrastructure capable of promoting sustained teacher growth in 14 districts. This project, composed of four to six teacher leaders and administrators from each district, formed cadres who took responsibility for leadership and ongoing support for state, district, school site, or university sponsored mathematics initiatives within their respective districts. In addition, districts received assistance in designing, selecting, supporting, and evaluating effective professional development in mathematics in order to provide high-quality mathematics education programs for all students.

These initiatives occurred in times of increasing dissent in mathematics education in the state. The initiatives provided leadership support so teachers could provide high-quality instruction in spite of pressures to reduce the academic rigor of the mathematics programs.

A common thread across each of these efforts was the need to develop and support teacher leadership. We recognized this as a national need, and the National Science Foundation funded our efforts to develop materials aimed at supporting the development of leaders of professional development. We recognized that leaders of professional development are more than good classroom teachers—they require specific support aimed at developing their skills and sensibilities to design and enact thoughtful, worthwhile experiences for teachers. We developed a case-based set of leadership materials, published as the *Learning to Lead Mathematics Professional Development* (Carroll & Mumme, 2007). They are designed to support mathematics professional development leaders K–12. The materials consist of 44 videocases organized into a series of modules addressing key issues faced by leaders of professional development. These are the set of materials we wish we would have had to support our work throughout the Renaissance.

In these materials, we present a revised set of guiding principles that evolved from the Renaissance:

- ***Purpose*** *guides the design and enactment of mathematics professional development.* Mathematics professional development is designed to achieve specific goals and purposes. This involves keeping long-term goals in mind as well as the purpose for a specific activity.
- *The **mathematics** must be important and worthwhile.* Throughout both the design and enactment of professional development the PD leader continually keeps an eye on the mathematical trajectory—how is this activity leading teachers to consider big mathematical ideas?

- *Robust **sociomathematical norms** are essential for productive mathematical work.* Leaders use these norms to cultivate mathematically rich environments that press for teachers' understanding of mathematics.
- ***Sense making** for teachers drives design decisions in mathematics professional development.* Professional development experiences are designed and enacted so that the teacher is continually being asked to think and reason—about mathematics and about mathematics teaching and learning.
- ***Access and equity** are lenses through which all work is considered in mathematics professional development.* Leaders create opportunities for teachers to confront issues of equity that arise in mathematics learning situations—for adults and children, all the while considering teachers' own experiences and those of their students.

Although we believe most of the guiding principles we established during the Renaissance work still hold true, our recent research on developing leadership suggests a change in one of these principles. We would reword the original Renaissance principle that suggested that the pedagogy of professional development is self-similar to classrooms to now state that *whereas doing mathematics in professional development is similar to doing mathematics in classrooms, it also has some important differences.*

Doing mathematics with teachers in professional development differs from what one does with students for several reasons. Teachers hold mathematical knowledge differently than students—teachers often already have some background experiences with the mathematical ideas they engage in professional development. They are not necessarily learning *new* mathematics but expanding or deepening their understandings of the mathematics and learning the mathematics needed for teaching. Teachers' motivation for being in professional development is different from their students'—teachers are there because they are learning about mathematics for teaching. Students, on the other hand, are not engaging in mathematics for the purpose of teaching it to their students. Therefore, the purposes for doing mathematics in professional development are different, and teachers should not expect that their experiences in professional development are directly relatable to those that their students might have engaging in similar work. This has implications for how leaders help translate their professional development experiences to the classroom.

Mathematics Renaissance: Context and Desired Outcomes

The Middle Grades Mathematics Renaissance was a component of the California Alliance for Mathematics and Science, an NSF-funded State

Systemic Initiative. Using professional development as its central strategy, the Renaissance was designed to help schools transform their mathematics programs so that all students, especially those historically underrepresented in mathematics, become empowered mathematically. During 1995 and 1996, eighteen hundred teachers from approximately 350 schools participated in the academic year and summer or off-track work, which focused on professional development issues: discussing mathematics education, experiencing hands-on mathematics, learning how to teach new state-of-the-art curriculum "replacement" units, and exploring the conditions that create opportunities for learning.

The Renaissance was developed against the backdrop of California, a state with a rich and complex environment for mathematics reform. At the time of the Renaissance's development, the state had more than five million students, 230,000 teachers (140,000 of whom taught mathematics), 7,000 schools, and 1,000 districts. Average class size was approximately 30 and per-pupil spending was $4,874, placing California 38th among states ($1,000 less than the national average). Approximately half of California's students were from Latino, African American, or Asian American backgrounds. There were more than 100 languages spoken, and 22% of the student population spoke limited English. Approximately 2.2 million children lived in poverty.

Several critical decisions were made early in the planning. First, professional development was chosen as the vehicle to achieve goals. Reaching the large numbers of California's teachers and students, however, required resources beyond the available funding (approximately $1.1 million annually). Therefore, a second decision was made: Middle school mathematics was selected because it acts as a gateway to future access to higher-level mathematics courses. Moreover, curriculum at this level has traditionally been a wasteland, and this area seemed ripe for development and exploration. Third, it was decided that the program would use a school-based rather than an individual teacher focus. Collaboratively, work among faculty members can provide a support system that provides opportunities to address the school structures that promote and inhibit reform. It was believed that by working with schools as the unit of change, a process that would sustain the effort beyond program funding could be established.

Designing the Work

With middle grades as the target, schools as the focus, and professional development as the implementation approach, the Renaissance was born. The challenge became the creation of professional development experiences that would create the fundamental transformation of middle grade mathematics, helping teachers meet the challenges of reform.

Leveraging Resources

Resources in education are rarely sufficient and are less so in a state the size of California. Consequently, plans were formulated to ensure that efforts not only maximized the available resources but also established an infrastructure designed to sustain and expand the efforts throughout the system.

To maximize the leveraging of resources, the Renaissance asked schools to support their own costs. Indeed, the approximately $1.1 million in funding barely supported the statewide leadership infrastructure (one director and 10 regional directors). Schools paid a $3,000 annual participation fee to cover the costs of local teacher leadership. Establishing an expectation that schools annually allot a sizable sum for professional development increased the likelihood that the process will continue once the initiative ceases.

Large numbers of schools were enrolled statewide to take advantage of a "tip-point strategy," which suggests that systemic reform begins with a small vanguard of schools taking the lead in reform and gradually expands to include more schools. Once a critical mass of one-fourth to one-third of the schools is engaged in the reforms, the argument states, the system will "tip," and the majority of the other schools will follow. During the five years of the Renaissance, more than 500 schools participated, well beyond the one-third envisioned.

Teacher Engagement

At the heart of the Renaissance is the belief that such change takes time. The 8 to 12 professional development meetings a year and the summer experience allowed time to deal with a wide range of issues. Teachers discussed current research on learning and effective instructional strategies, the nature of mathematics, and the redefinition of basic skills. Teachers learned how to teach new state-of-the-art curriculum replacement units. They taught these units in their classrooms and returned to debrief their experience with other network members. The replacement strategy provided an opportunity for teachers to have direct, firsthand experience with reform curriculum. Often, teachers engaged in direct mathematical experiences as learners. It is not enough to talk about what can be. Teachers must experience a broader version of mathematics themselves to break their traditional views.

Although there is much that is common about what teachers need to learn, the Renaissance work was also responsive to regional and local demands. In a district near San Diego, the issue of algebra in middle school was a crucial discussion point, whereas another district nearby was grappling with effective methods for engaging parent and community support. Topics of interest ranged from the place of algorithms in the middle grades to cobbling together a whole curriculum from available pieces. Agendas in one cluster included gender bias, portfolio assessment, and the effects of tracking. Regional agendas grew to meet the interests and needs of the cluster participants.

It was also learned that two of the program's commitments—fostering fundamental change and responding to teachers' needs—are sometimes in conflict. There is often a tension between challenging teachers to consider new ideas and being responsive to what teachers want. For example, one teacher commented, "I do not want to be gone from my classroom for days where I am not taught a specific unit that I can take back and use. My students lose every time I am gone." This teacher's comment is typical of many. How does one develop an in-depth understanding of the issues in mathematics education when teachers have a strong desire for things to take back—to add recipes to their files? Time spent exploring constructivism may not feel like a day well spent to some participating teachers. Short-term gains often limit long-term growth opportunities.

Even when teachers take back curriculum units, the opportunities for reflection often begin with managerial issues. These tensions are part of the inherently paradoxical nature of constructivist teaching. How does one respect what teachers want while pushing them to reinvent themselves? Time is part of the answer. Bit by bit, discussion by discussion, clusters begin to become communities of learners, reflecting on practice in critical ways and learning to ask tough questions and to push individual and collective thinking deeper. Over time, teachers' comments shifted to "I appreciate all the time allowed for discussion."

Leadership

The two-tiered structure of the Renaissance provided both statewide and local leadership. The 10 full-time regional directors interacted as a statewide team while directing and designing the unique work of the individual regions. Selection criteria for this role were experience in teaching middle grade mathematics and background in leadership for mathematics education. They played the role of a "critical friend," possessing both an understanding of the research and broad experience in schools attempting to change. Monthly three-day regional meetings and constant communications provided an immediate feedback mechanism.

Each regional director worked with a team of teacher leaders called cluster leaders, who were classroom teachers with the personal experience and credibility to help their peers change classroom practice. Typically, a cluster leader was released from the classroom 35 days during the academic year and worked five weeks each summer to serve in this professional development role. The ratio of cluster leaders to teachers was kept small to allow for the crucial development of relationships with the participating teachers (see Figure 6.5).

Figure 6.5   Renaissance Leadership Structure

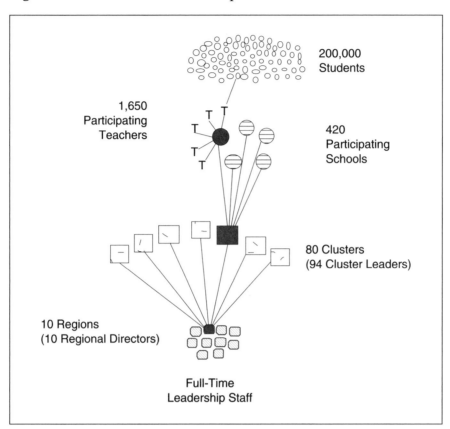

Cluster leaders were key to the quality of the professional development. Their credibility stemmed from the fact that they grappled with the same issues as those of the teachers with whom they worked. It gave them acceptance into the school, cluster, and regional learning communities. These cluster leaders did not simply emerge from the classroom as leaders. California has a long history of leadership development in mathematics. Many cluster leaders came from the California Mathematics Project or other reform projects. A good majority of them came from the ranks of participating Renaissance teachers—many from the first schools to join.

Their work was challenging and demanding, requiring the development of skills beyond those that make one a good teacher. Therefore, another complication arose. The Renaissance design required professional development for both teachers and the teachers who led those teachers. The need for ongoing professional development for leadership cannot be overstated. This is perhaps one of the central lessons that was learned. Leaders must have opportunities to reflect on their work, learning from one another the crucial lessons of leadership for reform. They constantly need to be challenged as learners, expanding their own understanding of mathematics, teaching, and learning. The initial design of the Renaissance failed to account for this need, and much of the statewide professional growth opportunities have been funded catch-as-catch-can.

Cluster leaders created their own version of professional development for participating teachers, and regional directors provided guidance, inspiration, and support. Here, another tension emerged. The program's commitment to shared leadership and delegated authority did not always produce results matching its goals. Messages sometimes got distorted as individual cluster leaders constructed their own understanding of the reform and the Renaissance. The program continued to struggle with the degree of control and guidance cluster leaders received. Does one intervene and risk damaging a cluster leader's credibility and opportunity to learn? How is quality maintained while leadership develops?

Supporting Reforms

Other important elements supported the Renaissance efforts. Enlisting parents as partners is one example. Schools throughout the Renaissance pilot tested the middle school version of Family Math, anticipating that more than 500 parent nights would be conducted during the 1995 and 1996 school year. Administrative support offers yet another example. Principals need time with teachers and other principals, and district administrators must understand and support the reforms.

Efforts of the Renaissance also moved beyond the middle school, in part due to conflicts that arose between some Renaissance middle schools and high schools they feed. Middle school teachers expressed concerns that their students went on to high school eager and excited about mathematics only to have their enthusiasm squelched by the high school placement tests and traditional course work. In many districts, these conflicts were seized as opportunities to promote discussions between middle and high schools. As a result of these discussions, some high schools began to revise their programs using new innovative high school curricula.

Guiding Principles

As the Renaissance engaged in this process, much about teacher change and professional development was learned. Principles that guided the Renaissance program, and all future Renaissance programs, are elaborated on in the following sections.

Teachers should be part of a professional learning community. The NCTM's *Professional Standards for Teaching Mathematics* (1991) and *Principles and Standards for School Mathematics* (2000) call for "classrooms as mathematical communities." Likewise, we believe that teachers need to belong to learning communities that place inquiry at their center and focus on building capacity for further learning.

Beliefs and behaviors are interdependent. Belief systems guide behaviors. It is the examination of belief systems that encourages us to rethink our actions. Behavior, however, provides the grist for examination of beliefs. Without concrete experience, discussions of beliefs can remain empty talk untethered to practice.

The pedagogy of professional development must be self-similar to the pedagogy desired in classrooms. Just as students construct their understanding of mathematics, teachers construct their understanding of the processes of teaching and learning mathematics. One's current views of teaching and learning are grounded in one's own experiences as a learner and teacher. Most teachers have learned mathematics in traditional ways. They know of no other recourse. The mold must be broken. People need ample opportunities to construct new understandings of mathematics, teaching, learning, and schooling. As learners, teachers must see firsthand how interaction with others increases opportunities to learn so that they can provide similar opportunities for their students. Unless effective collaborative work has been a personal experience, how can teachers be expected to establish an environment in which collaboration plays a pivotal role in increasing the quality of the classroom discourse?

Issues of equity must permeate the fabric of professional development. At the very heart of the reform is one simple standard: None of it will matter unless it improves learning for all students, regardless of race, gender, or class. Changing beliefs about who can do worthwhile mathematics must be central to the efforts.

Professional development must be grounded in classroom practice. The real hope for making broad-scale change is the ability to tie professional discussions and examinations to what is happening in classrooms. Teachers must experience reform in their own classrooms and have opportunities to grapple with those experiences.

All teachers are capable of making the changes. We believe that the driving force for the majority of teachers is the dream of helping children to become successful, productive adults. They want to do the best for their children. Teachers need opportunities to rethink their practices in light of new information. Given opportunities to share current professional thinking and findings, teachers can begin to make shifts. These changes must occur in all classrooms, not just the classrooms of the innovative teachers. Teachers who are new to the profession and teachers who have taught for 30 years can engage in reflective practice.

Conclusion

The Renaissance leveraged significant resources. It used networks of teachers and created new ones. Teachers engaged in high-quality professional conversations about practice. The program's cadre of teacher leaders demonstrated its capability to support school-based professional development. The Renaissance clearly had an impact, but this is a complex agenda that will take years to assess.

GLOBAL SYSTEMS SCIENCE: A PROFESSIONAL DEVELOPMENT PROGRAM FOR HIGH SCHOOL TEACHERS

Cary I. Sneider, Portland State University, Portland, Oregon, Former Director of Global Systems Science at the Lawrence Hall of Science, Berkeley, California

Table 6.4   Design at a Glance: Global Systems Science

Level and content	High school science
Knowledge and beliefs	*National Science Education Standards,* the nature of science
Context	Current practices in science teaching and curriculum, teacher knowledge, students' access to quality science programs, national audience and participants
Goal	Enable teachers to develop and implement a new course of integrated studies
Primary strategies	Curriculum development, curriculum implementation, institutes, professional networks
Critical issues	Developing leadership

Principal: Diane, I understand that you're excited about this new integrated program called Global Systems Science, but I'm concerned that some of our parents will worry that their children will do poorly on standardized tests if it replaces the usual science curriculum.

Diane: Then it's about time we educate some of our parents about the need for science literacy concerning environmental issues. The *National Science Education Standards* and our state science framework say we should spend less time teaching science vocabulary and more time helping our students relate science to the real world.

Jim: I'm not convinced that students who take integrated science will miss out on chemistry, physics, and biology. We plan to present the same concepts we taught before, but in a meaningful context. Students will still have labs, but they'll also debate the social implications of science and technology.

Principal: Now I didn't say I was against it, but I'll be the one to take the heat if our community is not convinced it's a good idea. Are you willing to present your ideas at the Parent-Teacher Association next Thursday evening? (Sneider, 1995, p. 1)

The previous dialogue did not take place in a real principal's office. But it did take place during a summer program for teachers at the University of California in Berkeley. Zooming our "camera lens" back from the small group seated around the table, the field of view reveals 20 other teachers listening intently as their colleagues role-play scenes that might actually occur when they return from the 1995 Summer Institute in Global Systems Science (GSS). Previously during the institute, the participants met with colleagues from throughout the nation and compared notes with other science and mathematics teachers who field-tested the student guides and laboratory activities. Later, they helped to create new activities and assessment instruments that would eventually be used in hundreds of other classrooms.

As codevelopers of this new science program, the 125 teachers who participated in the GSS programs increased their understanding of how studies of the planet are actually conducted and how resulting insights can best be communicated to diverse groups of students. They also returned to their school districts with a mission to change the current emphasis of high school science departments from preparing a small segment of the population for college to providing all of the nation's students with the skills that they will need to thrive in the modern world. The GSS program is one vehicle for accomplishing that, and the GSS professional development strategy, in which teachers learn to develop, implement, and disseminate new instructional materials, is one way to prepare them to change the course of science education.

Although the professional development aspects of the GSS program took place in the 1990s, its genesis can be traced to the context of the 1980s, when the national agenda began to focus on global change and science education reform.

The Context of Global Environmental Change

The worldwide climatic disturbances of 1988 (no less than an epidemic of droughts, famines, severe storms, and forest fires) focused attention on the danger of global warming—the theory that increased carbon dioxide in the atmosphere, due to the burning of fossil fuels and other human activities, is warming the entire globe. The potential for the industrial revolution to cause global warming had been predicted more than 100 years ago, but it was not until 1988 that the prospect was finally taken seriously, although scientists were by no means in complete agreement about whether global warming was under way and, if so, what it would mean for the future.

The prospect of global climate change was not the only environmental problem on the horizon at the end of the 1980s. The ever-increasing use of the world's resources to provide energy, food, and housing for a rapidly increasing human population was clearly changing natural environments, resulting in a loss of biodiversity. Also, new developments in technology were found to be influencing the global environment in unexpected ways, such as depletion of ozone gas in the stratosphere, exposing all life on the planet to higher levels of ultraviolet radiation from the sun.

Although men and women of every age probably consider themselves to exist at a unique time in history, during our lifetimes we are witness to the transformation of millions of square miles of natural habitats into farms, cities, industrial parks, and malls. The world's growing population and its tendency to become even more urbanized and industrialized is affecting the environment on a global scale. Although these changes have been under way for decades, only recently have a large number of people become aware of the scope of these changes and their implications for future generations.

Now the environmental issues are still high on the national agenda, and the case for global warming as a consequence of human activities has been strengthened. There continues to be a pressing need for curricula that enable high school students to apply what they learn in science class to real-world problems.

The Context of Science Education Reform

The 1980s were characterized as the decade of "crisis" in science education and the 1990s were characterized as the decade of "change." Project 2061 from the American Association for the Advancement of Science (1993) and the *National Science Education Standards,* created by the National Research Council (1996), challenged the status quo and identified the most important scientific concepts, theories, and attitudes that should form the core of the school science curriculum. These projects and other studies of our science education system have emphasized the need to teach fewer topics in greater depth and to teach not only what scientists have learned about the world but also how they have learned it. There is even strong support for an inquiry-based approach, recognizing that students bring their own ideas to the classroom, and that students construct new meaning from these prior ideas.

Since the passage of the No Child Left Behind (NCLB) Act in 2001, there has been increasing pressure on states to develop science standards and assessments and for school districts to strengthen science programs to meet new accountability measures. While many districts have hunkered down and focused on "the basics," other districts have sought courses that increase motivation, especially among students who might not choose to study science. Integrated science courses have become especially popular in states that have science requirements in all of the major science disciplines through tenth or eleventh grade.

Responding to the call for change, many administrators are directing teachers to spend the summer "writing a new course" that integrates the sciences and meets their state's standards. Global change has been a popular subject for these courses because relevant topics appear in the news almost every day. Environmental protection is of concern to high school students, and the subject lends itself to an inquiry-based approach in which depth is emphasized over breadth. Although many creative teachers developed excellent activities and assembled useful reading materials, most of these efforts have been conducted in isolation. The problem with developing instructional materials in isolation is that the same work must be repeated by many individuals, the opportunities for testing activities with students are limited, and the potential benefit of teachers working together to share their knowledge and build on each other's ideas and strengths is entirely lost.

Development of the GSS Program

Development of the GSS materials started in 1990, when the Lawrence Hall of Science was awarded grants from the National Institute for Global Environmental Change, with funds from the U.S. Department of Energy and the NSF. The product of that effort is an interdisciplinary course for high school students that emphasizes how scientists from a wide variety of fields work together to understand significant problems of global impact. Big ideas of science are emphasized, such as the concept of an interacting system, the coevolution of the atmosphere and life, the goal of a sustainable world, and the important role that individuals play in both influencing and protecting the vulnerable global environment.

The GSS course materials involve students actively in learning. They perform experiments in the classroom and at home. Students read and discuss background materials. They "meet" a wide variety of men and women who are working to understand global environmental change. They work together to dramatize their ideas for working toward solutions to worldwide environmental problems. They are challenged to make intelligent, informed decisions and to take personal actions, such as conserving energy, recycling, and preparing for their roles as voting citizens in a modern industrialized society. The course is frequently updated with short summaries of news articles related to global change via e-mail (and archived on the GSS Web site) to the network of teachers who are using the course.

The GSS Professional Development Program

The goal of the GSS professional development program was not just to implement a new course of integrated studies but also to enable teachers to actively carry out the new educational reforms. The key strategy selected to achieve this goal was teacher-as-curriculum-developer. According to nearly all the teachers who attended the institutes, the experience of working intensively with colleagues for three weeks to discuss what to teach and how to teach, within a framework of guiding principles, was a valuable educational experience in itself. In addition, their creative work in helping to shape and improve the program increased their commitment and their understanding of the principles on which it is based. In the GSS program, this strategy played out in five distinct phases:

Phase 1: Pilot testing. Unlike many professional development programs that begin with an institute or workshop, this strategy begins by asking the teachers to help pilot test new course materials. During the four- to six-week period of pilot testing, the teachers do what they usually do—teach science. However, they substitute a new unit of instructional materials in place of what they normally teach at this time of year. The materials themselves are quite different from the usual textbook, and the accompanying teacher's guide offers suggestions for teaching methods and supplementary activities. During this phase of the program, teachers become familiar with and develop opinions about the new approach.

Phase 2: Summer institute. Having pilot tested the GSS materials, teachers arrive at the summer institute with a common experience. During the first week, they share their insights about the content and process of teaching the new materials and provide critical feedback to the GSS staff. In the second and third weeks of the institute, the teachers focus their creative energies on making the course better by inventing new activities and assessment tasks. They present these to their colleagues and receive affirmation of their efforts and constructive feedback. They also visit laboratories and meet scientists involved in GSS research. Finally, they learn how the GSS program fits into the context of science education reform, and they participate in activities such as the role-play session described at the beginning of this case study.

Phase 3: Assessment of impact on students. For teachers to commit to an innovative approach, they need to be convinced that it is making a positive contribution to their students' learning. The teacher's guide provides several ideas for testing student understanding before and after teaching a unit so that it is possible for teachers to see what their students have learned. The guide also provides ideas for maintaining portfolios of student work. Many of the teachers also provide student test data to the GSS staff in Berkeley for analysis.

Phase 4: Networking. Experiences in working with other teachers to develop innovative approaches often lead to a desire for continued contact with the growing community of teachers who share an interest in the program both to find out about new activities developed by others and to share their own innovations. Electronic bulletin boards, newsletters, and reunions at teachers' conferences are used to support the network of teachers using the GSS materials.

Phase 5: Dissemination. The strategy of teacher as curriculum developer is by no means a new approach to professional development. Federally funded curriculum development projects have traditionally involved teachers both in the early brainstorm phases of materials development and in trial testing experimental activities. Teachers have contributed very important ideas to many of the science programs used in today's schools, and some sets of classroom activities have been entirely developed by teachers. The focus of these programs, however, has generally been on the products of the instructional materials that were developed rather than on the value to the teachers who helped to develop them. Recognizing that teacher-as-curriculum-developer is a strategy for professional development should make it easier to export it to new situations. This strategy is especially effective for experienced teachers who are being asked to expand their capabilities and adopt new approaches and perspectives.

Notes

1. In the first edition of this book, curriculum development was specified as a teacher learning strategy. In the third edition, curriculum work such as that described in this case is discussed in terms of curriculum and instructional materials alignment.

2. The Global Systems Science course for high school students is now online (www.lhs.berkeley.edu/gss).

Professional Development Case E

PROFESSIONAL DEVELOPMENT FOR ELEMENTARY SCHOOL SCIENCE CURRICULUM IMPLEMENTATION: THE CASE OF CAMBRIDGE, MASSACHUSETTS

Karen Worth, Senior Scientist, Education Development Center for Urban Science Education Reform, Newton, Massachusetts, and Faculty, Wheelock College

Melanie Barron, Director of Science, Cambridge Public School System, Cambridge, Massachusetts

Table 6.5   Design at a Glance: Cambridge, Massachusetts

Level and content	Elementary science
Knowledge and beliefs	*National Science Education Standards*, science for all, students learn science through inquiry, change process
Context	Past professional development efforts, teacher knowledge, levels of student learning, national and local standards, local mandates and structures
Goal	Improve science learning through curriculum implementation
Primary strategies	Curriculum implementation, workshops, institutes, study groups, professional networks, mentoring, coaching, immersion in inquiry, content courses
Critical issues	Developing leadership, building capacity for sustainability, and developing professional culture

Reflection and Update: Cambridge Since Then

The Cambridge case study ends with a number of questions, two of which are "What is the long-term picture after the Teacher Enhancement grant is over?" and "How will the progress be sustained?" What follows is a response over a decade later. Many changes have taken place at the national, state, district, program, and school levels. These have impacted the

Cambridge science program in multiple ways. At the national and state level, NCLB and the emphasis on testing literacy and mathematics have significantly eroded the support for the teaching of science at the elementary level. Testing in science has been helpful in keeping science in the public eye and a district focus. But the heavy focus of the test on information makes coverage more important than the depth that is at the core of the Cambridge inquiry-based program. At the district level, administrative turnover has also made maintaining the program difficult. Three superintendents and an interim superintendent were in place in Cambridge between 1993 and 2008.

Curricular and Structural Changes

Despite and because of the complex interaction of these external forces, there have been some positive developments in Cambridge, and many aspects of the original program have been maintained in some fashion. Perhaps the most significant positive change has been the carefully structured move from a reform program originally focused heavily on the elementary years to one that now reaches from prekindergarten through high school. Ten years ago, there was no specific junior kindergarten through second-grade (JrK–2) focus as there is now. At this youngest level, there is increased interest in and implementation of science with a new curriculum and a science mentor committed to that grade-level span. At the middle school level, science is still taught by full-time middle grade science teachers and the curriculum now consists of standards-based national NSF supported curriculum units providing a curriculum for junior kindergarten through eighth grade (JrK–8).

The high school also went through significant change as the reform effort moved up the grades. The curriculum went through major revisions resulting in physics being taught first to all incoming freshmen in heterogeneous classes by a group of physics teachers who met weekly to discuss and review this innovative course. While the high school program reverted to leveled classes in 2008, the experience, knowledge, and skills of the staff remain. In addition to focusing on the high school science program, lessons learned from the elementary and middle school experience were applied to the professional development and support at the high school. Science department coaches (part-time teacher assignments) worked with biology, physics, and chemistry teachers to provide opportunities for work groups, in-class professional development, and individual support. More recently, the science coaches have become part of a group of high school curriculum coaches from all subjects and less a part of a K–12 science department.

The elementary program, the original exemplary program of Cambridge's reform efforts, has experienced more problematic changes. While the new JrK–2 focus is very positive, the elementary program as a whole has become more fragile. The district policies on time allotted for science remain but gone is an expectation that every classroom teacher will teach the districtwide science curriculum. The curriculum is overcrowded with the demands of literacy and mathematics; the halo effect of the grant has faded, and the staff support for teachers has been reduced. The reality on the ground is that it is the decision of the principal or the teacher which, if any, of the units will be taught. This situation exists despite the fact that every teacher has the appropriate teacher's guides for the curriculum units and receives the materials needed.

In addition to this expansion of the science program in Cambridge, it is important to note that although resources and some program elements have declined, significant components of the original program are still in place. There are 3.5 coaching positions for JrK–8 (originally there were 6.5 positions for K–8); a biology, chemistry, and physics coach and a department chair at the high school; a full-time K–12 science director; and a part-time community agency liaison in the science department. These all testify to success in Cambridge in sustaining the reform effort. However, it is in the changes in the professional development program where the threats to future sustainability lie.

Professional Development

Professional development is a key element in sustaining a program of any kind in any subject area for many reasons, including (1) the thinking about teaching and learning changes with new research, (2) curriculum innovations reach the market, (3) new ideas about science and societal issues influence what is important, and (4) perhaps most important, new teachers continuously enter the system. Yet it is in professional development that there has been the most dramatic scaling back in Cambridge over the past 10 years, threatening the quality of the science program. Only time will tell the full story of the nature and seriousness of the impact on teaching and learning science in Cambridge.

Part of the reduction in professional development is the result of reduced funding. The National Science Foundation dollars that supported the original design and implementation of the Cambridge program were expended by 1997. State, district, and private funds enabled professional development to continue for a few years, but the expenses were never fully assumed by the district, especially as the funding for professional development in general was more and more devoted to the key Annual Yearly Progress subjects of mathematics and literacy. It is at best unclear whether current professional development efforts can sustain an innovative inquiry-based program in Cambridge even at its current level, much less the level at which it used to operate.

When science reform began in Cambridge in 1993, the district culture was very school based. Each school developed and implemented its own instructional and professional development program leading to enormous inconsistency in content and quality as well as serious inefficiencies in the use of resources. During the years of the reform efforts, the science program had made great progress implementing the districtwide science curriculum in Grades K–8 supported by in-depth professional development.

In 2004, the superintendent, returning to previous practice, mandated a change in the responsibilities of the principals to increase their role as instructional leaders. They were to orchestrate curriculum change and assume responsibility for school-based professional development. One consequence of this change was that teachers had less time during the school day or mandatory afterschool time to devote to professional development that was designed and offered by the district curriculum and instruction departments.

Decreased time and access to teachers has resulted in a smaller role in guiding district-based professional development for curriculum and instruction personnel. In science, this in turn has led to a reduction in the number of science staff development teachers and a change in the structure and substance of their work. Reduced in number, they have become mentors or coaches providing individual one-on-one coaching to individual classroom teachers if and only if they are invited into the classroom. In addition, the mentors have shifted from being school based, working with one or two schools, to being districtwide, with one science mentor for each grade span, JrK–2, 3–5, and 6–8. While these changes allow for each science mentor to focus his or her professional development support on the limited number of science units assigned to their grade levels, they diminish the possibility for the mentors to establish schoolwide relationships and programs.

As a result of the change in locus of control of professional development, there is less consistency in the delivery of professional development to all teachers at a grade level and fewer opportunities to provide in-depth and enrichment experiences across grade levels, both of which were hallmarks of the earlier successful efforts.

Fourteen years ago, with national funding, there were 10 to 15 different two- to three-day K–6 workshops on science units offered every summer. Teachers were paid to attend, and their expectations were high. Almost 80% of all classroom teachers took part in the summer workshops. Science staff development teachers followed through in the classrooms, and there were professional development opportunities offered during and after school.

Currently, the science department offers little more than one- or two-hour workshops to introduce the full science curriculum to all new teachers at the beginning of the school year: one unit-based workshop for teachers new to that unit and a brief overview of current science education.

An additional loss to the science professional development program has been a significant decline in partnerships that provided opportunities for teachers to participate in a variety of professional development experiences, including workshops and institutes with outside experts, national groups, and scientists. At one point, over 20 different institutions or individuals were working with the science department to support inquiry-based science instruction. These experiences, another hallmark of the original program, deepened teachers' science and science education knowledge in multiple areas and exposed them to innovative ideas from across the country. Cambridge does continue to develop and use partnerships with local universities, colleges, museums, and private scientific institutions to provide professional development opportunities for teachers but at a much lower level.

The causes of these changes in staff development certainly include a decrease in funding and the need to devote time and dollars to mathematics and literacy, but there has also been a reduction in school and central administrative support for a central role for science in the curriculum and a lack of explicit strong school committee statements and policies on science curriculum and instruction in schools.

The Cambridge story is ongoing. The reform efforts in the early 1990s as described in the case study were exciting and innovative. They provided the foundation and momentum for continued growth in some areas particularly at the high school and preschool levels. Many important elements are still in place despite all odds, including the Maynard Environmental Center, the Materials Center, and some coaches and mentors. And significantly, a culture of inquiry-based science and a curriculum that reflects that culture are still in place. Other elements, professional development in particular, have been seriously compromised. The next decade is likely to see more change. Whether the district will abandon all that was done, sustain and build on what still exists from the past, or move in new and different directions remains to be seen.

The Cambridge Case

Context

This case describes the professional development components of an effort to reform science education in a district through implementation of a districtwide core of in-depth science inquiry-based units of study. The setting is Cambridge, Massachusetts, which is a city of 72,938 people with an elementary student population of 5,725 in kindergarten (K) through sixth grade and an elementary teacher population of 300. Fifty-six percent of the children are minorities and 43% percent come from poor homes. The city has 15 kindergarten through eighth-grade schools and one large high school. The program described in this case is for elementary schools only; the district, however, is also implementing reform in Grades 7 through 9 with the goal of having a fully articulated kindergarten through ninth-grade program in place within the next several years.

In the early 1990s, the city hired a new science director who came with the charge and mission of reforming science education throughout the district. At the start, she undertook four key initiatives, which laid the foundation for the professional development plan that has been in place since the mid-1990s.

The first initiative was the redeployment of science specialists who had been teaching science classes in the elementary grades. The role of teaching science specialist was eliminated. To support the district reform effort at the classroom and school levels, five teachers were selected to become science staff development teachers. Each works in up to three schools with approximately 50 teachers and provides a wide range of support to individual teachers, groups of teachers, and school-level planning teams.

A second initiative was the development of a conceptual framework for science in the elementary years. This framework, based on the state framework, the *National Science Education Standards* (National Research Council, 1996), and the *Project 2061: Benchmarks for Science Literacy* (American Association for the Advancement of Science, 1993), was brief and to the point, providing an outline of basic concepts that students were to have studied by the second and sixth grades. This framework is providing the necessary guidance for the gradual selection of hands-on, inquiry-based science units at every grade level—the curriculum itself.

A third initiative was the decision to require all teachers at each grade level to teach four units of science per year, with three to be determined by the district and the fourth to be selected at the school or classroom level. A plan was set into place in which a wide variety of curriculum units were to be pilot tested in classrooms throughout the district. Out of this process would come a set of criteria for selecting units and information that would lead to the list of required units at each grade level. Teachers would be asked to begin with one unit and then, during a period of three to five years, incorporate all four. This process is currently ongoing.

Finally, a plan for a centralized resource center was initiated to provide teachers with the necessary materials for teaching the science units.

As these efforts were proceeding, the district science director prepared and submitted a proposal to the NSF for an intensive multiyear teacher enhancement program to support the entire elementary teaching staff in the implementation of this modular, inquiry-based science program. The following were the goals of the plan:

- To improve science learning for all elementary students in the Cambridge public schools
- To implement an inquiry-based, modular science curriculum across the district

- To build teacher leadership and expertise within the system
- To develop a structure that would permanently sustain the science program

The following assumptions were made as the program was designed:

- Districtwide reform of science education must be systemic with strong support structures at the central and school levels, real support for classroom teachers, and support and engagement from the community.
- District-mandated reform reduces the risk of teachers and administrators at the school level.
- Professional development must support different tiers of teachers, different levels of expertise among teachers, and different areas of interest among teachers.
- Implementation of materials-rich, inquiry-based curricula is often a staged process during which teachers move from awareness to mechanical use, to inquiry teaching, and to ownership and adaptation.
- Building capacity for growth and renewal within a system is critical to sustainability.

The professional development plan that was funded followed a structure that, in various guises, is quite common throughout the country where systems are attempting to put into place a centrally determined modular curriculum. It is a three-tiered approach with five science staff development teachers, two liaison teachers acting as point people at each school but with full classroom responsibilities, and the remaining staff teaching in their classrooms. The professional development program had to address the needs of these three different groups of professionals. In addition, the program had to consider the reality that teachers in the district and in each category were very diverse. For some, teaching from an inquiry perspective was unfamiliar; others were already skilled in the instructional strategies of inquiry teaching but did not apply them in science; and still others, although fewer in number, were skilled in teaching inquiry-based science.

Program Description

The following sections present a brief description of each group of teachers, the professional development program for each group, and some of the reasoning behind the design.

The Science Staff Development Teachers

It was clear from the start that the staff development teachers were critical to the success of the reform effort. The district had to develop a cadre of experts from within who could lead the implementation process. The science staff development teachers were the frontline professional support people; their skills and knowledge would be critical in helping the district, schools, and teachers implement the district plan. It was important to build an intensive professional development program with and for them from the start so that they would be supported on a continual basis.

The science staff development teachers all came from classroom teaching. All but one had been a science specialist within the district's more traditionally structured program. Each was chosen for his or her experience and interest in teaching science. All were interested in moving from working directly with children to playing a role supporting other teachers.

The professional development program for the staff development teachers needed to address several areas. It had to systematically and continuously enhance their knowledge of inquiry-based science and science teaching. It had to develop their knowledge of the curriculum materials that were under consideration and those being used in the system. It had to provide them with skills in working with others, both individually and in groups; skills in leading workshops, institutes, and presentations; and skills in taking responsibility for the design and implementation of a variety of activities within the district.

The following four professional strategies were selected:

1. *Weekly meetings.* These three-hour meetings provide the opportunity for reflection, communication, sharing, and problem solving. They are facilitated by one of the program consultants.

2. *Ten professional days.* The professional development days provide an opportunity for intensive work in science inquiry and curriculum, peer support and mentoring, and group leadership. These days are facilitated by individual experts but are structured and designed by the five science staff development teachers.

3. *Apprenticeships and mentoring.* Learning to be a staff development teacher also requires clinical experience. Working with more experienced facilitators and workshop leaders allows the staff development teachers to develop the skills they need before assuming the full responsibility for such activities themselves.

4. *Access to individual professional growth opportunities.* The local community offers many opportunities for individual professional growth, including courses, workshops, and conferences. Making the science staff development teachers aware of these and assisting with access and, at times, cost is an important component of this program.

Liaison Teachers

The reform effort in the district could not rely on the work of just five people to support the implementation in every school and every classroom; therefore, school-based liaison teachers were critical. With limited resources, it was impossible to provide release time for the liaison teachers. Therefore, the program planners felt it was critical at the start that the liaison teachers focus their time and development on their own science teaching so as to create exciting science classrooms within each building. At the same time, this plan would begin the process of developing a cadre of classroom experts within the system.

There are two liaison teachers in each building who work with the science staff development teacher to support schoolwide implementation of the reform. They are not released from their classrooms but receive stipends for their work and for their professional development time. To become a liaison teacher, teachers must submit an application. Some do so because of their particular skill and interest in science teaching, some apply because of their interest in something new and in working in a new way, and some apply because they were asked to do so by a building administrator.

The professional development program for this group needed to address the skills of good science teaching. The liaison teachers needed experiences with the concept of inquiry, the teaching of inquiry-based science, and the curriculum units that were being identified by the district. In the long run, they also needed the skills to work as a liaison within the building, supporting colleagues and supporting school-level planning.

The following four professional development strategies were selected:

1. *Four-day institute.* A four-day institute each summer, jointly led by the staff development teachers and selected external consultants, provides the opportunity for the liaison teachers to engage in inquiry, discuss and share ideas about teaching and learning science, and study the Cambridge frameworks and the modules that are under consideration for the Cambridge curriculum. These four days also bring the group together to discuss and reflect on the many demands of their role as liaison.

2. *Unit workshops.* All liaison teachers are given the opportunity to participate in two types of unit workshops: (a) afterschool meetings and (b) mentoring and coaching.

   Six afterschool meetings take place during the academic year. These maintain the networking and communication among the members of the group and provide opportunities to familiarize the liaisons with a range of resources for their buildings and particular aspects of science teaching, such as assessment and adaptation of units.

The staff development teachers provide mentoring and coaching to support the liaison teachers in their growth and development. They coach the liaisons in their classrooms, meet with them to discuss school issues, and cofacilitate activities at the school with other teachers.

3. *Apprenticeships.* Some liaisons have begun to apprentice themselves to workshop leaders, engage in leadership in other science projects in the district, and take advantage of resources made available through the district.

4. *Study groups.* During the second year, small study groups of 6 to 10 liaison teachers were formed to allow liaisons to pursue issues of particular interest and to become experts in a particular domain.

Regular Classroom Teachers

For the reform effort in the district to reach the classroom level, support was necessary for every teacher. All the classroom teachers are being asked to eventually teach four units of study per year. They are, as in any system, a diverse group of people with many different levels of expertise and experience. Some are very knowledgeable in the teaching and learning of inquiry-based science; others are less comfortable with science but teach from a child-centered, inquiry-based philosophy; and some teach from a more traditional belief system.

Because of limited resources, it is not possible to provide intensive professional development experiences for everyone. The decision was made to provide the intensive development support to the leadership cadre—to build the leadership capacity within the district—and limit the program for the rest of the teachers. The program planners, however, feel it is essential to provide teachers with a significant introduction to each of the units. Once familiar with a unit, teachers could turn to the staff development teachers, the liaisons, and one another for ongoing in-school support.

The following professional development strategies were selected:

1. *Two-day institute.* A two-day summer institute was developed for each unit selected for the district. These two-day institutes are designed to take teachers through an entire unit, exploring the materials themselves, the science content, the nature of the inquiry, and the teaching strategies required. In addition, time is spent exploring ways in which each unit might be enriched by local resources and connected to other areas of the curriculum. The institutes are led by the

science staff development teachers and external consultants and include scientists from the community for each unit.

2. *Individual school-based support.* This support is available to all teachers through the science staff development teachers who are present in each school at least one day a week. The support they provide varies in response to teacher and school needs and includes model teaching, classroom assistance, leading grade-level discussions, being members on schoolwide science action committees, and helping to access community resources. The liaison teachers are not freed from classroom responsibilities, so they have a limited role in direct classroom support. They are, however, available for such things as answering questions, providing resources, and coordinating meetings.

Neither the overall program in Cambridge nor the individual components have remained static during its years of operation. As the groups have matured, a number of interesting developments have occurred. This growth and development is a powerful sign of success. As each group changes and becomes more diversified in strengths, needs, and interests, the program leaders must reexamine the design and make new decisions to meet a new set of strengths, needs, and interests in a changing context.

Status of the Program in Its Third Year

The staff developers began to broaden their activities, engaging in grant writing and program management. One coordinated the volunteer students from two local universities, one wrote a successful grant to the National Gardening Association and is coordinating the infusion of this program into the system, and another was responsible for a program of mini-sabbaticals at the local science museum. Their work in the schools had become increasingly sophisticated. Weekly meetings and professional development days for the science staff development teachers now focused on in-depth issues of teacher change, school reform, and the role of a staff developer. They had become leaders of institutes and workshops and cofacilitators of liaison study groups. There was a trade-off in this change. As they took on new tasks and their roles changed, the staff development teachers spent less time in their schools and in classrooms providing the site-based support for reform. Care needed to be taken so that the shift away from direct classroom support did not move more quickly than the building of capacity of liaison teachers and the overall capacity of the teaching staff.

The liaison teachers had become more comfortable in the classroom and in their roles, and many had begun to develop interests in different areas as well as interest in becoming more involved with the design of their own professional development activities. A uniform professional development plan for them was no longer possible. The study groups described previously reflected one adaptation to their request. In addition, opportunities such as the museum fellowships, courses at local institutions, and intensive institutes provided additional possibilities. Full-group meetings still occurred, although less frequently, to maintain the sense of community deemed critical by the liaisons themselves.

The kindergarten through sixth-grade teachers had been introduced to many of the kits. The individualized and small group support they received at the school was, of course, constantly changing to meet their needs as the science staff development teachers became increasingly skilled in their roles. Some teachers were considering the adaptation and enrichment of the kits; others were looking forward to a second institute with the materials to increase their understanding of a particular unit. A number were becoming involved in new initiatives within the district and growing professionally through these. This development was powerful and a sign of success, but it required that program designers reexamine decisions and realign the components to meet a new set of needs and groups within groups.

Many questions confronted the Cambridge team as it moved forward. Much had been accomplished. There was now a foundation that included a framework and a curriculum, a materials center, a growing cadre of teacher leaders, a powerful relationship with the Massachusetts Institute of Technology, and a partnership with several key consultants at the EDC. Every Cambridge school and teacher at the elementary level had been influenced by the work in science. To no one's surprise, however, true inquiry-based science teaching and learning in every classroom was not yet a reality.

As the Cambridge team members moved into their fourth year, they continued to reexamine the progress made, what needed to be done to continue progressing and growing, and how to do so with the resources available. The questions they grappled with included, "Is the decision to focus on leadership development still a good one?" "What is needed now for the liaison teachers in their work at the school level?" "Should the balance of efforts be shifted to the classroom teachers?" "What is the nature of professional development for classroom teachers once the kits are in use?" "Should building administrators be the target of some of the professional development efforts?" "Are the efforts at the seventh- through ninth-grade level moving forward so as to support the students as they emerge from the elementary years?" "What is the long-term picture after the Teacher Enhancement grant is over?" "How will the progress be sustained?" "Who will pay for the efforts needed to sustain the work?" "What will those efforts look like?"

References

Acheson, K., & Gall, M. (1987). *Techniques in the clinical supervision of teachers.* New York: Longman.

Acquarelli, K., & Mumme, J. (1996). A renaissance in mathematics education reform. *Phi Delta Kappan, 77*(7), 478–484.

American Association for the Advancement of Science. (1989). *Science for all Americans.* New York: Oxford University Press.

American Association for the Advancement of Science. (1993). *Benchmarks for science literacy.* New York: Oxford University Press.

American Association for the Advancement of Science. (2001). *Atlas of science literacy* (Vol.1). Washington, DC: Author.

American Association for the Advancement of Science. (2007). *Atlas of science literacy* (Vol. 2). Washington, DC: Author.

Anderson, J. R. (1995). *Learning and memory.* New York: Wiley.

Anderson, R. D., & Pratt, H. (1995). *Local leadership for science education reform.* Dubuque, IA: Kendall/Hunt.

Andrew, D., & Lewis, M. (2002). The experience of a professional community: Teachers developing a new image of themselves and their workplace. *Educational Researcher, 44*(3), 237–254.

Appleton, K. (2003, July). *Pathways in professional development in primary science: Extending science PCK.* Paper presented at the annual conference of the Australian Science Education Research Association, Melbourne, Australia.

Asbell-Clarke, J., & Rowe, E. (2007). *Learning science online: A descriptive study of online science courses for teachers: Executive summary.* Cambridge, MA: TERC.

Ball, D. L. (1996). Teacher learning and the mathematics reforms: What we think we know and what we need to learn. *Phi Delta Kappan, 77*(7), 500–508.

Ball, D. L., & Cohen, D. K. (1996). Reform by the book: What is—or might be—the role of curriculum materials in teacher learning and instructional reform? *Educational Researcher, 25*(9), 6–8, 14.

Ball, D. L., & Cohen, D. K. (1999). Developing practice, developing practitioners: Toward a practice-based theory of professional education. In L. Darling-Hammond & G. Sykes (Eds.), *Teaching as the learning profession: Handbook of policy and practice* (pp. 3–32). San Francisco: Jossey-Bass.

Ball, D. L., & Cohen, D. K. (2000). *Challenges of improving instruction: A view from the classroom.* Retrieved from www-personal.umich.edu/~dkcohen/ws1999ball.pdf

Banilower, E., Boyd, S., Pasley, J., & Weiss, I. (2006). *Lessons from a decade of mathematics and science reform: A capstone report for the local systemic change through teacher enhancement initiative.* Chapel Hill, NC: Horizon Research, Inc.

Banks, J., Cochran-Smith, M., Moll, L., Richert, A., Zeichner, K., LePage, P., et al. (2005). Teaching diverse learners. In L. Darling-Hammond & J. Bransford (Eds.), *Preparing teachers for a changing world: What teachers should learn and be able to do* (pp. 232–274). San Francisco: Jossey-Bass.

Barnett, C. (1991). Building a case-based curriculum to enhance the pedagogical content knowledge of mathematics teachers. *Journal of Teacher Education, 42*(4), 263–272.

Barnett, C., & Friedman, S. (1997). Mathematics case discussions: Nothing is sacred. In E. Fennema & B. Scott-Nelson (Eds.), *Mathematics teachers in transition* (pp. 381–399). Hillsdale, NJ: Lawrence Erlbaum.

Barnett, C., & Sather, S. (1992, April). *Using case discussions to promote changes in beliefs among mathematics teachers.* Paper presented at the annual meeting of the American Education Research Association, San Francisco.

Barnett, C., & Tyson, P. (1993, April). *Mathematics teaching cases as a catalyst for informed strategic inquiry.* Paper presented at the annual meeting of the American Educational Research Association, Atlanta, GA.

Barnett-Clarke, C., & Ramirez, A. (2008). Case discussions. In L. Brown Easton (Ed.), *Powerful designs for professional learning* (2nd ed., pp. 85–94). Oxford, OH: National Staff Development Council.

Barnett-Clarke, C., & Ramirez, A. (2009, April). *Rethinking the design of discussion-based mathematics lessons to strengthen and broaden participation.* Paper presented at the annual meeting of the American Educational Research Association, San Diego, CA.

Barth, R. S. (2001). *Learning by heart.* San Francisco: Jossey-Bass.

Bennett, B., & Green, N. (1995). Effect of the learning consortium: One district's journey. *School Effectiveness and School Improvement, 6*(3), 247–264.

Berry, B., Johnson, D., & Montgomery, D. (2005, February). The power of teacher leadership. *Educational Leadership, 62*(5), 56–60.

Betts, J. R., Rueben, K. S., & Danenberg, A. (2000). *Equal resources, equal outcomes? The distribution of school resources and student achievement in California.* San Francisco: Public Policy Institute of California.

Black, P., Harrison, C., Lee, C., Marshall, B., & Wiliam, D. (2003). *Assessment for learning: Putting it into practice.* Berkshire, England: Open University Press.

Blanchett, W., Mumford, V., & Beachum, F. (2005). Urban school failure and disproportionality in a post-Brown era. *Remedial & Special Education, 26*(2), 70–81.

Blank, R. K., de las Alas, N., & Smith, C. (2008). *Does teacher professional development have effects on teaching and learning? Analysis of evaluation findings from programs for mathematics and science teachers in 14 states.* Washington, DC: Council of Chief State School Officers.

Bolam, R., McMahon, A., Stoll, L., Thomas, S., & Wallace, M. (2005). Creating and sustaining professional learning communities. *Research Brief* (Research Brief No. RB637). London: Department for Education and Skills, General Teaching Council for England.

Borko, H. (2004). Professional development and teacher learning: Mapping the terrain. *Educational Researcher, 33*(3), 3–15.

Bransford, J., Darling-Hammond, L., & LePage, P. (2005). In L. Darling-Hammond & J. Bransford (Eds.), *Preparing teachers for a changing world: What teachers should learn and be able to do* (pp. 1–39). San Francisco: Jossey-Bass.

Bransford, J. D., Brown, A. L., & Cocking, R. R. (Eds.). (1999). *How people learn: Brain, mind, experience, and school.* Washington, DC: The National Academies Press.

Brickhouse, N. (1990). Teachers' beliefs about the nature of science and their relationship to classroom practices. *Journal of Teacher Education, 41*(3), 53–62.

Britton, E., Paine, L., Pimm, D., & Raizen, S. (2003). *Comprehensive teacher induction: Systems for early career learning.* Dordrecht, Netherlands: Kluwer Academic & San Francisco: WestEd.

Britton, E., Raizen, S., Kaser, J., & Porter, A. (2000). *Beyond description of the problems.* Madison, WI: National Institute for Science Education.

Bruner, J. (1966). *Toward a theory of instruction.* Cambridge, MA: Harvard University Press.

Bybee, R. W. (1993). *Reforming science education: Social perspectives and personal reflections.* New York: Teachers College Press.

Bybee, R. W. (1997). *Achieving scientific literacy: From purposes to practices.* Portsmouth, NH: Heinemann.

Bybee, R. W. (2006). Leadership in science education for the 21st Century. In Jack Rhoton and Patricia Shane (Eds.), *Teaching science in the 21st century* (pp. 147–162). Arlington, VA: National Science Teachers Association Press & Prescott, AZ: National Science Education Leadership Association.

Caccia, P. F. (1996, March). Linguistic coaching: Helping beginning teachers defeat discouragement. *Educational Leadership, 53*(6), 17–20.

Campbell, P. (1995). *Project IMPACT: Increasing mathematics power for all children and teachers* (Phase 1, Final Report). College Park: University of Maryland, Center for Mathematics Education.

CampbellJones, B., CampbellJones, F., & Love, N. (2009). Bringing cultural proficiency to collaborative inquiry (pp. 80–95). In N. Love (Ed.), *Using data to improve learning for all: A collaborative inquiry approach.* Thousand Oaks, CA: Corwin.

Carlson, M. O., Humphrey, G., & Reinhardt, K. (2003). *Weaving science inquiry and continuous assessment.* Thousand Oaks, CA: Corwin.

Carnegie Corporation of New York. (2009). *The opportunity equation: Transforming mathematics and science education for citizenship and the global economy.* New York: Author.

Caro-Bruce, C. (2008). Action research. In L. Brown Easton (Ed.), *Powerful designs for professional learning* (2nd ed., pp. 63–70). Oxford, OH: National Staff Development Council.

Carr, J., Carroll, C., Cremer, S., Gale, M., Sexton, U., & Laganof, R. (2009). *Making mathematics accessible to English learners: A guidebook for teachers.* San Francisco: WestEd.

Carr, J., Sexton, U., & Laganof, R. (2007). *Making science accessible to English learners: A guidebook for teachers.* San Francisco: WestEd.

Carroll, C., & Mumme, J. (2007). *Learning to lead mathematics professional development.* Thousand Oaks, CA: Corwin & San Francisco: WestEd.

Chi, M. T. H. (2005). Commonsense misconceptions of emergent processes: Why some misconceptions are robust. *Journal of the Learning Sciences, 14,* 161–200.

Chi, M. T. H., Bassok, M., Lewis, M. W., Reimann, P., & Glaser, R. (1989). Self-explanations: How students study and use examples in learning to solve problems. *Cognitive Science, 13,* 145–182.

Chi, M. T. H., DeLeeuw, N., Chiu, M., & LaVancher, C. (1994). Eliciting self-explanations improves understanding. *Cognitive Science, 18,* 439–477.

Chi, M. T. H., Feltovich, P., & Glaser, R. (1981). Categorization and representation of physics problems by experts and novices. *Cognitive Science, 5,* 121–152.

Clermont, C., Krajcik, J., & Borko, H. (1993). The influence of an intensive in-service workshop on pedagogical content knowledge growth among novice chemical demonstrators. *Journal of Research in Science Teaching, 30*(1), 21–43.

Cobb, P. (1994). Where is the mind? Constructivist and sociocultural perspectives on mathematical development. *Educational Researcher, 23*(7), 13–20.

Coble, C. R., & Koballa, T. R., Jr. (1996). Science education. In J. Sikula, T. J. Buttery, & E. Guyton (Eds.), *Handbook of research in teacher education* (2nd ed., pp. 459–484). New York: Simon & Schuster/Macmillan.

Cochran, K. F., DeRuiter, J. A., & King, R. A. (1993). Pedagogical content knowing: An integrative model for teacher preparation. *Journal of Teacher Education, 44*(4), 263–272.

Cohen, D., Raudenbush, S., & Ball, D. (2003). Resources, instruction, and research. *Educational Evaluation and Policy Analysis, 25*(2), 119–142.

Cohen, D. K., & Ball, D. L. (1999). *Instruction, capacity, and improvement* (CPRE No. RR-43). Philadelphia: University of Pennsylvania, Consortium for Policy Research in Education.

Cohen, D. K., & Ball, D. L. (2006). Educational innovation and the problem of scale. In B. K. Schneider & S. K. McDonald (Eds.), *Scale-up in education: Ideas in principle* (Vol. 1, pp. 19–36). Lanham, MD: Rowman & Littlefield.

Cohen, D. K., & Hill, H. C. (1998). *State policy and classroom performance: Mathematics reform in California* (CPRE No. RB-23-May). Philadelphia: University of Pennsylvania, Consortium for Policy Research in Education.

Cohen, D. K., & Hill, H. C. (2001). *Learning policy: When state education reform works.* New Haven, CT: Yale University Press.

Corcoran, T. B. (2007). *Teaching matters: How state and local policymakers can improve the quality of teachers and teaching* (CPRE No. RB-48). Philadelphia: University of Pennsylvania, Consortium for Policy Research in Education.

Costa, A. L., & Garmston, R. J. (2002). *Cognitive coaching: A foundation for Renaissance schools* (2nd ed.). Norwood, MA: Christopher-Gordon.

Costa, A. L., & Kallick, B. (1993, October). Through the lens of a critical friend. *Educational Leadership, 51*(2), 49–51.

Council of Chief State School Officers. (2009, June 1). *Forty-nine states and territories join common core state standards initiative* [Press release]. Retrieved from www.ccsso.org/whats_new/press_releases/13359.cfm

Crowther, F., Kagan, S. S., Ferguson, M., & Hann, L. (2002). *Developing teacher leaders: How teacher leadership enhances school success.* Thousand Oaks, CA: Corwin.

Darling-Hammond, L. (1997). *Doing what matters most: Investing in quality teaching.* New York: National Commission on Teaching and America's Future.

Darling-Hammond, L. (2000). Teacher quality and student achievement: A review of state policy and evidence. *Education Policy Archives, 8*(1). Available from http://epaa.asu.edu

Darling-Hammond, L. (2004). What happens to a dream deferred? The continuing quest for equal educational opportunity. In J. A. Banks & C. A. M. Banks (Eds.), *Handbook of research on multicultural education* (2nd ed., pp. 607–630). San Francisco: Jossey-Bass.

Darling-Hammond, L., & McLaughlin, M. W. (1999). Investing in teaching as a learning profession: Policy, problems and prospects. In L. Darling-Hammond & G. Sykes (Eds.), *Teaching as the learning profession: Handbook of policy and practice* (pp. 376–412). San Francisco: Jossey-Bass.

Davenport, L. R., & Sassi, A. (1995). Transforming mathematics teaching in grades K–8: How narrative structures in resource materials help support teacher change. In B. S. Nelson (Ed.), *Inquiry and the development of teaching: Issues in the transformation of mathematics teaching* (pp. 37–46). Newton, MA: Education Development Center, Center for the Development of Teaching.

Davis, E. A., & Krajcik, J. S. (2005). Designing educative curriculum materials to promote teacher learning. *Educational Researcher, 34*(3), 3–14.

Dede, C., Breit, L., Ketelhut, D. J., McCloskey, E., & Whitehouse, P. (2005). *An overview of current findings from empirical research on online teacher professional development.* Cambridge, MA: Harvard Graduate School of Education.

Denmark, V. M., & Podsen, I. J. (2000). The mettle of a mentor. *Journal of Staff Development, 21*(4), 18–22.

DePree, M. (1989). *Leadership is an art.* New York: Dell.

DiRanna, K., Osmundson, E., Topps, J., Barakos, L., Gearhart, M., Cerwin, K., et al. (2008). *Assessment-centered teaching: A reflective practice.* Thousand Oaks, CA: Corwin.

Donovan, M. S., & Bransford, J. D. (Eds.). (2005). *How students learn: History, mathematics, and science in the classroom.* Washington, DC: The National Academies Press.

Drago-Severson, E. (2004). *Helping teachers learn: Principal leadership for adult growth and development.* Thousand Oaks, CA: Corwin.

Driscoll, M. (2001). *Fostering algebraic thinking toolkit.* Portsmouth, NH: Heinemann.

Driscoll, M., & Bryant, D. (1998). *Learning about assessment, learning through assessment.* Washington, DC: National Research Council.

Driver, R., Asoko, H., Leach, J., Mortimer, E., & Scott, P. (1994). Constructing scientific knowledge in the classroom. *Educational Researcher, 23*(7), 5–12.

Driver, R., Squires, A., Rushworth, P., & Wood-Robinson, V. (1994). *Making sense of secondary science: Research into children's ideas.* London: Routledge-Falmer.

Duckworth, E. (1986). Teaching as research. *Harvard Educational Review, 56*(4), 481–495.

DuFour, R. (1999). Taking on loneliness. *Journal of Staff Development. 20*(1), 61–62.

DuFour, R. (2001). In the right context. *Journal of Staff Development, 22*(1), 14–17.

DuFour, R. (2004, May). What is a professional learning community? *Educational Leadership, 61*(8), 6–11.

DuFour, R., DuFour, R., Eaker, R., & Karhanek, G. (2004). *Whatever it takes: How professional learning communities respond when kids don't learn.* Bloomington, IN: National Educational Services.

DuFour, R., & Eaker, R. (1998). *Professional learning communities at work.* Bloomington, IN: National Educational Service.

Dunne, K., & Villani, S. (2007). *Mentoring new teachers through collaborative coaching: Linking teacher and student learning.* San Francisco: WestEd.

Duschl, R. A. (1990). *Restructuring science education: The importance of theories and their development.* New York: Teachers College Press.

Duschl, R. A., & Osborne, J. (2002). Supporting and promoting argumentation discourse in science education. *Studies in Science Education, 38,* 39–72.

Duschl, R. A., Schweingruber, H., & Schouse, A. (Eds.). (2007). *Taking science to school: Learning and teaching science in grades K–8.* Washington, DC: National Academies Press.

Dyasi, H. M. (1990). Assessing imperfect conceptions. In K. Jervis & C. Montag (Eds.), *Progressive education for the 1990's: Transforming practice* (pp. 101–110). New York: Teachers College Press.

Dyasi, H. M. (1995). *The City College Workshop Center program for reculturing teachers to teach inquiry-based science in the elementary school.* Unpublished manuscript.

Eaker, R., & Keating, J. (2008). A shift in school culture: Collective commitments focus on change that benefits student learning. *Journal of Staff Development, 29*(3), 14–17.

Educational Research Service. (1999). Professional development for school principals. *The Informed Educator Series* (WS-0350*).* Alexandria, VA: Author.

Eisenhower National Clearinghouse. (1998). *Ideas that work: Mathematics professional development.* Columbus, OH: Author.

Elmore, R. F. (1996). Getting to scale with good educational practice. *Harvard Educational Review, 66*(1), 1–26.

Elmore, R. F. (2002). *Bridging the gap between standards and achievement: The imperative for professional development in education.* Washington, DC: Albert Shanker Institute.

Elmore, R. F., & Burney, D. (1999). Investing in teacher learning: Staff development and instructional improvement. In L. Darling-Hammond & G. Sykes (Eds.), *Teaching as the learning profession: Handbook of policy and practice* (pp. 263–291). San Francisco: Jossey-Bass.

English, F. W. (2000). *Deciding what to teach and test: Developing, aligning, and auditing the curriculum.* Thousand Oaks, CA: Corwin.

Epstein, J. L., Sanders, M. G., Sheldon, S. B., Simon, B. S., Salinas, K. C., Jansorn, N. R., et al. (2009). *School, family, and community partnerships: Your handbook for action* (3rd ed.). Thousand Oaks, CA: Corwin.

Evans, R. (1996). *The human side of school change: Reform, resistance, and the real-life problems of innovation.* San Francisco: Jossey-Bass.

Fernández-Balboa, J. M., & Stiehl, J. (1995). The generic nature of pedagogical content knowledge among college professors. *Teaching and Teacher Education, 11,* 293–306.

Ferrini-Mundy, J. (1997). Reform efforts in mathematics education: Reckoning with the realities. In S. N. Friel & G. W. Bright (Eds.), *Reflecting on our work: NSF teacher enhancement in K–6 mathematics* (pp. 113–132). Lanham, MD: University Press of America.

Fichtman Dana, N., & Yendol-Hoppey, D. (2003). *The reflective educator's guide to classroom research: Learning to teach and teaching to learn through practitioner inquiry.* Thousand Oaks, CA: Corwin.

Filby, N. N. (1995). *Analysis of reflective professional development models.* San Francisco: WestEd.

Fishman, B., Marx, R. W., Best, S., & Tal, R. T. (2003). Linking teacher and student learning to improve professional development in systemic reform. *Teaching and Teacher Education, 19,* 643–658.

Ford, D., Grantham, T., & Whiting, G. (2008). Culturally and linguistically diverse students in gifted education: Recruitment and retention issues. *Exceptional Children, 74*(3), 289–306.

Frances, D., Rivera, M., Lesaux, N., Kieffer, M., & Rivera, H. (2006). *Practical guidelines for the education of English language learners: Research-based recommendations for instruction and academic interventions.* Retrieved from www.centeroninstruction.org/files/ELL1-Interventions.pdf

Fredericks, J., Blumenfeld, P., & Paris, A. (2004). School engagement: Potential of the concept, state of the evidence. *Review of Educational Research, 74*(1), 59–109.

Friel, S. N. (1996, January). *Teach-Stat: A model for professional development in data analysis and statistics for teachers K–6.* Paper presented at the Professional Development Project of the National Institute for Science Education, Madison, WI.

Friel, S. N., & Bright, G. W. (Eds.). (1997). *Reflecting on our work: NSF teacher enhancement in K–6 mathematics.* Lanham, MD: University Press of America.

Friel, S. N., & Danielson, M. L. (1997). Teach-Stat: A key to better mathematics. In S. N. Friel & G. W. Bright (Eds.), *Reflecting on our work: NSF teacher enhancement in K–6 mathematics* (pp. 197–206). Lanham, MD: University Press of America.

Friel, S. N., & Joyner, J. (1991). *Teach-Stat: A key to better mathematics.* Arlington, VA: National Science Foundation.

Friel, S. N., & Joyner, J. (Eds.). (1997). *Teach-Stat for teachers: Professional development manual.* Palo Alto, CA: Seymour.

Frost, D. L. (1995). *Elementary teachers' conceptions of mathematics staff development and their roles as workshop leaders.* Unpublished doctoral dissertation, University of North Carolina, Greensboro.

Fullan, M. (1991). *The new meaning of educational change* (3rd ed.). New York: Teachers College Press.

Fullan, M. (1993). *Change forces: Probing the depths of educational reform.* London: Falmer Press.

Fullan, M. (2000, April). The three stories of education reform. *Phi Delta Kappan, 81*(8), 581–584.

Fullan, M. (2001). *Leading in a culture of change.* San Francisco: Jossey-Bass.

Fullan, M. (2002, May). The change leader. *Educational Leadership, 59*(8), 16–20.

Fullan, M. (2005). *Leadership and sustainability: System thinkers in action.* Thousand Oaks, CA: Corwin.

Fullan, M. (2007). *The new meaning of educational change* (4th ed.). New York: Teachers College Press.

Fullan, M., & Hargreaves, A. (1991). *What's worth fighting for? Working together for your school.* Andover, MA: Regional Laboratory for Educational Improvement of the Northeast and Islands.

Fullan, M., & Miles, M. (1992). Getting reform right: What works and what doesn't. *Phi Delta Kappan, 73*(10), 745–752.

Garet, M. S., Birman, B. F., Porter, A. C., Desimone, L., Herman, R., & Yoon, K. S. (1999). *Designing effective professional development: Lessons from the Eisenhower program.* Washington, DC: U.S. Department of Education.

Garet, M. S., Porter, A. C., Desimone, L., Birman, B. F., & Yoon, K. S. (2001). What makes professional development effective? Results from a national sample of teachers. *American Educational Research Journal, 38*(4), 915–945.

Garmston, R. J. (1987, February). How administrators support peer coaching. *Educational Leadership, 44*(5), 18–26.

Garmston, R. J., & Wellman, B. M. (2009). *The adaptive school: A sourcebook for developing collaborative groups* (2nd ed.). Norwood, MA: Christopher-Gordon.

Gee, J. P. (1990). *Social linguistics and literacies: Ideology in discourses.* New York: Falmer Press.

Gersten, R., Baker, S., Shanahan, T., Linan-Thompson, S., Collins, P., & Scarcella, R. (2007). *Effective literacy and English language instruction for English learners in the elementary grades: IES practice guide* (Report No. NCEE 2007-4011). Washington, DC: U.S. Department of Education.

Glanz, J. (2003). *Action research: An educational leader's guide to school improvement.* Norwood, MA: Christopher-Gordon.

Glazerman, S., Dolfin, S., Bleeker, M., Johnson, A., Isenber, E., Lugo-Gil, J., et al. (2008). *Impacts of comprehensive teacher induction: Results from the first year of a randomized controlled study* (Report No. NCEE 2009-4034). Washington, DC: U.S. Department of Education.

Gleason, J., Vesilind, E., Friel, S. N., & Joyner, J. (Eds.). (1996). *Teach-Stat for statistics educators: Staff developer's manual.* Palo Alto, CA: Seymour.

Glennan, T. K., Bodilly, S. J., Galegher, J. R., & Kerr, K. A. (2004). *Expanding the reach of education reforms: Perspectives from leaders in the scale-up of educational interventions.* Santa Monica, CA: RAND.

Goe, L. (2007). Linking teacher quality and student outcomes. In C. Dwyer (Ed.), *America's challenge: Effective teachers for at-risk schools and students* (pp. 7–23). Washington, DC: National Comprehensive Center for Teacher Quality.

Goldenberg, L. B., & Outsen, N. (2002). Missed connections can be instructive: Project to link teachers turns setbacks into information. *Journal of Staff Development, 23*(1), 28–31.

Goldhaber, D. D., & Brewer, D. J. (2000, Summer). Does teacher certification matter? High school teacher certification status and student achievement. *Educational Evaluation and Policy Analysis, 22*(2), 129–146.

Goldstone, R. L., & Son, J. Y. (2005). The transfer of scientific principles using concrete and idealized simulations. *Journal of the Learning Sciences, 14*(1), 69–110.

Grady, A. (1997). Elementary and middle school math and technology project. In S. N. Friel & G. W. Bright (Eds.), *Reflecting on our work: NSF teacher enhancement in K–6 mathematics* (pp. 207–214). Lanham, MD: University Press of America.

Graham, A. (1987). *Statistical investigations in the secondary school.* Cambridge, UK: Cambridge University Press.

Grant, C. M., Nelson, B. S., Davidson, E., Sassi, A., Weinberg, A. S., & Bleiman, J. (2002). *Lenses on learning: A new focus on mathematics and leadership.* Parsippany, NJ: Seymour.

Grossman, P. (1990*). The making of a teacher: Teacher knowledge and teacher education.* New York: Teachers College Press.

Guskey, T. R. (1999). Apply time with wisdom. *Journal of Staff Development, 20*(2), 10–15.

Guskey, T. R. (2000). *Evaluating professional development.* Thousand Oaks, CA: Corwin.

Hall, G. E., & Hord, S. M. (2001). *Implementing change: Patterns, principles, and potholes.* Boston: Allyn & Bacon.

Hall, G. E., & Hord, S. M. (2006). *Implementing change: Patterns, principles, and potholes* (2nd ed.). Boston: Allyn & Bacon.

Hawley, W. D., & Valli, L. (2000, August). Learner-centered professional development. *Phi Delta Kappa International Research Bulletin, 27,* 1–7.

Haycock, K., & Robinson, S. (2001). Time-wasting workshops? *Journal of Staff Development, 22*(2), 16–18.

Hazen, R. M., & Trefil, J. (1991). *Science matters: Achieving scientific literacy.* New York: Anchor Books.

Heenan, B. (March 2009). *Reflections on the success of NWP teacher leadership: A dynamic cycle of teaching, learning and leading.* Inverness, CA: Inverness Research.

Heller, J. I., Kaskowitz, D., Daehler, K. R., & Shinohara, M. (2001). *Annual technical report to the Stuart Foundation.* San Francisco: WestEd.

Henderson, A., & Mapp, K. (2002). *A new wave of evidence: The impact of school, family, and community connections on student achievement.* Austin, TX: Southwest Educational Development Laboratory.

Hewson, P. W., & Thorley, N. R. (1989). The conditions of conceptual change in the classroom. *International Journal of Science Education, 11*(5), 541–553.

Hirsh, S., & Killion, J. (2007). *The learning educator: A new era for professional learning.* Oxford, OH: National Staff Development Council.

Hmelo-Silver, C. E., Marathe, S., & Liu, L. (2007). Fish swim, rocks sit, and lungs breathe: Expert-novice understanding of complex systems. *Journal of the Learning Sciences, 16*(3), 307–331.

Hord, S. M. (2008). Evolution of the professional learning community: Revolutionary concept is based on intentional collegial learning. *Journal of Staff Development, 29*(3), 10–13.

Hord, S. M., & Boyd, V. (1995). Professional development fuels a culture of continuous improvement. *Journal of Staff Development, 16*(1), 10–15.

Hord, S. M., & Sommers, W. A. (2008). *Leading professional learning communities: Voices from research and practice.* Thousand Oaks, CA: Corwin Press; Reston, VA: National Association of Secondary School Principals; & Oxford, OH: National Staff Development Council.

Horizon Research, Inc. (2001). *Local systemic change through teacher enhancement: 2001 teacher questionnaire: Mathematics (6–12).* Chapel Hill, NC: Author.

Houston, P. D., Blankstein, A. M., & Cole, R. W. (Eds.). (2007). *Out-of-the-box leadership.* Thousand Oaks, CA: Corwin.

Huberman, A. M. (1995). Networks that alter teaching: Conceptualizations, exchanges and experiments. *Teachers and Teaching: Theory and Practice, 1*(2), 193–211.

Hutchins, D. J., Sheldon, S. B., & Epstein, J. L. (2009). *National Network of Partnership Schools, Johns Hopkins University: Special report: 2008 School update data.* Baltimore: Johns Hopkins University, National Network of Partnership Schools.

Ingersoll, R., & Kralik, J. (2004). *The impact of mentoring on teacher retention: What the research says.* Denver, CO: Education Commission of the States.

Institute for Educational Leadership. (2000). *Leadership for student learning: Reinventing the principalship: A report of the task force on the principalship.* Washington, DC: Author.

International Society for Technology in Education. (2008). *The ISTE national educational technology for standards (NETS-T) and performance indicators for teachers.* Eugene, OR: Author.

Johnson, S. M., & The Project on the Next Generation of Teachers. (2007). *Finders and keepers: Helping new teachers survive and thrive in our schools.* San Francisco: Jossey-Bass.

Joyce, B., & Showers, B. (1988). *Student achievement through staff development.* New York: Longman.

Joyner, J., Pfieffer, S., Friel, S. N., & Vesilind, E. (Eds.). (1997a). *Teach-Stat activities: Statistics investigations for grades 1–3.* Palo Alto, CA: Seymour.

Joyner, J., Pfieffer, S., Friel, S. N., & Vesilind, E. (Eds.). (1997b). *Teach-Stat activities: Statistics investigations for grades 3–6.* Palo Alto, CA: Seymour.

Kadlek, A., Friedman, W., & Ott, A. (2007). *Important, but not for me: Parents and students in Kansas and Missouri talk about math, science, and technology education.* New York: Public Agenda.

Kaminski, J., Sloutsky, V. M., & Heckler, A. F. (2006). Effects of concreteness on representation: An explanation for differential transfer. In R. Sun & N. Miyake (Eds.), *Proceedings of the XXVIII annual conference of the Cognitive Science Society* (pp. 1581–1586). Mahwah, NJ: Lawrence Erlbaum.

Kaser, J., Mundry, S., Stiles, K. E., & Loucks-Horsley, S. (2002). *Leading every day: 124 actions for effective leadership.* Thousand Oaks, CA: Corwin.

Kaser, J., Mundry, S., Stiles, K. E., & Loucks-Horsley, S. (2006). *Leading every day: 124 actions for effective leadership* (2nd ed.). Thousand Oaks, CA: Corwin.

Katzenmeyer, M., & Moller, G. (1996). *Awakening the sleeping giant: Leadership development for teachers.* Thousand Oaks, CA: Corwin.

Keeley, P. (2005). *Science curriculum topic study: Bridging the gap between standards and practice.* Thousand Oaks, CA: Corwin.

Keeley, P. (2008). Introduction. In J. Tugel (Ed.). (2008). *Notes from the field: Teaching for conceptual change: Uncovering student thinking in science through action research* (pp. i–iv). Augusta, ME: Maine Mathematics and Science Alliance.

Keeley, P., Eberle, F., & Farrin, L. (2005). *Uncovering science ideas in science: 25 formative assessment probes.* Arlington, VA: National Science Teachers Association Press.

Keeley, P., Eberle, F., & Tugel, J. (2007). *Uncovering student ideas in science: 25 more formative assessment probes* (Vol. 2). Arlington, VA: National Science Teachers Association Press.

Keeley, P., & Rose, C. (2006). *Mathematics curriculum topic study: Bridging the gap between standards and practice.* Thousand Oaks, CA: Corwin.

Kegan, R., & Lahey, L. (2009). *Immunity to change: How to overcome it and unlock the potential in yourself and your organization.* Boston: Harvard Business School.

Killion, J., & Harrison, C. (2006). *Taking the lead: New roles for teachers and school-based coaches.* Oxford, OH: National Staff Development Council.

Klahr, D., & Nigam, M. (2004). The equivalence of learning paths in early science instruction: Effects of direct instruction and discovery learning. *Psychological Science, 15,* 661–667.

Klein, S. P., McArthur, D. J., & Stecher, B. M. (1995, February). What are the challenges to "scaling up" reform? In *Joining Forces: Spreading Successful Strategies, Proceedings of the Invitational Conference on Systemic Reform* (pp. 71–80). Washington, DC: Department of Education. (ERIC Document Reproduction Service No. ED381135)

Knowles, M., Holton, E. F., & Swanson, R. A. (2000). *The adult learner: The definitive classic in adult education and human resource development.* Houston, TX: Gulf.

Koba, S. B., Clarke, W. M., & Mitchell, C. T. (2000). Action research: Collaborative efforts in teacher change. In D. L. Jordan, M. A. Henry, & J. T. Sutton (Eds.), *Changing Omaha classrooms: Collaborative action research efforts* (pp. 90–102). Aurora, CO: Mid-continent Research for Education and Learning.

Kotter, J. (1996). *Leading change.* Boston: Harvard Business School.

Kouzes, J. M., & Posner, B. Z. (2001). *Leadership practices inventory: Participant's workbook* (Rev. 2nd ed.). San Francisco: Jossey-Bass.

Kruse, S. D., & Louis, K. S. (2009). *Building strong school cultures: A guide to leading change.* Thousand Oaks: CA: Corwin.

LaBonte, K., Leighty, C., Mills, S. J., & True, M. L. (1995). Whole-faculty study groups: Building the capacity for change through interagency collaboration. *Journal of Staff Development, 16*(3), 45–47.

Lave, J., & Wenger, E. (1991). *Situated learning: Legitimate peripheral participation.* Cambridge, UK: Cambridge University Press.

Learning Mathematics for Teaching. (2009). *Mathematical knowledge for teaching (MKT) measures.* Ann Arbor: University of Michigan.

Lee, O., & Fradd, L. (1998). Science for all, including students from non-English-language backgrounds. *Educational Researcher, 27*(4), 12–21.

Lee, V. E., Smith, J. B., & Croninger, R. G. (1995). *Another look at high school restructuring: Issues in restructuring schools.* Madison: University of Wisconsin, Center on Organization and Restructuring of Schools.

Leithwood, K., Louis, K. S., Anderson, S., & Wahlstrom, K. (2004). *How leadership influences student learning: Review of research.* Minneapolis: University of Minnesota, Center for Applied Research and Educational Improvement.

Lemberger, J., Hewson, P., & Park, H. (1999). Relationship between prospective secondary teachers' classroom practice and their conceptions of biology and of teaching science. *Science Education, 83*(3), 347–371.

Lemke, J. (1990). *Talking science: Language, learning, and values.* Norwood, NJ: Ablex.

Lewis, C. C. (2002a). Does lesson study have a future in the United States? *Nagoya Journal of Education and Human Development, 1,* 1–23.

Lewis, C. C. (2002b). Everywhere I looked—Levers and pendulums: Research lessons bring studies to life and energize teaching. *Journal of Staff Development, 23*(3), 59–65.

Lewis, C. C. (2008). Lesson study. In L. Brown Easton (Ed.), *Powerful designs for professional learning* (2nd ed., pp. 171–184). Oxford, OH: National Staff Development Council.

Lieberman, A. (1986, February). Collaborative research: Working with, not working on . . . . *Educational Leadership, 43*(5), 28–32.

Lieberman, A., & McLaughlin, M. W. (1992). Networks for educational change: Powerful and problematic. *Phi Delta Kappan, 73*(9), 673–677.

Lieberman, A., & Miller, L. (2004). *Teacher leadership.* San Francisco: Jossey-Bass.

Lindsey, R. B., Roberts, L. M., & CampbellJones, F. (2005). *The culturally proficient school: An implementation guide for school leaders.* Thousand Oaks, CA: Corwin.

Lindsey, R. B., Robins, K. N., & Terrell, R. D. (2003). *Cultural proficiency: A manual for school leaders* (2nd ed.). Thousand Oaks, CA: Corwin.

Little, J. W. (1982). Norms of collegiality and experimentation: Workplace conditions of school success. *American Educational Research Journal, 19*(3), 325–340.

Little, J. W. (1993). Teachers' professional development in a climate of educational reform. *Educational Evaluation and Policy Analysis, 15,* 129–151.

Loucks-Horsley, S. (1995). Professional development and the learner-centered school. *Theory Into Practice, 34*(4), 265–271.

Loucks-Horsley, S. (1999). Effective professional development for teachers of mathematics. In Eisenhower National Clearinghouse, *Ideas that work: Mathematics professional development* (pp. 2–7). Columbus, OH: Author.

Loucks-Horsley, S., Harding, C. K., Arbuckle, M. A., Murray, L. B., Dubea, C., & Williams, M. K. (1987). *Continuing to learn: A guidebook for teacher development.* Andover, MA: Regional Laboratory for Educational Improvement of the Northeast and Islands & Oxford, OH: National Staff Development Council.

Loucks-Horsley, S., Hewson, P. W., Love, N., & Stiles, K. E. (1998). *Designing professional development for teachers of science and mathematics.* Thousand Oaks, CA: Corwin.

Loucks-Horsley, S., Kapitan, R., Carlson, M. O., Kuerbis, P. J., Clark, R. C., Melle, G. M., et al. (1990). *Elementary school science for the 90s.* Alexandria, VA: Association for Supervision and Curriculum Development & Andover, MA: The NETWORK.

Loucks-Horsley, S., Love, N., Stiles, K. E., Mundry, S., & Hewson, P. W. (2003). *Designing professional development for teachers of science and mathematics* (2nd ed.). Thousand Oaks, CA: Corwin.

Loucks-Horsley, S., & Stiegelbauer, S. (1991). Using knowledge of change to guide staff development. In A. Lieberman & L. Miller (Eds.), *Staff development for education in the 90's: New demands, new realities, new perspectives* (pp. 15–36). New York: Teachers College Press.

Loucks-Horsley, S., Stiles, K. E., & Hewson, P. (1996). Principles of effective professional development for mathematics and science education: A synthesis of standards. *NISE Brief, 1*(1). Madison: University of Wisconsin, National Institute for Science Education.

Loughran, J. J., Mulhall, P., & Berry, A. (2004). In search of pedagogical content knowledge in science: Developing ways of articulating and documenting professional practice. *Journal of Research in Science Teaching, 41*(4), 370–391.

Louis, K. S., & Marks, H. M. (1998). Does professional learning community affect the classroom: Teachers' work and student experiences in restructuring schools. *American Journal of Education, 106*(4), 532–575.

Love, N. (2002). *Using data/getting results: A practical guide for school improvement in mathematics and science.* Norwood, MA: Christopher-Gordon.

Love, N., Stiles, K. E., Mundry, S., & DiRanna, K. (2008). *The data coach's guide to improving learning for all students: Unleashing the power of collaborative inquiry.* Thousand Oaks, CA: Corwin.

Magnusson, S., Krajcik, J., & Borko, H. (1999). Nature, sources and development of pedagogical content knowledge for science teaching. In J. Gess-Newsome & N. Lederman (Eds.), *Examining pedagogical content knowledge: The construct and its implications for science education* (pp. 95–132). N. Dordrecht, The Netherlands: Kluwer Academic.

Magnusson, S. L., & Palincsar, A. S. (2005). Teaching to promote the development of scientific knowledge and reasoning about light at the elementary school level. In M. S. Donovan & J. Bransford (Eds.), *How students learn: History, mathematics, and science in the classroom* (pp. 421–474). Washington, DC: National Academies Press.

Makibbin, S., & Sprague, M. (1991, December). *Study groups: Conduit for reform.* Paper presented at the annual meeting of the National Staff Development Council, St. Louis, MO.

Marks, H. M., Louis, K. S., & Printy, S. M. (2000). The capacity for organizational learning: Implications for pedagogical quality and student achievement. In K. Leithwood (Ed.), *Understanding schools as intelligent systems.* Stamford, CT: Jai Press.

Marzano, R. J., Waters, T., & McNulty, B. A. (2005). *School leadership that works: From research to results.* Alexandria, VA: Association for Supervision and Curriculum Development & Aurora, CO: Mid-continent Research for Education and Learning.

Massell, D. (2000). *The district role in building capacity: Four strategies.* (CPRE No. RB-32). Philadelphia: University of Pennsylvania, Consortium for Policy Research in Education.

Math and Science Partnership Knowledge Management and Dissemination Project. (2007). *Defining teacher content knowledge.* Retrieved from www.mspkmd.net/index.php?page=04_2b

McLaughlin, M. W. (1993). What matters most in teachers' workplace context? In J. W. Little & M. W. McLaughlin (Eds.), *Teachers' work: Individuals, colleagues, and contexts* (pp. 79–103). New York: Teachers College Press.

McLaughlin, M. W., & Talbert, J. E. (2001). *Professional communities and the work of high school teaching.* Chicago: University of Chicago.

McLaughlin, M. W., & Talbert. J. E. (2007). Building professional learning communities in high schools: Challenges and promising practices. In L. Stoll & K. S. Louis (Eds.), *Professional learning communities: Divergence, depth and dilemmas* (pp. 151–165). Berkshire, England: Open University Press.

Mendro, R., & Bembry, K. (2000, April). *School evaluation: A change in perspective.* Paper presented at the annual meeting of American Education Research Association, New Orleans, LA.

Merseth, K. (1991). *The case for cases in teacher education.* Washington, DC: American Association for Higher Education & American Association of Colleges for Teacher Education.

Mezirow, J. (1991). *Transformative dimensions of adult learning.* San Francisco: Jossey-Bass.

Mezirow, J. (1997). Transformative learning: Theory to practice. In P. Cranton (Ed.), *New Directions for Adult and Continuing Education No. 74, Transformative learning in action: Insights from practice* (pp. 5–12). San Francisco: Jossey-Bass.

Michigan Department of Education. (2001). *What research says about parent involvement in children's education in relation to academic achievement.* Retrieved from www.michigan.gov/documents/Final_Parent_Involvement_Fact_Sheet_14732_7.pdf

Miller, D. M., & Pine, G. J. (1990). Advancing professional inquiry for educational improvement through action research. *Journal of Staff Development, 11*(3), 56–61.

Minnett, A., Murphy, M., Nobles, S., & Taylor, T. (2008). Sharing evidence of student engagement sparks changes in teacher practice. *Journal of Staff Development, 29*(4), 25–30.

Muijs, R. D., & Reynolds, D. (2001). *Effective teaching. Evidence and practice.* London: Paul Chapman.

Mumme, J., & Seago, N. (2002, April). *Issues and challenges in facilitating videocases for mathematics professional development.* Paper presented at the annual meeting of the American Education Research Association, New Orleans, LA.

Mundry, S. (2003). Honoring adult learners: Adult learning theories and implications for professional development. In J. Rhoton & P. Bowers (Eds.), *Science teacher retention: Mentoring and renewal.* Arlington, VA: National Science Teachers Association Press & National Science Education Leadership Association.

Mundry, S., Britton, E., Raizen, S., & Loucks-Horsley, S. (2000). *Designing successful professional meetings and conferences in education: Planning, implementation, and evaluation.* Thousand Oaks, CA: Corwin.

Mundry, S., Keeley, P., Rose, C., & Carroll, C. (forthcoming). *A leader's guide to mathematics curriculum topic study: Designs, tools and resources for professional learning.* Thousand Oaks, CA: Corwin.

Mundry, S., Keeley, P., & Landel, C. (2010). *A leader's guide to science curriculum topic study: Designs, tools and resources for professional learning.* Thousand Oaks, CA: Corwin.

Mundry, S., & Loucks-Horsley, S. (1999, April). Designing effective professional development: Decision points and dilemmas. *NISE Brief, 3*(1). Madison: University of Wisconsin, National Institute for Science Education.

Mundry, S., & Stiles, K. E. (Eds.). (2009). *Professional learning communities for science teaching: Lessons from research and practice.* Arlington, VA: National Science Teachers Association Press.

Murphy, C. (1995). Whole-faculty study groups: Doing the seemingly undoable. *Journal of Staff Development, 16*(3), 37–44.

Murphy, C. U., & Lick, D. W. (2001). *Whole-faculty study groups: Creating student-based professional development* (2nd Ed.). Thousand Oaks, CA: Corwin.

Murphy, J. (2005). *Connecting teacher leadership to school improvement.* Thousand Oaks, CA: Corwin.

National Center for Education Statistics. (2001). *The condition of education 2001.* Washington, DC: Department of Education.

National Commission on Mathematics and Science Teaching for the 21st Century. (2000). *Before it's too late.* Washington, DC: U.S. Department of Education.

National Commission on Teaching and America's Future. (1996). *What matters most: Teaching for America's future.* New York: Author.

National Commission on Teaching and America's Future. (2003). *No dream denied: A pledge to America's children.* New York: Author.

National Council of Teachers of Mathematics. (1989). *Curriculum and evaluation standards for school mathematics.* Reston, VA: Author.

National Council of Teachers of Mathematics. (1991). *Professional standards for teaching mathematics.* Reston, VA: Author.

National Council of Teachers of Mathematics. (1995). *Assessment standards for school mathematics.* Reston, VA: Author.

National Council of Teachers of Mathematics. (2000). *Principles and standards for school mathematics.* Reston, VA: Author.

National Council of Teachers of Mathematics. (2003a). *A research companion to principles and standards for school mathematics.* Reston, VA: Author.

National Council of Teachers of Mathematics. (2003b). *Lessons learned from research.* Reston, VA: Author.

National Council of Teachers of Mathematics. (2006). *Curriculum focal points for prekindergarten through grade 8 mathematics: A quest for coherence.* Reston, VA: Author.

National Network of Partnership Schools at Johns Hopkins University. (n.d.). Retrieved August 21, 2009, from www.csos.jhu.edu/P2000/index.htm

National Partnership for Excellence and Accountability in Teaching. (2000). *Revisioning professional development: What learner-centered professional development looks like.* Oxford, OH: National Staff Development Council.

National Research Council. (1996). *National science education standards.* Washington, DC: The National Academies Press.

National Research Council. (2001). *Classroom assessment and the National Science Education Standards.* Washington, DC: National Academy Press.

National Research Council. (2006). *Rising above the gathering storm: Energizing and employing America for a brighter future.* Washington, DC: National Academy Press.

National School Reform Faculty. (n.d.a). *Guide for bringing student work.* Retrieved from www.nsrfharmony.org/protocol/doc/guide_bring_stud_work.pdf

National School Reform Faculty. (n.d.b). *Suggestions for bringing student work.* Retrieved from www.nsrfharmony.org/protocol/doc/sugg_bring_stud_work.pdf

National Science Teachers Association. (2006). *NSTA position statement: Professional development in science education.* Retrieved from www.nsta.org/about/positions/profdev.aspx

National Staff Development Council. (2001a). *E-Learning for educators: Implementing the standards for staff development.* Oxford, OH: Author.

National Staff Development Council. (2001b). *Standards for staff development.* Oxford, OH: Author.

National Staff Development Council. (2008). *NSDC strategic plan.* Retrieved from www.nsdc.org/standfor/strategy.cfm

National Staff Development Council. (2009). *NSDC's definition of professional development.* Retrieved from www.nsdc.org/standfor/definition.cfm

Nelson, B. S. (Ed.). (1995). Introduction. In *Inquiry and the development of teaching: Issues in the transformation of mathematics teaching* (pp. 1–7). Newton, MA: Education Development Center, Center for Development of Teaching.

Newmann, F. M., King, M. B., & Youngs, P. (2000). Professional development that addresses school capacity: Lessons from urban elementary schools. *American Journal of Education, 108*(4), 259–285. Retrieved from www.wcer.wisc.edu/archive/pdbo/grand-aje411.htm

Newmann, F. M., & Wehlage, G. G. (1995). *Successful school restructuring: A report to the public and educators.* Madison: University of Wisconsin, Center on Organization and Restructuring of Schools.

Newton, A., Bergstrom, K., Brennan, N., Dunne, K., Gilbert, C., Ibarguen, N., et al. (1994). *Mentoring: A resource and training guide for educators.* Andover, MA: Regional Laboratory for Educational Improvement of the Northeast and Islands.

No Child Left Behind Act of 2001. Public Law 108–110, 20 U.S.C. § 6301 et seq. (2002).

Norris, J. H. (1994). What leaders need to know about school culture. *Journal of Staff Development, 15*(2), 2–5.

Novak, J. D., & Gowin, D. B. (1984). *Learning how to learn.* New York: Cambridge University Press.

Noyce Foundation. (2007). *Silicon Valley Mathematics Initiative: Pedagogical content coaching.* Retrieved from www.noycefdn.org/documents/math/pedagogical contentcoaching.pdf

Nuri Robins, K., Lindsey, R. B., Lindsey, D. B., & Terrell, R. D. (2006). *Culturally proficient instruction: A guide for people who teach* (2nd ed.). Thousand Oaks, CA: Corwin.

Oakes, J. (1990). *Multiplying inequalities: The effects of race, social class, and tracking on opportunities to learn mathematics and science.* Santa Monica, CA: RAND.

Oakes, J. (2005). *Keeping track: How schools structure inequality* (2nd ed.). New Haven, CT: Yale University Press.

Oakes, J., & Saunders, M. (2002). *Access to textbooks, instructional materials, equipment, and technology: Inadequacy and inequality in California's public schools.* Los Angeles: University of California.

Obama, B. (2008, December 20). *Democratic Committee weekly radio address: Obama announces science and technology team* [transcript]. Retrieved from http://voices.washingtonpost.com/44/2008/12/20/obama_announces_science_and_te.html

Oehrtman, M., Carlson, M., & Vasquez, J. A. (2009). Attributes of content-focused professional learning communities that led to meaningful reflection and collaboration among math and science teachers. In. S. Mundry & K. E. Stiles (Eds.), *Professional learning communities for science teaching: Lessons from research and practice* (pp. 89–106). Arlington, VA: National Science Teachers Association Press.

Oja, S. N., & Smulyan, L. (1989). Collaborative action research. In *Collaborative action research: A developmental approach* (pp. 1–25). Philadelphia: Falmer Press.

Partnership for 21st Century Skills. (2008). *21st century skills, education & competitiveness: A resource and policy guide.* Tucson, AZ: Author.

Pashler, H., Bain, P. M., Bottge, B. A., Graesser, A., Koedinger, K., McDaniel M., et al. (2007). *Organizing instruction and study to improve student learning* (Publication No. NCER 2007–2004), Washington, DC: National Center for Education Research.

Patterson, J. L. (1993). *Leadership for tomorrow's schools.* Alexandria, VA: Association for Supervision and Curriculum Development.

Paulos, J. A. (1992). *Beyond numeracy.* New York: Vintage Books.

Pellegrino, J. W., Chudowsky, N., & Glaser, R. (2001). *Knowing what students know: The science and design of educational assessment.* Washington, DC: National Academies Press.

Perie, M., Moran, R., & Lutkus, A. D. (2005). *NAEP 2004 trends in academic progress: Three decades of student performance in reading and mathematics* (Publication No. NCES 2005–464). Washington, DC: Government Printing Office.

Phillips, J. (2003). Powerful learning: Creating learning communities in urban school reform. *Journal of Curriculum and Supervision, 18*(3), 240–258.

Posner, G. J., Strike, K. A., Hewson, P. W., & Gertzog, W. A. (1982). Accommodation of a scientific conception: Toward a theory of conceptual change. *Science Education, 66*(2), 211–227.

Pratt, H., & Loucks-Horsley, S. (1993). Implementing a science curriculum for the middle grades: Progress, problems, and prospects. In G. M. Madrazo & L. L. Motz (Eds.), *Sourcebook for science supervisors* (pp. 61–72). Washington, DC: National Science Supervisors Association & National Science Teachers Association.

Reeves, D. B. (2009). *Leading change in your school.* Alexandria, VA: Association of Supervision and Curriculum Development.

Regional Educational Laboratories. (1995). *Facilitating systemic change in science and mathematics education: A toolkit for professional developers.* Andover, MA: Regional Laboratory for Educational Improvement of the Northeast and Islands.

Remillard, J. T., & Geist, P. K. (2002). Supporting teacher' professional learning by navigating openings in the curriculum. *Journal of Mathematics Teacher Education, 5*(1), 7–34.

Rentner, D. S., Scott, C., Kober, N., Chudowsky, N., Chudowsky, V., Joftus, S., et al. (2006). *From the capital to the classroom: Year 4 of the No Child Left Behind Act.* Washington, DC: Center on Education Policy.

Robbins, P. (1999). Mentoring. *Journal of Staff Development, 20*(3), 40–42.

Roop, L., & Best, S. (2005). Making a real difference: Scaling up education reform. *Innovator, 35*(3), 12–15.

Rose, C. M., Minton, L., & Arline, C. (2007). *Uncovering student thinking in mathematics: 25 formative assessment probes.* Thousand Oaks, CA: Corwin.

Rosebery, A. S. (2008). *Teaching science to English language learners: Building on students' strengths.* Arlington, VA: National Science Teachers Association Press.

Rosenholtz, S. J. (1991). *Teachers' workplace: The social organization of schools.* New York: Teachers College Press.

Roy, P. (2006). Family involvement: A far cry from room mothers and cupcakes. *The Learning Principal, 2*(1), 3.

Russell, S. J., Schifter, D., Bastable, V., Yaffee, L., Lester, J. B., & Cohen, S. (1995). Learning mathematics while teaching. In B. S. Nelson (Ed.), *Inquiry and the development of teaching: Issues in the transformation of mathematics teaching* (pp. 9–16). Newton, MA: Center for the Development of Teaching, Education Development Center.

Sagor, R. (2005). *The action research guidebook: A four-step process for educators and school teams.* Thousand Oaks, CA: Corwin.

Sanders, W., & Rivers, J. (1996). *Cumulative and residual effects of teachers on future student academic achievement.* Knoxville: University of Tennessee, Value-Added Research and Assessment Center.

Saphier, J. (2008). *A district plan to improve student achievement through workforce excellence, strong curriculum, and data.* Unpublished manuscript.

Saphier, J., & Gower, R. (1997). *The skillful teacher.* Carlisle, MA: Research for Better Teaching.

Saphier, J., Haley-Speca, M. A., & Gower, R. (2008). *The skillful teacher: Building your teaching skills* (6th ed.). Acton, MA: Research for Better Teaching.

Schifter, D. (1994). *Voicing the new pedagogy: Teachers write about learning and teaching mathematics.* Newton, MA: Center for the Development of Teaching, Education Development Center.

Schifter, D. (1996a). A constructivist perspective on teaching and learning mathematics. *Phi Delta Kappan, 77*(7), 492–499.

Schifter, D. (Ed.). (1996b). *What's happening in math class?* (Vols. 1–2). New York: Teachers College Press.

Schifter, D. (1999). Reasoning about operations: Early algebraic thinking in Grades K–6. In L. V. Still (Ed.), *Developing mathematical reasoning in Grades K–12.* Reston, VA: National Council of Teachers of Mathematics.

Schifter, D., & Bastable, V. (1995, April). *From the teachers' seminar to the classroom: The relationship between doing and teaching mathematics, an example from fractions.* Paper presented at the annual meeting of the American Education Research Association, San Francisco.

Schifter, D., Russell, S. J., & Bastable, V. (1999). Teaching to the big ideas. In M. Solomon (Ed.), *The diagnostic teacher: Constructing new approaches to professional development.* New York: Teachers College Press.

Schlechty, P. (1997). *Inventing better schools: An action plan for educational reform.* San Francisco: Jossey-Bass.

Schmidt, W. H., McKnight, C. C., Houang, R. T., Wang, H., Wiley, D. E., Cogan, L. S., et al. (2001). *Why schools matter: A cross-national comparison of curriculum and learning.* San Francisco: Jossey-Bass.

Schmidt, W. H. (2001). Defining teacher quality through content: Professional development implications from TIMSS. In J. Rhoton & P. Bowers (Eds.), *Professional development planning and design* (pp. 141–164). Arlington, VA: National Science Teachers Association Press.

Schmoker, M. (1999). *Results: The key to continuous improvement.* Alexandria, VA: Association of Supervision and Curriculum Development.

Schmoker, M. (2002). Up and away. The formula is well known, now we need to follow it. *Journal of Staff Development, 23*(2), 10–13.

Schneider, R., & Krajcik, J. (2002). Supporting science teacher learning: The role of educative curriculum materials. *Journal of Science Teacher Education, 13*(3), 221–245.

Schön, D. (1983). *The reflective practitioner: How professionals think in action.* New York: Basic Books.

Schön, D. A. (1988). Educating teachers as reflective practitioners. In P. Grimmett & G. Erickson (Eds.), *Reflection in teacher education.* New York: Teachers College Press.

Senge, P. M. (1990, Fall). The leader's new work: Building learning organizations. *MIT Sloan Management Review, 32*(1), 1–5.

Sergiovanni, T. J. (2007). An epistemological problem: What if we have the wrong theory? In P. D. Houston, A. M. Blankstein, & R. W. Cole (Eds.), *Out of the box leadership* (pp. 49–68). Thousand Oaks, CA: Corwin.

Sheldon, S. B. (2003). Linking school-family-community partnerships in urban elementary schools to student achievement on state tests. *Urban Review, 35*(2), 149–165.

Showers, B., & Joyce, B. (1996, March). The evolution of peer coaching. *Educational Leadership, 53*(6), 12–16.

Shulman, J., & Kepner, D. (1994). *The editorial imperative: Responding to productive tensions between case writing and individual development.* San Francisco: Far West Laboratory. (ERIC Document Reproduction Service No. ED378182)

Shulman, L. S. (1986). Those who understand: Knowledge growth in teaching. *Educational Researcher, 15*(2), 4–14.

Shulman, L., & Shulman, J. (2004). How and what teachers learn: A shifting perspective. *Journal of Curriculum Studies, 36*(2), 257–271.

Shulman, L. S. (1992). Toward a pedagogy of cases. In J. H. Shulman (Ed.), *Case methods in teacher education* (pp. 1–30). New York: Teachers College Press.

Silva, D., Gimbert, B., & Nolan, J. (2000). Sliding the doors: Locking and unlocking possibilities for teacher leadership. *Teachers College Record, 102*(4), 779–806.

Silver, E. A., Kilpatrick, J., & Schlesinger, B. (1990). *Thinking through mathematics: Fostering inquiry and communication in mathematics classrooms.* New York: College Entrance Examination Board.

Singleton, G. E., & Linton, C. (2006). *Courageous conversations about race: A field guide for achieving equity in schools.* Thousand Oaks, CA: Corwin.

Skiba, R. J., Simmons, A. B., Ritter, S., Gibb, A. C., Rausch, M. K., Cuadrado, et al. (2008). Achieving equity in special education: History, status, and current challenges. *Exceptional Children, 74*(3), 264–288.

Smith, D., & Neale, D. (1989). The construction of subject matter knowledge in primary science teaching. *Teaching and Teacher Education, 5*(1), 1–20.

Smith, M. S. (2001). *Practice-based professional development for teachers of mathematics.* Reston, VA: National Council of Teachers of Mathematics.

Sneider, C. (1995, January). *Global Systems Science: A professional development program for high school science teachers.* Paper presented at the Professional Development Project of the National Institute for Science Education, Madison, WI.

Southern Regional Education Board. (2004). *Standards for online professional development: Guidelines for planning and evaluating online professional development courses and programs.* Atlanta, GA: Author.

Southern Regional Education Board. (2006). *Standards for quality online teaching.* Atlanta, GA: Author.

Sparks, D. (1994). A paradigm shift in staff development. *Journal of Staff Development, 15*(4), 26–29.

Sparks, D. (1996, May). How do we determine the effects of professional development on student learning? *NSDC's The Developer: Powerful Ideas for Promoting Improvement,* 2–6.

Sparks, D. (1997). Maintaining the faith in teachers' ability to grow: An interview with Asa Hilliard. *Journal of Staff Development, 18*(2), 24–25.

Sparks, D. (2001). *Time for professional learning serves student learning: Results.* Oxford, OH: National Staff Development Council.

Sparks, D. (2002). *Designing powerful professional development for teachers and principals.* Oxford, OH: National Staff Development Council.

Sparks, D. (2003, April). Advocate each day for powerful professional learning. *Results,* 1–8.

Sparks, D. (2005). *Leading for results: Transforming teaching, learning, and relationships in schools.* Thousand Oaks, CA: Corwin.

Sparks, D., & Hirsh, S. (2000). *A national plan for improving professional development.* Oxford, OH: National Staff Development Council.

St. John, M., & Pratt, H. (1997). The factors that contribute to the "best cases" of standards-based reform. *School Science and Mathematics, 97*(6), 316–324.

Stein, M. K., Silver, E. A., & Smith, M. S. (1998). Mathematics reform and teacher development: A community of practice perspective. In. J. Greeno & S. Goldman (Eds.), *Thinking practices in mathematics and science learning* (pp. 17–52). Hillsdale, NJ: Lawrence Erlbaum.

Stein, M. K., Smith, M. S., Henningsen, M. A., & Silver, E. A. (2000). *Implementing standards-based mathematics instruction: A casebook for professional development.* New York: Teachers College Press.

Stein, M. K., Smith, M. S., Henningsen, M. A., & Silver, E. A. (2009). *Implementing standards-based mathematics instruction: A casebook for professional development* (2nd ed.). New York: Teachers College Press.

Stephens, A. C. (2005). Developing students' understanding of variable mathematics. *Mathematics Teaching in the Middle School, 11*(2), 96.

Stigler, J. W., & Hiebert, J. (1999). *The teaching gap: Best ideas from the world's teachers for improving education in the classroom.* New York: Simon and Schuster.

Stiles, K. E., & Mundry, S. (2002). Professional development and how teachers learn: Developing expert science teachers. In. R.W. Bybee (Ed.), *Learning science and the science of learning* (pp. 137–151). Arlington, VA: National Science Teachers Association Press.

Stiles, K. E., Mundry, S., & Kaser, J. (2006). *Facilitator's guide: Leading every day: 124 actions for effective leadership* (2nd ed.). Thousand Oaks, CA: Corwin.

Stoll, L., Bolam, R., McMahon, A., Wallace, M., & Thomas, S. (2006). Professional learning communities: A review of the literature. *Journal of Educational Change, 7*(4), 221–258.

Strahan, D. (2003). Promoting a collaborative professional culture in three elementary schools that have beaten the odds. *The Elementary School Journal, 104*(2), 127–146.

Supovitz, J. A. (2002). Developing communities of instructional practice. *Teachers College Record, 104*(8), 1591–1626.

Supovitz, J. A., & Christman, J. B. (2003). *Developing communities of instructional practice: Lessons from Cincinnati and Philadelphia* (CPRE No. RB-39). Philadelphia: University of Pennsylvania, Consortium for Policy Research in Education.

Supovitz, J. A., & Turner, H. M. (2000). The effects of professional development on science teaching practices and classroom culture. *Journal of Research in Science Teaching, 37*(9), 963–980.

Talbert, J., & McLaughlin, M. (1994). Teacher professionalism in local school contexts. *American Journal of Education, 102*(2), 123–153.

Thompson, C. L., & Zeuli, J. S. (1999). The frame and the tapestry: Standards-based reform and professional development. In L. Darling-Hammond & G. Sykes (Eds.), *Teaching as the learning profession: Handbook of policy and practice* (pp. 341–375). San Francisco: Jossey-Bass.

Tugel, J. (Ed.). (2008). *Notes from the field: Teaching for conceptual change: Uncovering student thinking in science through action research.* Augusta: Maine Mathematics and Science Alliance.

U.S. Department of Education. (1996). *Pursuing excellence: A study of U.S. eighth-grade mathematics and science teaching, learning, curriculum, and achievement in international context* (NCES Publication No. 97-198). Washington, DC: Government Printing Office.

Van Driel, J., Verloop, N., & de Vos, W. (1998). Developing science teachers' pedagogical content knowledge. *Journal of Research in Science Teaching, 35*(6), 673–695.

Vescio, V., Ross, D., & Adams, A. (2008). A review of research on the impact of professional learning communities on teaching practice and student learning. *Teaching and Teacher Education, 24*(1), 80–91.

Villani, S. (2002). *Mentoring programs for new teachers: Models of induction and support.* Thousand Oaks, CA: Corwin.

Vosniadou, S., & Brewer, W. F. (1992). Mental models of the Earth: A study of conceptual change in childhood. *Cognitive Psychology 24,* 535–585.

Wagner, T., Kegan, R., Lahey, L. L., Lemons, R. W., Garnier, J., Helsing, D., et al. (2006). *Change leadership: A practical guide to transforming our schools.* San Francisco: Jossey-Bass.

Wandersee, J. H., Mintzes, J. J., & Novak, J. D. (1994). Research on alternative conceptions in science. In D. L. Gabel (Ed.), *Handbook of research on science teaching and learning* (pp. 177–210). New York: Macmillan.

Warren, B., Ballenger, C., Ogonowski, M., Rosebery, A., & Hudicourt-Barnes, J. (2001). Rethinking diversity in learning science: The logic of everyday sense making. *Journal of Research in Science Teaching, 38*(5), 529–552.

Waters. J. T., & Marzano, R. J. (2006). *School district leadership that works: The effect of superintendent leadership on student achievement.* Aurora, CO: Mid-continent Research for Education and Learning.

Waters, T., Marzano, R. J., & McNulty, B. (2003). *Balanced leadership: What 30 years of research tells us about the effect of leadership on student achievement.* Aurora, CO: Mid-continent Research for Education and Learning.

Watkins, J. (1992). *Speaking of action research.* Paper adapted from a presentation to the Board of Overseers of the Regional Laboratory for Educational Improvement of the Northeast and Islands, Andover, MA.

Wei, R. C., Darling-Hammond, L., Andree, A., Richardson, N., & Orphanos, S. (2009). *Professional learning in the learning profession: A status report on teacher development in the U.S. and abroad.* Oxford, OH: National Staff Development Council.

Weiss, I. R. (1997). The status of science and mathematics teaching in the United States: Comparing teacher views and classroom practice to national standards. *NISE Brief, 1*(3). Madison: University of Wisconsin, National Institute for Science Education.

Weiss, I. R., Banilower, E. R., McMahon, K. C., & Smith, P. S. (2001). *Report of the 2000 National Survey of Science and Mathematics.* Chapel Hill, NC: Horizon Research, Inc.

Weiss, I. R., Matti, M. C., & Smith, P. S. (1994). *Report of the 1993 Survey of Science and Mathematics Education.* Chapel Hill, NC: Horizon Research, Inc.

Weiss, I. R., & Pasley, J. D. (2009). *Mathematics and science for a change: How to design, implement, and sustain high-quality professional development.* Portsmouth, NH: Heinemann.

Weissglass, J. (1996). *No compromises on equity in mathematics education: Developing an infrastructure.* Santa Barbara: University of California, Center for Educational Change in Mathematics and Science.

Weissglass, J. (1997). *Ripples of hope: Building relationships for educational change.* Santa Barbara: University of California, Center for Educational Change in Mathematics and Science.

Wellman, B., & Lipton, L. (2004). *Data-driven dialogue: A facilitator's guide to collaborative inquiry.* Sherman, CT: Mira Via.

Wenger, E. (1998). *Communities of practice: Learning, meaning and identity.* New York: Cambridge University Press.

Wenglinsky, H. (2000). *How teaching matters: Bringing the classroom back into discussions of teacher quality.* Princeton, NJ: Educational Testing Service.

WestEd. (2000). *Teachers who learn, kids who achieve: A look at schools with model professional development.* San Francisco: Author.

WestEd & WGBH Educational Foundation. (2003). *Teachers as learners: A multimedia kit for professional development in science and mathematics.* Thousand Oaks, CA: Corwin.

Wheatley, M. (2002). *Turning to one another: Simple conversations to restore hope in the future.* San Francisco: Berrett-Koehler.

Wiliam, D. (2007). Keeping learning on track: Formative assessments and the regulation of learning. In F. K. Lester, Jr. (Ed.), *Second handbook of mathematics teaching and learning* (pp.1053–1098). Greenwich, CT: Information Age.

Wong, H. K. (2004). Induction programs that keep new teachers teaching and improving. *NASSP Bulletin, 88*(638), 41–58.

Yoon, K., Duncan, T., Lee, S., Scarloss, B., & Shapley, K. (2007). *Reviewing the evidence on how teacher professional development affects student achievement* (Publication No. REL 2007-No. 033). Washington, DC: U.S. Department of Education, Regional Educational Laboratory Southwest.

York-Barr, J., & Duke, K. (2004). What do we know about teacher leadership? Findings from two decades of scholarship. *Review of Educational Research, 74*(3), 255–316.

Index

CORWIN

A SAGE Company

The Corwin logo—a raven striding across an open book—represents the union of courage and learning. Corwin is committed to improving education for all learners by publishing books and other professional development resources for those serving the field of PreK–12 education. By providing practical, hands-on materials, Corwin continues to carry out the promise of its motto: **"Helping Educators Do Their Work Better."**